D1526688

A MAN OF MANY WORLDS

The Memoirs & Diaries of
DR. GHASEM GHANI

EDITED BY
CYRUS GHANI

TRANSLATED BY
CYRUS GHANI & PAUL SPRACHMAN

MAGE PUBLISHERS
WASHINGTON DC
2006

LIBRARY OF CONGRESS CATALOGING-IN-PUBLICATION DATA
Ghanî, Qâsim.
A man of many worlds : the memoirs & diaries
of Dr. Ghasem Ghani / edited by Cyrus Ghani ;
translated by Cyrus Ghani & Paul Sprachman.
p. cm.
Includes bibliographical references and index.
ISBN 0-934211-30-2 (clothbound : alk. paper)
1. Ghanî Qâsim. 2. Ambassadors--Iran--Biography.
I. Ghanî, Sîrûs. II. Title.
DS316.9.G475A3 2006
327.55'0092--dc22
2005024667

CLOTHBOUND ISBN 0-934211-30-2

Mage books are available at bookstores or directly from the
publisher. Visit mage on the web at www.mage.com.
Call 202-342-1642 or e-mail as@mage.com for a catalog

CONTENTS

For Vida and Ali, my father's grandchildren

Cyrus Ghani

✳

For Susan

Paul Sprachman

With all my love

Paul

INTRODUCTION
CYRUS GHANI

I FIRST PUBLISHED THE MEMOIRS and diaries of my father, Dr. Ghasem Ghani (1895–1952), in the original Persian during the period 1981–85 (London, Ithaca Press). They comprise thirteen volumes (5,237 pages). Haleh Esfandiari ably assisted me in the preparation of the first five volumes. The late scholar Mohammad-Jafar Mahjoub aided in preparing volumes nine and ten, and Dr. Hassan Amin helped with volume thirteen. The set was not sold commercially but given to interested individuals and a few institutions. Later, with my authorization and without any financial interest on my part, the late Ali Akbar Zavvar published them in Tehran, where they were a great commercial success.

After the London publication, several people approached me to assist in an English translation of some key volumes. I had by then started on an ambitious project, *Iran and the West*, an annotated bibliography of my own collection of some four thousand books and lengthy articles on Iran, which date from the sixteenth century. I subsequently went on to write other books and set aside any thought of translating the memoirs.

About two years ago Dr. Paul Sprachman, a scholar of Iranian language and literature at Rutgers University, approached me suggesting that together we translate segments of my father's memoirs. He had translated some forty pages, which evinced a superb knack for translating difficult passages, even the most delicate poetry. Dr. Sprachman

9

has great facility with several languages. Besides English, his mother tongue, and Persian, which he teaches at Rutgers, he is conversant with Arabic, Hebrew, German and Russian. We divided the translation and what you see in these pages is the resulting joint effort of some two years' duration.

My Father was an exceptional person. His life spanned many eras and cultures, and was a blend of the humanist traditions of both the East and West. He was a renowned physician, a man of letters and a diplomat. His wide range of activities includes establishing the first hospital in his birthplace of Sabzevar in northeastern Iran. His translations from French into Persian encompass three novels of Anatole France and segments from Buffon's *Discours sur le style.* He was an avid reader of Ralph Waldo Emerson and William James. He attended lectures by Sigmund Freud in Vienna in the late 1920s and taught psychology in one of the colleges of Tehran University. In the late 1930s he collaborated with Mohammad Ali Foroughi on an edition of Omar Khayyam, and through painstaking research they were able to separate the true works of the poet from verses that were written and attributed to him after the poet's death. In 1942 Dr. Ghani and one of the greatest scholars of Iran, Mohammad Qazvini, published an edition of Hafez's poetry that is still held to be the definitive anthology of the poet's work.

Dr. Ghani wrote a two-volume study, the first of which is a history of mysticism in Islam and the second is the historical background of the age of Hafez. He is the author of several other works, some of which are listed in this volume. He is regarded as one of the preeminent scholars of Iranian history and literature. He also knew Arabic, French, English and enough Latin to read Virgil. A perfect amalgam of Western and Iranian cultures, his comments on many aspects of Western life are relevant and incisive.

Dr. Ghani's diplomatic career was relatively brief. He enjoyed the trust and confidence of Reza Shah and Mohammad Reza Shah. He performed his assignments in Egypt, Turkey and the U.S. with efficiency and dedication. His diplomatic reports are still used by the foreign ministry as models for young Iranian diplomats.

Various people remember Dr. Ghani as a great conversationalist, raconteur and letter writer—all lost arts. One can better appreciate and see more clearly the breadth and depth of the man from the complete Persian memoirs and diaries. Dr. Ghani died at the relatively young age of fifty-nine. He suffered from various illnesses and mishaps during the last eight years of his life that curtailed his literary contribution and seem to have darkened his mood and outlook but did not affect his unquenchable intellect.

My colleague and I agreed that a translation of the entire work would be too onerous, even though an abridged volume cannot achieve the range and breadth of the original. Dr. Ghani's Persian writing is lucid and elegant. Coordinating the efforts of two translators with different styles and perspectives required great effort by both. I hope this translation has done him justice.

Gratitude must be extended to my wife, Caroline, who as always, has trained her critical eye on this effort and contributed much to its completion. I also wish to thank my publisher and valued friend, Mohammad Batmanglij, a man of intellect and integrity, who has advised and assisted me in more than one endeavor.

NOTE ON THE TRANSLATION
PAUL SPRACHMAN

CERTAIN PARTS OF DR. GHANI'S diaries do not present a challenge to the translator. The routine events in the life of an ambassador, the gatherings he attended, the places he visited become English easily. Many entries are about traveling from one place to another: Mashhad to Tehran, Tehran to Ankara, Istanbul to Beirut, and San Francisco to Washington, D.C. The logic of time and place determines how they translate from Persian to English. In this respect diary writing is similar regardless of language. Even part of a journey described in this volume, which relates how Turkmen bandits captured the young Dr. Ghani, lends itself well to translation. This kidnapping can stand on its own as a narrative. The traditional aspects of storytelling—chronology, character development and crisis resolution—lend the writing a structure and a texture that are akin to adventure tales in English. Other entries readily translate from Persian because they are about the author's physical health. Except for medical terminology, they do not pose many problems for the translator.

The writings of Dr. Ghani resist translation because they contain hundreds of proper names, some of which appear for the first time in print. At first glance, the transliteration of these names seems simple. The mechanical application of any of the available romanization schemes favored by archivists and scholars (The Library of Congress, *The Encyclopedia of Islam*, etc.) can convert Persian, a language (like Arabic, Hebrew and Urdu) written primarily with consonants, into English, a European language with a full set of vowels. At second glance, however, the task of clothing bare strings

13

of Persian consonants into fully voweled English goes beyond the mechanical application of rules and enters the realms of culture and history.

Those familiar with transliteration systems favored by scholars of Persian will immediately notice all sorts of irregularities and inconsistencies in this book. The form of the author's name, Ghasem Ghani, breaks one of the fundamental laws of romanization: there must be a one-to-one correspondence between English letters and the Persian letters they represent. To write "Ghasem Ghani" for قاسم غنی implies that the author's first and second names begin with the same consonant. But, as Arabic, Urdu and Persian readers know, the first name begins with "qaf" (ق) and the second with "gheyn" (غ). Though they sound the same to many Persian speakers,[1] they are not written identically. This means that rather than transliterating his name, the author transcribed it as it sounds in Iranian Persian.

To use "Ghasem Ghani" instead of "Qasim Ghani" (as The Library of Congress has it) is to assert a Persian (as opposed to an Arabic) written identity. An Iranian who uses "gh" in both parts of the name proclaims, "Though the Arabs invaded our land and imposed their religion and writing system on us, don't mistake me for an Arab." As the author notes in the first part, his family name is originally Arabic. The Qur'an often refers to God as *ghani* or "free of want," an attribute of the deity. After the Arab invasion of Iran in the seventh century, many Iranian converts became *abd al-ghani* (عبد الغنی) or "servants of God." Qasem (قاسم) meaning "one who swears," also comes from Arabic.

The Persian tendency to nativize Arabic produces other anomalies. Occasionally Persian speakers double consonants where they are not doubled in the originals. For example, *tadayyon* (تدیّن) is an Arabic noun meaning "being faithful." Ironically a man by this name, who eschewed a clerical career early in life and eventually went on to become minister of education, spelled it Taddayon. In other words, doubled consonants are nativized as single consonants. Thus, "navvab" (نوّاب) becomes "navab" and "vahhab" (وهّاب) "vahab."

---

[1] Speakers of Dari, the Afghan dialect of Persian, distinguish between the two consonants. In many dialects of Arabic they also represent two distinct sounds.

Another source of idiosyncratic transliteration is the cultural orientation of educated Iranians. Products of French schools tend to write the sound of English "j" as "dj."[2] Those influenced by Gallicisms also prefer to romanize long "u" as "ou." This is seen in the names of Cabinet Minister Mohammad Ali Foroughi[3] and Minister Vosouq al-Dowleh. The standard unit of currency in Iran is sometimes written "touman" for this reason.[4]

When not deferring to sound or personal preference, the translators have followed this scheme:

a = ´ and آ e = ِ i,y = ی o = ´ ow (aw Arabic) = وَ u = وُ
ey (ay Arabic) = یَ

b = ب ch = چ d = د f = ف g = گ gh = غ h = ح ه j = ج
' = ء (medial & final ع) k = ک kh = خ khw = اوخ l = ل m = م
n = ن p = پ q = ق r = ر s = ث ص س t = ت ط v,w = و
z = ز ظ ض eh = ه
-e, -ey = کتابِ خوب کتابهای خوب

---

[2] In French "j" would yield the sound of "s" as in "pleasure."
[3] Other Iranians who hold this name spell it "Forughi."
[4] In the text people spend "tomans" (closer to the sound of the original).

CHRONOLOGY

Important dates in Iranian history, 1896–1952

1896   Naser al-Din Shah (r.1848–96) assassinated by followers
       of the pan-Islamist Jamal al-Din Afghani; Crown Prince
       Mozaffar al-Din assumes the throne.

1900   New Zealander W. K. D'Arcy buys mineral rights
       concession for entire country.

1901   D'Arcy concession replaced by new concession from
       Iranian government for sixty years, which excludes five
       northern provinces.

1902
       Oil drilling begins near Khanaqin.

1903   Discontent spreads in the country over Shah's costly trips to
       Europe, the autocratic rule of Prime Minister Ayn al-
       Dowleh and the grant of concessions to foreign countries.

1906   Increasing number of petitions to the shah to implement
       reforms and curb the excesses of the prime minister.
       Prominent merchants take sanctuary in the British
       Legation and demand a constitution. Shah dismisses
       prime minister and in August proclaims a constitution
       primarily modeled on the Belgian constitution.
       Elections are held for first session of Parliament

(Majles) and representatives meet in October. Constitution is ratified in December. Mozaffar al-Din Shah dies in December.

1907   Mohammad Ali, eldest son of Mozaffar al-Din Shah, becomes king. He is hostile to parliamentary rule and attempts to dismantle Parliament.

Anglo-Russian Convention divides the country into spheres of influence. Iranian government has no choice in the matter. Tehran, the capital, is designated a neutral zone. Anarchy in most parts of Iran; bandits roam the countryside; tribal chiefs are ascendant. Prime Minister Amin al-Soltan (Atabak) is assassinated.

1908   Government troops led by the Cossack Brigade attack and shell Parliament; mass arrests and some executions; uprising in Tabriz and warfare between forces of the shah aided by Russian troops against the insurgents.

1909   Members of the Bakhtiari tribe together with forces from Mazandaran lead a drive to Tehran and the shah is deposed and forced to flee the country.

Twelve-year-old prince Ahmad, second oldest son of the shah, takes the throne. A regent is appointed to run the country. A new Parliament is convened.

1911   American advisor Morgan Shuster is employed as treasurer general to bring order to the finances of the country. Deposed king Mohammad Ali attempts to reclaim his throne. He is defeated and flees. When Shuster attempts to confiscate the properties of a brother of the shah in lieu of back taxes, the Russians force him to leave the country.

1914–15   British Admiralty acquires majority of shares and
              controlling voice in the Anglo-Persian
              Petroleum Company.
           New elections for Parliament.
           Turkey enters World War I on German side and its forces
              occupy northwestern Iran. Iran declares neutrality, but
              Russia lands troops and occupies Iranian ports on the
              Caspian Sea and adjacent land. British forces occupy
              southern parts of the country.

1915   In July Ahmad Shah comes of age and is crowned.
           Russians land troops in the northern provinces. Iran
              Democrat Party (the nationalists) set up "National
              Defense Committee"; leave Tehran for Qom and, later,
              set up a government in exile in Kermanshah. Most
              members are forced to flee to Beirut, Damascus and,
              later, Istanbul.

1916   Russians troops occupy Esfahan and Kermanshah.
           Britain forms South Persian Rifles with mostly
              Indian troops.
           Tribal unrest in eastern parts of the country.

1917   Russians link with British forces in eastern Mesopotamia.
           Iranian prime ministers are chosen by Britain. Revolts in
              Gilan led by Kuchek Khan and in Azerbaijan led
              by Khiabani.
           Bolsheviks assume power in parts of Central Asia. Russian
              troops evacuate Iran.

1918   New government in Russia renounces all tsarist
              concessions and privileges in Iran.
           Britain sends military forces to Tblisi to expel Bolsheviks.

Vosouq al-Dowleh becomes Prime Minister.
Armistice between Allies and Germany and Turkey.

1919   Iran denied hearing at the Paris Peace Conference for
losses suffered.
Britain proposes Anglo-Iranian Agreement permitting
British control over the military and fiscal affairs of the
country and bringing British experts to Iran. Public
opposition in Iran to the proposed agreement
intensifies. Vosouq al-Dowleh resigns and leaves the
country. Successive Iranian governments argue that
only the Iranian Parliament has the authority to
approve the Agreement.

1921   Sayyed Zia al-Din Tabatabai, former journalist, and Reza
Khan, head of the Cossack Brigade, stage a coup d'état.
Sayyed Zia becomes prime minister.
Anglo-Iranian Agreement is repudiated by
new government.
Mass arrests of notables and repression by Sayyed Zia lead
to unrest. Sayyed Zia is dismissed and goes into exile.
Qavam al-Saltaneh, formerly governor of Khorasan
who had been arrested by Sayyed Zia, is appointed by
Ahmad Shah as prime minister. Reza Khan becomes
minister of war in successive governments.

1922–24   Reza Khan quells revolts in Azerbaijan, Lorestan,
Kurdestan, Fars and Khuzestan.
First U.S. financial mission to Iran under Arthur
Millspaugh.

1923   Ahmad Shah appoints Reza Khan prime minister and
leaves for Europe, never to return to Iran.

Campaign for the establishment of a republic with Reza Khan as president. Strong protest by religious elements forces Reza Khan to abandon attempt.

1925   Parliament deposes Ahmad Shah and Constituent Assembly gives the throne to Reza Khan who adopts "Pahlavi" as the name of the new dynasty.

1926–31   Last tribal and separatist movements are quelled and government is centralized.

1927–41   Reform and reorganization of judiciary and finance under Ali Akbar Davar. Students sent abroad on government scholarships. National Bank formed. Trans-Iranian Railway built. Extra-territorial rights of foreign powers (capitulation) cancelled. Growing secularization of society and corresponding reduction of the clergy's power.

1928–31   Treaties with neighboring countries. Sections of a civil code completed; secular laws are applied by the judiciary.

1932–33   Anglo-Persian Oil Concession is revoked. New Concession is signed.

1934   State visit to Turkey. Close relationship between Reza Shah and Mustafa Kamal Atatürk. Religious riots in Mashhad protesting Western-style attire for men are quelled.

1935   Tehran University founded. Iranian airline formed for intercity service.

1936   Veil abolished.

1937   Sa'adabad pact between Iran, Iraq and Turkey.

1938   Trans-Iranian Railway completed.

1939   Marriage of Crown Prince Mohammad Reza to Princess
        Fawzia of Egypt.
        World War II. Iran declares neutrality.

1941   British and Russian forces invade Iran. Iran capitulates.
        Reza Shah forced to abdicate; succeeded by Mohammad
        Reza Shah.
        Formation of the Tudeh (Communist) Party.
        Britain arms southern tribes.
        Iranian National Railway expropriated to transport arms
        and material to Russia.

1942   Tripartite Treaty among Iran, Britain and Russia
        constrains Allies to leave Iran after the war.

1943   Iran declares war on Germany.
        Tehran Conference attended by, Winston Churchill,
        Franklin Roosevelt and Joseph Stalin. Three powers'
        declaration guarantees Iran's independence.

1945   Iran requests Allied troops evacuate and hand over state
        railways.
        By October all foreign troops leave Iran.
        Ja'far Pishevari with Soviet backing forms Democrat Party
        and takes over Tabriz. Refuses to admit Iranian troops.

1946–7   Prime Minister Hakimi appeals to the UN to force
        Russians out of Azerbaijan.
        Prime Minister Qavam includes Tudeh Party members in
        his Cabinet. His government reaches agreement with

Russians granting autonomy to Azerbaijan and promising oil concessions in northern part of the country. Russians complete their withdrawal of troops. Seven Year Plan for economic reconstruction drafted. Separatist Democrat movement in Azerbaijan collapses. Tudeh members of the Cabinet are dismissed.

1948　Parliament rejects agreement of Qavam and Russians. Qavam resigns.
　　　First U.S. loan of $26 million. Russians protest U.S. involvement in Iran.
　　　Shah divorces Fawzia.

1949　Unsuccessful assassination attempt slightly injures the shah.
　　　Senate elections as provided in the 1906 constitution.
　　　Minister of Court Hazhir assassinated by religious zealot.
　　　Shah is invited to U.S. on state visit.

1950　National Front led by Dr. Mohammad Mosaddeq gains seats in Majles elections.
　　　Loan from Export/Import Bank.

1951　Shah marries Soraya Esfandiari.
　　　Prime Minister Razmara assassinated.
　　　Dr. Mosaddeq becomes prime minister.
　　　Majles votes for nationalization of the oil industry. Anglo-Iranian Oil Company and British government appeal to International Court at The Hague; inconclusive decision. British staff at oil installations are dismissed.
　　　UN Security Council holds meeting on dispute.
　　　Mosaddeq arrives in U.S. to defend nationalization.
　　　Tensions between shah and Mosaddeq increase.

CHILDHOOD AND YOUTH
Written in 1948

AS MY MOTHER OFTEN TOLD ME, I was born after the cholera epidemic of 1891–92. That is almost one year after the epidemic, for she says that they had been summering at the Kuh Mish heights outside Sabzevar, and I was born about several months later in 1893 in Sabzevar. The house where I was born was a humble and cramped place that I remember well. In the neighborhood of Gowdanbar opposite a lane that leads to Sabriz, there is a lane that has remained exactly the same as it was in the old days.

Along the passage there were three houses. One, belonging to a merchant whose name escapes me, was the first house on the left. The first house on the right belonged to Aqa Mirza Ali Akbar Arabshahi, one of the famous Sabzevar Arabshahi Seyyeds who were considered my relations, because the family of Sabzevari Seyyeds were all from one line of the Arabshahi tribe. Mirza Ali Akbar's advanced age earned him guardianship of the Shrine of Yahya, the original Arabshah, who lived in the thirteenth or fourteenth century (according to Khafi's history *Mojmal-e Fasihi*)[1] and is buried in the shrine.

These Seyyeds, who are related to the prophet Mohammad through his grandson Hoseyn, comprise about a hundred families or so living in Sabzevar and its environs. While they may have had their internal quarrels, they had always presented a united front. Whenever an outsider intruded, it would be all for one and one for all to the death. They also always had a leader whom they obeyed. Among Iranian cities Sabzevar is exceptional in that almost all of its

25

inhabitants' ancestors had been Shiites (those that believed in twelve imams) from the very beginnings of Islam. At the time when the majority of the people were Sunni, some cities were considered centers of Shiism. Besides Sabzevar, they include Saveh, Qom, Gorgan (Astarabad) and, it appears, the Taleqan district. In any case since the first century of Islam, Sabzevar was known as one of Shiism's important centers. A tale Jalal al-Din Rumi tells in Book V of the *Masnavi* attests to the city's adherence to this sect. According to the tale, a Kharazmshahi amir surrounded the town and demanded a punitive tax from the people. When a delegation from the town went before the amir and asked the reason for the tax, he eventually explained that contrary to the majority of the people in other towns, the Sabzevaris were Shiite. The Sabzevaris, practicing dissimulation, demurred, claiming that all manner of Moslems lived in town. The amir tightened his siege, and a number of people were killed. Finally, when the Sabzevaris gave up and agreed to pay the tax, the amir said that he only wanted one piece of tribute from them: if they could show him someone named Abu Bakr. He told them:

> *Never shall you escape from me alive,*
> *Unless you present an Abu Bakr to me.*

The people offered to pay the money again, saying,

> *Since when is there an Abu Bakr in Sabzevar?*
> *He would be rarer than a dry clod in a river.*[2]

Finally they

> *Raced about three days and nights,*
> *And found a scraggly Abu Bakr.*
> *He was a wayfarer who had fallen ill,*
> *Staying in a run-down corner full of death.*

This man who was incapable of going on,

> *They raised on the corpse-bearers' plank*
> *And bore him to Kharazmshah.*

In Sabzevar, there is a popular legend about this Abu Bakr. People say that he was from a small village about four and a half kilometers northeast of town officially called Izi. But they changed the name of the village to Badnam (ill-repute), because the man called Abu Bakr had lived there.

The Sarbedaran revolt, a devout Shiite movement, also originated in Sabzevar. Several histories contain detailed accounts of Hasan Juri, the leader of the uprising, and his lieutenants.

Not only did the city rank among the important Shiite centers, the Seyyeds of Sabzevar, especially the Arabshahi family, always enjoyed the utmost in respect and influence. Originally during the Daylamid dynasty they were in Fars Province, but with the decline of the dynasty some Shiites migrated to Saveh, and another group came to Sabzevar. The first Arabshah and his brother Mokhtar Shah (as he was known at the Daylami court of Fars) lived in Shiraz. The second Arabshah is buried in Sabzevar, and Khafi in his *Mojmal*, which was written in the first half of the fifteenth century, mentions his death and burial.

The Arabshahi Seyyeds took a kind of special pride in their lineage. All of them—even those who were Arabshahi from their mothers' family—insisted that their lofty status be universally acknowledged. However, people often made distinctions when identifying them: "He is not pure Arabshahi, his father is not Arabshahi, only his mother."

The clerics, rulers, functionaries, and influential people sought ways to affiliate themselves with the Arabshahis and earn their backing. Opposition from this family, given their solidarity, spelled trouble for a governor, a religious leader or anyone else. The people of the city also held them in the highest esteem. Their words carried considerable weight, and whenever the Arabshahis held gatherings, a great many flocked to them. The city administrators also helped them out at these times, expecting Arabshahi help and backing in return.

As a child, I witnessed some of these gatherings. Very few other groups displayed such solidarity. Even if the most ordinary member of the family or one related to him or under his protection were to be injured, the entire clan from the youngest to the oldest and those affiliated with them would gather in an instant. They displayed remarkable discipline; the commands of the head of the Arabshahis were to be followed like God's commandments. Deferring to age was always an important tradition among them.

Until the reign of Reza Shah, the Arabshahi Seyyeds had a kind of tribal status and exercised a local authority that would later come to an end. Though most members of the family were landowners and farmers, they were also to be found among the ranks of scholars, clerics, seminarians and merchants, who were accorded a special form of respect and regarded as leaders. This served to spread the family's influence.

Another reason for their prestige and authority was a characteristic type of chivalry known in Persian as *javanmardi*. An Arabshahi Seyyed was known for fidelity, honesty, bravery, forbearance, kindness and for protecting to the death those seeking sanctuary. Those qualities had become second nature to them. The weight of custom made it impossible for them to act in any way that violated the code of *javanmardi*. If an Arabshahi Seyyed gave his word, one could rely on it. They acted as protectors of their neighbors, women and the weak and downtrodden. All of this meant that when Arabshahi Seyyeds took action on some matter, the people would follow, closing down the bazaar and carrying out their every command. Heaven help the times when the Seyyeds gathered to hold a conclave.

They made the most influential Hojjat al-Eslams[3] cower in awe. The most powerful administrators respected their wishes and maintained friendships with their leaders, otherwise they could not get anything done. Of course, owing to their code of chivalry, the dictates of reason and their interest in maintaining their authority and family prestige, the Seyyeds never misused their influence. Their close ties to rulers always served the interests of the people, the oppressed and the wronged. This family practice became part of their nature.

Another very interesting side of the Arabshahis was the extraordinary pride they took in their lineage and honor. This was ingrained in me from childhood. Being an Arabshahi Seyyed was synonymous with the terms "excellence," "leader," etc., and they were incredibly proud of this association. Their self-esteem reminded me of the way heads of the ancient Arab clans boasted of their ancestry.

History records the following example of Arabshahi pride. One of the Seyyeds named Mirza Mahmud,[4] who died some fifteen years ago at the age of eighty, was one of the most remarkable individuals I have ever known. Unfortunately the broad sweep of world history fails to mention the names of such individuals. They only remain alive in the memories of a few contemporaries, but as those few pass away nothing remains to mark their existence. I consider it my moral duty, therefore, to speak about this great man. Aqa Mirza Mahmud was one of those individuals in whose existence humanity should take pride. I am absolutely certain that this Seyyed never lied in his entire life—what's more he never contemplated a lie. His was a mountain of moral courage, candor, and simplicity, with a natural, unadorned grandeur. <...>

Mirza Mahmud was a tall, strong figure with a full beard and thick mustache. Slight red lines marked the whites of his striking and penetrating eyes. His brow was broad and deep. His commanding looks were those of an amir or a leader, and on his shaven head a black, worn turban sat carelessly. He wore a shirt with a high collar, which was often unbuttoned and showed his broad, sunburnt chest. He had a long tunic over the shirt and wore a mantle draped from his shoulders. His appearance inspired awe and reverence. He spoke quite eloquently in a fluent Persian with a thick, manly accent. When he became agitated, small specks of foam gathered at the corners of his mouth. He was conversant in Islamic history and sciences, the Qur'an and legends about the Prophet, and he was also familiar with the epic pre-Islamic sagas of Persia. His words were cogent, and what was most evident when he spoke was his complete honesty and sincerity, his fearless devotion to the truth. He owned a bit of land a few kilometers outside of town in a village known as Kaskan. He would visit the property that had some fields and a garden, and toward the end of his life until his death he spent his entire time there. He also had a modest home in Sabzevar on Sarsang Lane in the southern part of the city. The room he occupied was the model of a simple Sabzevari home. The floor was covered with a few strips of felt, and some Baluchi and local carpets. There were also several large leaning pillows at the head of the room. In niches in the walls and in squinches were assorted lamps, lanterns and several books.

During the Constitutional Period the people, because of their complete faith in him, virtually forced Mirza Mahmud to become their advocate in matters related to law and justice. But it was his practice first to be absolutely certain of the truth of his petitioner's case before accepting. Once he did, he would bring all his might and passion to bear. He was well-briefed, persuasive, extraordinarily eloquent. These traits combined with the mere fact that he had taken on a particular case convinced almost everyone in town of the validity of his client's cause. The judges of the judiciary did not dare split hairs with him nor did the opposing attorneys find it advisable to argue. Mirza Mahmud's good character, however, led him to take extraordinary pains to settle cases peacefully, which he often did. He was not concerned in the slightest with his fee. He either took nothing at all or would give it to some needy person. Occasionally he would accept something for himself.

Once on a religious holiday, perhaps Eid-e Ghadir, I visited the home of the late Hajj Mirza Hoseyn Sabzevari, the venerable ayatollah of Sabzevar. Both his house and the large room where he received guests were crowded with people of various classes. It was the time when the late Abdolhoseyn Teimurtash, the minister of justice, had closed the courts in most jurisdictions for reorganization. In any case, Sabzevar's court was closed. The clerics and religious jurists, as a group sworn opponents of the secular justice system, rejoiced. Mirza Mahmud, who was also present to convey his felicitations, sat near his host. With a smirk on his face, Hajj Mirza Hoseyn said sarcastically, "So, Mirza Mahmud, they've shut down your judiciary, too." Mirza Mahmud did not like his tone. He was, moreover, generally not well

disposed to Hajj Mirza Hoseyn because the cleric was not particularly pious, and his sons, the overseers of the household, were not exactly honest. With his typically assertive tone and persuasive eloquence,
he answered, "Yes, Hajj, it's just like the story of the thief who broke
into someone's house. The thief spread his bedding cover on the floor
to fill it with goods he thought he would find there. After searching
the house and finding nothing to steal, he returned to gather the cover; but in the meantime the homeowner, a shameless, naked repro-
bate, had discovered the cover and happily stretched out upon it.
When the thief saw the owner on the cover, he changed his mind
about retrieving it. But as he was tiptoeing from the room, the owner
purposely let out a derisive fart. The thief then turned on him saying,
'You un-self-respecting dolt—I've found nothing here to steal, but I
will go elsewhere, and eventually something will come my way. But
you, you spineless creature, why don't you look at your own life
because no one would call what you have here a home.' You're right,
Hajj, I too will have to find another way of making a living; if it isn't
the courts, it will be something else. But you should think about a
better way of making a living yourself." This was a Seyyed that
enjoyed the unquestioned respect and popularity among the modest
and good people, but he cared little for such clerics. It was clear what
happened to Hajj Mirza Hoseyn at his own gathering. I was present
when Mirza Mahmud had begun his story. I thought it unseemly
and, as one of his kin, wanted to change the subject, but his tone of
voice precluded any interruption. He finished the story and made an
utter fool of the religious elder.

Mirza Mahmud possessed all the admirable traits of a
javanmard—he was a fearless protector of the weak, devoted to the
truth, candid and incorruptible. Of course, not every member of the
Arabshahi clan was a Mirza Mahmud, but they did produce, more or
less, outstanding individuals. I remember from childhood hearing
my father occasionally praising Mirza Mahmud in connection with
something or other. <...>

Every member of the family, no matter what their line of work,
always enjoyed superior status. For example, if a certain Seyyed from

the family was an apothecary, his shop in the bazaar would become a meeting place for groups of merchants and others. He himself would automatically be a trusted member of the community. If any family member were to step out of line, the entire clan would set him straight, not allowing him to dishonor them.

My father was the head of the clan, a very popular and influential leader, to whom all were devoted. His name was Abd al-Ghani, which, as was customary among the Seyyeds, became Mirza Abd al-Ghani. He owned property that consisted of some water rights and the land of the Abd al-Rahman Qanat, one of the most reliable underground irrigation channels in Sabzevar.[5] The greater part of the channel belonged to Hajj Mirza Seyyed, my father's great-ancestor. After his death, it was apportioned and part of it came to my father through inheritance. In addition to the property, there was a mill on the channel and living quarters in the Gowdanbar neighborhood in which the three of us, my brother Hoseyn, my sister and I, were born. These properties provided enough income for a family like ours but were not considered a means to wealth or riches. In the years that I remember the mill produced thousands of pounds of flour, some of which was brought to the house for our use. The land also produced several thousand kilos of barley, wheat and cotton. <...> Father had no money worries; he lived comfortably but not in luxury. Our lives were like those of the rest of the Sabzevaris. In those days, luxury had not reached today's heights. Life was simple and all those with something to their names lived more or less equally.

Father named me after my grandfather Mirza Ghasem. He told me that Mirza Ghasem had been a man of letters and learning, devout and with a fine bearing. Of course, I never saw him, but Father was always relating things about him. The elders of Sabzevar would remember him with respect, and I repeatedly heard Father's friends and others confirm that people would ask the Lord to make my life as useful and decent an existence as my grandfather's. During my years of practicing medicine in Sabzevar I often heard this blessing.

<...>

The cleric Hajj Mirza Hoseyn was the son of Hajj Mirza Seyyed, who, unlike his son, was celebrated for the purity of his intent and his devotion. He lived like the companions at the time of the Prophet; many famous stories circulated about him in Sabzevar that reminded people of such legendary Moslems as Salman Farsi and Ovays Qarani. He was the owner of considerable property and our own land had originally been part of his. Like other farmers he would dutifully go to the fields and reap just enough to meet his own needs and no more. He considered God the real landowner, farming as a duty, and felt his efforts entitled him only to what he and his family truly needed to feed themselves. It is widely known that wherever he stopped for midday prayer, hundreds would follow his lead in search of divine favor. <...>

My father was strong and tall with features that I, his son, found very handsome. He had dignity and, at the same time, was loving and kind. He wore a black turban and also sported the full complement of a long shirt, tunic and mantle. He shaved his head and wore his beard trimmed short. He was extremely neat and went to the public bath every morning. His taste was impeccable and he loved flowers and brooks.

One of my earliest memories (I was four or five) is hearing that the "Aqa," as Father was called, was going to set up a garden outside of town. One day my mother brought me to the garden when they were building the house. At that stage in childhood when everything seemed overly large, I saw the garden, which was probably no more than two thousand square meters, as a huge jungle—the garden house reservoir seemed like one of the wonders of the world. I gaped at the trees and flowers. It was not long before we moved to our new home, to the garden outside the city, as it was known.

Sabzevar is and was particularly devoid of trees. Few compounds had them. The home of Amir Hasan Khan and his son-in-law boasted a few cypresses and pines that were the marvels of the city. In the northern part where water was more plentiful, one saw a few mulberry trees and willows. Some compounds had these and a few fruit trees. If one had taken a tree census, the total would probably not have exceeded two hundred. The city was likewise very short of flowers. A few individuals with flowerpots were the green thumbs of the city. Ordinary geraniums and carnations were considered miraculous. More common were the mirabilis, sunflowers, oleanders, nasturtiums, and, to a lesser extent, morning glories.

Our garden had these and other blooms like petunias and chrysanthemums. There were a few broom, Judas and fruit trees, common and weeping willows, and several grapevines that they had trained to arch forming what is called in Sabzevar a *cheft*. This vine shaded a part of the garden and we would sit in its shade during the summers.

Most important was that the garden had a steady water source that would feed it every week for three or four days and nights. The water, known as *qasabeh*, would rush into the compound through a small waterfall and gurgle into an oval pool that Sabzevaris called a *daryacheh* [lake]. The channel ran the entire length of the house and reached the property next to ours, which we later purchased. This became my brother's house, and now it belongs to our maternal aunt and cousins. Early in the morning when Father woke, as soon as he emerged from the bath he tended to each flower and tree lovingly. Today I can appreciate how much pleasure he took from this. I was also an early riser, and, as soon as I opened my eyes, I would fly out of the house. Father would tell me: Ghasem, come and see this flower that was so small yesterday and tomorrow will become this way or that. Look at this part, he would say, look at this genista, how it resembles the broom. <...> In constant motion, he would circle the garden, visiting the Judas tree and all the greenery. He would walk along the water channels and without thinking dip his hand into the water to enjoy its feel, as if merely seeing it was not sufficiently satisfying.

In those morning hours, Father also enjoyed visiting his vats of wine, which were kept in two cellars. Early in the morning he would see to all the vats himself. Later he would tell his friends that he had just opened such-and-such vat, describing to them the wine's intoxicating rumbling and foaming; how this white wine gleamed like a diamond or that batch shone ruby red. He would say which vat had the best young wines, which grapes were good, which were bad. Some of these wines Father and his friends drank at home. Those were simpler times when there weren't any excise taxes or other formalities.

Another of Father's favorite pastimes was reading. I especially remember the books he always kept near his chair: Mowlana's *Masnavi*, Hafez and other poets' works (if there were other books, I was not that familiar with them). The *Masnavi* was an old edition published in India with the calligraphy of Hakim or Vesal. Later he bought the Ala al-Dowleh edition with the concordance.

As soon as I could read, father set verses from Sa'di and the *Masnavi* for me to memorize. For each line he gave me a coin that I deposited in the slot of a metal (most likely tin) bank that I kept buried on the grounds. He delighted in listening to me recite and correcting me. At that time I remember learning the first story in the *Masnavi*, "The King and the Slave Girl," which I would recite mechanically, understanding little. I owe my present command of the entire tale to his encouragement.

I remember once father's friend Hajj Aqa Ebrahim, a large landowner and member of the Sabzevar elite, was at our home. Father called me, explaining to Hajj Ebrahim that I had memorized a few things. He encouraged me to recite from the *Masnavi* and Sa'di. Hajj Ebrahim praised me and then turned to father and said something that I can only imperfectly recall now: "He'll never get the meaning right. What's the point of this? "Father answered, "The point is to develop or fortify his retention." His response was a mystery to me. What did "fortify" mean? What was "retention"? After Hajj Aqa Ebrahim left, I repeatedly asked father to explain. He put it in a way that I could understand, but for years the true meaning of what he had said puzzled me. Even now the word "retention" resonates strangely in my mind. Throughout my studies of psychology, the subject of memory and retention has exerted a special pull. Even when I lectured on mental illness and psychiatry in Tehran at the theological college and the medical school, I made this subject one of the mainstays of my lectures, for I was inexorably drawn to it.

Another thing I recall happened when I was a boy about ten years old. Father took me to the home of one of his dearest friends, Hajj

Mirza Mohammad Ali Sadr al-Ashraf Sabzevari. While I was there, Father had to leave to meet someone and then return. During the interim, Hajj Mohammad Ali, who was sitting with a number of people in the outer quarters of his home, began singing my praises to his guests: "Master Mirza Ghasem, the son of Aqa Mirza Abd al-Ghani, is a fine boy. He studies hard and knows many poems by heart." Then he asked me to recite. So I began to rattle off some pieces or odes, whatever I knew from Sa'di. Among the group in attendance, all of whom were cheering my performance, was a cleric wearing a large white turban. In my childish imagination I inflated that turban into a huge millstone, and today it might be difficult to persuade my recollection that it was not as immense as I had thought then. In any case, the cleric gruffly said, "What's the meaning of this? Why have they given him Sa'di's verses to memorize? Sa'di was Sunni." At that time I was not familiar with the last word. From his tone I gathered that it meant something bad, and he was objecting to my knowing a bad person's poetry by heart. I found his speech and presence so hard to take that I burst out crying. With Father not there, I felt estranged and terrified. Sadr al-Ashraf brought me close to him, took my hand and soothed me. At the same time, he started to argue heatedly with the cleric. I don't remember his exact words, but the gist was that he was castigating him. At this point Father entered and asked, "What's this all about? Why are you crying, Ghasem?" I didn't feel like answering, but Sadr al-Ashraf, who by nature was a mischief-maker (later I saw him toying with people and even provoking them), said dryly, "Reverend Molla Mohammad objects to your son's reciting Sa'di. Why, he asks, did you make him learn the poetry of a Sunni?"

Father loved me dearly; I was his first son and now as I judge the intricacies of his behavior toward me, I know the depth of his affection. I also know him to have been especially fair-minded. He said to me, "No need to cry, dear boy, this cleric is an utter fool." Then he turned to Molla Mohammad and asked half-jokingly, "Why are you such an ass, Molla Mohammad?" Even the cleric laughed. Though I had had my revenge, his laughter bothered me. Deep down I wanted him to cry or to be embarrassed, too. <...>

Father had a group of close friends that often would visit us. In this group, which met every night, was Mirza Esma'il Taleqani, known as Eftekhar al-Hokama or "Pride of Physicians," who lived to over a hundred until succumbing about twenty-one years ago to liver failure and virulent jaundice. He is buried in the tomb of his teacher Hajj Molla Hadi Sabzevari.[6]

Eftekhar al-Hokama had met Molla Hadi around 1868–69, five years before the renowned philosopher's death (February 1873). A physician by profession, Eftekhar al-Hokama had a firm grounding in science and also was a skilled mathematician. He practiced medicine for several years in Barforush and Tehran and accompanied a Qajar prince to St. Petersburg as companion and doctor. He had taken up the study of Illuminist philosophy. He went to Sabzevar to study with Hajj Molla Hadi, who, after an interview, encouraged him to become one of his students. He would say to his students, "Most of you are weak in mathematics. Learn from this Mirza Taleqani, who knows the subject well." The grounding in the preliminaries of philosophy and other learning allowed Eftekhar al-Hokama to take full advantage of his teacher's lectures, and he became one of his most accomplished disciples. At the same time, being Hajj Molla Hadi's student enhanced his reputation as a physician. After his teacher's death, Eftekhar al-Hokama, while famed as a skilled practitioner, also taught Illuminist philosophy and other subjects. This regimen continued until the final weeks of his life. In addition to the philosophy and works of Hajj Molla Hadi, he taught traditional medicine, mathematics, rhetoric, jurisprudence and music.

The man's grasp of classical learning was encyclopedic and, by virtue of years of teaching, well rehearsed. He was also familiar with new medicine and knew a little French. He was very patient and forbearing. He wore the turban of a physician and, in winter, a splendid fur mantle, while in summer, a magnificent printed cloth and a spun silk cloak. His walking stick was embellished. When mounted on his donkey, at least one person preceded him on foot. Eftekhar al-Hokama would go to his clinic early and assume his place on a fine Turkman carpet covering a raised platform near the lower entryway bench. Before him were his penholder, a scroll, and several small pieces of paper for prescriptions. A number of books were also on each side of him. To his left there was a curtain behind which his female patients sat. His male patients sat on the bench at the lower entry. There was no waiting room, no physical examinations—it was old-fashioned medicine. With his dyed beard, distinguished bearing, and fine clothes, Eftekhar sat like an amir at times, smoking aromatic tobacco in a water pipe that a servant kept filling. He had someone call out to the patient, "So-and-so Hajji, what do you say, what ails you?" The patient explained his complaint, and Eftekhar would ask him to come forward. He would take his pulse, examine his tongue and over-all appearance, and ask a few questions. Then with a reed pen he would write a prescription in his fine hand, tell the patient what to eat and dismiss him. Then he would call the next patient. In the same way, he would feel a female patient's pulse and, when near to him, examine her tongue from behind the curtain and write a prescription.

Because of his advanced years, Eftekhar was like a father to the city. He knew young and old and joked with everybody. With the gravity of an old-time doctor, he would laugh and tell little amusing tales. After hours, the clinic became a school. At noon he would go to the inner quarters, in the afternoon he would hold court outside. His courtyard was wetted down and swept of dust, and had a working water-pantry. He would seldom go out—anyone inclined to see him had to visit his premises. When the doors closed at sundown, he would begin to drink his wine. He drank a lot, becoming drunk quickly, and he was one of those awful drunks who passed out every night without exception. The next morning he awoke not knowing when or how he had gone to bed nor who had put him there. He had two wives: one old, one young. The young one was the older one's niece. He had no children.

In one of the rooms of his own compound near the tomb of Hajj Molla Hadi he had a crypt constructed. There were three graves in it—the middle one was for him, the ones on either side for his wives. Though he was a freethinking physician who had no faith in any-thing, he endowed a caravanserai next to the tomb where on

Thursday nights they would perform the Passions of the Karbala saints. He found this necessary to forestall accusations of blasphemy and apostasy.

After I returned from Beirut and was practicing medicine in Sabzevar, my respect for Eftekhar al-Hokama was almost limitless. As he was one of Father's closest friends, my esteem for him was filial. I did whatever he wanted of me. After he had become elderly, I sent people by to see if he needed anything. Whenever I traveled out of town, I made it a point to call on him and, upon my return, would also see him. One day when I was about to go to Bojnurd, I sent word that I would visit him that afternoon as my trip would last several days. I arrived late in the day, about half an hour before sunset. The compound door was open and, as soon as I entered, Eftekhar got to his feet so abruptly that he appeared to have vaulted into the air. Then he wrapped his cloak around himself and sat down. I asked him, "Hajj Aqa, what were you doing?" He changed the subject. I then repeated, "What were you doing when I came in? It seemed as though you had jumped in the air." "Let's drop the subject, shall we?" he suggested. I persisted, "Aqa, the more you evade the question, the more you arouse my curiosity, so please." "If I tell you," he answered, "I will confirm my own stupidity." But he eventually said, "I was waiting for you. When you came early, I noticed that the door was open and thought someone might come by, so to fool them I stood pretending to pray. But you entered and spoiled my act, so to cover up I hurriedly put on my cloak and sat down." "Aqa," I asked him, "if your prayer was sincere, why didn't you continue, and, if it was a sham, then who are you trying to fool?" He said, "I told you myself that it is my own stupidity that has been confirmed, so no more criticism."

He had this kind of wit, but his drinking sessions were awful for he quickly became drunk, making everyone uncomfortable. He began by cursing God and all that was holy and sacrosanct. Sometimes he would cry excessively. My presence at several sessions led him to recall his closeness to my father and weep over his memory. He was hard to take, and I would try to avoid being with him at night when he would insist that everyone drink. <...> However, all in all, Eftekhar al-Hokama was a very good man who spent a lifetime helping others.

<...>

Father's large circle knew only one way of being friends. They were a free-living, nonconformist group, who cared little for what others said. They enjoyed themselves and did not believe in squandering life's capital. They formed a united front, agreeable comrades always ready to help one another. Their get-togethers were all about drinking, music, singing, books, travel, and walks in the gardens and surroundings. Because Father was the very model of independence and indifferent to established codes, and unafraid of the hypocrites, he was the leader of this group. He was also the head of the Arabshahi clan, who were not known for hypocrisy. He enjoyed complete authority among the people for whom he was protector and advocate. So it was only natural that he be considered the protector of this large group of friends. <...> They behaved in short with a kind of freedom and latitude rarely found elsewhere.

Everyone is likely to form an image of a great person from the past and to liken it in his mind to some contemporary. After searching repeatedly for the historical figure most like Father, being wholly objective and avoiding a son's natural prejudice, I have reached the conclusion that he was the perfect image of the poet Hafez. In my mind, Hafez's behavior, way of life and thought were Father's. He associated with everyone, liked one and all, sympathized with their suffering and had a kind of universal vision. Most of what I know about him came after his death, and this was later sharpened after I got to know his surviving friends. From them, I heard details of how he had lived. His wide circle of acquaintances took in the high and the low. He valued every moment of life, and was a man who had reached a certain mystical state of ecstasy. He faced the world with courage.

Everybody in Sabzevar knows the story of Father's courageous death. Several months before the cholera of 1904–05, he traveled to Tehran to attend to some business regarding his lands. Hajj Mirza Mohammad Ali Sadr al-Ashraf had already journeyed to Tehran for a similar purpose. This was at the end of the reign of Mozaffar al-Din Shah, when Ayn al-Dowleh was prime minister. While Father was completing the business in Tehran a cholera epidemic spread from Baghdad to the city. Every day hundreds of people were perishing. Riding in several horse-drawn carriages, wagons and coaches, Father and Sadr al-Ashraf along with a group of Sabzevaris and servants set out from Tehran. Before reaching the first winter campground about 130 kilometers outside of town, Father came down with cholera and became very weak. Everyplace they went people were infected and succumbing, but there was no one to gather their bodies. Wherever they tried to camp they found the dying and the dead. It was not possible to set up camp near them and, at the same time, take care of their own sick. Finally they reached a caravanserai where there were the infected in every corner and chaos reigned. They got to the roof where they found a dead body. They removed it and put people in charge of seeing to the shroud and burial. Then they cleared a space for my father. They said that he insisted that his friends keep journeying a few more kilometers and perhaps outpace the epidemic. Sadr al-Ashraf and the others told me that Father was constantly urging them to move on as his time was up. Despite his illness, he said with a smile, "Don't bother about me. Did anyone imagine that we'd be around forever? It's as I've always told you, live while you can for death is coming at a gallop and will shortly overtake us." This was his own particular way of referring to death. He continued, "We've been on the move for four days. You must move quickly. I'm going to die here, so leave some money with the owner of this place to bury me." Then with consummate realism he said, "There's nothing to dying, think about yourselves." He asked Sadr al-Ashraf only to take some papers from his pocket and briefcase and make sure they reached his children. Several hours later he passed away and was buried in that place. Sadr al-Ashraf and the others got back to Sabzevar where several weeks later cholera broke out. But Father's lightheartedness in the face of death, and his equanimity and poise became legendary. In this he was for me a modern-day Hafez, a liberated soul. He had a philosopher's outlook. He appreciated the arts and poetry. At the time of his death he was a man of about fifty-five.

MY BIRTH

As was said, I was born in Sabzevar (apparently on 20 March 1893) in that very house in Gowdanbar that we later rented out and, after Father's death, sold. My mother, Roqiyeh, was the daughter of Molla Ali Sabzevari. At the time of my writing this (September 1948), she is about seventy-five and lives in Sabzevar with my youngest brother Mahmud and my sister.

In his youth, Father married an Arabshahi woman, one of his own kin who bore him a daughter. But that wife died several years later, and he married my mother perhaps around 1890. I remember my stepsister well, as one who loved me very much and cared for my mother. My mother also loved her. When I was perhaps seven she died, most likely committing suicide by taking opium. I heard that she had wanted to marry a neighbor's boy, but social considerations stood in the way making the marriage impossible. The girl's maternal aunt and uncle were particularly opposed, and Father, who himself was not altogether happy about the match, left the decision up to the maternal aunt. In the end, the inexperienced girl lost hope and killed herself. It was said at the time that she died of natural causes, but I think it was most likely suicide. When it happened, they only told me that she had died, but I was too young to know about death. I recall her as being a tall girl with a broad forehead and fine features, always a willing companion to me.

My mother was greatly affected by her death, becoming depressed because they were about the same age and were very close. For years afterward, I noticed that whenever her name came up, my mother lamented her death and always spoke well of her.

I have a sister two years younger than I named Aqa Bibi. There was also a brother who died when he was a few months old. Then another brother, Hoseyn, followed. In 1902, two years before father's death, my youngest brother Mahmud was born.

On my mother's side there was my grandmother who died of cholera a few months after my father in our home outside of town. I have the most wonderful memories of this fine woman who was like a bird of paradise. She embodied whatever the world has written on affection and tenderheartedness, love and motherly attachment.

When news of Father's death reached Sabzevar, she said she could no longer go on and would soon be gone. She was extraordinarily fond of my father, and he returned her affection. Several days later when cholera had spread in the city, my aunt Robabeh, the next-oldest daughter after my mother, also came down with the disease. Grandmother, whom we called Naneh, was always at her daughter's bedside. When Robabeh's condition became critical, she said with a devotion and natural directness and simplicity that recalls the shepherd's prayer in Moses' time that Rumi describes in the *Masnavi*, "Lord, my daughter is too young to go and I am old. Save her and take me instead." In the pure world that woman inhabited, it was as though a voice assured her the exchange would be made, that Robabeh would get better, which is what happened. After her daughter's recovery, Naneh became ill, died and was buried in the Nishapur Gate cemetery. One can put everything in the world into words more or less except emotions and impressions on the psyche. It is impossible for me to describe that woman whose frail body contained all the love in the world and whose heart was pure devotion.

My earliest memories of Naneh go back to a time when we were living in the old Gowdanbar house. A few paces to the south of our lane near a neighborhood called Sarsang was the modest home she shared with her oldest son, Aqa Mohammad Hasan, and her youngest child Hoseyn. Aqa Mohammad Hasan had a wife, while Hoseyn was a child about three years older than I. Naneh's other son, next oldest to Aqa Mohammad Hasan, was a student in Eshqabad. Her daughter Robabeh also lived in Eshqabad with her husband, the son of her paternal uncle Aqa Mohammad Ebrahim Tajer.

Naneh's affection was a magnet that drew me to her. Deep down I wanted to be near her, and it was clear that she returned the feeling, in part because my uncle Hoseyn and I were so close in age. I would go there often to be around Naneh. <...>

I had no relatives on my father's side. He had no siblings, his only relative being my late stepsister. I never saw my paternal grandmother who died two years before I was born. But on my mother's side was an extensive family.

SCHOOL

When I was around six, still living in the Gowdanbar house, there was an old woman named Naneh Aqa near us. She was called "the mother of Aqa" because her two sons were "Aqas"; one, a seminary student, was Aqa Seyyed Reza and the other, a preacher of the passion of the martyrs of Karbala, was Aqa Nezam al-'Olama. She ran a school in her house where she taught reading and writing to several boys and girls my age. Every student had an alphabet primer, and the more advanced ones had a reader with the last chapters of the Qur'an. With a switch made of a pomegranate branch in her hand, Naneh Aqa sat in the front of her humble basement, while we were on the ground on both sides of her. Often the children would supply a piece of carpeting or hide to sit on. The students learned the sounds of the alphabet and spelling. Several would recite out loud with their Sabzevari accents the three possible pronunciations depending on how each letter of the alphabet beginning with "alef" was voweled. Then they would graduate to the Qur'anic reader, and after students had mastered that they were given a certificate of completion from Naneh Aqa. Every month students paid a few cents in tuition. They brought a lunch box with food like chopped meat, bread, cheese, fruit, and sweets. They ate some of the food and gave some to Naneh Aqa.

When I went to the new house there was another teacher lady near us called "Daughter of Hajji Arab." I was at this school longer than at Naneh Aqa's. My new teacher was called Arab after her father who had been resident in Karbala and Najaf ("Arab" generally meant

Iraq). She was an old woman; so old did she appear in my childish mind that I imagined that no one in creation could have preceded her. Any thought I had about ancient times was coupled with her image. For example, I imagined that her hair was white even at the time of Noah's flood. When they spoke about the Prophet and the Imam, I imagined that they knew Daughter of Hajji Arab. I don't know why no other elder made such an impression on me. With her very large, red face and pronounced cheekbones, and her head and eyebrows of thick, unkempt hair white as billowing snow, the old lady was ill-formed and hard to look at. She had a daughter who was also ancient. Her grandchildren were grown and some of their children were our classmates.

This Daughter of Hajji Arab had a huge appetite. She watched what we ate like a hawk, and whoever ate their fill early, she would praise by saying that this was an intelligent student not like those others who ate too much. Those that brought the most generous and varied lunches became her favorites. We quickly learned to have our families pack ample lunches as we dashed out the door and to eat as little as possible while in school. Our fevered competition for her attention reached such a pitch that some of us would not eat altogether. Naturally this did not please her, and she forced us to eat something. The daughter of Daughter of Hajji Arab collected our leftovers, sorted them, and presented them to her mother. This was part of our schoolhouse diversions. The Daughter of Hajji Arab also kept a hefty cane in front of her, which, of course, she did not use on anyone but waved from time to time.

We memorized the book of Qur'an selections without understanding a word, of course. But we were always reciting it even in the alleys. In the wintertime besides the monthly tuition, we also paid fuel money. The school was heated with a coal brazier and sometimes would fill with smoke.

Soon thereafter, Father brought around a preacher to tutor me named Aqa Sheikh Abbas Damghani who lived in a humble dwelling near us. He had a study cell at the Shari'atmadari Seminary. Though a seminarian, he lived outside the seminary with a Sabzevari wife, who was my mother's frequent guest. Childless and often alone, the wife spent hours at our house until her husband came by and told her that it was time to go home. Aqa Sheikh Abbas was very ill-tempered and exceedingly ugly and morose. In my whole life, I have never seen a brow more furrowed with anger and hostility than his. He inspired dread. Though he never hit me himself, I was so frightened of him that when I was being lazy and it took me too long to wake on school mornings, the maid had only to say "Aqa Sheikh Abbas" and I would leap from bed perfectly alert. I associated the name Abbas with words like lightning, storm, thunder, disaster, catastrophe, omen. This Aqa Sheikh also visited a number of other homes to teach. He did not carry a cane or a stick but kept a chain in his pocket with which he beat a student when necessary. Though I never actually felt the sting of this chain, I dreaded it so much that I learned well. The Sheikh taught the *Golestan* and made us memorize the rhymed Arabic lexicon *Nesab al-Sebyan*. Of course I was at an age when I did not gain anything from memorizing the hundreds of lines of poetry in it. I merely recited them like a parrot.

Educators identify a variety of factors that influence students' intellectual growth and development. Each factor plays in its own way an important role in shaping the mind and in developing the natural talents of students. They include teaching methodology—making the subject commensurate with the intellectual level of the student; speaking with young students in ways that do not exceed their grasp and patience and explaining things to them in their own language with comparisons and analogies to things from the places in which they were raised; the appeal of the learning environment; whether their teachers are neat and good-looking or ugly; whether they treat students kindly and respectfully or brutally and callously.

In one of his books, Anatole France[7] says that when he was about seven his mother took him to a nearby schoolhouse run by a mademoiselle. She entrusted her son to the mademoiselle, who was responsible for teaching reading and writing to a number of children in the neighborhood. France describes his teacher's beauty and charm. What he sees through the prism of a seven-year-old's memory amounts to this: the young boy's natural eye for beauty recognized in the mademoiselle a shapeliness and grace not found in others. He recounts the way she looked when deep in thought and says this transfixed him. Looking at her, which he did constantly, gave him pleasure. When he returned from school and his mother asked him what he had done that day, he said, "Mother, I looked at mademoiselle." She laughed at him, not attaching any importance to his childish response. But, France writes that he must admit if he had learned anything, it was in the aura of that very "gazing at mademoiselle," which as the first step in the life of his intellect taught him the meaning of proportion and elegance. This made such a deep impression on him that when he went off to the Stanislaus School where the teachers had tried hard to twist his mind, the lasting stamp of mademoiselle's education negated their efforts. The impression those first lessons made was sturdier than what the priests had tried to superimpose on it. Anatole France was educated, as Hafez would say, "in the school of truths from the teacher of love."

The contrast between France's initial education and my own is the difference between night and day. The three teachers I had during that time when the young mind is at its most impressionable consisted of Naneh Aqa, a poor old lady of sixty, ancient enough to be Noah's sister; the Daughter of Hajji Arab, the ill-natured she-devil; and Molla Abbas Damghani, the father of frights, whose face, surliness and foul temper will always epitomize for me everything I heard about the villains that ordered and carried out the martyrdom of Imam Hoseyn at Karbala. I studied with them in cellars that were as dank as black holes, with filthy dirt floors covered with sections of nasty felt and gelims. My classmates were unwashed innocents, each dressed in ridiculous clothing of haphazard colors and shapes. To the sensitive young people these classrooms were humorless places where there were no smiles, kindly faces, nor softness. Any student that laughed was branded ill-bred, castigated and sometimes beaten. After class, as we headed for home through the alleys and breathed the fresh air, we flew past the walls and doorways, as though nature, which had been bottled up inside us, was now trying to escape.

The worst part of that education was that I did not understand what I memorized. As I returned from school I would recite—either alone or chorally with the other students—the things we had learned from the Qur'an. <...> Our recreation came when a baby was born at the home of a classmate or a well-known family of the town. They would bring the whole class around so we could sing the *Salam Allah* [God's blessing] to the baby: "O you with the face as lovely as the moon, may Ali the Prince of Believers protect you." Our host would greet us warmly and give us candy. This basically provided an excuse to get outside and was a red-letter day in our childhood. Of course the ever vigilant schoolmarm would always get some loaf sugar or fabric or money from the host.

However you look at it, Iranians are an odd alloy. Unlike other children of God, nothing about them from cradle to grave makes any sense. With those filthy cities, those cramped surroundings, the ruin and desolation everywhere you look, the dust and dirt, the flies and mosquitoes, the crooked and lopsided doors and walls and twisting lanes, the exclusion of any beauty whether natural or artificial, that ignorance, poverty and deprivation, disease, unsightliness and unseemliness, the state of education, and that breed of instructors, teachers and tutors, it's a wonder that we survived at all. The education of European and American children begins partly at home, in the society around them. With each new stage what they know grows and grows. Their environments are neat and clean; they hear the irrelevant and useless less than we do and they see the ugly, the objectionable and the repulsive less than we. Each period in their lives comes with the appropriate form of entertainment and recreation. The children can learn from their museums, churches, theatres, books, the streets, neighborhoods and one another. The upshot of this is enthusiasm, moderation and proportion.

Such was my wretched childhood and such were those to whom I am indebted for teaching me. May God bless them all, for they were in their own way products of that same environment.

Of course, we were among the more fortunate and privileged who had parents, servants and maids. They provided books, paper and food, and, no matter the sacrifice, managed to educate us, make us literate. Thousands and thousands of the rest of the people were denied these privileges and regarded us with envy. Praise God, they would say, so-and-so's son has learned his ABCs, can read and write, and is educated. So our guardians would pin charms against the evil eye on our sleeves or hang them around our necks, and burn wild rue incense. We were among the fortunate few.

In any event, I soon managed to become literate and, with Father's encouragement, practiced my calligraphy. I memorized prose and verse selections and recited and wrote them fluently, which made father ecstatic as I was his eldest son. <...>

My literacy had reached the point that Father occasionally would have me write compositions and bring them to him—also some simple things like the receipt for flour for the mill. I now appreciate how his face was brimming with joy and satisfaction that his son could read and write. He would tell everyone about my latest accomplishment. Perhaps it was father's encouragement that was the main factor in shaping my mind and fortifying my spirit, the thing that got me started on the road to learning and engendered in me a sense of self-respect. This feeling always remained with me in later years, when I did well studying in Tehran and Beirut. I sensed from teachers that same spiritually nourishing encouragement that I had gotten from Father. I would always get to school before the others and help any student who had problems with that day's lessons. In the morning I noticed several people waiting for me to explain the complexities of a variety of subjects. This was an endless source of pleasure. The students' admiration reinforced my sense of self-respect and self-reliance.

I was twelve years old when Father passed away. It was the middle of a summer day, and Mother and I were resting in the basement. Sabzevar has fierce summers that make these basement refuges from the heat a necessity. They are basements that go down two or three steps. Hajji Qorban, Eftekhar al-Hokama's servant, came by and said to Mother, "Eftekhar al-Hokama sends his greetings and says it has been a while since he's heard from you and your children. So he sent me around." A little later Eftekhar entered. My mother had had a carpet spread in the compound before the entrance to the basement. There she welcomed Eftekhar al-Hokama as I stood near the doorway listening to them. His face strained in grief and his voice sorrowful, he said that a telegram had arrived saying that *Aqa* (Father) had fallen ill while on the road. Of course, news of the cholera in Tehran had reached us and every day the terrified people were getting word that someone had died. My mother began to cry. Listening at the basement doorway, I also immediately started to cry though until that time the only experience with death in my family was the passing of that sister when I was very young. I reasoned that if someone had died, they wouldn't tell us all at once. They would prefer to say that he was sick and then let the truth out gradually. This made me sure that father had actually died. Eftekhar said a bit more that I did not understand and Mother continued to cry.

After Eftekhar had left, Mother entered the basement and, seeing me crying, kissed me and said, "Don't cry, Father has only been taken ill." But it wasn't long before the family gathered. My grandmother entered crying, and my maternal uncles came. I imagine that from that point on Grandmother, Uncle Mirza Azizollah Khan, Uncle Hoseyn, Uncle Aqa Mohammad Hasan and his wife, and my maternal aunt all began staying with us. Three or four days later, Sadr al-Ashraf and Father's other companions arrived. As soon as he got there, Sadr al-Ashraf took me away to his home. The next day they held the memorial service and mourning. They gathered Father's possessions, papers and documents, and Sadr al-Ashraf was designated my guardian. Not more than a few days later cholera came to Sabzevar. My maternal aunt came down with it and survived, but Grandmother did not. In the city thousands were dying and there was chaos. Everyone tried to flee to the far mountain villages, but many died on the plains, proving the truth of the verse, "Wherever ye are death will find you out."

After the cholera passed, thoughts once again turned to continuing my education. By this point I could read and write fluently. They sent me to study at the Molla Hadi Sabzevari school with Aqa Mirza

Ruhollah Sabzevari, a Sufi of the Gonabadi lodge. This man was always in a state of contemplative self-renouncement, sitting cross-legged in his cell, holding his knees with eyes on the ground and shaking his head slowly from side to side. Occasionally he would also place his head on his knees and, after a while, lift it and sigh, intoning things like "There is no power or might but with the Lord" or "O, Truth!" or "O, He!" This man was a fine calligrapher. He made a living by taking on several students and getting a few coins monthly from each—at this time (more than fifty years ago) a few coins was a considerable income. This was how some ten to fifteen children of Sabzevar's well-to-do came to study with him. Mirza Ruhollah was affiliated with Molla Hadi Sabzevari by family connection.

Aqa Mirza Ruhollah is a very good man—"is" because I believe he is still alive. He was calm, sedate and a devotee of the path toward mystical understanding. While he was in contemplation in his cell, the students sat quietly. Those with books read. When he reached a certain state, he would smoke his long-stemmed pipe. His mind elsewhere, he would absently ask one of the students to fill the pipe or one of them would do so on his own. He started teaching us the standard works: *Hedayat*, Mir's *Grammar*, the *Golestan*. He also taught us how to shave the nib of a reed pen and how to hold it, how to make ink with lamp soot, how to starch paper and how to color it and make it shiny, how to write with onion water, saffron and the essences of other hues, and how to extract them. He gave each student examples of calligraphy to copy and praised their efforts. He had attractive features and we all liked him. He was also humane; there were no switches or canes in his class and none were treated harshly. Because he maintained equal respect for all, his students behaved reasonably, treating their teacher and classmates with the same respect, which was why we attended his classes with pleasure. <...>

It was not long before another school had become famous: the Aqa Sheikh Abd al-'Azim Academy. This Sheikh was a forty-or fifty-year-old merchant with premises at the Aqa Serai, a trading place where many of the reputable merchant houses rented space. <...>

Aqa Sheikh Abd al-'Azim rented a spacious room at the serai for a school. They sent the three of us—me, my maternal uncle Hoseyn and my brother Hoseyn—to this school. This Sheikh was stricter than Aqa Ruh. Every day he would give us calligraphy exercises to complete and give back to him. Besides these exercises and the standard grammars, there was also the considerably more useful reader *Tarikh-e Mo'jam*, which he explained word for word and whose more difficult expressions he would say in Persian as we wrote them down. We had to memorize the poetry in the book. Among the innovations at this school was letter writing and composition. The teacher himself would provide sample letters and then assign us topics: requests, appeals for friendship, congratulations on the occasion of a birth, commiserations for the death of a friend.

This Sheikh was particularly fastidious; his clothes were always neat and freshly pressed. He sat on a soft, bright pillow and his charcoal brazier was spotless. There was a small, finely wrought samovar with two immaculate teacups, all meticulously arranged. In the late afternoon he would make tea and drink it. He rolled his own cigarettes of fine Rasht tobacco that he kept in a tin under his mat so it would not spill. The room was also immaculate, and he became very upset if a student made a mess. There was a cane in front of him, but I never saw him use it, though he would shake it sometimes. When he was in a bad mood he would say something in Turkish meaning, "Boy, do you want me to knock your teeth in?" The Sheikh married a woman from Sabzevar with whom he lived in a modest home.

Years later, after I had become a physician, I returned to Sabzevar and asked about this teacher. They said that he was ill and could no longer manage a school. In addition, the Ministry of Education, which had opened several primary schools, closed the old-fashioned ones. This robbed the Sheikh of his living. Owing to a strongly held belief he was not prepared to become a teacher in a government school. Instead, he worked as a scribe near the entryway benches outside the Molla Hadi Seminary, writing letters for the illiterate and getting something in return. The Sheikh did not come to visit me, rather I went to him one day at his place of work and showed him great respect. I also visited his home at night and invited him to come by. Sometimes he would and do some work I had commissioned. On holidays and other such occasions, I would send him some money in gratitude for his teaching. The Sheikh took pleasure in this and would boast to the Sabzevaris that he had been my teacher, and that I was the only one who appreciated him. He passed away some years ago.

Gradually a keen desire for learning grew in me. I was reading a great number of books; I loved poetry and various other subjects, especially history. I copied passages into notebooks, imagining that I was making my own anthology. I wish I had those notebooks today to see what kinds of things appealed to a boy of thirteen or fourteen. That love of reading has never left me, and I habitually copy down things that I read.

Another source of encouragement was cousin Fatemeh, the daughter of my maternal aunt. Fatemeh knew Persian literature well and was an enthusiastic writer, reader and note-taker. My cousin lived with her younger sisters, little brothers and parents in a house that was attached to ours. Fatemeh and I were inseparable, bound by a deep regard for one another. To me she was a kind of confidante and soul mate. Mother and my aunt, everyone, wanted us to wed— become engaged, that is, and after a few years, married. That this was common knowledge made Fatemeh and me overly shy and modest; it robbed us of the freedom and spontaneity of just being ourselves. We had to be very careful not to let anyone think that we were in love.

The thought process is strange. The rumors about Fatemeh and me, our relatives' occasional glances, turned what was one of the most spiritual and purest types of love into something sordid, making us feel suspicious and anxious. Despite this, Fatemeh left a miraculous impression on my emotional makeup, on my heart and soul. Indeed, I owe her my ability to form attachments. It is as if she nurtured in me the capacity to love others purely and unselfishly, to want their happiness without expecting anything in return. I have always needed friends like these. <...>

I have been close to a number of women throughout my life. Only I know to what extent these relationships have been simply

Platonic and how much I have dreaded that physical desires would contaminate them. Of course, very few people are capable of such friendship. <...> To sit and talk with a true companion is paradise for me. Both Fatemeh and I benefited from being together—how much we read and wrote to one another.

After I left Sabzevar, Fatemeh went to Eshqabad with her family. There she married a man who is now [1948] a merchant in Sabzevar. Both are in good health and have several children. Their eldest daughter Zia'ieh is herself married with children. Fatemeh's younger sister, Monireh, was married to my brother Hoseyn in Eshqabad. They now have three children and live in Mashhad; their oldest boy, Ruhi, is married and has a child. There is a son Amin, and their youngest, Firuz, both students in the United States.

Among the things I read those days was *Habl al-Matin*, a Persian newspaper published in Calcutta to which my uncle Aqa Mirza Azizollah Khan had a subscription. He also got newspapers from Tehran and Mashhad, some books and other publications, all of which I read avidly. These I more or less understood, but whatever the case they made good reading practice. The random general information I got from reading made me eager to sit and listen when the adults would gather to discuss the events of the day. Whether they spoke of the Russo-Japanese War, of foreign countries, or told the stories of individuals and nations, I was able to derive something from their conversations because of this background information. Reading these newspapers also gave me a stock of high-sounding words and phrases like "knowledge and education," "sciences and learning," "arts and crafts," "rule of law," "progress" and "civilization." I vaguely understood them to be positive and this encouraged me somehow to become "learned." The dream of education became a desire that intensified daily.

When I was fourteen, I heard people saying that the shah had decreed that Iran become a constitutional monarchy. Science and learning were to prosper, and, to prevent tyranny and injustice, the rule of law was to be established. This news created a sensation among the people. Every face beamed with excitement and enthusi-

asm. Hope breezed through the land. But, several months later, we
learned of Mozaffar al-Din Shah's death. Those who knew him as the
founder of the constitutional monarchy, loved him. The Sabzevaris
gathered at the congregational mosque to mourn. <...>

Several months later, when news of the shelling of Parliament
spread, the people gave in to despair. Before the news reached us, my
family, including my two maternal uncles Aqa Mohammad Hasan and
Aqa Mirza Azizollah Khan, had agreed that I ought to go to Tehran.
Considering my love of learning, Tehran with its great number of new
schools was the best place for me. I was also determined to go, so finally Uncle Aqa Mohammad Hasan sacrificed his time to accompany me
there. While in Tehran, he was to establish his own trading company.
He had just divorced his wife (why, I don't know) and had no children.
But the shelling of Parliament and news of unrest in the city caused
the trip to be postponed. In the meantime, I could hardly wait for my
dream to come true. Finally, during the reign of Mohammad Ali
Shah—known in history as the Minor Tyranny—Uncle Aqa
Mohammad Hasan and I went to Tehran. We set out one day in a
coach belonging to a driver from the Caucasus called Safar Deli
(Crazy Safar). It was a brand-new and clean carriage pulled by a team
of four fine horses. These Caucasus people were Russian subjects and,
because of the protection they enjoyed, had become quite numerous
in Iran, especially in Khorasan. Merchants hired them to transport
their goods because they were less likely to be robbed, and if they were,
the Russians would insist that the loot be returned. Passengers favored
the Russian conveyances because thieves and highwaymen refrained
from attacking coaches belonging to them.

ON TO TEHRAN

Uncle and I along with Crazy Safar set out and spent the first night at
Sulvand about fifty kilometers outside of Sabzevar. This Safar, true to
his nickname, was unbalanced. He would be belligerent and very
abusive. He would also bully shopkeepers and feed-sellers with his
rage and would dismiss grooms who served us for a day or two with-

out paying them. This was why all the tradesmen and coffeehouse owners cursed him. The next morning we had only gone eighteen kilometers when we camped again because he wanted to baby his team of horses. He had coddled these animals and they had become fat. Every fifteen kilometers, he would tend to the beasts, giving them water and caressing them, speaking to them in Turkish, stopping and playing with them idiotically. Then we would set out again, but whenever he tugged one of the horses' reins, he would console it softly, whispering confidences to it. In very broken Persian, he praised his team, mumbling endearments, and would at times even sing to them. Then suddenly he would shout like a man possessed and strike the groom for no apparent reason.

In the afternoon of the second day, we reached a village called Mehr, ninety-two kilometers from Sabzevar. No one dared ask Safar why our progress was so slow, least of all I, but he did volunteer that after Mazinan, the distance between stages would be longer. We would have to go about fifty kilometers without water and feed. He wanted to travel less in the more settled areas to accustom the horses. In any case, that morning he hitched up the coach and, just as we were about to go, brutally kicked the groom and punched the coffeehouse owner, without paying either.

He emerged in that same lunatic state, but just as he was about to enter the carriage, the side horse kicked him in the head so hard that he was thrown at least two meters and seemed dead. One of the things I will never forget as long as I live is hearing the entire crowd near the coffeehouse suddenly sing the Lord's praises, thanking Him for finally giving the Godless savage what he deserved. As we had learned, one of his habits when he was in a bad mood was to curse the Lord. The Turkish driver's obscenities would typically begin "Goddamn…!"—one of the impieties he used that day. The only humanity and kindness in that brute was reserved for his four horses. With no one to help him the task of nursing Safar's wounds fell to Uncle and me, and we begged people to find someone to help. A villager with medical experience turned up to cauterize the wound and stop the bleeding, applying a felt bandage to it. They massaged Safar's body. We melted a bit of sugar, added rose water, and fed it to him when he could swallow. The village mollah came to absolve him and pray over his body. As soon as he could speak, the first words out of his mouth was "horses." His voice cracking a little, he kept crying out to his "beloved" animals.

In the meantime, an itinerant surgeon from Mazinan that had been sent for arrived. He opened the wound and rebandaged it. I imagine that he also had a variety of drugs with him like potassium permanganate, iodine, white bandages and forceps. We nursed Safar all day and night and he got better. The next morning, the groom that Safar had kicked hitched up the coach and took control of the reins himself. We loaded Safar into the coach with difficulty and tried to keep him stable while we proceeded at a slow measured pace. In the afternoon, we reached Mazinan where the surgeon who had joined us had his clinic. He heated some water and washed the wound. Then he sterilized some felt and spider's web and worked them for an hour until they became malleable. He cleaned the wound, stitched it and applied ointment. Safar was given some medicine. The surgeon also had them get about seven pounds of meat, cook it and feed the thick broth to him. That night while the surgeon remained with us, Safar slept peacefully. In the morning, he was well enough to take the reins himself. But we hadn't gone more than several kilometers when his pain seemed to return. Whatever it was, we noticed that he had begun to howl and curse the heavens. We had to stop about twenty-five kilometers from Mazinan at a village called Kaheh, where the surgeon treated him again. The pain subsided and he slept. Uncle paid the surgeon handsomely for the treatment and the drugs, and he gave us extra medicine, ointment, and bandages for the road. At every station Uncle with my help cleaned and rebandaged the wound as the surgeon had instructed. Finally, after twenty-four days on the road, we reached the outskirts of Tehran. When we were about fifty kilometers out, Safar began to pressure us for more than the agreed fare, which we gave him. This was our thanks for saving his life.

ENTERING TEHRAN AND ON TO SCHOOL THERE

We parted from Safar at the Jalilabad Street (today Khayyam Street) coach station. Uncle immediately sought out a Tehrani merchant named Aqa Mirza Nasrollah. We stayed with him for the first two or three days and then moved to the home of one of Uncle's acquaintances, Mirza Taqi Khani, near the Qazvin Gate. This man, who was from Qazvin, apparently had spent some time in Khorasan and had gotten to know Uncle there. Two or three days later we rented a modest house on Jannat-e Golshan Avenue. An old woman was found to be the maid. The house was an outer residence with a locked door leading to the landlord's inner quarters. We had two rooms and a very small space that served as a kitchen.

I enrolled in Tarbiat, one of the government schools with good teachers that was very famous at the time. I couldn't have been more enthusiastic and excited. Of course, there was no comparison between Tarbiat and Sabzevar-style education. There were regular classes and instruction, things that were new to me. This novel world that I had entered had real order and discipline, where the minutes and hours counted. Students knew exactly what their schedule was each day. There were four morning classes: first period, math; second, Persian; third, Arabic; and then calligraphy. School recessed at noon for lunch and resumed at two. The two afternoon classes might be geometry, algebra, art or foreign languages. They gave us homework exercises in all of the subjects. At specific points in the day the bell rang and all the students went outside. In the afternoons they had us line up.

Because to that point I was a willful child raised without discipline and indifferent to time, the orderly spirit of the school was a welcome lesson. In class, they questioned us on our lessons and a student's answers not only affected his grades, but also determined whether his peers treated him with respect or shamed him. The school had instituted a sense of friendly competition and rivalry among the students. Teachers both encouraged and chided us. They would reward us with pens, pads of paper or books. They were conscientious and genuinely fond of learning. During those first days of the Constitutional Period, when people's spirits were high, no group was more engaged in reforms than the teachers.

I have the fondest memories of the teachers from this school, and it is with heartfelt respect that I write about some of them here. Sheikh al-Ra'is Taleqani was a learned man of about fifty or sixty. He was single and lived at school. He appeared lofty and dignified and was a spirited man who laughed and joked freely. He wore the robe of a disheveled preacher and often kept food in his pocket, usually some bread and cheese. Before sunrise he would leave the school grounds and sit beside the gullies along Amiriyeh or Farmanfarma Avenues and have his bread and cheese breakfast. In those days Tehran had more trees than today and small streams ran beside the roads. He would return to school before the students arrived. Later they would gather round him and start poetry competitions. He would cheer on the winning teams and occasionally give pens as prizes. The poetry at these contests had to be from the greats—no unknowns were allowed. He never tolerated mistakes when we recited. Students formed two lines, one to the left, one to the right of him, and he would always root for the front-runners. One day Mahmud Khan Morshedzadeh, who was known for his prodigious memory and was virtually the leader of one side, lost. The next day Mahmud Khan challenged anyone to match him in lines from Ferdowsi that ended in "g" and defeated all comers.

Sheikh al-Ra'is taught in a clear and fluent voice, and would insist that the students speak the same way. He was very strict when he gave dictation. The maximum grade one could receive in dictations was twenty, and he would subtract one whole number for every mistake, like writing *shotor*—"camel"—with an Arabic "t." The same applied to a misplaced dot or any other minor writing error. He allowed no exceptions; a mistake was a mistake. He instilled the habit of writing carefully and precisely in his students. He was likewise extraordinarily meticulous about reading aloud. The readers used in class consisted of a variety of texts, both prose and poetry selections. Newer books were introduced like science, history and some translations from foreign languages.

Hajj Mir Seyyed Ali Esfahani taught Arabic. His textbooks were the standard grammar used in Beirut and a series of readers designed specifically for schools. Seniors studied *Moghni* with him.[8]

The French teacher was Mirza Farajollah Khan Pirzadeh, known as "Monsieur." This man was a walking dictionary. He was a good teacher though he had a slight stammer.

The literature and composition teacher was Mirza Azizollah Khan Mesbah, who was a poet and writer in his own right. He gave us many selections to memorize and taught us writing and composition exceptionally well.

Soltan al-Khattatin taught calligraphy. Mirza Seyyed Mohammad Khan Mohandes Homayun, who is now in Tehran at the Ministry of Education, was the math, geometry and algebra teacher. There was an American called Mr. Preag and a Parsi from India who taught English. All of them were conscientious, learned and devout.

After three years at Tarbiat, I returned to Sabzevar for summer vacation. Upon my return to Tehran, I entered the Dar al-Fonun (Polytechnic), which was the most prestigious and oldest school in Tehran at the time. The Polytechnic went back to 1851, the year it was established by Mirza Taqi Khan Amir Kabir, becoming the first school to employ a cadre of European professors. It contained a kind of secondary school, a military academy, and colleges of engineering, surveying and medicine. During the two years I spent at the Polytechnic the faculty were:

Mathematics: Mirza Gholamhoseyn Rahnama;

Geometry and Trigonometry: Mirza Reza Khan Qarajeh Daghi Mohandes al-Molk.

Geography and History: Aqa Mirza Abolhasan Khan Foroughi.

History: Mirza Asadollah Khan Tarjoman al-Saltaneh, famous as "Alu" (or "plum") because he often pursed his lips when he spoke or listened.

French: Monsieur Richard Khan Mo'addeb al-Molk;

Chemistry: Dr. Mahmud Khan Shimi (the son of Mirza Kazem Shimi Mahalati).

<...>

At that time Beirut was famous in Iran as a center of learning, and a number of Iranians had already been studying there. Many books published in Beirut circulated in Iran. The example of two of my elementary school classmates, Abdolhoseyn Dehqan and his brother Ali Mohammad,who went to Beirut, also motivated me to go. Both were among the top students whose accomplishments earned my respect and fascination. Moreover, my passion for knowledge was growing by the day, occupying all my senses, and I thought that were I to go to Beirut, I would reach the highest rungs of learning. Letters traveled between Tehran and Sabzevar, but I was adamant. Finally, they wrote me to come to Sabzevar when school was over and prepare for the trip to Beirut.

While I was away, my sister had reached maturity and married a man from Sabzevar named Aqa Mohammad, who owned property some fifty kilometers from Sabzevar. <...>

RETURN TO SABZEVAR

Around the end of the school year, Aqa Mohammad came to Tehran on business. When the school year was over, he and I traveled back to Sabzevar together along with a man from Kuh Mish. My maternal uncle Aqa Mohammad Hasan remained behind in the city to see to his trading business.

At that time bandit gangs were operating around Miandasht, a town between Shahrud and Sabzevar. Because of them, the caravanserais were built like fortresses. As Miandasht was a caravan stop on the road to Turkestan, most of the Turkmen attacks occurred around there. Apparently during the reign of Naser al-Din Shah,

Hoseyn Khan Shehab al-Molk Shahsavan had built a network of caravanserais and had underground channels dug to provide water. More than just safe havens for travelers, these serais served as defensive outposts in case of attack. Thanks to the channels, which surfaced in them, they had reliable water supplies. The serais also contained numerous storerooms.

All these things also made them ideal hideouts. At the time of our journey an Iranian living in southern Central Asia by the name of Hoseynzadeh commandeered the serais and with a band of thieves who at that time had styled themselves "freedom fighters" terrorized the surrounding countryside. They attacked merchants, robbing them of their goods, and then extorted money from them for the return of their property. Other bandit gangs from the region had joined forces with Hoseynzadeh. The bandit leader and rebel in his own right, Ali Khan Savadkuhi, brought horsemen from Khaar, Varamin, and other places. Savadkuhi made one of the large caravanserais his, while Hoseynzadeh took over another. The two gangs had joined to extort money from both seasoned travelers and any innocent passers-by who happened to fall into their clutches.

When we reached Shahrud, we naturally asked about security on the roads. Everyone said that they were fine—travelers had come and gone. So off we went, but when we entered Miandasht in the afternoon of the next day, Hoseynzadeh's men stopped us and went through all our possessions taking many things belonging to Aqa Mohammad. They demanded that we buy them back, but we did not have much money. Two days later, they decided to let me go to Sabzevar while Aqa Mohammad remained behind as a hostage to be ransomed.

The thought of being a prisoner to the gang in the first caravanserai terrified Aqa Mohammad, because their leader, Hoseynzadeh, was not just a highwayman but a bloodthirsty killer. Ali Khan, though a thief, was a tribal bandit that observed certain proprieties. So we threw in our lot with him and moved to the other caravanserai. As Ali Khan's partner, Hoseynzadeh evidently gave his approval. In any event, at daybreak on the third day I was allowed to leave on the post stagecoach and to take a trunk of schoolbooks for which the bandits obviously had no use.

At sunrise when we had gotten about nine kilometers east of Miandasht, suddenly there was the sound of gunfire, about forty or fifty shots in rapid succession. The postman Asadollah Beyg and the driver, who had experienced this before, halted the coach and began to wave white and other colored cloths in the air to signal their surrender. Then a number of Turkmen spilled out of the hills along the road and led the coach to a hill. When we reached the other side of the hill, we saw hundreds of women and men seated on the ground and several coaches, horses and pack animals. What had happened was clear: they had waylaid all the coaches traveling in either direction and secreted them behind the hill. Having robbed the passengers of their belongings, they packed up the loot and were waiting for the last haul of the day—our coach. In a split second they had our baggage on the ground and had repacked it for loading onto the horses. Some of the things they threw away, including the mail and my trunk, which were beneath their contempt.

The baggage out of the way, they stripped the passengers of their personal possessions and hung them from their saddle horns. They had the men undress down to their pants but did not remove the women's clothing. After the loot was loaded onto the coach horses, the bandits had the women (about ten in all with two or three children) ride with them. Then they ordered us to run with the pack north of the road, a dry and desolate expanse, full of thorns and desert brush. It was a sandscape, or, properly speaking, a rocky elevated plain. No matter where one looked there wasn't a road or track in sight. But the thieves, who knew every inch of the way, moved quickly forcing us to race alongside them as they cracked their whips menacingly. After about six kilometers, our bare feet and legs were covered with cuts and bruises. These wounds along with the sun, which was now scorching, sapped our strength considerably, but the ordeal had only begun. Anyone who fell behind they whipped, and soon the naked backs of the captives were covered with black lash marks. There couldn't have been a worse time for this march, but we had no choice. Because Aqa Mohammad and I had to wait for my final exams at school to end, we were traveling during the first days of summer. The dry rockscape was especially hot, and the closer it got to noon the worse the heat became, making us even more exhausted. Thirst was also becoming an unspeakable torment.

Speaking from experience, Asadollah Beyg and his driver urged us to use all the strength we had left to run because the thieves would kill anyone that fell behind. They feared that if one of us reached the road, he would put the authorities on their trail. The postman and his driver explained, "The bandits will go about twenty-four kilometers before letting the horses have a breather. After setting up their tents and seeing to their own people, they will either kill or free us—and it seems more likely that they'll let us go seeing they've brought us this far."

Naturally, the fear of being killed and the Turkmen's whips were great incentives. Fear of death made all the other agonies, the gashes on our legs, the exhaustion, the thirst and even the blazing sun, seem nothing. Fortunately, in that heat, the horses were also tiring. They lacked the vigor they had when galloping to the first stage. We ran until around noon, when we reached a reddish hilltop, which according to Asadollah Beyg was about twenty-four kilometers from the road. The Turkmen positioned lookouts on the surrounding hills and then unloaded the animals. After dividing us into two groups separated by a small distance, men on one side and women and children on the other, they watered the horses.

Recessed within the hill there was a sort of hollow with a vaulted ceiling, from which water was dripping. Over the centuries this dripping had formed the vault. Water collected in a rock basin at the bottom of the recess. The Turkmen kept dipping their water bags into the basin and lugging them to the horses. Otherwise, they were very miserly with the water. After the horses had had enough, the Turkmen themselves drank. Then they filled some cast iron kettles and placed them on a fire made from thorn and scrub kindling to prepare their green Turkman tea. By this time, there was nothing left in the basin for us to drink. We would have to wait hours for enough water to collect there again. Happily, I was seated close enough to the cave to dig out a few moist clods of earth, which I sucked greedily and then rubbed all over myself to quell the blaze burning inside me. Of course, I was acting purely on instinct, as this could not possibly help.

To describe my mental and physical state at this time is extraordinarily difficult. I had no idea about the others and was so disoriented and distraught that words can hardly do justice to my feelings. Life, my future, existence itself, all meant nothing. The only thing that mattered in my life then was a drink of water, even a gulp of the wastewater from the sewers by the road. Just one cup, nothing more, was my here and hereafter, my now and my future, my hopes and aspirations, my desire, the object of my obsession, my very beloved. Even today, decades later, I can still taste how sweet those red clods were on my fingertips. The lovely sight of water trickling from that crack in the hill is still with me, and those damp clumps of soil that I rubbed on my chest, stomach, and arms are to this day like the most comforting, most soothing of salves.

After the Turkmen had finished their meal, they began to argue among themselves. Again we had to rely on Asadollah Beyg and the driver, a boy from a village east of Miandasht called Abbasabad, for our information. Both knew a smattering of Turkman and Kurdish. They listened to the Turkmen intently and the expressions of horror that played on their features were enough to tell us what was being said.

Who were these bandits? Thirty-three men belonged to the gang, seventeen Turkmen and sixteen Kurds from the Khorasan borderlands (around Bojnurd). The Turkmen had to be partners with the Kurds because they passed through their territory, which was on the boundary with Russia. The Kurds knew the territory well and, besides being armed, were highwaymen, too. The curious thing was that the Turkmen were enthusiastic Sunnis, while the Kurds were Shia. So to the extent that a band of ignorant and savage desert-dwellers can hold religious sentiments and beliefs, they were devout in their own way. <...>

The Kurds and the Turkmen were also debating about what to do with us. The Turkmen were in favor of keeping the women prisoners and killing the men, more than twenty people. The Kurds, on the other hand, wanted to free the men so that they could return with money to ransom the women and children. The bickering between the two factions was getting sharper. Asadollah Beyg and the boy driver, who were eavesdropping, surreptitiously told us what they were saying. The expressions on their faces were bizarre; what they heard made their eyes dart constantly and their facial muscles twitch. Their features expressed hope then fear and anxiety, and then again surprise and resignation. I was also listening, but if you were to ask me today how I felt then, I would say that ninety percent of my attention was on the water collecting in the basin. The rest was of secondary importance to me. <...>

The bandits' discussions ended around three o'clock in the afternoon. Asadollah said a prayer of thanks as they had decided to let us go. The Turkmen packed up their baggage and headed for the desert while several lookouts stood watch from the surrounding heights. Their leader, a man called Sardar Qorban, ordered them to break camp. Left behind were some pieces of mail that they scattered about the campsite. A half-blind (one-eyed) Turkman remained with a sack of cornbread, which he was to distribute among us. He warned us that if anyone strayed from the spot before the Turkmen were out of sight and any trace of them had disappeared from the horizon, the men on the hills would kill us. He explained that the lookouts would wait until the main band got some distance away, whereupon they themselves would catch up at a gallop. We were to wait until we could not see them and then leave. They took the women as hostages, however, and said they would hold them until their relatives brought enough ransom to retrieve them at Astarabad. When the men asked whom they should see in Astarabad to ransom their women, the bandits said, "You will know when you get there. Now kiss the stirrups of Sardar Qorban and the Kurdish chief to say goodbye and thank them for sparing your lives." The "blind" Turkman even extended his hand for us to kiss and then set us free. Meanwhile each of us drank from the pool of water that grew muddier the more we crowded around it. They also gave each man a round loaf of stale cornbread. Now we only had to deal with the cuts and bruises on our feet and legs that drained our strength. Our bodies were so numb and worn out that moving was difficult.

One of our fellow passengers on the coach was a Mirza Hasan Khan from Kashan. He evidently was an employee of the telegraph office in Mashhad. With him were his wife and eight-year-old daughter. Most of the baggage on the coach had belonged to him. This consisted of several Kashan rugs wrapped in burlap and some silk fabric also from Kashan. The Turkmen tried to get his wife and daughter onto their saddles and take them away, but his wife managed to jump off three times. The fourth time they beat her viciously and bound her feet. Her husband went over and I clearly heard him assure her in his Kashan accent, "Dear, don't worry, I'll give them what they want. Now go." There was an ineffable look of grief and terror on his face as he added to his daughter, "Go with them, baby." The other passenger was a man from Qom, whose profession I didn't know. He also had his young wife with him. This fellow was an opium addict. Along the way and even when we were camped behind the hill, all he could think of was the opium in his suitcase. He kept swearing to Asadollah Beyg and the driver that he would die if they didn't give it to him. He approached the bandits, but when they growled at him, he began to whimper and beg. His wife, on the other hand, did not seem that perturbed. She seemed to take in what was happening with the vacant gaze of someone watching a film or a play.

The few women prisoners were far better off than the men. They were on horseback all the way to the encampment, and as soon as they arrived, the Turkmen fed them. So when the bandits ordered the addict's wife to share the saddle with one of the riders, she complied as though she were off on an outing to one of the Saints' shrines around Tehran. Before she left, her husband edged close to her, pleading with her to get the bandits to give him his suitcase. His wife, who couldn't speak their language, naturally said nothing. The other females, who were not among our party, were villagers with two or three children.

The men from our coach were Mirza Hasan Khan Kashi whom I mentioned before, the addict from Qom, my servant Mohammad Taqi, Asadollah Beyg and his young driver. I can't recall anyone else.

There were also several villagers and men from the small caravan that they had captured before us. The last group could think of nothing but the donkeys they had been forced to abandon by the main road.

As the Turkmen had instructed, we waited until they were out of sight before, at Asadollah's urging, we prepared to go. In the meantime we drank all the water we found and wrapped our feet in scraps of paper, sackcloth and hide that the Turkmen had left behind. But I soon realized that the rough hide and paper shoes were harder on my feet than the desert and threw them away. None of us felt like moving anyway. Kind by nature, Asadollah Beyg was particularly good to me. When he was an apprentice coachman, he frequently passed through town and had gotten to know my family. He probably was looking forward to a reward they would give him when I came home. He had no clothing or food to offer, but he did try to cheer me up by saying that at least we had escaped death. He also gathered up the mail and put it into a makeshift knapsack on his shoulder. How wonderful it was, he kept repeating to himself, that they didn't take the "government mails."

The phrase he used and others like "grand post office" and "august telegraph" were in vogue in those days. Occasionally some postmaster would even threaten the governor or military commander of a region with closing the "government mails." The deliverymen at the post and telegraph offices and the apprentice postmen proudly wore the government insignia (a lion and sun) on their caps, which were rimmed in scarlet. Earnest postal official that he was, Asadollah Beyg could not leave the government mails behind.

The return trip was downhill. The weather had cooled and, as it became dark, we even felt a chill. Asadollah Beyg warned that if we fell while traveling at night, we would die. Having escaped the Turkmen, it would be a shame, he said, to fall prey to the wild animals, the snakes and even the ghouls that lived in the desert. So he marched us along quickly to reach the road before nightfall.

Around sunset we reached a place called Kurds' Well. Here they had excavated a path that led a couple of meters below the surface to the water. Kurds' Well was a staging point where thieves stopped to drink and water their horses before attacking the main road some seven kilometers away. Asadollah and the boy, both of whom knew the place well, drove us on with promises of water. But after descending into the well, we saw that it would be impossible to scoop it with two hands. We had to grip the roof of the well with one hand, while trying to reach some of the water with the other. This was so difficult that we only managed to wet our hands. Thank God the bandits had not taken Mirza Kashi's cap.

Tribal bandits, especially the Turkmen, are known for not overlooking any object no matter how useless and shapeless. Being the meanest and most rapacious people on earth, they won't even pass up a worn pair of shoes or a soiled, moth-eaten kerchief. One can imagine, then, how useless Mirza Kashi's cap was for them to have left it behind. It was a ragged thing, made in Iran of felt stained with patches of sweat, grime and mud. The average Iranian faced with a long, dusty coach trip would probably not choose to wear his best hat. But even supposing Mirza Kashi's cap was new when he left Kashan, one can only imagine the state it was in when we reached Kurds' Well. Picture the sweat and salt that poured from his head for days or the dust that had the misfortune to land on the thing. From this cap, now a cup, we drank as much as we could.

Poor Asadollah Beyg kept warning us in vain not to drink too much, afraid we might burst. But we survived and the incident has taken its place among my indelible memories. We then followed the path out of the well and headed for the road. An hour later we were on the main road and found that [the caravanserai people] had brought us several horses from the stables at Miandasht. It was now about ten at night, and everyone was asleep. Asadollah Beyg obtained a pleated overshirt from the driver and the kind of shirt that goes under it for me to wear. Mine was woven in Damghan of coarse, yellow cotton that was tattered. Though it was something thrown away, the shirt proved a blessing during the scorching days and at night when I nearly froze in the cold and the wind. The only problem was that it had no buttons, which I remedied by putting holes in it and stitching the sides together with a length of rough yarn.

The sole person to take pity on me was Aqa Mohammad, whom I saw at a distance, but he had nothing, no food, no money, to offer. It didn't take long for them to hitch up another coach and we prepared to go. Because this coach had no cargo but us with our bruised feet and legs, the resident thieves ignored it. They even had the nerve to express their sympathy with the hypocritical submissiveness of a person without self-respect. I asked Asadollah Beyg to stop at the place where we were captured and retrieve my books. When we got there, he gathered the books in the battered trunk and loaded it onto the coach. When we arrived in Abbasabad, some villagers acting out of charity and the duty to feed travelers gave us milk, tea and bread. Asadollah Beyg was determined to move on, explaining that his only thought was to restore me to my family. That afternoon we reached Mazinan where one of the local hajjis brought us some grapes. Though they were unripe, I have never enjoyed anything more in my life. After the agonies and the privation of the last few days, each grape was like a precious jewel. The same humane hajji also lifted our spirits considerably with tea with milk and some bread and butter. That evening when we started up again, Asadollah Beyg said that he had planned to enter Sabzevar the next night to spare me the embarrassment of appearing in town barefoot and bareheaded in a derelict undershirt. I declined the offer, saying the sooner we arrived the better. In any event we reached Sabzevar the next afternoon. I left the coach at the station and went home, having told Asadollah Beyg to send my trunk along later.

When I reached my door and knocked, a servant girl answered and asked what I wanted. I told her who I was. When I stepped in, she ran away and a coachboy appeared. He announced to the rest of the household that the Aqa had returned. When my mother, sister and the rest of the household saw my condition, they immediately had a bath prepared. But before cleaning up, I insisted that they photograph me as I was. In those days camera equipment was not as available as it is today, so we had to wait for a time. Eventually I was "divested" and bathed. They had found some of my uncle's clothing for me to wear. His oversize robe made me look like one of those old-fashioned accountant's assistants. A few days later I came down with a high fever, which lasted two months. It may have been the result of a tick bite or something like that. In any event, it left me very weak and worn out.

In the meantime, the family took steps to ransom Aqa Mohammad. Money was sent through intermediaries to Ali Khan Savadkuhi, who set him free. But by this time things had gotten so bad between the two gangs, Savadkuhi's and Hoseynzadeh's, that they had posted sentries on their respective caravanserais expecting an attack. The conflict grew worse by the day, so when they released Aqa Mohammad, Hoseynzadeh decided to make an example of him that would teach people they could do nothing without first getting his approval. The gang ambushed Aqa Mohammad's coach and dragged him out. Then they tied him to a telegraph pole and shot him, burying him in the desert where he fell. The news of his death created an uproar, throwing the entire household into mourning.

My first education in how miserable life in Iran can be came through incidents such as these. One must be an Easterner, an Iranian, and have spent some time in that world to realize how deprived Iranian society is of the requisites of human existence. It is impossible for someone from Europe or the West in general to appreciate it. Normally people do not have the power to conceive something that is entirely alien to them. Our imagination cannot derive from nothingness; it is composed of sensations and experiences from the world around us. The average Westerner, especially one that has never been to the East, cannot imagine such deprivation.

I remember in 1924 when I was the Iranian delegate to the International Conference of the Red Cross, General Paux, the head of the French Red Cross, invited representatives from various countries to a dinner at the General Secretariat in the Interalliée Building. Hundreds of guests sat ten or twelve to a table. I found myself next to Mademoiselle Heget, the daughter of famous Belgian scholar Professor Heget. She was around twenty or twenty-two years old and had accompanied her father to Paris where he was the head of the Belgian delegation. During dinner, she was the typical student, full of curiosity and questions that I duly answered. I mention two of them here as they illustrate what I mean by imagination and experience.

"Dr. Ghani," she asked, "do the women of Iran have the right to vote?"

"No, Mademoiselle," I said, "Persian women don't have the right to vote for representatives of Parliament."

"So," she concluded, "they are just like the women of France and Belgium who are still denied the right to vote."

I agreed and she was satisfied, having enlightened herself on this point. But I immediately saw how hard it is for people to understand one another fully. Those who imagine that this is merely a matter of language are mistaken. We both knew French. The question she posed was also simple, but the conclusion she reached, namely that Iranian women were the same as the French and Belgians, was absurd. How, I asked myself, could she conceivably compare herself to us? Iranians did not even have the right to a life that can be called humane, let alone the right to vote. The Mademoiselle, of course, would have been raised in Brussels by Professor and Madame Heget, in a milieu befitting her father's social position. Her surroundings would have been predictable, orderly, a place where rights and justice existed. The best and most refined things society had to offer enriched every stage in her short life, her childhood, adolescence, education, and social life. What could she possibly know about a woman like Mirza Hasan Kashi's wife, or about people like the addict from Qom? How could she appreciate Sardar Qorban, post coaches or "the government mail"? Kurds Well and Turkmen? The Abbasabad Gap? What would she make of the mauser-toting thief Hoseynzadeh and the homicidal beasts known collectively as murderous highway-men?

While I was lost in these thoughts, her next question took me totally by surprise: "Dr. Ghani, do you still travel by caravan in Iran?"

"Yes, Mademoiselle," I said, "most of the time we travel that way."

Now she was all excitement and enthusiasm. Though speaking gracefully, she could hardly contain herself as she congratulated me on the life I led traveling by caravan. This naïve young girl had seen camels and donkeys with the finest saddles at the zoo. In her mind were the fully groomed horses and donkeys decked out in bells and ribbons at amusement parks. She probably thought all the roads in Iran were just like the trails in European parks, except for added heaps of roses, Persia's national flower. She had read the novels of Western writers who raved about the beauties of desert tracks in the moonlight, under the stars, and the crystal skies of the Orient. Mounted on those camels, donkeys and horses, a few fortunate boys and girls would ride alone or by twos, seeking answers to life's problems.

In the expressions and sayings of any people are certain covert truths that reflect the reality of their lives. Outsiders, those who live different lives, cannot appreciate such expressions. In Arabic one says, "Travel is part hell." The Easterner equates travel with the horrors of hell because of the hardships involved in going from one place to another. The Arabs also say, "The traveler is like a lunatic." The average traveler in the East has a right to his insanity, for he cannot be certain that he will reach his destination alive. In Persian, we speak of the "pain of travel" and the "journey's tortures." There are a thousand such expressions. About to leave Shiraz, Sa'di wrote:

As I turn to go, my heart twists like my feet;
The more I load up, the more I am weighed down.

All the benedictions we say when setting out to travel or the lucky charms and the thousands of other superstitions we have are part of a reality in the East not experienced on a trip from New York to Washington or on Mademoiselle Heget's journey from Brussels to Paris.

All the celebrations and singing, the animal sacrifices and the offering of sweets that one sees when the traveler returns reveals a bitter truth. Until several years ago, caravan leaders would go about Mazandaran and Astarabad crying that they were taking travelers to Mashhad and would guarantee their chances of returning safely at fifty percent. Another would up this and announce sixty percent. Of course, this was not the guarantee that European insurers make. Rather, even if everyone were to perish, the caravaner could cover his losses with such phrases as "tragedy from heaven," "will of God" or "it was their time." He might also quote the Qur'an: "O mankind, you know not when death will come." But this hue and cry itself tells the story of what it was like to travel in the East. <...>

Only in a country like Iran, a cradle of disease, epidemics, bands of thieves, and chaos, can one find these and other such expressions. When I returned to Iran from Europe once, I went to Sabzevar. Mirza Ali Akbar Arabshahi, who had never set foot out of town, paid a call and asked whether the places I had been to were safe and secure. I told him that they were. He was silent for a bit and then asked, "So, in those parts there was no famine—plenty of rain?" "Yes," I said. The amazing thing is that despite the regularity of tragedy, the inhabitants of Iran believe that their particular town is heaven on earth, with fine weather, few diseases and plenty of elderly people. Though there were rumors one year of cholera, their particular town remained immune or less vulnerable than other places.

Sabzevar is a town of scorchingly hot summers and many fierce dust storms. Varying in severity from year to year, these afternoon wind storms begin around the second month of spring. There is little rainfall, which makes farming like drawing blood from a stone. Because the lands to the south of town are very saline, few plants and trees can grow. Sabzevaris, however, say so many good things about the town's climate, about its "blessings," and voice their satisfaction with life in so many ways that they defy description. One of the town's Sufis, Hajj Sheikh Emad al-Din, would go on in this vein and his audience would agree automatically as though he had stated the absolute truth. The confirmation of his scholarly opinion gave the Sheikh considerable pleasure. He said something like this: "There is no question that Iran enjoys the most temperate climate and most plentiful riches in the world. And the foremost province in the country is Khorasan, with its superb crops, cotton, fruits and water. And Sabzevar is the queen of Khorasan's cities, excelling all others in climate and natural gifts. Sabzevar, in fact, is heaven on earth." With this everyone issued thanks to the Giver of those bounties.

ON TO BEIRUT

After my recovery, Uncle Mirza Azizollah Khan Khazra'i (really a spiritual father to me) and I readied everything necessary for the Beirut trip and my studies there. At the end of summer we traveled by carriage to Quchan and then via Bajgiran to Eshqabad. There we stayed with Hajj Abdol Rasul Tajer Yazdi, head of an Iranian concern called the Omid Company. Uncle was to marry his daughter Tahereh as soon as we settled in. After about forty days I went by rail to Tazeh Shahr on the Caspian. From there a boat for Baku where I stayed three days. Then a train to Batum, and after two days, I boarded a ship for Istanbul.

At this time, the beginning of summer 1914, the city was in an uproar because a group of senior Turkish politicians had assassinated the head of government. The conspirators who were well-known figures, including the former interior minister and a son-in-law of the sultan. They were hanged, the day we arrived, at the orders of Enver Pasha, the minister of war. We learned that we would have to wait a week for the next ship to Beirut. Several resident Iranians at the Valide Market advised me to leave the next day for Izmir where there would be more ships going to Beirut. I did this but couldn't disembark for two days because the Italian and Balkan ships had yet to sweep the Bay of Izmir of mines. Several boats came alongside our ship and took the Izmir-bound passengers aboard. This was around sunset with the sea so stormy that the closer we got to shore the higher the waves became. The boat was close to capsizing as they kept bailing the water that constantly poured into it. For three hours the waves toyed with us, but finally we managed to reach shore. We were still soaked when we found a hotel. A troop of Jewish dancers happened to be performing at the hotel, and this was the first time that I saw a woman dance. Three days later, I boarded a Russian ship bound for Yaffa that was ferrying Jewish pilgrims to the Holy Land. Hugging the shore all the way, the ship reached Beirut. <...>

In Beirut I made some Iranian friends, for those days there were many of us there, almost two hundred students or more. Though schools were closed for the summer, I managed to get the curriculum of the French Lycée St. Joseph so that I could spend the summer preparing for the exams. Knowing only French ruled out the American University for my education. My Persian friends and I decided to take a vacation. The Dehqans, Azizollah Bahador (who died just this spring—1948—in Qolhak in Tehran), two or three others and I went touring in Egypt. We spent several days in Alexandria, Port Said and Cairo.

We returned to Beirut when school opened. I went to St. Joseph and after taking the exams, was told that I should enroll in the pre-medical college. It was a Jesuit school administered by a man named Père Pascal, who was the one who tested me thoroughly and recommended I attend the last year of college to get ready for the medical school entrance examinations. The oral and written results showed that my math, physics, and chemistry were sufficient, but that my French was weak. I was also ignorant of French literature, geography, and history. So I enrolled and got down to work.

The teachers were Jesuit priests, generally very learned men that devote their entire lives to study and learning. Because of their religious affiliation, they do not have that much latitude when it comes to teaching the humanities. Père Pascal, an old man, taught astronomy two days a week (Saturday mornings and one weekday). He said that we must attend the church services that he conducted on Sunday. Consequently, every Saturday he would lecture enthusiastically, demonstrating gravity and Newtonian principles in scientific detail, while on Sunday he would preach about the ascension of Christ.

I was an inquisitive student with a genuine thirst for learning. One weekday after Pascal had finished teaching and, as was his habit, solving problems the students couldn't, I went up to his desk with a question. "Father," I said, "last Saturday, you explained the forces of gravity, attraction and repulsion, and using the laws of mathematics and physics you proved that Newton had been right. Sunday you said that a man weighing some 170 pounds broke those laws by levitating to heaven after his death. You also said that for a time after his death he appeared to his disciples and then returned to heaven. Now, I am just a new student, but which should I believe: what you say on

Saturday or what you preach on Sunday? They contradict one another and I can't believe both, can *you*?"

Pascal said, "Yes, I believe both and don't see any contradiction. It is as if my mind has two separate compartments: in one I have stored science and scientific laws, in the other my faith and religious beliefs. The logic of one, the way I perceive it, is wholly different from the logic and the way I understand the other. So for me, there is no conflict."

I benefited a great deal from my time at the Jesuit school. It was orderly and well run. I had entered with many gaps in my general education, which I filled by listening carefully and taking extensive notes. I spent virtually every waking hour studying French literature, history, psychology and astronomy, subjects that I had never studied in Iran. New to me also were the premedical courses: botany, zoology, general biology, physics and chemistry for medical students. I was interested in all of them, and it didn't take long before my teachers and classmates started to notice that I had become a student in every sense of the word.

I rented a room from a Druze, which was near the school on Fern al-Shebbak Avenue. It came with breakfast and was furnished only with a bed, a chair, a lantern, a ewer and a drinking glass. Though the room was dark and damp, the landlord was very kind. The Druze are generally humane, especially to Iranians, though they practice a mysterious offshoot of Islam considered heterodox (some Orientalists, among them Gobineau, have studied them extensively). In any event, I would leave my room in the morning for school and have my dinner in the neighborhood restaurants. In those days living in Beirut was cheap and easy.

<...>

My studies went so well that out of the 116 students who took the medical school entrance exam, I placed among the top of the thirty-two admitted. After vacationing that summer in Palestine, I entered St. Joseph's Medical College in the fall, thrilled to be finally studying at a school of higher learning. I should make it clear that the decision to study medicine was entirely my own. Neither my uncle nor my mother nor anyone else encouraged me to become a doctor. When I first came to Beirut, I had no idea what I wanted to study. After giving the matter some thought, I decided not to pursue literature or philosophy, because these one could study outside of school. But the sciences, including medicine, were another matter—they would be difficult to study on one's own. If I were going to be a student, why not choose the most difficult subject, rather than literature, law or the social sciences, which were by degrees easier than the sciences. Besides this, I found myself growing more curious about scientific research, but despite not having much experience with the various fields, I thought medicine had the most potential. <...> It turned out to be the best choice; it is both a science and an art. Its scientific aspects engage the mind, while the craft and practice of medicine are practical. In a place like Iran, it would be the best way to serve people.

I couldn't have been more elated about starting my studies at the medical college. I rented rooms in the neighborhood, at the end of Fern al-Shebbak Avenue. But three weeks later, when the Ottoman rulers of Lebanon entered the war on the German side, naturally all French schools closed. The entire French expatriate community, including the Jesuits, packed up and returned to France, leaving me with nowhere to study. Most Iranian residents, students at various French schools, returned to Iran via Aleppo. Others went elsewhere, but I was determined to stay in Lebanon whatever the cost. I knew that if I returned to Iran, my family would not be able to send me back to resume my education. The only place I could continue was the American University, which had various colleges. The medical college was famous for its faculty, hospitals and affiliated institutions. The problem was that I knew no English, the college's language of instruction. For a week I fell into a deep depression. My hopes were gone and the world seemed a dark place.

On the advice of the Dehqans and Azizollah Bahador, I visited the American University and explained my problem to its chancellor, Howard Bliss, a man with an excellent command of French. He looked at my records and was quite sympathetic. He saw my situation clearly, concluding that had I known English, I would have been accepted as a first-year medical student at the university. But now I had to study English until I reached the same proficiency as any other graduate student. I had, he said, one year to achieve this and might well succeed because of my knowledge of French.

The closing of the French-run schools had put many people into the same situation as I. This caused the American University to open English classes to help them. These classes were specially designed for adults who had already been to college. Having enrolled in the language program, I wasted no time in moving my few belongings to the same place the two Dehqans, Abdolhoseyn and his younger brother Ali Mohammad, were living. They had rented rooms near the university with Azizollah Bahador Shirazi and offered one to me. Each of us had his own bedroom in the building, and we shared a sitting room and kitchen. The landlord, a Beiruti Arab named George, occupied the first floor with his wife and mother. The local grocery store was nearby.

The language program consisted of six hours of English a day on various topics. After considerable effort, I was able to read books on a variety of subjects using a dictionary. By mid-year I was tackling college texts and other books on that level. My one and only goal was passing the university language exam in the fall. Failure meant waiting another whole year before I could retake the exam, as no one would be admitted two weeks after the term began. There have been few times in my life that I have studied harder or read more. As the object was to learn the language, I devoured everything in English no matter what the subject. Finally, in the fall of 1915, I passed the exam and entered medical school.

That year has to be considered one of the most fortunate in my life—I felt like I had won a hard-fought contest. The individual is a world unto himself, made up of personal triumphs that have no relation to the world outside. To the rest of the world it was as if nothing had happened. In any case, I emerged from the previous year's ordeals a confident young man with a self-respect that lifted my spirits considerably <...>.

When I was studying English and during the first year of medical school, we would eat at the restaurants near the university. There was no problem getting food when the Ottomans first entered the war and the Germans still had enough for themselves. Little by little, though, it became difficult as the Germans began to take the Ottoman reserves. The resulting panic caused people to hoard food. There was an Iranian merchant named Hajj Mohammad Yazdi, a very fine man with a wife and a child. Because British and French warships threatened areas along the shore, anyone who could reach the interior of Lebanon or Syria escaped. Hajj Mohammad decided to move his family from the city. One night this noble man visited us saying that since he could not take his hoard with him, he would sell it to us at a reasonable price. We thankfully bought several sacks of sugar and rice, some tea and other goods from him.

Now that we had the raw materials we had to decide what to do with them. Servants were out of the question, because we spent the day at school, and, considering the famine that was to come, they would definitely steal the lot. Merely having it known that there was food, moreover, might prove dangerous. We finally decided to do the cooking ourselves, though none of us knew how. With the determination and eagerness typical of young people, we set out for the market to buy an aluminum pot and pan, a kerosene stove, utensils and other necessities. We also bought a large white samovar from Enayatallah Khan, the owner of a coffeehouse.

Over tea, we divided the housework. I was to be the cook, Abdolhoseyn Dehqan, nicknamed "Abi," was to do the washing, Ali Mohammad Dehqan, "Ali," would set the table and tidy the rooms, and Azizollah Bahador, "Aziz," the oldest and most experienced of us, would do the daily grocery shopping. He also was to do the accounts, keeping track of how much each of us spent.

We tackled our jobs with boundless energy and enthusiasm. When I applied what little I had learned about cooking from various people, the results were at times burnt, other times soggy, and others undercooked. Occasionally there was too much salt or too little, but I finally got the hang of it. Our main meal was a stew of meat, potatoes, onions, tomatoes and green beans seasoned with salt and pepper, which I heated over a low flame on the kerosene stove. I would start the stew around seven or eight in the morning. After breakfast we went to school and returned that afternoon. Abi washed the dishes, Ali set the tablecloth we put on the floor, Aziz supplied the bread, vegetables, cheese and fruit, half of which we had for lunch, saving the rest for dinner. We also kept other things on hand like yogurt, halva and fruit.

Saturday afternoons when school was out, we lit the samovar, and other students would often join us for tea. We also held teas on Sunday, but we boiled some rice, added leftovers and, starting in the morning, picnicked outside of the city.

Ask me what was the best food I have ever tasted, I will say without hesitation those stews that I cooked myself. Those were the happiest times that any of us ever had. We were so set in our routines that as soon as the meal was over, each did his assigned chore and then went to his room to study. Like four considerate brothers acting as one we were careful not to make any noise that might disturb the others. The two or three Persian books we had were the *Works* of Sa'di or the *Divan* of Hafez. These we would read together on holidays or especially during the summer vacations. My Persian friends were from Shiraz and most of the Persian books available were the works of masters from that city. The Shirazis, by nature prejudiced toward their own town, loved to tease the Khorasanis by proudly quoting from Hafez or Sa'di, lines that everyone knew, on the beauties of Shiraz. I could never win these contests, because none of the books of the poets from Khorasan were available. One day after school, I just happened to go by the shop of Hajj Qasemi, a second-hand goods dealer from Tabriz, who had been in Beirut for years. After we exchanged greetings, I noticed a large volume among the odds and ends in the store. I asked about it and he told me it was a "Ferdowsi" that was among the goods that a pilgrim to Mecca had sold him. The book was a bunch of loose pages, one of those folio editions printed in Bombay. I asked him to sell it to me, immediately adding that all the money I had in the world was one gold French franc. After he agreed, I went straight to a bookbinder who was to bind it for a fifth of an Ottoman pound. I borrowed that amount from the school credit fund. A week later I brought the elephantine volume home. From that moment on, Ferdowsi's *Shahnameh* was one of the books we studied and read aloud together.

It wasn't long before signs of the food shortages appeared in Beirut. The government confiscated everything. War engulfed the vast Ottoman Empire from one end to the other. Its ports were blockaded and its allies, Germany and Austria, needed all the available food. Forces commanded by Ahmad Jamal Pasha, the minister of naval forces, mounted an attack on the Egyptian front. Jamal Pasha became commander in chief of Ottoman armies in Syria and Palestine. The effects of the war grew more severe daily, causing panic among the populace. A number of merchants were busily hoarding food and bleeding people dry. Most of the hoarders were under the protection of Ottoman officials, who were also their silent partners. Bread was rationed to one loaf per person daily, and tea and sugar disappeared altogether.

These were very bleak times for us. Communicating with Iran by mail became difficult as country after country entered the war. Banking ties were now cut because Iran did not have commercial relations with Beirut in the first place. Egypt was in British hands, Baghdad was a war zone and, to make matters worse, Russia was also now at war. From time to time people would transfer funds from Tehran to Istanbul via the American Embassy, but when the United States entered the war in 1916, it recalled its ambassador.

We were in a bind: on one hand our supplies had run out and, on the other, goods that had been available in the market before—fruit, milk, yogurt, vegetables, halva, etc.—were now scarce. The scarcities forced us out of the house and into the college dormitory. The Russian banks that had sent money to me from Khorasan and Eshqabad now cut their relations with Beirut. After the war, we discovered that a lot of the money had disappeared in those banks <...>. The Austrian consul, an apparent opium and morphine addict, was nominally in charge of Iranian affairs. But the actual Iranian consul was Dr. Ali Khan Farahmandi (Alim al-Molk, now assistant minister of education), who by that time had completed his education at the French medical school. There was also Hajj Ali Beyg, an employee of the Iranian Consulate, who had become knowledgeable about local conditions and helped. The family of Mo'ezz al-Soltan Hesabi, his wife and two sons Drs. Mohammad and Mahmud Hesabi who had been students in Beirut, lived at the consulate.

We were now dependent on the American University, which loaned us money that we were to repay in dollars after the war when international banking resumed. The university was very frugal, however. Of course, they gave us tuition and room and board, but as for pocket money or expenses for clothing and laundry they acted with extreme austerity. We found ourselves in tight circumstances, economizing wherever we could. The things we wanted were not to be found, and even if they were available, we had no money to buy them. For four years there was no sugar; we drank our milk, tea and coffee unsweetened. At some point I had bought less than four pounds of grape syrup for an Ottoman pound. On special occasions, we would ceremoniously invite a few select friends to share this syrup and some bread, and these experiences became important events in my life. The slight satisfactions of this austere student life made it easier to focus better on my studies than I ever had. My academic ranking rose so high that many of the professors exempted me from the finals in their specific subjects as well as from the general tests taken before a board of examiners.

The food at school was not good, but there was no use in complaining as the University did all it could to feed us. In the face of famine and the anti-American attitude of the Turks, the university had to see to the needs of some several thousand people: one thousand students; five hundred university employees and workers; the occupants of about two thousand hospital beds throughout the city; and more than 230 American professors, instructors, doctors and their families. For this we were grateful. The year 1915 saw no changes in the situation; our only consolation was that despite the oppressive days of war, we maintained an orderly academic life.

In 1916 we fell prey to a strange uneasiness. We learned that Ehtesham al-Saltaneh Alamir (son of Mohammad Rahim Khan Ala

al-Dowleh), then Iranian ambassador in Istanbul, had secretly negotiated an agreement with the Ottoman government that allowed the
drafting of able-bodied Iranian residents of the Ottoman Empire. At
the time, the Iranian government (if it could be called that) was in a
state of turmoil. The Russians and the British were pressuring the
country to enter the war on their side, becoming what they politely
called their "ally"—in effect their coolie. The plan was to station their
armies in Iran where they would take a number of "volunteers" and
help themselves to all the crops grown in the country. The Germans
and the Ottomans had the same idea. Meanwhile emigrating from
Tehran was a group of respected and popular politicians, mostly
allied with the Democrat Party; people like Seyyed Hasan Modarres,
Seyyed Mohammad Reza Mosavat, Mirza Mohammad Ali Khan
Farzin, Moshar al-Dowleh Shirazi (Hekmat), Soleyman Mirza, Aref
Qazvini, Seyyed Abol Hasan Alavi, Naser al-Eslam Nadamani, Aqa
Hoseyn Sami'i (Adib al-Saltaneh), Mirza Soleyman Khan Maykadeh
and Yar Mohammad Khan(Sardar Koll). There were hundreds of
others. Several thousand Iranian gendarmes and their Swedish officers joined them creating a new force that engaged in guerrilla operations around Qom, Saveh and Esfahan. Finally they fled toward
western Iran to join Ottoman and German forces that were coming
through Iraq. The governor of Khuzestan and Lurestan provinces,
Rezaqoli Khan Nezam al-Saltaneh Mafi, also joined them. They
formed a provisional government with Nezam al-Saltaneh at its head
and Farzin, Soleyman Mirza, Modarres, Alavi and others in the cabinet. Eventually with the situation hopeless, they immigrated to Iraq
and dispersed throughout the Ottoman territories. Some remained
in Istanbul and a number went to Berlin.

These events set the stage for the Ottomans to join forces with the
Iranian government in exile, which they claimed was free of Russian
and British influence, and the true representative of the Iranian people. They urged all Iranians living throughout the Ottoman empire to
defend their mutual interests. Ehtesham al-Saltaneh went along with
this charade, giving the Turks a free hand. Now I do not credit the
rumors that he received so many thousand pounds and the like. But,

as we say sarcastically, a Shahsavan tribesman may have every fault, but he could never be a thief! The Iranian public servant also, no matter how impoverished, would never take a bribe! The upshot of this was that with their customary ferocity, the Ottomans rounded up all the Iranian subjects in their territories, from the shores of the Mediterranean to the outskirts of Khanaqin and Mt. Ararat. They would extort money from these people under the pretext of having them buy their way out of military service. None were exempt because, for the most part, they were living from hand to mouth as porters, shoeshine boys and itinerants who had neither protector nor any means of escape.

In Beirut Azmi Beyg, the Turkish governor of Syria (which subsumed Lebanon at the time), requested that the consulate provide a list of all Iranian residents, including those at the American University. The school dragged its feet as much as possible. At the outset the American ambassador in Istanbul protested, representing the interests of small states, and the request was suspended. But several months later, when relations between the United States and Turkey were broken and the U.S. entered the war, the school lost this recourse. We Iranian students didn't dare set foot off campus lest the Ottoman police press us into military service. We were becoming so anxious that we were losing our appetite for study and the pleasures of student life.

Two Iranian exiles living in Beirut at the time were Mirza Soleyman Khan Maykadeh and Yar Mohammad Khan (Sardar Koll). The former had joined his brother Gholam Ali and his son Abol Hasan who had already been there<...>. Both Mirza Soleyman Khan and Sardar Koll, who knew the facts, advised us to contact the embassy in Istanbul. So despite our dire financial straits, we would send daily telegrams to the ambassador detailing our predicament. In time-honored formulas Iranians have honed over a six-thousand-year history, he would answer some of these telegrams "serious steps shall be taken"; "it will be seen to"; "the result will be known shortly." Even in our student naïveté, none of these empty phrases were the slightest consolation or comfort.

Meanwhile something unexpected happened that spared us the honor of joining the Ottoman rank and file. There is a pointed Persian saying that captures exactly how we as Shiite Moslems felt about the Sunni Ottoman government's request for our services. It goes something like this: for the love of Omar, why don't you go down into a deep well and without being paid bring out as many snakes as you find there.[9] In other words, they were asking the impossible and giving nothing for it.

What happened to save us was that Asghar Pasha, an Ottoman grandee in Damascus, suddenly became deathly ill. Two doctors, a German with the rank of brigadier general and Dr. Fakhraddin Pasha, considered at the time the leading internist in Istanbul, went to Syria to treat him. They found symptoms of renal poisoning and the like, but no matter what they did, they could not arrive at an exact diagnosis and gave up hope of curing their patient. At this time the absolute ruler of the area was Ahmad Jamal Pasha, who also happened to be extremely fond of Asghar Pasha. They told Asghar Pasha that he ought to call in Dr. Harris Graham, for years an internist at the American University Hospital in Beirut, who had a reputation for treating these types of diseases. (Professor Graham was Canadian and therefore considered a British subject by the Turks.) The Ottoman minister of war Enver Pasha had ordered Jamal Pasha to put pressure on the American University in every way he could: for example, by cutting the food rations. This way without officially closing the university they could force the administration to shut it down voluntarily. One of the punitive measures Jamal Pasha took at this time was to order several Canadian and English professors expelled from Beirut and sent to Syria. They were forbidden to stay in areas along the Mediterranean. These professors included two Englishmen, Drs. Watson Smith and Derry (head of the dental school), and two Canadians, Drs. Webster and Harris Graham.

The order to expel the professors happened to come at the same time Jamal Pasha was told to call in the Canadian doctor. He telegraphed the chancellor of the university, Dr. Bliss, to have Dr. Graham report to Syria immediately to treat the patient. He also ordered the governor of Beirut, Azmi Beyg, by telegram to arrange a car to get Graham there as quickly as possible. Three hours later Graham was in Damascus examining the patient. His diagnosis was malignant malaria. The two attending physicians debated this with Graham, and the German, insulted, asked whether he thought him incapable of recognizing malaria. Graham replied, no, he was not incapable, but it was possible that he had never encountered this strain of the disease. Jamal Pasha told them to give Graham a free hand in the treatment since they had already given up. Graham gave him twenty-five centigrams of quinine intravenously as well as the requisite liquids and nutrients. He repeated the injections after three or four hours and the patient regained consciousness. After two days, he recovered. To Jamal Pasha the recovery was miraculous and Graham now personified Christ's healing powers. This caused him to change his mind about Americans and the university. Disobeying the express orders of Enver Pasha from Istanbul, he defended them saying that one should not confuse the issue. Though the professors were Americans, Englishmen and Canadians, they had already helped the Turkish cause. Were there not hundreds of graduates from this very American University serving in the Ottoman ranks?

Graham returned to Beirut and resumed his teaching and clinical duties. At the time the students did not know where he had been; all we knew was that he had gone to treat someone high in the Turkish hierarchy. Several days later, Jamal Pasha, always on the move between Syria, Lebanon, and Palestine, came to Beirut. Around 11:00 A.M., I saw Dr. Bliss in official attire and a top hat rush by. Though obviously in a great hurry, he called me over to explain that he was meeting with the pasha to discuss the Ottoman intention to draft the Iranian students. He told me to be in front of his residence around noon when he would let me know the outcome of the meeting and so I could inform the other students. I paced around the grounds until noon and when he appeared, he summarized his meeting with the pasha this way:

Jamal Pasha: Entrust the Iranians to me—we have common interests.

Dr. Bliss: They are far from their country and the school has assumed financial responsibility for them.

Jamal Pasha: I pledge that I will take personal charge of them and find a suitable place at the front for each one.

Dr. Bliss: Let us agree that they finish their studies as they are not ready to assume positions of responsibility at this age.

In the end the pasha said he would consider what Dr. Bliss said and inform him of his decision when they met at four o'clock that afternoon when he was to pay a formal visit to the University. At five o'clock the pasha was invited to tea with the professors and their wives at Dr. Bliss's residence. He told me to delegate the oldest Iranian student to appear at his home then. The student was to present the pasha with a petition for military exemption that we were to have translated into Turkish and written in the finest Persian hand.

I immediately gathered all the Iranians to tell them that there was still a window of hope. I wrote the petition, which Professor Haratounian, an Armenian, translated into Turkish and Azizollah Bahador rendered in his fine nasta'liq handwriting. In the petition the Iranian students acknowledged that the Ottomans entered the war to defend the sanctity of Islam (the Ottomans had declared a Holy War and the minister of war traveled with the hair, mantle and other parts of the Prophet's reliquary to all Ottoman dependent states). Though we avowed that all Moslems—including Iranians— had the duty to support the Ottoman cause, we requested an opportunity to complete our studies so that we might serve the effort in an even worthier way. Bahador, as the oldest among us, was delegated to take the petition before the pasha. He was perfect for the job because of his proper demeanor and his dignified presence.

The very soul of wit and reason, Dr. Bliss gave the best speech I have ever heard in my life. In all the international meetings, assemblies, parliaments, etc. I have attended, never have I heard anyone argue more effectively than he did that day. He charmed Jamal Pasha. Dr. Bliss was blessed with all the assets a great orator must have. His Ph.D. was in the humanities, and not only was he widely read, he could also retrieve what he read from a strong memory. He was, in addition, remarkably quick-witted and had a delightful voice. He was also quite attractive; his eyes were especially penetrating. He shaved his beard but kept a mustache. The way he gestured when he spoke was elegant and effective; when he made a point with his finger, it would strike his listeners as if jolting them with an electric charge. There were times that one would think he had enlisted his entire body to express what was on his mind as eloquently as possible. His speech was the model of clarity and brevity; he avoided bombast. In addition to all of this, more than thirty years' experience had honed him into a true master of public speaking. <...>

What I remember of Dr. Bliss's speech is still vivid because it represented the one true hope amid all the lies and meaningless replies to our telegrams to Istanbul. As the chairman of the meeting, he sat in the center of the hall with Jamal Pasha to his right. The pasha's retinue, the high-ranking Ottoman officers and the important professors sat in the first row of chairs and people of less importance sat behind them in rows that filled the hall. Dr. Bliss turned to the pasha and said:

> Honorable Ahmad Jamal Pasha, supreme commander of Ottoman land and naval forces in Syria, Palestine and the Egyptian front. Many other great and learned people have occupied the chair where you now sit. This is not the first time a general or a minister has sat here. [Here Dr. Bliss mentioned the names of specific personages, statesmen and military leaders.] But I am sure that if this chair could speak or if we had the power to heed its inner voice, we would sense the immense pride and pleasure it feels in your presence. Your being here today, it would say, is the cause of such great honor and rejoicing because, unlike those other great generals, statesmen and scholars who came here during times of peace, you have rewarded us with your presence, Ahmad Jamal Pasha, in the throes of a devastating world war. You have come on a day when American soldiers are using their very teeth to tear at the throats of their German adversaries, spilling their blood on the battlefield—at a time when all relations between the United States and Turkey are severed. Your visit

teaches the students at this cradle of learning the great lesson that the present war, a war between the interests of two opposing political ideologies, is a struggle between the commercial concerns of two groups that are ravenously attached to their own particular interests. It is a war between the two satanic forces of avarice and greed, but American and Ottoman learning are at peace. Truth, science, and spirituality are united in every land; they are one, inseparable, admitting no duality. Truth is indivisible and by coming here, Jamal Pasha, you have shown that you are prepared to demonstrate that fact in person.

Then he pointed to the students and said:

Rise in honor of the individual that has taught you this unforgettable lesson. Learn what the great Ahmad Jamal Pasha is communicating in the most eloquent way possible, through his presence here.

Dr. Bliss then addressed the pasha directly and regaled him with so many references to the truth and spirit of learning from great authors that he shook the doors and walls.

As Jamal Pasha rose to his feet to respond, it was clear how much he had been moved. Transported to an otherworldly state, he said in Turkish:

Today is one of the most fortunate in my entire life. I am a soldier. I have come to you in a Turkish military uniform with medals on my chest and an Ottoman sword at my side. With a soldier's sincerity and honesty, I loudly proclaim this university to be a spiritual and cultural institution established to serve the lofty principles of all humankind. It is a great honor to enroll my name among those who have served this institution. It is our wish that you students, who represent hope for the future, will be successful and ignite the fires of science and learning in the East...

A stenographer recorded Jamal Pasha's speech and, as soon as the meeting was over, wrote it out longhand on a scroll. They brought it to the chancellor at his home where the pasha was having tea. Dr. Bliss gave it to him while he was surrounded by the teachers, their wives, and daughters, and said that we must preserve it in the university library to commemorate this historic day. He also requested that the pasha sign his speech to enhance the value of the already precious document. After the pasha signed it, the chancellor had several thousand copies written, sending them to everyone and everywhere. This in fact was a canny way of proving that an Ottoman vizier and amir had recognized the university as a spiritual and educational institution that he was proud to serve. It would prevent any ne'er-do-well Turk from flexing his muscles against it. Then Bahador presented the pasha with the Iranian students' petition, whose phrasing and calligraphy pleased him greatly. He asked Bahador to approach him and, taking his hand, the pasha said:

> Go and join hands with the other Iranian students of this university and assure them from me that they are our spiritual children. The soul of this petition has delighted me immensely. Tell them to devote themselves wholeheartedly to completing their studies, confident of our best wishes for their success in the future.

We had all assembled outside the president's home, waiting for Bahador's words. The moment he told us the good news, there was pandemonium. I don't know when I have been happier. In short Dr. Graham's timely diagnosis and treatment and Dr. Bliss's magical words were enough to save the Iranian students and a colony of some five thousand people from all those miseries.

A few years later in 1919 after I had finished my studies, my return trip to Iran took me to Istanbul where I stayed for a week. One day I called on Ambassador Ehtesham al-Saltaneh at the embassy. He was very encouraging, saying that now that I had gotten an education, especially as a physician, I could serve my country. He asked where I was from in Iran. When I said Sabzevar, he went on about Hajj Molla Hadi and his accomplishments. During our conversation, he said that it was gratifying to have saved me from the Ottoman draft. I replied in all candor and schoolboy naïveté that he had done no such thing, that it was in fact the Americans who engineered our salvation. Ehtesham al-Saltaneh immediately changed the subject, going on again about the virtues and disciples of Molla Hadi. At that point I left the embassy.

No longer threatened by the Ottomans, I became absorbed in my studies again. But that fall when school opened I caught a chill that developed into bronchitis. For several days I remained in bed with a fever. The school doctor, an Englishman named Piper, looked in on me a few times. When my condition did not improve, they transferred me to the university hospital where I remained for two weeks. I got a little better, but the weakness and fatigue would not go away. That was the third year of medical school, a particularly difficult one. At the end of it there are board exams that cover two and a half years of material. There is in addition a great deal of dissection. Students are responsible for describing all the parts of two cadavers, inside and out, from head to toe. They must demonstrate their practical knowledge before the anatomy teacher by spending hours on end in a well-ventilated room working over bodies laid out on marble slabs colder than the cadavers themselves. This work is very tiring because it involves long hours and comes on top of several periods of class work. <...>

During that year of work and anxiety I was always ill and feverish. Coughing kept me awake at night. I became hypersensitive and lost weight. My appetite was so diminished that I could not stomach any food, much less what they served in the cafeteria. I finally managed to get permission from the university authorities to have two liters of milk a day. That milk, which along with a few other things was all I had every day, I grudgingly drank without sweets. I visited Dr. Graham a few times, and he prescribed some special medicines, which exhausted the little pocket money I got from the school. Soon they began to speak about tuberculosis and sent me to a specialist who examined my phlegm and did other tests used to diagnose the disease. Proving that a little knowledge can be a dangerous thing, my medical student's suspicions did nothing to calm my nerves. I spent hours on end scouring medical texts for symptoms of the disease and comparing them to my own.

In short, everything conspired to wear me down in body and spirit—fever, sleepless nights, a strange loss of appetite, my studies, which continued despite my condition, apprehension about final exams and the terror evoked by the word "tuberculosis," which in the East especially is synonymous with "death." Despondent, I began to view living and dying philosophically. What was the point of existence, I asked myself, if it was to end this way? My life was now like a play and I was a spectator watching it go by.

By nature and psychology, the Easterner is a subtle thinker and keen observer. His mind is capable of many flights of imagination, of jumping in an instant from the natural to the metaphysical, of covering the entire gamut of creation in less than a second. <...> The Persian New Year [which coincides with the vernal equinox] is a historic day, the most ancient national tradition that plays an unusual role in the life of every Iranian. That New Year was a strange one for me. This was when I played the philosopher, as I thought it might be the last I would ever celebrate. One aspect of this philosophizing was an odd feeling of resignation. I had become so used to suffering that it became my natural state. The strange thing was that my greatest fear was failing the final exams. One day in May with the exams some thirty-five days away, I went to the school cafeteria at 5:30 when they rang the dinner bell. After having a couple of glasses of milk, I went straight to a bench near the medical school. Sitting there I sank into the old despondency and worries about my studies. Before me was a small stand of spruce trees overlooking a hill that ran down to the Mediterranean. One after another, the waves rushed in throwing up a foamy spray that covered the rocks along the shore and then fell back toward the sea. The recurrent pounding of the surf may have made me ready for soul-searching, and it was almost as if the waves and my thoughts were synchronized.

As I sat there, oblivious to the world around me, in a way depersonalized and lost in a sea of unsettling visions, there was a voice calling me as if to wake me from that state. It was Dr. Van Dyke, the distinguished professor of biology and physiology.[10] With those ethereal features of his and in that commanding voice he asked, "Ghani, what's the trouble? What's plunged you into these depths of despair?" I moved and said hello, adding that there was nothing unusual—I was just sitting and getting some air. "Don't you eat at school?" he asked. "Why are you here?" I said that I had eaten and gone out. He said, "Be candid with me, what's wrong?" "There's nothing wrong, Doctor," I replied. He said, "My wife is waiting for me and would be upset if I came late. So accompany me as I walk home and we'll talk." I went with the thoughtful old man as he walked with his accustomed slowness and I fell in behind him. After he repeatedly asked me what the problem was, I finally said, "How can I put it Doctor—it's not one thing but a whole chapter." "Tell me about it," he said. I told him, "Doctor, I have become ill, getting weaker every day. I can't relax and there's a strong possibility I have tuberculosis. This year is the hardest in school and at the end I have preliminary exams. Because of the war, there's no contact with my country, no word of my family, no way to tell them how I'm feeling, and no money even reaches me."

Van Dyke suddenly stopped and stood straight, and said sharply, "My son, get a grip on yourself. Be a man. How can you start out in life so weak and timid? Are you supposed to give up just when life's struggles are beginning? You're sick, but you will recover. You're weak, but you will become stronger. You're tubercular, but you will be cured. You have exams, but you will pass them. You're a student, but you will be a teacher. There's war, but it will end. You've no news from your family, you will hear from them. You're out of money, but you will receive some. Are these difficulties worth mentioning? No! Now stand up like a man and master them. Life has more difficult problems in store that you will have to prepare yourself to confront. Being a man does not mean that one can surrender when faced with the difficulties that are part of the ordinary fabric of life."

In the lives of all individuals there are special moments that amount to momentous events and make the deepest impressions on their hearts and minds; however, they are of little import in the larger scheme of things. Of course seen through my eyes, this moment assumed an importance that is hard to express. That sage old man meant so much to me that I have no choice but to express my feelings, however inadequately.

I am unable to explain the magic Van Dyke's words worked on me, but this much I can say. It was as though my weakness and distress for the

Dr. William Van Dyke

most part were gone having given way to strength and hope. My heart was steeled and I was ready to battle the world. It was as if a new chapter in my life had opened, a chapter I must call "hope and aspiration." As we were about to reach Dr. Van Dyke's home, he said to me, "My son, tomorrow at four o'clock come to West Hall (where his study was) so I can examine you."

I returned with all the excitement and anticipation in the world, especially now that I sensed I was not alone and that a person of substance was going to use his skill to treat me. This pleased me more than any other feeling. In any event, I went to the doctor's study at four sharp. Dr. Van Dyke, who had brought his instruments, examined me for a full hour and listened to my symptoms. Then he said, "You don't have tuberculosis, but you have a condition that could lead to it. We must be serious about your treatment and build up your strength. You have to go to the mountains outside of Beirut immediately and take a complete rest. I will give you medicine that will nourish you and build up your strength so you can prepare for your studies." At that point there were some thirty-three days left to the school year, meaning until the juried final examinations began.

He said, "I will arrange an exception so that you can take the exams in the fall."

"Doctor," I said, "these exams are so important in the life of a student that I won't be able to rest for the five months before next fall. Day and night while I'm in the mountains, my thoughts will be on those exams, so nervous that my treatment will not progress. If you can make an exception in my case by postponing the exams, why not make another exception and let me take them now? I've finished studying and am just reviewing what I have already prepared. I'll take the exams now regardless of the outcome. I'll have peace of mind whether I am accepted or rejected. Even if I fail there will be one year to rest, because I'll have to repeat. Then I can rest without any extraneous worries." Van Dyke considered this for a while and said, "You're right. Now go rest and come back at four o'clock tomorrow to see me." I left.

The next day when I returned it was clear that Professor Van Dyke had gone to the home of Chancellor Bliss just after dismissing me the previous day. As soon as Van Dyke had entered he started chiding Bliss, saying that as university chancellor he was like a father to the students, especially those far from their homelands. It was a matter of conscience that one of the good students, Ghasem Ghani, was in a terrible state, and if nothing was done immediately, he might be gone. Bliss was convinced. The chancellor asked what should be done. Dr. Van Dyke asked him to convene an emergency meeting of the Medical School Council at 7:00 P.M. so that he could bring the matter up with them. He did this immediately, having the professors, all of whom lived in the area, appear. Dr. Van Dyke explained the situation. He was held in such high esteem that everyone agreed to the following proposals without the slightest opposition: (1) in two days the board of examiners convene to examine me; (2) one hundred English pounds from school funds be given me now to relieve me of money worries;

and (3) the administrative offices of the university be ordered to see to my needs immediately in a way that would not cause me any concern and that any medicines Van Dyke ordered be sent without delay to Behamdoun in the mountains. The next day Van Dyke told me to be ready for the examinations at nine o'clock the following morning. He gave me a letter addressed to Sister Anastas of Behamdoun, who ran a guesthouse and retreat, explaining that I was his son and requesting that she personally treat me with special care. He recommended that I take a number of books from the library. Finally that fine old man said that there was one task he could not do for me and that was to have my Iranian friends hire a horse to carry me to Behamdoun. The railways of Lebanon and Syria were in the hands of the military and one had to go there on horseback.

I went at nine the next morning. As I was a good student and most of the examiners on the jury were themselves my professors, they encouraged me, saying that the exams for me were a formality—otherwise there was no need for me to take them and they would have exempted me. These seemingly unimportant words were the most precious things to a student. In any case the examination started, questions on various subjects were asked, and in the end a paper was issued that promoted me to the next class. I left the building and the next day was on my way to Behamdoun on the horse rented by my friends. I arrived at night. Van Dyke's remedies were very simple, a solution of arsenic and energizers and appetite enhancers. He had complete faith, which was born out, in air, sun, rest and nutrition. Upon my arrival at Sister Anastas's retreat, I gave them Van Dyke's letter, which they treated as sacred. They found a room with a beautiful view for me and I slept. I rose in the morning before sunrise and had some fresh grapes and then stretched out in the sun streaming through my window. At eight I ate a breakfast of milk, eggs, butter and fruit. At ten I rested for an hour. At noon I had lunch in the restaurant of the retreat and around three had to rest again for at least an hour. In the evening I would walk a bit and at night I ate dinner in the restaurant. At ten I would be in bed.

As the days went on, I became better. I began to eat and sleep well. Dr. Van Dyke wrote to me regularly, saying at the outset that two months' rest would suffice, but at the end of the two months he wrote that the city was very hot and humid and advised me to stay another month. At the end of the third month, he told me not to come to the city and to continue to rest. By the end of the fourth month when school was reopening, he wrote that I had two and a half years of medical school ahead of me, I had to build my strength completely. Since there was little done in the first two weeks of class—registration and various tasks—and as I was a good student, there would be no problem were I to come several days late. He suggested I stay another month. In the meantime, he had privately written to the rest home to keep me busy lest I become bored. <...> In the end I stayed five months, regained my strength and have never had the slightest lung problem or general weakness since.

I finally returned to school and my studies. Two years later on 18 June 1919, I graduated with an M.D. degree and was awarded accreditation from the State of New York.[11] Throughout my studies until the end of the war, the school, as it had before, provided me with loans. After I returned to Iran at the end of 1919 and the beginning of 1920, I repaid those loans. <...>

Speaking of Van Dyke, here I would like to give some sense of his personal attainments and qualities. When one reviews his own past carefully, through introspection he can identify and analyze various stages in life. He sees a process of evolution and realizes that a number of people have left impressions of varying degrees on him, influencing his spiritual and intellectual life. After hereditary factors, instincts, and environmental and social circumstances, these people are the shapers of an individual often without his being aware.

The first to make a deep impression on my psyche were Mother and Father. Father especially was always the model of spiritual and intellectual greatness, independence, selflessness, strength and innate distinction for me. There were also a number of other individuals who left a deep impression on my spiritual and intellectual growth. Whenever appropriate I will always remember them, for above all else I enjoy doing so. Recalling them and mentioning their qualities bring me to a kind of ecstatic state. For another thing I consider it repayment of a debt; when I say their names I express my thanks. Van Dyke was one such individual. Having known him and having been in his presence were blessings that enriched my life.

William Van Dyke was the second son of Dr. Cornelius Van Dyke, who came to Beirut in the first part of the nineteenth century. In addition to medicine, this man's understanding encompassed other branches of science and a further variety of subjects including Hebrew and the other Semitic languages. With his knowledge of Arabic, he was one of those whom God created to serve learning and scholarship. He was among those marvels who formed the heart and soul of human society. Arriving in Syria and Lebanon as a young man, Cornelius Van Dyke established schools and study centers in Beirut and the surrounding villages. He wrote a series of concise and abbreviated books in Arabic on various sciences called *The Image on the Stone*. Among the topics were astronomy, chemistry, physics, botany, zoology, etc. He completed the Arabic translation of the Torah and the New Testament that the British Dr. Smith had started but passed away after completing half of it. Van Dyke worked on the translation about seven or eight years, consulting with experts in Arabic. He wore Arab clothing: a robe, a turban, a long cloak and open-toed sandals. He sat on the floor smoking a water pipe, thoroughly enjoying life as the Arabs lived it. Among those he educated was Petros Bostani, the compiler of the Arab encyclopedia.

When the American Medical School was founded in Beirut, Van Dyke joined the faculty. He translated medical texts and labored hard to find indigenous Arabic equivalents for modern terminology. These significant and classic works were highly scholarly in their nomenclature and lexical standards. He wrote some independently and a number in collaboration with Dr. Wortabet, an Armenian who established the weather observatory in Beirut and apparently passed away in

1895. When Cornelius Van Dyke went to the United States, people were adamant, offering him the best inducements to remain and teach Semitic languages, which he ultimately agreed to do. But on the day of his departure from the U.S., he requested that they give him time to think, after which he told them, "To be frank I must say that my heart resides in the East, in Lebanon. Were I to stay, I would lose that heart, so I can't." In the end he returned to Beirut.

William Van Dyke, who grew up at the feet of such a father, completed his medical education in America. This was during the lifetime of Charles Darwin, and Van Dyke was very receptive to the great British naturalist's theories. He conducted research in biology, including genetics and Mendel's laws. He corresponded with Darwin on the results of his research, and Darwin, greatly appreciating his efforts, encouraged him. At the International Congress of Biologists held in London one year before his death, Darwin, its president, presented William Van Dyke's views and the results of his research to the participants, the world's leading scientists. Darwin's biographers have recorded this event in their works.

I was privileged to study under Van Dyke for four years (1915–1919) when he was about sixty-five. He died in Beirut in 1939 at eighty-seven and was buried there. He was a man of average to above-average height, broad-shouldered, strong, of consummate build with a long face accentuated slightly more than normal by a pointed beard. He had a long, thick mustache that made his features intimidating, austere and monkish. But he also possessed the simplicity, charm, natural sympathy and feelings that innocent children have. His nose was well-proportioned and his eyes were very penetrating; his high forehead was attractive, furrowed in a way that bespoke nervous energy and passion. He was very, very conscientious. For example, during the four years I was his student, he taught us every single day without exception from three to four in the afternoon.

He taught in a large amphitheater adjoining his private office where he kept his books, cane, hat and necessities. It also contained a water pitcher and a glass, several chairs and a couple of benches. As soon as it was three, as the large university clock struck but once, the door to his office would open and he would rush toward where the students were entering the amphitheater and lock the door so that no one else could enter. With the same haste he would go to the professor's chair and, with one foot on the chair, would start to lecture. His teaching, in other words, would start precisely at three. When the clock sounded four, he would apologize for ending his lecture; of course, he would run over for a minute or two to complete something he was explaining. I never knew any of his lectures to last fifty-nine minutes, as he always made it a practice to go an hour. He began the first lesson we had with him by saying:

> At the outset I would like you gentlemen to keep several things in mind. First, there is an attitude among students that goes against the true spirit of learning and, more important, contradicts reality and logic. Students seem to feel deeply that the teacher is of a different substance than they are; they consider him a man who has mastered all science, especially the subject he teaches. This in itself causes them to see him as a species apart from their own and to accept a distinction between him and themselves.
>
> The only difference between me, the teacher, and you, the students, is the fact that I am older than you. I have become involved in the matters we are about to discuss and debate before you did. <...> However, don't imagine that you will only learn from me; I for my part will also learn from you. In my experience one question from a student has opened my eyes in an instant to a wide world that I had never seen before; because the student brings a particular point of view to a problem, sees it from a special angle. <...> In short our sessions are ones of give and take. <...>
>
> <...>

Van Dyke had office hours immediately after his class. Students were free to ask him questions about the subject of the lecture and he would answer.

In short the man's class began with astronomical precision at three and not the slightest sound was heard while he was teaching. He had our complete attention. On the quality of his teaching I can say wholeheartedly that I have never seen anyone exercise greater mastery or control or show a greater gift for explanation. When he lectured, not only did he address the topic, but it was as though his whole body vibrantly took to the task. His respect for learning and scholarship was so great that it made people sit up and take notice. The love of learning manifested in him, made him alive; he would become curious, selfless, self-effacing and engaged.

Thinking of that transcendent man, remembering his divine bearing, gives me a certain spiritual lift. He was the perfect image of the grand, heroic figures of science. He was so committed to precision and accuracy, so wedded to truth, that it defies description. Everything about him, his demeanor, thought, behavior and speech, conformed to rigorous standards, akin to the principles taught in such exact sciences as mathematics and astronomy. This man had no concept of leniency or indulgence. In what he said, thought and did he was the model of rectitude. Even with his encyclopedic grasp of the subject, preparing a one-hour lecture actually took him several hours, because his concern was how to explain a topic to a group of entry-level students—how to portray it; where to begin; how to make the transition from one issue to another; what sources to use; what logic to choose; what was the easiest path toward engaging the students; how to arouse their curiosity; how to present the elegance of scientific principle; what device to use to lessen the topic's dryness; and how to paint it in a charming and alluring color. In sum he fully typified what the Sufis call an Elijah of the path, a venerable wayfarer on the road to enlightenment, and a spiritual guide.

The courses he taught in first and second year were general biology (zoology and parasitology), health (general and specific, i.e. healthcare related to various ages, social groups, occupations, places, etc.), statistics, genetics and physiology. In the last years of medical school, he taught general medicine, symptomology, Freudian psychology and psychoanalysis. For each of these subjects he published précis that though concise were so inclusive and to the point that I have yet to find their like in medical publications.

In my time as a student I trained myself to listen attentively, and consequently I did not need to resort to notes. I would jot down a specific point or write captions that later helped me to remember the order and the flow of the material. Unlike many students that take down what the teacher says like dictation machines, I relied on my memory and logic. I am completely indebted to Van Dyke for this exercise, which later became second nature. In many cases it was as if I had gained such complete control over my memory that I was able to keep the irrelevant from entering and inhabiting it.

Van Dyke's lectures and delivery were captivating, profound and valuable; they forced one to listen carefully, eventually to absorb what he said. I was one of the last students to emerge from his office sessions and I would occasionally leave with him.

Van Dyke also had his own style of testing students in class. Never did he ask a direct question, rather he would pose problems and seek the student's opinion on them. This way he found out whether the student had digested the material or whether he was just parroting something he had memorized. To put it another way, teaching had become part of Van Dyke's being, like a color that no water could wash away. <…> I always had the highest grades in his classes, outpacing the other four or five students in contention.

<…>

Once my excessive curiosity astonished him, for I tried to reconcile philosophy, metaphysics, religion and spirituality with the natural sciences. Van Dyke said, "Do you know what Thomas Huxley, the naturalist contemporary of Darwin and one of the great developmental biologists of the nineteenth century, said about the difference between science and myth, between truth and superstition? Huxley said that the difference was that scientific truth progresses gradually and cannot sustain, not even at a single point, a break in the continuity or order of events. But superstition allows astounding leaps from the natural to the supernatural, from earth to heaven.

Another time he said, "I am prepared to accept anything you say as long as you do not overstep the bounds of 'nature.' These boundaries are vast. This is the nature that astronomers teach, proving that it takes light radiating from some bodies millions of years to reach us. In the context of nature such as this the dimensions of time and space are inconceivable." <...> "Let us proceed step by step and whenever we reach the limits of nature, then enter into the discussion about where the metaphysical lies." <...>

<...>

I was intent upon learning as much from him as my capacity would allow. Van Dyke by nature was a great leader; one could see how his search for truth and learning had shaped his mind. It had also made him humble, modest, cordial and friendly. How much he enjoyed being a friend to a group of students. He would listen and speak to us as a comrade and colleague.

Having sensed that I had a thirst for learning, Van Dyke soon developed a special affection for me, calling me "my son." He introduced me to his wife, a fine and pure older woman who became a true mother to me. <...> On Sunday mornings at ten I would regularly visit them at home where I would stay until twelve asking various questions. This woman, who is still alive, lives at an old-age home in Cambridge, Massachusetts. Three years ago I managed with some difficulty to find her address and wrote saying that, as her son, I felt it my filial duty to do whatever I could for my loving mother. I sent a variety of presents and then went to see the old woman, who is now eighty-six. When she saw me she kissed me fondly and cried, saying that her husband spoke of me until the very last moments he was alive. I am still in correspondence with her.

Van Dyke's paternal affection and love for me went so far that our friendship approximated the relationship between Mowlana Jalal al-Din Rumi and his student and disciple Hosam al-Din Çalabi. Of course to forestall the wrong conclusion, let me immediately quote Mowlana himself: "Do not apply one's own standards to the acts of the purehearted"; though if I compare Van Dyke to Mowlana, it is no exaggeration.

Both were cut from the same cloth in the way they served the truth—naturally each had his own way. The comparison between me and Hosam al-Din is an overstatement. Comparisons, however, require only one point of similarity. The point is that a great teacher like Van Dyke had a respect and special regard for me that I did not truly merit. Let me illustrate this with an example. Once Bahador and my dear friend Abdolhoseyn Khan Dehqan, a student at the Faculty of Humanities and Social Sciences at the American University, came and told me that Professor Wilson wanted to see me at a certain time in his office. (Wilson, now a professor at the University of Chicago, is a specialist in Egyptian history and every year spends a season in Upper Egypt researching and excavating.) I knew him only by sight. He shook my hand and thanked me for coming. Then he said that he and a number of other university professors needed a favor that I alone could do for them. "What is it?" I asked. He said, "Professor Van Dyke is a prominent scientist in the field of evolution and the principles of Darwinism. We would like him to hold a series of symposia so we can benefit from his expertise. We have asked him a number of times, but he has refused saying he was too busy. We thought we would impose upon you to ask him, being sure that he would not refuse you any request." In all modesty I said, "I am nothing more than an ordinary student, while you are his colleagues. If he has refused you, how can I ask him?" He said, "No, he has a special regard for you and will agree. Dr. Van Dyke is entirely committed to training you in the best way and to satisfying your intellectual curiosity." I promised that I would try—eager myself, of course, as I was a third-year medical student, ecstatic at the prospect of a regular series of symposia on the subject, especially by a distinguished authority like Van Dyke.

I went to Van Dyke and explained exactly what happened, neither adding nor subtracting anything. He thought for a moment and said, "My son, tell them that my time, which is completely taken up during the school year, will not allow me to work more. However, I am prepared to forsake my vacation and spend the first six weeks of the summer in Beirut to hold symposia two or three times every week in the museum's large lecture hall." I went to Wilson who became so happy he couldn't contain himself. When summer arrived, they prepared the large lecture hall, filling it with chairs. A group of the leading university scientists and scholars including Chancellor Bliss, a number of local learned men and theologians, and several advanced medical students including myself assembled there. With the expertise, mastery and command that he brought to the subject, Van Dyke worked his customary magic. The detailed notes I have of those lectures are among my trove of personal treasures. In that great hall it was as if those experienced men of learning had become a group of beginners with their pens and notebooks in hand, taking in that man's sea of learning. All of them gave up their vacations and not a day went by that several of those in attendance did not thank me at the end of the lecture. Mowlana called his *Masnavi*, which is one of humanity's enduring works, the "Hosami-nameh." Were it not for Mowlana's affection for this man and his dedication of the poem, history would absolutely never have taken notice of him; but, as scripture says, "That is the Grace of Allah, which He bestows on whom He pleases." My dealings with Van Dyke were about grace; otherwise, judging honestly, I never considered myself worthy of the attention and paternal love he lavished on me.

Among Van Dyke's characteristics was a modesty and a genuine humility. Of all the things he said, "I don't know" was most often on his lips. Of course implicit in that "I don't know" were a thousand "knows," but the line he drew between the known and the unknown differed from the one the rest of humankind drew. I have seen several individuals like him in my life and infer that this is characteristic of great people. The erudite literary scholar Mirza Mohammad Khan Qazvini also has these characteristics and the sentence that most readily came to his lips was "I don't know." <...> Another individual I have seen with that humility and modesty was Professor Albert Einstein about whom, if these recollections continue, I shall write something.

Van Dyke's humility was not the ordinary or polite variety. Once I recall having borrowed a biography of Darwin from the library whose British author I cannot recall. The final chapter of the book describes the last public lecture Darwin gave the year before he died. This was when he presided at the International Congress of Biologists held in London. Darwin's remarks were mostly in support of the experiments and research on genetics that Dr. William Van Dyke of Beirut had conducted, which had shed light on some scientific uncertainties. I was astonished that the whole time this great man was lecturing in class or talking in his office on genetics and Mendel's laws, he never mentioned this. I even thought that it was a case of mistaken identity, that there was another William Van Dyke in Beirut.

I raised the issue one Sunday morning when I was at his home. "Is this you that I read about in some biography of Darwin?" I asked. Van Dyke looked stunned, as if he had received a blow; like a child he did everything to avoid answering the question. With shock registering on his features, his voice strained, he said, "Where did you read that?" I told him the name of the book. He said, "Yes, my son, that author has it wrong. He portrays me as Darwin's 'colleague.' I am too insignificant to be put in a class with him. Darwin's ideas did indeed fascinate me; I had studied, worked and experimented with them. I wrote to Darwin of my findings, and he wrote back with guidance and encouragement. That which distinguishes great people, those passionate about the truth, is how they guide novices and encourage future servants and devotees of knowledge—regardless of who they are or what their station in life. All Darwin was doing in mentioning my research and experiments at that congress was encouraging me. I have never been and will never be important enough to be considered one of Darwin's colleagues. He is one of the leading lights of science and learning, and we are as far apart as the stars and the earth." Then in that same impassioned state he called out and his wife came from the adjoining room. He said, "Dear, Ghani is quite enthusiastic about Charles Darwin. Bring that packet of the great man's letters so he can see them." She went and returned with the packet, which was a large handkerchief containing some papers and knotted in the traditional Middle Eastern way. Holding the handkerchief with two hands, she entered as if bringing Holy Writ to a congregation. Dr. Van Dyke rose in honor of the packet, forcing me to rise with him. Then with a special reverence he took it from his wife and untied it. One after another he showed me his own letters and Darwin's. We read a portion of them while he explained and then, as if to exculpate himself, he said, "The term that biographer used was entirely inappropriate. Darwin had to call me his colleague just to encourage me; but one should get the spirit of events right and not stray from the truth."

Dr. Van Dyke was widely informed on many subjects. In addition to his knowledge of biology of plants and animals, his command of medical and other sciences, he was also a scholar of French literature, Arabic poetry and prose, and had a philosopher's sensibility in his literary taste. He was catholic in his opinions on all of these topics. <...> He believed in a kind of universal knowledge, knowledge in its absolute and broad sense. For this reason every branch of human understanding attracted him; of course the sciences were at the core and all other matters revolved around them.

Among contemporary European writers he was particularly fond of Anatole France. I first heard this author's name from him. It was during one of my regular Sunday morning visits when he ranged from subject to subject and said at one point, "To explain this further let me read you excerpts from Anatole France." He brought out some typewritten selections from France's writings, looked for a particular section and read. Knowing French, I enjoyed them very much but today cannot remember the specific sections. "Doctor, who is this person?" I asked. He said, "Perhaps the greatest writer, thinker and man of talent of our time." "Is he still alive?" I asked. "Yes," he said (this was around 1917). He suggested that I read his books. "You know French and there are few writers better at developing the mind of a student and a reader."

In January 1924 I had returned from Iran and was traveling to France via Beirut where I spent several days with Dr. Van Dyke. As I was about to go, I asked him, "Doctor, what do you want from Paris?" He said, "Send me all the books Anatole France has written from 1914 when the war broke out until now." At that time Anatole France was still alive, but he died toward the end of that year. As soon as I arrived in Paris, I sent all those books to him.

One of Van Dyke's character traits was his humanitarianism. His affection and sympathy for all mankind, human society, smaller nations, oppressed minorities, and his pacifism, were limitless. He had nothing but love for the truth, believing in science and the future of science; that science would ultimately render war impossible and elevate human life to such a level that people will be able to live in peace.

<...>

He had the faith of a freethinker. As the poet says, "the lover's religion is unlike any other." His religion was science and truth; wherever he found truth he revered it. Moses, Jesus, Mohammad were all the same to him. He worshipped the god of science, which in his definition was so broad that it was impossible to imagine anything beyond its confines. Consequently his god was limitless, as was his conception of God. His deity was not the debased and mean or the popular conception, but the Creator of Greater Existence. <...>

If during the course of writing these memoirs (which are free of any plan or systematic approach or method, like a stream of words in which I record whatever comes to mind in no particular order), I remember other matters that came during the course of my conversations with that great man, I will note them.

My student days were over and at the end of that period my health was fully restored. In those years the two professors who occupied the highest positions in the university were Drs. Van Dyke and Graham. Of course, Van Dyke was a unique amalgam: philosopher, spiritual guide, man of infinite heart and one of the wonders of his age. He personified the great men of the past who encompassed whole universes within themselves. Graham was pure physician but also a complete man of medicine, having trained in various specialties. He was a clinician possessing vast experience and a sixth sense, and many took advantage of his skills as a pathologist. He was also a great personality.

One of the famous teachers during my time was Jabr Zoumet, professor of Arabic literature. Zoumet was one of those walking encyclopedias of Arabic that comprise all Semitic languages. He was a very unpretentious man and, though a Christian, one more interested in Islam than any Moslem. He was a man of wide interests, all of which, as the saying goes, "formed a single light." The poet says,

Where there's a vine the flower will blossom;
Where there's a bubbling vat the wine will flow.
Reckon whoever comes from fine stock as good;
Whether he stems from Ali or Omar.

Islam sealed the heterogeneity of the Arabs; were it not for Islam and the Qur'an, the Arabic language and the Arab nation would not have survived. They would have been absorbed into other nations. The Qur'an maintained the Arabic language, and the Islamic religion in turn preserved the language and the Arab peoples. If Islam were to disappear, the Arabs would also go.

University life is very enthralling. One can forget anything in life but one's school days. I enjoyed myself so much during that time that I remember everything about it with pleasure. I even recall Asad the Doorkeeper, an old man who had a room by the gate. It delights me to think of that fine, earnest and responsible man who faithfully carried out his duties as gatekeeper. He dressed in full Lebanese finery, with his homespun mantle and wide shawl, his fez and, Arab-style slippers. He sat on his stool keeping watch over who came and went.

In 1938 when I was going to Egypt with Mr. Mahmud Jam, the minister of court, and Dr. Ali Asghar Mo'addab Nafisi, head of the Office of the Crown Prince, I spent six days in Beirut, three on my way and three days on my return trip. Before entering the city, I told Mr. Jam that I would be seeing very little of him, not participating in any of the gatherings and receptions given by the Lebanese government. Nor would I appear at the French High Commissioner's because I wanted to spend all my time visiting the university, the professors and my schoolmates. I was staying at the Iranian consulate, and early every morning when I got started I would dismiss the government car waiting for me and go for a walk in the streets. There was a memory behind every rock, every doorway and wall. Sometimes as I traveled back and forth on the very city trams I used when I was in university, I remembered those days.

—◆—

That year, 1938, was the last time I saw Dr. Van Dyke, several months before that great man's death. The first day I went to see him we had a talk that was actually the best souvenir of that trip. Since what he said could apply to the life of every individual, I shall record it here verbatim, adding things by way of explanation.

As soon as I entered Van Dyke greeted and hugged me. I said, "Doctor, I don't want to tire you, so just act as though I'm not here."

He said, "That is a good idea. Normally I would be stretched out on the bed, busy reading with a blanket over my legs."

I said, "Why don't you do that," mindful that Van Dyke had a weak heart and at this time was almost eighty-six years old. So we went to his bedroom and I spread a blanket over him. He said, "Very well, instead of reading I will talk with you."

Then he asked me questions about my life, one of which was "Do you have any children?"

"A daughter and a son," I replied. Then he asked, "Are you still studying Freudian psychology?"

"Yes," I said. "I happen to have the sort of work that makes this a necessity."

"How so?" he asked.

I said, "I teach normal and abnormal psychology, psychopathology and Freudianism at the medical school in Tehran. I have to stay current to prepare my lectures, which I am happy to do."

I had not seen Van Dyke from the middle of 1919 before I returned to Iran via Istanbul until January 1924 when I visited him at his modest home. On that trip I brought a pair of large antique carpets with me as gifts for Dr. Van Dyke. They were of very fine design, the best examples of Turkman work. Azizollah Khan Sardar Mo'azzez Bojnurdi, chief of the Shadlu tribe, had given them to me. He had written that as I was so fond of objects of art, he was presenting the two carpets, which had been in his family. I gave them to Van Dyke along with some silverwork and inlay pieces from Shiraz. He was so pleased with the carpets that he made detailed studies of them, their dyes and the process of extraction, how they were woven, etc. After being in his company for several days, I traveled through Palestine and Egypt to Port Said and then on to Marseilles and Europe. <...>

While on that trip around the middle of 1925, Van Dyke wrote saying that he was now old and probably would not see me again. He suggested that, as long as it didn't upset my plans, I come and see him on my way back. I returned through Beirut and met him in the modest summer place he had. I noticed the pair of carpets there, one draped over the sofa, the other fixed to the wall near it. He wished to sleep on one and keep the other nearby so he could touch it. He said, "Though I have not brought many things from town, as I told my wife, I must never be separated from Dr. Ghani's gifts." I spent several days with him.

The next time I saw him was in 1938, the year he died, while traveling to Egypt with Mr. Jam. I was in his company for three days going and three on my way back. After I returned to Iran, he sent me a published biography of his father that contained marginalia and notes that Van Dyke had written himself. He wished me to keep it so that it would avoid being damaged.

A heart alive with love will never die;
It's graven on the world's lasting journal.

My student days were over. On 18 June 1919 I received a medical degree from the American University at Beirut (under the aegis of the State of New York). Americans call the time when one receives diplomas the "commencement." What an appropriate name, for graduation is the start of education not the end of it. While in school a person can gain the bent for learning, exercise it, master the way to learn, mature and become established. He can also develop a thirst and a curiosity in preparation for true education. I once asked Van Dyke where I should go to specialize. He answered:

> My son, having traveled this road I can advise you from
> experience not to go right after a specialty. What you have gained in
> medical school is still raw, not part of you. You ought to return to
> Iran, practice medicine two or three years and get some experience.
> Learn your own weaknesses; discover your instincts; understand the
> needs of your country; give yourself some time to learn what

working in a clinic with patients is like. In the meantime you will digest what you have learned, making it a part of your being. Afterward you can decide what you want to specialize in and complete your education. But I don't recommend studying where you went to medical school, because it's preferable that your education not be entirely American. It would be better for you to go to France where you can add a Latin flavor to your Anglo-Saxon training. Knowing French will allow you to take full advantage of that setting.

I followed this advice and prepared to return to Iran, but the roads were closed making the trip difficult. The chancellor arranged with the British and French, who were in control of Beirut, for a travel permit and a passport, and in July 1919 I embarked on the thirteen-day boat trip from Beirut to Istanbul.

ENTERING ISTANBUL

The boat traveled along the coast stopping in, at Tripoli, and then went on to Iskenderun, Cyprus, Khos, Izmir and other places. After thirteen days it finally reached Istanbul, at that time under French, British and Italian occupation. The Ottoman Empire had collapsed and there was not even a ghost of the central government or the caliphate.

I had boarded with all the hopes and expectations in the world. A student in spirit with a thousand dreams and ideas that all students have, I was on, so to speak, a tour of the horizons. I read a great deal and engaged anyone I met in conversation. In Istanbul I found a room at the Valide Market, where the Iranian community congregated, and searched for a ship that would take me to Batum. I finally found an Italian ship that was going there.

<...>

Before leaving I bought some medical equipment including a sphygmomanometer, a stethoscope, a percussion hammer, paraphernalia for injections, a medical bag and first aid materials. The promised day came, and I boarded the Italian ship for Batum and was there

four days later. I took a room in a run-down hotel by the sea. In 1919
Batum was in the hands of the Italians, meaning it was a restive city
with a number of Italian troops. Batum had been left to its own
devices and was full of thieves and killers, who would commit murder for as little as part of a ruble. After sunset, nobody dared leave his
house, as there were constant reports of murder and robbery, and the
municipal police were under Italian control. To frighten the Italian
police the thieves had killed a number of them, which forced the rest
to remain in hiding to be out of their reach. The unfortunate part was
that I had to obtain another travel document here and visas for
Armenia, Georgia and Azerbaijan. I purchased currencies of the three
places at the moneychangers.

I stayed in Batum for three days to obtain my ticket to Tblisi. By
chance I met an Iranian merchant named Hajj Hoseynqoli Tabrizi, a
very fine man. This man, who was constantly traveling between
Istanbul and Tblisi, knew Russian, Turkish and other languages; but
he was not only very clever he was also a decent person. We arranged
to travel together on the nonstop train to Tblisi that left around midnight. But a half hour before sunset, Hajj Hoseynqoli hurried to my
room and said, "Quick, we have to leave immediately for the station
<…>."

When I asked him about this, he said, "This place becomes very
dangerous as soon as it is dark. We must go to the station and wait
there." We waited, then, for several hours at the station, where I was
nervous and everyone looked like a thief or a criminal to me <…>.
When we boarded the train, it was very crowded. We had a four-
person compartment and we each took an upper berth. Hajj
Hoseyn, who to this point had been moving constantly, now went
to his place very deliberately. He immediately sat in his seat. When
the conductor entered, he secretly gave him some loaf sugar from a
pouch. The man was clearly very appreciative; sugar, the best present one could offer in those days, was like life itself to these people.
This was to ensure the inspector would treat us with a certain consideration. I later learned that Hajj Hoseyn had sewn some gold
coins that he wanted to carry to Tblisi into the lining of his long

wool trousers. When we arrived at the station, Hajj Hoseyn left me and, having removed the gold coins, he bundled them up with some soiled clothing. He put the bundle under his arm and quickly went to give it to a local associate. His mind at ease, he rushed back and gave the rest of his luggage, which he had entrusted to me, to a porter. We left the station together and obtained rooms at a hotel. <...>

Our whole plan was to leave on a train that would reach Baku during the day, because we had heard stories that bandits were in league with the locals. We stayed in Tblisi for a week. I met some of the local merchants whose names I have forgotten. I dealt with a firm owned by the Milani family, who were decent people. <...> They changed money and invited me to their home. They also arranged a ticket on the express train that would arrive in Baku the afternoon of the next day. For the journey from Tblisi they had informed one of the local young hoodlums of the town who was Iranian, apparently from the Sarab neighborhood in Tabriz, to accompany me. Though he was one of the town's disreputable people, he possessed a certain *javanmardi*. The Milanis paid him to look after their interests, and he was of service to them from time to time. This person came to the station and, without a second thought, gave my luggage and my seat number to the porters. Then he sat me at a table at the station coffee-house, ordering tea, lemonade, etc. for everyone. When I offered to pay, Hajj Milani stopped me, saying that if I did the young man would take offense as we were his guests. The train arrived from Batum at three o'clock and I boarded and entered the compartment where I met my traveling companion, a Greek silk merchant who had been in Iran for years and was on his way to Rasht. I was happy to be traveling with a reliable person.

Unfortunately this feeling did not last long as, after a half hour, we entered the station on the Qafri desert. Two people boarded the train and one of them began to inspect the bags. When he found the medical equipment, he said that there was duty on them and took them down. I got off the train to retrieve my bags, but the train start-ed moving, leaving me behind at the desert station house with a number of the thieves. I was terrified and actually feared for my life. I shouted, "I am a doctor and have a perfect right to have a reasonable number of medical supplies with me. If there is a question of customs, they must look into it at the border between Georgia and Azerbaijan. At this point I rushed about asking where the railroad telephone or telegraph were so I could contact the head of the railway in Tblisi or Baku. My brashness terrified everyone.

Someone approached and said in English that was more comprehensible, "Sir, you should have told this man that you were a doctor on the train or have shown your medical degree <...>." I took out my diploma and showed it to the young man who had spent a year in St. Petersburg where he studied medicine. He read the diploma out loud, but mistranslated it to mean that I was an American from New York. This sent them into a panic. I was wearing the Iranian headgear that I had bought in Istanbul, but now they realized they were dealing with an American. At the time Baku was in British hands, and the British and Americans enjoyed a great deal of prestige in those parts. Ultimately I had to wait two hours for another train to come, afraid only that the delay would cause me to reach Baku at night.

After a few minutes on the train, I left a compartment in which there were several Armenian men and women, and stood in the corridor before a window. On the train a vendor was selling ice cream. I bought a cup and was eating it when I noticed a passenger standing beside me. He was a British officer, perhaps a major or a colonel. Two other soldiers from the adjoining coach would join him from time to time. After the ice cream man had gone by, the officer called out to him. Knowing a little Turkish, I attracted the man's attention and bought a cup of ice cream for the officer. He thanked me and offered a cigarette and we began to talk. He was very surprised that I spoke English and the first question he asked after we had spoken a bit was: "Your teachers were American, were they not?"

"That is the case," I said.

"I assumed as much from your accent," he said.

We traded stories about Beirut and General Allenby.[12] He said, "At the beginning of the war I was an officer with Allenby's army." I took the presence of this kind man as a good omen. During our conversation, he asked, "How did you come to be at the station where you boarded?" I explained what had happened <...>. He elaborated critically on how the people in the region were uncivilized. Finally he suggested, "Why don't you transfer your bags to my compartment. I am alone and you can stay with me." After he insisted, I accepted this fine man's hospitality.

I said, "Not knowing Baku, I had wanted to arrive during the day."

He said, "If they do not keep this train too long on the Georgia-Azerbaijan border, we shall get there during the day. Besides, you can come to our camp at Baku and stay with us until you arrange your ticket, or, if you wish, I can offer you one of our British officers who knows Russian as a guide. He will accompany you and show you a safe place to stay. He will also arrange a ticket for you on a ship to Iran." This was very comforting to hear. So after arriving an hour before sunset, I went to the hotel, purchased a ticket the next day and left for Enzeli the day after.

At that time Mohammad Sa'ed Maraghe'i, Iranian consul general in Baku, was making preparations for the visit of Ahmad Shah, the Qajar king who was on his way to Europe. A few hours after I was to leave Baku, the king's ship was scheduled to arrive. I happened to see Mr. Sa'ed, and Mahmud Sepasi, who was to be my traveling companion, introduced me to him. Later in Tehran we became friends and colleagues and now are very close.

Sepasi was in Baku to purchase printing presses in his role as the director of Rowshna'i Publications, publisher of the newspaper *Ra'd*. During the voyage I became ill, and Sepasi took it upon himself to nurse me back to health.

In book collector's terms Mirza Mahmud Khan Sepasi was a unique copy. Most people having many things in common fall into certain broad categories; but Sepasi was one of those rare individuals who defy categorization <...>. He was a very handsome man, refined, reasonable, cultured and aware of his limitations and what was his due. His actions were exact; he behaved as though he were a mathematician who would not brook the least imprecision in meas-uring the universe. He spoke softly and gently, always polite in his gestures, observant of every nicety. Though his speech was measured and detailed, his eyes and features betrayed a world of emotion, a core of affection and sincerity. His respect for learning, the learned and artists bordered on sanctification. He was extraordinarily kind and good-natured, never self-serving. He sighed when he spoke, sometimes suppressing a sob, but would apply a scientist's exactitude to the smallest matters. He loved poetry, music, companionship, con-versation and drinking, but he always observed the same propriety and politeness that were basic to his nature—exemplifying the adage "wine merely made him more like himself."

Some ten years ago (1938), when Amir Showkat al-Molk Alam (Mohammad Ebrahim Khan Qa'eni) was governor of Fars Province, two of my friends, Colonel Alinaqi Vaziri and Dr. Ali Akbar Fayyaz, and I went to Shiraz. The day before we left, we learned that Mahmud Sepasi was also in town. As soon as he telephoned, I said, "Some friends and I are going to the Dehqans' Enayatabad gardens today. Why don't you join us? We'll spend the day in the Bordi Mosque grounds." He agreed and we all went together, bringing Shiraz wine with us. The colonel played the tar so well that he moved heaven and earth with his music. We all drank including Sepasi who had more wine than anyone. We stayed until sunset and then returned to the city. That night the colonel said to me, "Today was an unusual outing for me. Mahmud Sepasi is remarkably well-man-nered. I noticed that the more he drank, the more refined and con-siderate he became; good manners and civility must be part of his true nature, not an affectation."

Sepasi's sister was married to the late Mortezaqoli Khan Sani' al-Dowleh (Hedayat); they had one daughter named Fatemeh, now the wife of my friend Ali Mohammad Dehqan. But Sepasi was so scrupu-lous that eight years ago when Dehqan had wanted to marry Fatemeh and asked me to obtain her uncle's consent, he said, "I don't think it would be right because Dehqan is an extraordinarily fine young man, while my niece is short-tempered and moody."

A few years before, in the early days of Pahlavi rule, he served at the Ministry of Justice but disliked the work and begged Davar to let him resign. <...> Sepasi ultimately established Rangin Publishers. His ideal was to produce error-free publications, and Iranian printers and their illiterate, irresponsible workers became his bêtes noires. In any event he was a close and faithful friend. He was even on good terms with Aref [of Qazvin] when friendship with the poet was extremely difficult; Aref was an abnormal man verging on insane, and twenty-four hours in his company was more than a chore for anyone. <...>

ENTRY INTO ENZELI AND ON TO RASHT

Sepasi and I eventually arrived in Enzeli and went on from there to Rasht conveyed in an ancient vehicle—this was my first ride in an automobile. It was 1919 and automobiles were very rare. It belonged to a Frenchman who had been chauffeur to Mozaffar al-Din Shah and had brought the new vehicle to Tehran. We stayed at the Europa Hotel on Sabzeh Meydan in Rasht. I immediately telegraphed Sabzevar for money as my funds had run out. I stayed in Rasht for a week. At that time Abdolhoseyn Khan Teimurtash (Sardar Mo'azam-e Khorasani) was governor. He was the son of Karimdad Khan Nardini (Mo'azzez al-Molk) <...> and had been sent as a child to Russia to be educated. He completed primary school and learned Russian in Eshqabad. <...> From there he went to St. Petersburg where he studied at an exclusive military academy. <...> He completed his education and returned to Sabzevar when his father was governor. As a child I saw Abdolhoseyn Khan in the streets or the market. He was a tall, good-looking young man—much like his son Hushang today. After a time, his father appointed him deputy governor of Juvayn region, an important part of Sabzevar, whose county seat was Jogtai and which comprised some seventy villages. Having gone to Russia as a child Abdolhoseyn Khan did not receive a proper Persian education and consequently was unfamiliar with official or religious titles. He once wrote Hajj Mirza Hoseyn Alavi, the well-known Sabzevar theologian, and, in a way that became famous throughout town, addressed the envelope to the "Blessed Highness, Source of all Emulation" [a term reserved only for the highest ranking ayatollahs]. <...>

In Sabzevar at this time was also a turban-wearing Qajar prince named Mohammad Hashem Mirza Afsar. The prince was a seminary student, one of the scribes at the home of Hajj Mirza Hoseyn, but in actuality he served as a go-between with the religious courts and, as we say, was known to "arrange things" for a fee. He had a clownish side and a bizarre way of speaking—of course, a turbaned prince was a novelty in itself. In addition, since his maternal ancestor Prince Jenab, was one of Molla Hadi's respected students, his family enjoyed some prestige. His father, Nurollah Mirza, was a parasitic prince who affected saintliness and piety <...>. He was the one in the mosque who loudly proclaimed, "And the time of prayer has come," and was always ready with a recitation of the martyrs at every religious gathering. He had reservations about sugar, as it was produced in infidel countries, and would have Iranian-made rock candy instead <...>. He let his beard grow and shaved his head, and in open-toed sandals he was the consummate cleric. Nurollah Mirza made a living by following divines and prayer leaders around.

When the son Mohammad Hashem came into his good looks, he became a veritable Adonis. He was the leading light of a band of the Sabzevar mavericks that enlivened Eftekhar's banquets and revels. He was the wit around whom discriminating men gathered, and, despite a rudimentary literacy, learned something from every group. A clever prince with a poetic disposition, he extemporized quatrains and fragments, but these short pieces aside, he did not have the stamina for longer verse like odes and sonnets. He was just like a sparrow—how apt it was for the Tehranis to call him "sparrow of the Olema." Like the bird he would sing one light beakful but could not continue versifying because, as the Khorasanis say, his "breath ran out."

<...>

The free-living prince eventually became Abdolhoseyn Khan [Teimurtash] Nardini's favorite companion; as his Persian language and literary tutor he accompanied him to Juvayn where they were

busy carousing and became fast friends. In the second session of
Parliament, after the dethronement of Mohammad Ali Shah, Afsar
and Teimurtash became deputies. At that time parliamentary elections had two rounds and there was a dearth of candidates because of
the recent shelling of the Parliament. Some considered constitutional
government irreligious, others were afraid to run for Parliament; only
a group of agitators bothered to get involved. Mohammad Hashem
Mirza Afsar was elected from Sabzevar with an apparent thirty-two
votes. <...>

The friendship between Afsar and Teimurtash continued their
entire lives, and after Teimurtash's death, Afsar maintained his affection and closeness to the family, which was a credit to his character.
After the end of the second session of Parliament, Prince Nayer al-
Dowleh became governor of Khorasan. Teimurtash married Sorur
al-Saltaneh, daughter of Hajj Khazen al-Molk, who was the son-in-
law of Nayer al-Dowleh. <...> They had four children: Iran
Khanom, who became the wife of Hoseyn'ali Khan Qaraguzlu and,
after Teimurtash's death, was divorced; Manuchehr; Hushang; and
Mehrpur, who died in an automobile accident at the age of twenty
and was buried in Tehran beside his father. Afsar married Nayer al-
Dowleh's granddaughter, the daughter of Fath al-Saltaneh. Both
Teimurtash and Afsar, now related to Nayer al-Dowleh by marriage,
went to Khorasan where the former became commander of the garrison and the latter head of religious endowments. Later when they
were reelected to Parliament, Teimurtash resigned his office and
both became deputies. Teimurtash was always representative from
Nishapur and Afsar from Sabzevar. Teimurtash distinguished himself as a deputy and became a skilled speaker, courageous and quick-
witted; he was handsome, possessed an innate nobility and was
candid. He was also well to do, came from a good family and was liberal with his personal fortune, all of which contributed to his fame
<...>.

During the time of the second session of Parliament Sattar Khan
and Baqer Khan came to Tehran after the defeat of Mohammad Ali
Shah. Despite the fact that both, especially Sattar, were becoming

national icons and were greeted with a lavish welcome when they entered the city, it did not take long before the formerly cheering Tehranis began to desert them. Sattar Khan took up residence at Atabak Park. To centralize the armed forces, the government demanded that they surrender their arms, but Sattar resisted. In Parliament during the many debates that broke out, one deputy, a backer of Sattar, took the podium and glowingly praised his sacrifices and battles for freedom. He described how Sattar rose to defend constitutional government when Parliament had been dissolved and a tyrant like Mohammad Ali Shah was persecuting the constitutionalists. After Sattar Khan risked his life day and night battling the forces of tyranny and saved the vestiges of constitutional government, it was not right that his forces be disarmed. Teimurtash, a remarkably quick-witted man, went to the podium and, while all present were still under the spell of the former speaker, said, "To fight for what is right for the nation and the people is the responsibility of every Iranian Moslem. But one who fights for freedom should never expect to be rewarded with special privileges. Ali b. Abu Taleb, for example, the greatest freedom-fighter of Islam, never expected to be exempt from so much as two prostrations in his morning prayers or to be excused for even one day of the Ramazan fast." As religious passions ran high during that session, Teimurtash's compelling logic and his use of Ali's name neutralized the effect of the previous speech, and the deputies ultimately voted to have Sattar's men disarmed. When the situation turned violent, Sattar was shot in the leg during the melee. He later died in Tehran <...>.

Teimurtash had all the requirements for a rapid rise to power. The same Abdolhoseyn Khan whose Persian was so elemental that he called a Sabzevari cleric "Source of Emulation" became learned and a connoisseur of Persian literature: He knew Russian and French and was generally well-informed. As a result of these personal attributes he rose very quickly. He was a deputy for several terms. He was governor of Rasht and Kerman, served as minister of justice and public works, and through his many efforts became a key player in the establishment of the Pahlavi reign. He became court minister and, at the height of his power, the absolute ruler after Reza Shah, but internal and external political factors eventually caused his downfall. He was immoderate, and immoderate people either rise to absolute power or are obliterated. During the reign of powerful monarchs, survival depends on caution and moderation. In the reign of an overbearing and powerful king like Reza Shah, if one were to remain aloof and cautious, staying on the sidelines, he would gradually be forgotten. While those who went too far, got too close, became a second skin to the king in whatever way, whether it be in Teimurtash's style or Davar's, would finally be removed. <...>

In the Pahlavi period, individuals like Hajj Mokhber al-Saltaneh, Mirza Mohammad Ali Khan Foroughi (Zoka al-Molk), Mahmud Jam and Amir Showkat al-Molk remained safe and immune because they were moderate and prudent. Another group of individuals like Amid al-Saltaneh Semnani were so cautious, stayed so far out of the picture that they gradually disappeared from view and were forgotten. Another group of men like Asadi (Mohammad Vali-Khan Birjandi) became so close to power, so desirous of pushing all others out of their way, that they were removed <...>. When Davar finally thought of caution, it was already too late; he had become so close to the Shah that he was gripped by fear, so weary and depressed that he eventually took his own life. As a result of a brashness stemming from the success in everything he did, the self-confident Teimurtash lost his bearings and he was eventually put away. A number of men also became close, but their lack of presence and talent and their mediocrity kept them secure. With his remarkable political intuition, Reza Shah realized that nonentities like Taddayon and Soleyman Mirza had no popular base <...>, left to their own devices, they eliminate themselves. <...>

Teimurtash had two or three weaknesses. He was a hedonist, and so extreme was his love of pleasure that when his eyes fell on a woman it was as if his entire being and all his wits were focused on her conquest. And win her he did for he possessed all the tools needed for conquest: good looks and a persuasive way of speaking, a variety of charms and enticements, generosity, and above all social position and prestige, which are important inducements to surrender. When he was drunk he did not pass up on any woman, white or black, good or evil, they were the same to him, and he would change them often. At the outset of the coup d'état, Tatiana Tomanians, an Armenian woman from the Caucasus, who had a husband and children, became the object of his affection. (The woman now lives in New York with the two daughters that she bore Teimurtash.) The beautiful Tatiana divorced her husband to become Teimurtash's second wife. Shortly afterward when Teimurtash was on a mission to Kerman, she accompanied him. Thereafter she was with him everywhere he went as his official wife. During his tenure as court minister when he traveled in Europe, he was received in very grand style and wherever he went heads of state treated him with the utmost respect. However, when he went to prison, Tatiana sued for divorce. <...>

Teimurtash was also inordinately devoted to a liberal society. Of course the motivation behind all this desire for freedom, license and liberty—beyond the obvious factors and the rhetoric—was that very hedonism of his and nothing more. If anyone entertains doubts about Freud's pleasure principle, he has only to look at Teimurtash's life to have it confirmed <...>. This instinct was his whole life, his actions, his thoughts, his intelligence—all were subject to that one great appetite; his sexual drive left no room for any other motive.

Teimurtash's other faults were his severe addiction to alcohol and his gambling. He drank to excess and he was a prodigious gambler. To Teimurtash the world and life were nothing but a gamble; women, society, property, children, the earth, the sky, prestige, all for him were a gamble. His prolonged gambling bouts were legendary. Now this man needed extraordinary self-control during times when he was under stress, which was why he became very disagreeable toward the end.

Another of his social failings was his extravagant rashness; in none of his actions did he take the demands of time and space, the exigencies of the situation, into account. By nature autocratic and selfish, he was unjustifiably self-confident and had become arrogant. He was in short a strange blend of contradictory traits and qualities.

Of course Teimurtash played an important role in the social progress of Iran, its development and modernization, a fact that even his enemies cannot deny. Another flaw that caused him untold grief was that he surrounded himself with a group of vile men. Teimurtash had poor judgment when it came to selecting intimates, and he was notorious for remaining faithful to them, almost irrational. The more people advised him against such friendships the more inflexible he would become. <...> As happens in the case of a man as famous as he, people ignored his good associates and judged him by his bad ones—he was excessively attached to many shameless buffoons and fools, womanizers, gamblers and cheats, and to those who flaunted their immorality and irreverence. Though he fully understood all of this, nothing could be done—it was his nature. <...>

Teimurtash maintained a strong hand in all matters; the government, the prime minister, Parliament all obeyed his dictates. Elections went exactly the way he wanted, and foreign policy actually both in detail and direction was in his hands—ambassadors, ministers, governors were not appointed unless he approved. Naturally these successes brought a measure of pride and complacency, which blind even the brightest people and cause them to commit acts that are ill-advised and rash, acts that not even the most sordid and dim-witted creature would commit. A good example of this was Teimurtash's behavior with the Russians, who not only wouldn't have minded creating turmoil in Iran, but wanted to overturn Pahlavi rule. What is absolutely certain is that Teimurtash became unfriendly to the British; so much so that on his recent trip to Europe, they were hostile to and threatened him. Teimurtash's daughter Iran has described to me the openly hostile negotiations he conducted with John Cadman, chief operating officer of the Anglo-Persian Oil Company. Others have also related to me how the British cooked up a thousand schemes and plots to prepare the ground for his downfall, beginning in a very genteel way; for example, by publishing in a Bucharest newspaper an article about Reza Shah's greatness. It went on a great deal about modern Iran under the leadership of a strong man like Reza Shah; how on every front this infant state was moving rapidly toward advancement; but though Reza Shah was forceful, capable and in control, the only troubling thing was his advanced age, that he did not have a long future—his son, the crown prince, was a child who needed years to mature and come into his own. There was cause for hope, however, because a man like Teimurtash was at the heart of and the force behind this resurgence; a young man with a firm constitution, and were Reza Shah to die, the Iranian people could be confident that the threads of his reforms would remain intact under Teimurtash's leadership and guidance, until the Crown Prince reached his majority, etc. In the European capitals that Teimurtash visited, naturally behind the scenes and with the requisite discretion, they had grand receptions prepared for him, which were publicized, and people were forced to write of Teymur's greatness and nobility. On the other hand, the British, by treating him so treacherously and being so unwelcoming, forced him to move toward the Russians, who naturally would court him all the more with their own receptions in Moscow.

Of course it was as clear as day that these measures would make a very bad impression on Reza Shah, who himself had a cautious and suspicious disposition and worried about the dynasty he had founded. The British being cannier than other people about individual and mass psychology, understood this; moreover, their administrative apparatus was organized to implement their intentions in the most unobtrusive and thorough ways possible. The plan worked. The Russians gravitated toward Teimurtash and received him lavishly, and the enticements for Teimurtash were already there; he knew Russian well and had spent the best years of his youth in Russia—he was also fond of women and having a good time. During the whole affair, British intelligence services related what was happening both in detail and general terms, indirectly and directly, to Reza Shah. Employing a woman of beauty, they managed to steal Teimurtash's briefcase containing his private correspondence and send it abroad.

To Reza Shah every mole hill was a mountain. He was aware of Teimurtash's ambitions and feared that they threatened to undermine the very dynasty that he himself had founded. The people he regarded as dangerous often were. His suspicions were justified. He instinctively knew who his opponents were, understood their characters thoroughly. When Teimurtash returned to Iran, the basis for his nearness to Reza Shah was in ruins. Within the country itself, Teimurtash had made a number of enemies, some of whom were jealous, which is common for those who hold high office, especially in the Middle East. Another group of religious and bigoted men considered him godless, openly libertine and contemptuous of religion; despising him in their hearts, they saw him as the lone architect of all the modernizing reforms in Iran. Another group was on bad terms with him over women, for reasons of personal honor; while yet another group that had fallen from favor thought him to be the agent of their frustration. Teimurtash's friends and close associates took advantage of his power, thereby creating more enemies for him. A number of people opposed him for political reasons, on principle, and a number were instruments of foreign powers. Above all, there were the suspicions of Reza Shah himself, who saw Teimurtash as an energetic man of great ambition, which could never sit well with the autocratic nature of a dynasty founder. All of these factors conspired to undermine Teimurtash when he returned from Europe. Reza Shah was a remarkably seasoned, patient and farsighted man. I heard that during their conversations about Teimurtash's trip to Russia, he asked innocently—as if merely seeking information—who the minister of war was. Teymur said Voroshilov. Reza Shah asked whether Teimurtash had seen the man, and he responded that he had at receptions along with the other ministers; but British agents had informed the shah that Teimurtash had met privately with Voroshilov. Soon after his return Teimurtash realized what was happening—unfortunately it was too late. Not long afterward, a bout of depression caused him to ask for leave and he spent several weeks resting in Gilan. When Teimurtash returned to Tehran, his enemies, each in his own way, acted to bring about his downfall. The worst of them was Mohammad Hoseyn Khan Ayrom, the powerful chief of police at the time who ruled over everything, everyone and every situation. Finally on a Thursday around noon, after Teimurtash had finished work and gone home, the Ministry of Court issued the order for his dismissal and he was confined to his house.

In 1942 Iran Khanom, Teimurtash's daughter, told me in Tehran what had happened a few days before his dismissal. She had just returned from Europe with her husband, Hoseyn'ali Qaraguzlu and there was a birthday party for her with her in-laws: the wife of the late Naser al-Molk; Hoseyn Ala and his wife, the daughter of Naser al-Molk. Also present were Davar and his wife, and Sardar As'ad Bakhtiari and his wife. Davar had come before her father returned from court and appeared anxious. As soon as Davar arrived he phoned the court to ask where the minister (Teimurtash) was. They told him that he was with the shah. A short time later, they called to say that the minister had departed and it was not long before Teimurtash entered visibly upset and, after asking the guests to forgive his late arrival, asked if he could have a few words with Davar in private. They went to his office and later came to the table where they finished dinner. After the guests had left, <...> he told his daughter that it was all over, that he had reached a dead end. She asked how and he replied that for some time his relationship with the shah had been becoming more clouded. That night something had happened that told Teimurtash the last act of the tragedy was coming to an end and the curtain was about to fall. He explained that around sunset Davar was with the shah. After this audience, Davar came to his office at the ministry where they talked. Davar wanted to leave, but Teimurtash told him to stay so they could go together and that he would send the car for Davar's wife who could come on her own. Davar agreed. Suddenly the door opened and Reza Shah entered the room unannounced, whereupon they rose to their feet. The shah asked what he was doing and Teimurtash told him that night was his daughter's birthday party and that he and Davar were going to join the other guests for dinner. "Very well," said the shah, "but I need you for something." Davar bowed and left the room. The shah came close to Teimurtash and said something along these lines: "Teymur, you are everything to me, my best aid and associate. Not only do you handle all the affairs of state for me, you also take care of private matters and what happens at court also runs smoothly because of you. I hate to think what would happen if you were not around, and I sincerely wish you to remain faithful to me forever." Then he took Teimurtash's hands in his and made him swear that he would always be loyal. Teimurtash answered with the appropriate assurances. Iran Khanom then said to her father, "The shah's words should not worry you, rather they seem to augur well." Teimurtash said, "No, daughter, what he said tonight indicates that my doom is just over the horizon." "How?" she asked. "He knows that I am worried, so he wants to assure me, give me a false sense of security until the hour of decision is at hand. Having seen Davar in my office at court, he may have thought that I was in despair and that, God forbid, I was consulting with him to find a way out, that I might do something that would cause him a problem. So he tried to put my mind at rest tonight, but I am absolutely certain that my downfall is near." And Teimurtash was right, for he was dismissed that Thursday.

Sardar As'ad Bakhtiari had gone hunting outside of the city that morning, consequently when he returned on Friday afternoon, he was not aware of what had happened. As soon as he learned of Teimurtash's dismissal, he rushed to the minister's home. On Saturday morning Sardar As'ad had his audience with the shah who asked him what the news was. He replied that he had been away for two days hunting, but that he had seen Teimurtash on his return. He said to the shah, "As Teimurtash has been a dependable and perceptive servant of yours, why not appoint him to some ambassadorship? The shah's cold-blooded reply was "No, Teymur is capable of much more impor-tant duties and ought to be in a position of significant responsibility." So a few days later security agents came to Teimurtash's home, and no one knew what would happen next. At the time I was in Mashhad treating Mohammad Vali Asadi who was troubled with liver problems. Asadi was extremely agitated because his son had telegraphed him from Tehran explaining the situation and Asadi, as one close to Teimurtash, feared that the same flames that had engulfed Teimurtash might singe him. <...>

Now Teimurtash confronted charges of embezzlement and cur-rency speculation. This was the time that the German Lindenblatt, head of the newly established Melli [National] Bank, was under investigation. Teimurtash was charged with profiting from an agreement that Amin al-Tojjar Esfahani negotiated that pegged the price of the rial to the British pound. His dossier went to the Ministry of Justice where Mohammad Soruri was the prosecutor and, subsequently, Abdol Ali Lotfi the judge. Teimurtash was found guilty and sentenced to three years' imprisonment. This was also the time when the oil question had been raised, i.e., Reza Shah cancelled the oil agreement and the issue was taken up by the League of Nations in Geneva. Justice Minister Davar traveled to Switzerland to argue the validity of Iran's case and considered the trip a great blessing because his friendship with Teimurtash was well known, and during this period his position as minister troubled his conscience considerably. He faced the possibility that judges under his authority would prosecute his friend, and that Reza Shah might regard him with the same suspicions that he viewed Teimurtash. Greatly distraught, Davar completed his work in Geneva and though he confided to a friend that he had resolved not to return to Iran, his love for his two small children weakened that resolve forcing him to return.

When he came back to Iran, Teimurtash's trial was coming to a conclusion anyway. He was in Qasr Prison, his Armenian wife had divorced him and his life was a shambles. Teimurtash's son-in-law tried his hand at betrayal. He petitioned Reza Shah to the effect that his family had always been the shah's faithful servants, living honorable lives and not only had his father-in-law forced him to marry his daughter, but he also had asked for and received a large bride price (25,000 tomans). He requested that he be allowed to divorce the woman to remove the stain of dishonor from his family's good name. Reza Shah was so infuriated that he used many obscenities and called for his justice minister at the time, Mohsen Sadr (Sadr al-Ashraf). The shah instructed him to remind the "bastard" that his clan had enlisted the entire city to make the girl his wife, and now that his father-in-law was in prison he was going to do something so unworthy. In any case he told the minister to protect the woman's rights because if they could no longer live together, they were to be treated according to the law (and what was right). Not only did Reza Shah have a noble streak, he also kept the issues separate, judging people on the basis of their individual merits and characters. Sadr settled the divorce, ordering the husband's family to pay ten thousand tomans from the bride price.

<...>

In any case Teimurtash's hard prison existence was a lesson in misfortune and the vagaries of fate. All at once he had fallen from the pinnacle of power to manacles, becoming open to abuse by any sort of person, while his beautiful daughter had to do a thousand things just to see him for a few minutes in the presence of the guards and security people and to endure the foul looks and behavior of the crudest forms of humanity as she passed them. His children came from Europe; Manuchehr was able to get a glimpse of him through the barred window and they looked at one another with tears in their eyes. Sorur al-Saltaneh, his wife, visited him once and he asked her forgiveness, admitting that he had not been a good husband. Expecting peril every day, he finally died in the most abject way or, as it was universally rumored, was injected with poison and strangled. Whatever the case, one day when they telephoned that Teimurtash had died and that his corpse was at a certain morgue, his survivors buried him temporarily at Emamzadeh Abdollah. Several years later his son Mehrpur (who had died in a car crash) was buried next to him, and one year after that both the son and Teimurtash were buried in a permanent grave. I was present at the burial. Nothing remained of the late Teimurtash but a few bits of broken and decayed bone, and of his son, a few better-preserved pieces.

After Teimurtash's death, his wife and children were sent into internal exile in Khorasan. Through the adverse reports of Colonel Nava'i, the head of the police, they were subsequently exiled to an area near Torbat-e Jam. They spent some time in those salt wastes and then were transferred to Kashmar (Torshiz), and later, after Reza Shah's abdication, they returned to Tehran. <...>

We arrived in Tehran from Rasht at sunrise on the second day, and Sepasi got off before his family home near the Qavam al-Dowleh market. I stayed at the Hotel France on Ferdowsi Avenue, actually a casino and tavern with neither a place to relax nor a bath. This was why I transferred to the Grand on Lalezar Avenue, which belonged to Seyyed Nasrollah Khamsi (Baqeroff) and at the time was perhaps the finest hotel in Tehran. I stayed two months at that establishment. This was the end of fall 1919 when Vosouq al-Dowleh was Iran's powerful prime minister and his brother Qavam al-Saltaneh the powerful and benign governor of Khorasan. <...>

I spent those two months in Tehran studying conditions there, all of which were new to me having spent many years abroad. This was during the months of Moharram and Safar when people from various walks of life held commemorative processions that I would watch during my frequent walks. Having rented a coach, I finally set out for Khorasan. About thirty-six kilometers outside of Sabzevar, my brother Hoseyn, my uncle Azizollah Khazra'i and several others came to greet me. <...> It was daybreak when I entered Sabzevar and went to see my mother, sister and the rest of my family. <...> After sleeping until dawn, I left the house to make my first visit to a Sabzevari suffering from a terrible earache caused by fever. That night, at his request, I visited Mir Seyyed Hadi Khan Amir Farrokh (Amir Arfa'), at the time titled "Salar Heshmat." Amir Farrokh, who was the governor of Sabzevar, was in bed suffering from cardiac neurasthenia. He had written his will and sent it along with a chest of documents to Hajj Mohammad Hoseyn Owlia, a Sabzevari merchant, while he himself, terrified and having given up all hope of living, intended to travel to Tehran. After examining him that evening and the next day, I determined that his condition was not somatic; his heart muscle was sound and with a treatment of diet and drugs I was able to change his life completely. He found it difficult to have confidence in me, as I was a young physician, while Dr. Mozayyen al-Soltan, the head of Mashhad Hospital, and Dr. Amir Alam, considered a one-of-a-kind physician, had diagnosed his cardiac muscle as infirm and prescribed certain remedies. But he gradually came under my care, was cured and today—after twenty-nine years—is still alive and active at the age of eighty-five or ninety. <...>

Now that I have mentioned Amir Arfa', a sense of gratitude impels me to write about him, for Mir Seyyed Hadi Khan Amir Farrokh was among those individuals who—each in his own way—left a lasting impression on my own character. Based on what he told me, I can summarize his life as follows.

He came from a well-known family of Tehran Seyyeds (the Akhavis) that had always been prominent and favored during the Qajar period. Amir Arfa' had an older brother, Mir Seyyed Mohammad Khan, who was known as "Aql" (wisdom) and worked as a comptroller. Mir Seyyed Mohammad Khan was the son-in-law of Hakim al-Mamalek Farzaneh; his son, Mir Seyyed Mehdi Khan Farrokh (Mo'tasem al-Saltaneh), became Iranian ambassador to China in 1948. During his childhood, Amir Arfa' came under the tutelage of his older brother, but as an adolescent, he fell in with a group of stalwart young men known as *Dash* that protected the unprotected and worked in or headed traditional gymnasiums known as Houses of Strength. Owing to the noble ancestry of Arfa, these Dash were honored by his association with them. Mir Seyyed Mohammad Khan, who did not want his younger brother to become too set in his Dash ways, found positions for Amir Arfa' in the government: first in the armory, where with a band of riflemen behind him he became even more of a Dash, famed throughout Tehran for his stateliness. He arranged for Amir Arfa' to enter the service of Mirza Ebrahim Khan Mo'tamed al-Saltaneh (father of Vosouq al-Dowleh and Qavam al-Saltaneh) in Shiraz. Amir Arfa' rose in Mirza Ebrahim Khan's household to become his trusted steward, receiving the title of Heshmat-e Divan. Later he held important positions in government. <...>

<...>

Amir Arfa' must be considered, with justification, one of the great men of Iran, for he had the characteristics shared by the elite all over the world. He was extraordinarily intelligent, quick-witted, keenly aware of popular sentiment, a problem-solver and gifted. As a governor, his word was so unquestioned and so committed was he to justice that it defies description. <...> His governorship of Sabzevar coincided with Aporsof's term as consul in Mashhad when the Russians, were trying to agitate the masses throughout Khorasan with their propaganda. Amir Arfa' had to restore order and combat these machinations. In those years (1919 and 1920), he was responsible for all the activities of the judiciary, police, etc. in the province. <...>

In Sabzevar at this time there was a high-ranking cleric, a *mojtahed*, named Hajj Mirza Hoseyn Sabzevari who was a distinguished old man. <...> He was the mojtahed whose word was very influential in the city. He was also a learned man who had taught all his life and was teaching theology in Sabzevar. All of the religious endowments were entrusted to him and he exercised religious authority over all. The Seyyed himself was a good man, but was weak in character. His son, Aqa Mirza Hasan Aqazadeh, would affix his father's "Hoseyn the Alavite" seal to any sort of document, valid or not, for a small consideration. The son, who was indifferent, very simple and weak himself, was surrounded by a group of men, all of them corrupt. They forced him to get involved in everything that happened in the city, no matter how small or large. For example, when an unscrupulous baker was found to have sold bad bread, the son would immediately write a letter or send a go-between to effect his release. When the governor prosecuted a certain butcher who was a price gouger, the Aqa would introduce himself as one of his relatives and request that he be exempt from prosecution. <...> Amir Arfa' quickly realized this practice made administering the city impossible, and he determined to put the Aqa in his place as a lesson for the people. One day he was sitting in the administration chamber, which was full of city people. At that time provincial governors generally sat on the floor and, there being no waiting room, anyone who wanted to see them would approach. A number of prominent men, merchants, landowners, clergymen, etc.—without any specific business—would take turns coming into the governor's presence and have coffee or tea to demonstrate—so to speak—their privilege and importance. Some, the governor summoned himself. This was why when the governor went to his office it was usually full of people from various classes. On one such occasion Abolqasem Kuh Mishi, a lackey and go-between in Aqa Hajj Mirza Hoseyn's household, entered and said, "Hajj Mirza Hoseyn, the mojtahed, says that you have a certain man in custody on such and such a crime. Please order his release and the Aqa will settle the case and satisfy the complainant himself." Always in control of his bad temper, Amir Arfa' was now visibly upset and shouted, "Today among the Shiite, of all the leaders of the twelve imamis no one has a higher place nor is more venerable than the Reverend Ayatollah Hajj Mirza Hoseyn, whose word is law. Now why, you stupid bastard, have you merely said 'Hajj Mirza says' instead of 'the Reverend Ayatollah commands' or 'it is the desire of the embodiment of Islam that…'?" He then ordered the official attendants to remove the man's turban and beat him about the head, which they did so hard that the man fainted. The governor then sent his private secretary to respectfully suggest to the ayatollah that he might preserve the dignity of Islam and his own position as the unquestioned arch-Shiite by ridding his household of such creatures. Of course everybody in the city secretly knew that the governor—in the slang of the day—was "a real man." That night the governor admitted Aqa Mirza Hasan into the inner room of Government House. When the Aqa entered, Amir Arfa' ordered Ali Asghar, his Lor servant, to bring an iron chest. He opened the lid and extracted his own order of appointment, placed it before the Aqa and said, "Give this order to your father and tell him that Amir Arfa' is transferring the governorship of Sabzevar to him and leaving town. <…> What is your father thinking? Doesn't he know that the province is on the brink of chaos? I am responsible for maintaining the public order and if your father interferes in every administrative matter, then why should people obey any of the injunctions my office issues?" The son began to apologize, not knowing what to say. Finally Amir Arfa' said, "From this day on if your father has something to say on a certain matter he is only —and not too often— to send you personally to me. You are to come secretly to this private chamber at nightfall and say what you have to say and I will honor Hajj Aqa's age and prestige. If his request is not warranted, I will explain why." Soon thereafter every thief and miscreant knew where to draw the line.

Amir Arfa' was able to govern well, extraordinarily attached to the welfare of the citizens as he was. <...> He spared no effort for the common good, seeing to the people's supply of bread and meat, water and other necessities, closing the door to price gouging. The Heshmatiyeh Hospital was, in fact, established through his determination and efforts; not a day went by that he would not come by and lovingly and enthusiastically see to its needs. <...>

During Ramazan, one of the preachers of Mashhad, Hajj Qavam al-Va'ezin Lari, came to Sabzevar to preach. At that time clergymen were political agents who took the pulpit to speak on issues of state, both domestic and foreign. This preacher's attention was on foreign matters. Among other things, he said that one of the signs of the coming of the End-of-Time Imam is the conquest of the world by Gog and Magog, whom he identified as the Russian Bolsheviks. Their victory was, it seems, divinely ordained and the harbinger of the Twelfth Imam's appearance. Amir Arfa', who knew this game well, summoned Qavam al-Va'ezin. He came early at night when I was also present. As soon as he entered Amir Arfa' said, "Sheikh, I am a Seyyed and a believer in Islam. Your sermons are robbing people of their hope and enthusiasm; they are disregarding what is good for the country. You are also the kind of mollah who is only out for himself, to make money. Know that this kind of willfulness and the idiocy you spout on the pulpit will not make you rich because I will use every power at my command to bring you down. Islam has thousands of moral teachings. Go and preach the kind of advice that will be a credit to your pulpit, guide the people on the right path, and I will reward you a thousandfold. I will order them to pay you out of the religious endowments; but if you continue, what happens will be your own doing." The priest acquiesced and Amir Arfa' said, "Very good, go and transfer your belongings to Government House and live right here with me. You can preach during the day." The Sheikh did this and every night would tell Amir Arfa' what he was going to say the next day on the pulpit. Though the month of Ramazan during those years were generally filled with outbursts, ferment and political machinations, that Ramazan passed uneventfully.

My friendship with Amir Arfa' went beyond medicine and my practice. We were genuine companions, spending most nights together, often at his residence. Besides us, the gatherings ordinarily included Mirza Hoseyn Khan Shaybani, Prince Abbas Mirza Sahami, Sheikh Mohammad Malvandi the Passion reciter and also a singer with a very fine voice, Hajji Khan the tar player and sometimes Zia al-Haqq Hakimi (a traditional healer) who played the drum well. At times there was no music and song and we would come together to talk or, other times, listen to poetry. <...>

ARRIVAL AND RESIDENCE IN SABZEVAR

When I first arrived in Sabzevar I had intended to stay for a few months, seeing my family, and then travel to Mashhad where I would practice medicine, or go back to Tehran. But, as fate would have it, there was at that time (fall 1919) a serious influenza epidemic that actually spared none of the townspeople. In addition to this, there were the endemic diseases like malaria and typhus. These serious diseases were greatly similar to ordinary ailments and were seldom diagnosed. Furthermore, if surgery were necessary, there was no one to perform it; equipment was very rudimentary and insufficient; pharmacies were in short supply and no drugs were available. There was a handful of old-style apothecaries. Worst of all, there were no hospitals to bed down the patients.

The town had a few doctors, traditional practitioners like Mirza Esma'il Eftekhar al-Hokama. He had come to Sabzevar sixty years earlier having learned to prescribe medicines under a doctor in Barforush in Mazandaran. Another was Sheikh Mohammad Hoseyn Gonabadi who was originally a seminary student and later became a servant to a traditional Sabzevari doctor called Mirza Abdolhoseyn. In the cholera epidemic of 1904 when all doctors fled the city, Sheikh Mohammad Hoseyn visited the sick and more or less employed the remedies he had learned from Mirza Abdolhoseyn. When his teacher died, he married his daughter and went to Tehran. <...> Another was originally an apothecary who obtained a certificate to practice medicine and was called Mirza Abolhasan Ehtesham al-Atebba. There was also a Seyyed called Qavam al-Atebba Torshizi, who also had a certificate.

When the influenza epidemic spread, they came to me from everywhere and I was working perhaps eighteen hours a day treating people. From the dawn call to prayer with the mosques still closed, I would begin work, going from house to house on horseback and admitting hundreds to my own office. I worked afternoons and nights, having no alternative. In this predicament, beset by medieval conditions without doctors or medicines, I thought, after all I was a Sabzevari, born and bred and had used the money of this town to go abroad and receive an education. I owed it to the town to remain and repay the people as best I could. <...> When I told Amir Arfa', himself adamant about my staying, he was overjoyed.

I began to think of establishing a hospital. Amir Arfa' was very receptive to the idea and offered a great deal of help. He convened a meeting and collected funds. The people bought a house outside of Sabzevar from my uncle Mirza Azizollah Khazra'i for a low price; that is, he agreed to accept a low price for a common cause. Equipment, furniture and beds were provided. We bought surgical instruments from Dr. Hoffman, an American residing in Mashhad on his way to India, who agreed to sell them for a nominal amount. <...> The structure was extensive and had running water and a bath. <...> Several thousand square meters of land next to the house belonging to the Hajj Molla Hadi Sabzevari religious trust were purchased. The property was well wooded with cypress and firs from Torbat-e Jam. <...> Other buildings were constructed to expand the hospital. The city mojtahed, Hajj Mirza Hoseyn, put a section of the municipal waterworks at the hospital's disposal. <...> The fee for the water was some 800 tomans, which Amir Arfa' initially helped to defray by levying a tax on every head of sheep slaughtered in the city. This amounted to some 2,000 tomans. In addition there was an icehouse at Zafarani, some of the ice from which was endowed to pilgrims, while some was sold. The yearly income from ice sales was 700 tomans; thus the hospital was assured approximately 3,000 tomans per year (about $3,000 at the time). I myself received no pay and also contributed something on my own. Most of my time was spent in the hospital. In addition to this many of the elite and propertied people helped the hospital in appreciation of the medical services I had rendered to them. I also trained a number of the young people of Sabzevar as nursing staff. At first this took some time, but soon several of them became familiar with the work and carried out a variety of tasks like applying medicine to the eyes of trachoma victims, dressing wounds, bursting fever blisters, administering injections, washing patients, sterilizing surgical instruments, bandages, etc. <...>

The hospital grounds were famous for their cleanliness. When Colonel Hall,[13] an American financial officer in Khorasan, visited with a party, the Americans continually asked how we were able to keep the place so immaculate and free of flies.

I gathered all the traditional apothecaries to give them instruction in practical chemistry that they could use in their own pharmacies. This included preparing medicine—vaporizing, dissolving, distilling, etc.—safeguarding poisons, registering and authorizing prescriptions, and preserving the privacy of patients. It was ordered that they use precise scales in measuring required doses, and I myself would drop in on their shops to personally assure myself of the quality of their work.

The hospital was the only place where everyone in the city came when they were sick. <...> Once they brought in an old man from Forumad whose leg had become gangrenous. Amputation well above the knee was the only way to save him. I anesthetized him with chloroform and began the operation. After cutting through the flesh and tying off the arteries, I tried to cut through the thigh bone with the one saw I had, a small, delicate instrument suitable for cutting teeth and fine bones, but not the femur. In the middle of cutting the bone the blade snapped, and I quickly sent one of the orderlies to buy a larger saw from a carpenter. That instrument was sterilized, and I completed the operation on the old man successfully. From that time on as long as I was in Sabzevar, he sent me several pounds of barberries, which grew in the wilds around his hometown, in gratitude for having saved his life. <...>

The hospital soon attracted a steady stream of patients from the entire province of Khorasan. The nurses and my colleagues proved to be very good. I pressed one or two local doctors like Ehtesham and Shafa al-Molk into service. There was also Aqa Rajab'ali, a surgeon who was completely illiterate but had assisted a Polish doctor and had become expert in treating gunshot and other wounds. <...>

Every year I would face outbreaks in the city of various types of malaria, at times its most acute form. At one point I was working night and day saving hundreds of people with injections of chloroquinine. Other endemic diseases were typhoid, typhus, various kinds of grippe, trachoma, skin diseases <...>. There were also conditions that required immediate operations like hernias and gunshot wounds. <...>

Dr. Ghani never completed this autobiography. His diary entries of 1948 in Egypt indicate that he had no time.

Dr. Ghani went to Paris in 1924 for a stay of some twenty months. He received specialized training in internal medicine after which he returned to Sabzevar. In late 1926 he again went to Paris working in various hospitals and attending lectures on psychiatry, returning in late 1928. He married Maryam Ghaffouri, the granddaughter of Hajji Molla Hadi Sabzevari. His son, Cyrus was born in November 1929. Dr. Ghani moved to Mashhad in early 1930 and set up a medical practice. His daughter, Nahid, was born in Mashhad. In 1934 he was elected to the tenth session of Parliament and moved to Tehran. He was elected to three further two-year terms. In 1935 he was elected a member of the Iranian Academy of Culture. In 1944 he briefly served as minister of health and later as minister of education. In 1945 he was appointed as a delegate to the founding session of the United Nations and thereafter kept a daily journal, parts of which have been translated in the present volume.

NOTES
CHILDHOOD AND YOUTH

1. A general history of Islam to the year 1441–42 by Fasih al-Khafi (born 1375).

2. Abu Bakr (caliph 632–34) was the Prophet Mohammad's immediate successor. Very few Shiites are called Abu Bakr because they believe that he usurped the caliphate from the Prophet's rightful successor, Imam Ali.

3. Hojjat al-Eslam (Proof of God) is the title of a high-ranking cleric, only one rank below ayatollah (Sign of God) in terms of authority.

4. "Mirza" is a word that appeared in Sabzevar in the fifteenth century at the time of the Sarbedars. A Sarbedar amir had a young son and successor named Lotfollah. Because Lotfollah was not old enough to rule, a regent ruled in his place. Lotfollah thus became Amirzadeh (son of the amir) Lotfollah. This was later shortened to Mirzadeh. Later, "mirza" was used among the successors of Timur: e.g., Mirza Shahrokh, Mirza Bysonqor, etc. During the Safavid period, "mirza" came at the beginning or end of names. In the Qajar period, they put it at the end of a name that carried a princely connotation. At the beginning of Islam in Iraq, "mirza" was reserved for the literate and learned class.

5. These underground channels, called *qanat* in Persian, are found in many parts of the Middle East and North Africa. They carry fresh water from mountains to fields that can be thirty kilometers away.

6. Hajj Molla Hadi Sabzevari was one of the most important Islamic philosophers of the nineteenth century.

7. Anatole France (1844–1924). Major French novelist. Nobel Prize in Literature, 1921. Dr. Ghasem Ghani translated into Persian three of his novels and a few of his essays.

8. Probably *Moghni l-Labib 'an Kotob al-A'arib* by the grammarian Jamal al-Din 'Abdallah b. Yusof b. Hesham (died 1359).

9. It is difficult to capture the bitterness of the original. To have some sense of it, the reader should know that Omar (ruled 634–44) is despised by Persians for being caliph when Islamic armies overran Iran and by all Shiites for having assumed the caliphate that they believe rightfully belonged to Ali.

10. Dr. William Van Dyke (1852–1939). Darwinist. Professor of biology and physiology at the American University of Beirut.

11. The Medical College of the American University of Beirut(A.U.B.) had a close relationship with Cornell University Medical School. Hence, New York State at that time licensed A.U.B. graduates.

12. Field Marshal Edmund H. Allenby (1861–1936) commander of British forces in the Near East, 1917–19.

13. Colonel Melvin Hall, an American who served in World War I. He later was sent to Iran where he served as acting treasurer-general as a member of the Millspaugh Mission (1922–1927).198

FIRST TRIP TO THE UNITED STATES
18 April 1945 to 12 August 1947

TO AMERICA

WEDNESDAY 4 APRIL 1945

This afternoon Court Minister Hoseyn Ala telephoned to say, "Prime Minister Bayat [Saham al-Soltan] will propose that you represent Iran at the San Francisco Conference for the founding of the United Nations that will take place on 25 April. I suggest you accept this post because it is His Majesty's desire that you be in America on the mission until the order for your appointment as ambassador to Washington is issued." Since I had been somewhat aware of this posting, I accepted. <...>

The background of the proposed ambassadorship is as follows. I resigned as minister of education in May of 1944. After HIM [His Imperial Majesty] reluctantly accepted the resignation, I left the cabinet. <...> But two weeks later His Majesty determined that I replace my old friend Mahmud Jam as ambassador to Cairo, and Hoseyn Ala communicated this decision to me officially. I said that I had no objections to the posting on principle, as long as my one reservation, not to displace my old friend, be satisfied. I insisted that a suitable position be found for Mr. Jam before I accepted. After two months of discussions, it was decided that Jam become ambassador to Turkey in Ankara and I become his replacement in Cairo. <...> In the meantime Reza Shah passed away in Johannesburg. Jam was delegated to go to Cairo to handle the transportation of the coffin and see to placing the late shah's children in schools in Europe and America. After he completed these tasks, Jam was to go to Ankara and I was to take his place in Cairo.

Two months later, after all this had been sorted out, at the outset of the Bayat government and with Nasrollah Entezam as foreign minister, His Majesty summoned me to the Marble Palace and instructed me to prepare for the trip to Egypt. The next day I went to the Ministry of Foreign Affairs to become familiar with the dossiers related to Egypt and with pacts and treaty conferences Iran had had in the last years. The minister took his time in providing these documents. In the meantime the government had resolved to elevate the Washington post to an ambassadorship. However, Zoka al-Molk (Mohammad Ali Foroughi), who had been appointed to this post, passed away. No successor was named. The American government, having upgraded its ministerial-rank offices in Tehran to full ambassadorial status, expected Iran to do the same. At this point HIM changed his mind and told the foreign minister that it would be better to send me to Washington instead of Cairo. The next day the foreign minister officially communicated the news to me. After many discussions, I agreed. But as this was happening, the Bayat government became unstable and received a no-confidence vote in Parliament. Then the court minister informed me that HIM decided that I become prime minister and form a cabinet. After conferring for two and a half hours, I convinced Ala that given the current state of the country and Parliament, and with foreign troops in most provinces, I would be unable to accept the position. HIM was not satisfied and ordered further talks with Mr. Ala. After discussing the matter for three hours with Mr. Ala at my home, I managed to convince him that it would be better to find someone else. During these days they renewed the offer of a Washington ambassadorial appointment, saying I was to be a member of the Iranian delegation (to San Francisco) so that the order for the ambassadorship would come when I was in the United States. I agreed once more.

The night that Dr. Ali Akbar Siasi officially made the offer and I accepted, there was a dinner party at the royal palace. The English actress Mary Ney, who specialized in Shakespearian roles, had also been invited. I was among the twenty Iranian and foreign guests. Around 8:30 as the actress was performing, His Majesty inquired through Mr. Ala whether or not I had accepted the San Francisco mission. When he learned that I had, he expressed his satisfaction and during dinner that night spoke in detail about my assignment to the UN and subsequent appointment as Iranian ambassador to the U.S. I accepted the UN delegation post in anticipation of being made ambassador to the U.S.

<...> The members of the Iranian delegation to the UN Conference were the following:

> Mostafa Adl (Mansur al-Saltaneh), the minister of justice, head of the delegation
>
> Seyyed Baqer Khan Kazemi (Mohazzeb al-Dowleh), former minister of foreign affairs and education
>
> Seyyed Nasrollah Entezam, former minister of foreign Affairs
>
> Dr. Ali Akbar Siasi, minister without portfolio
>
> Alahyar Saleh, former minister of justice
>
> Dr. Ghasem Ghani, former minister of education
>
> Dr. Rezazadeh Shafaq, member of Parliament
>
> Dr. Jalal Abdoh, member of Parliament
>
> Dr. Abdol'hoseyn E'tebar, member of Parliament
>
> Mohammad Shayesteh, minister plenipotentiary in Washington
>
> General Ali Riazi, HIM's special adjutant and head of the royal military corps
>
> Dr. Ghasemzadeh, doctor of law and professor at the University of Tehran, legal advisor to the delegation
>
> Fazlollah Nabil, one of the senior members of the ministry of foreign affairs, head of the delegation's secretariat.

<...>

From left to right: General Ali Mo'arefi, Dr. Rezazadeh Shafagh, Mostafa Adl,
Dr. Aliakbar Siasi, Major General Ali Riazi, Dr. Ghani, Alahyar Saleh

MONDAY 9 APRIL 1945

At 11:00 A.M. there was a briefing session for the delegates with the prime minister and the minister of foreign affairs. Mr. Anushirvan Sepahbodi resigned as a delegate. Sepahbodi is around fifty-two and has spent his entire career at the Ministry of Foreign Affairs as ambassador to Paris, Berlin, Moscow and Ankara. He knows French well, has considerable general knowledge and is a thoughtful, decent man. <...> He knows most of the key people in foreign governments. I had believed that he was the best man to head the delegation and had recommended his appointment, but the Bayat government, which had been weakened, was unable to help.

WEDNESDAY 11 APRIL 1945

The entire delegation had a meeting with HIM. <...>

SUNDAY 15 APRIL 1945

At 8:00 A.M. our American military airplane (the first flight of my life) took off from the American airfield at the head of New Karaj Road near Amirabad. My brother Hoseyn and daughter Nahid were there to say goodbye. We arrived in Cairo at 1:30 P.M., 3:00 P.M. Tehran time, after a seven-hour flight. Mr. Mahmud Jam, who had been informed of our arrival, was there to greet us at the airport and our party had lunch with him. <...>

At 4:30 P.M., after a pleasant three hours in conversation with my dear friend Jam, we were off to Tripoli on an improved military plane. Six hours later we entered Tripoli and, after a one-hour stop for dinner were on our way to Casablanca. Four hours later, past midnight local time, we entered the city and found rooms at the Hotel Anfa. This was the same hotel where Roosevelt and Churchill met for several days.

In the morning we toured the city by automobile and realized somehow that the driver had been instructed not to take us into the native Arab quarter so we would not become aware of the poverty and misery there. Casablanca, which has a population of 700,000, is a city of some size with a number of prominent buildings like the Eskanderia, and with squares and tree-lined, sedate boulevards. The weather at this time of year was delightful. On the avenue we met an Arab man dressed in the fashion of an Iraqi. He also had an automobile and followed ours and wherever we stopped, guided us. We toured the palace of the Moroccan king and the other royal buildings with him. Then at one o'clock he invited us for tea at a home, a very beautiful and ornate Moroccan house where he himself was a guest. He instructed the servant girl to prepare tea. Meanwhile the owner of the home, a patrician and well-to-do Moroccan, entered with his brother and children. Our companion told him in Arabic that he had met our group on the avenue and knew that we were Iranian. So taken with our being fellow Moslems, he attached himself to our party and like a dog obedient to its master followed behind. <...> Their driver, he explained, would not allow him to take us to places where the natives live in abject poverty, deprived of the most basic needs. Later, in tears he spoke eloquently on the suffering of the Arabs. Among other things, he said that they did not admit local children to the schools so that at least they could learn to read and write their native language. He also spoke a great deal about "Black Colonialism," "French exploitation" and "tyranny." At the end he begged us to help Morocco at the San Francisco Conference and point out the abject poverty of the country. <...>

At 8:30 we flew from the Azores to Bermuda. The flight lasted thirteen hours. We slept at night and woke the next day, 17 April 1945, and entered Bermuda. <...> There to meet us were some American officials. We toured the island, seeing, among other things, the building where Roosevelt and Churchill and the military leaders had met. We took off around noon and arrived in New York at 3:00 P.M. <...>

WEDNESDAY 18 APRIL 1945

Meeting us at customs were Messrs. Hoseyn Navab, the consul general; Emad Kia, consul; Mahmud Ameri; Aliqoli Khan Nabil al-Dowleh; Khosrowshahi; Manuchehr Marzban; Esfandiari (son of Mer'at al-Saltaneh Kermani); Kashef; Pur Reza Bushehri; Dr. Taqi Nasr; Habib Sabet; several other Iranians; and a couple of representatives from the State Department who took us to the Waldorf-Astoria Hotel.

THURSDAY 19 APRIL 1945

<...> Lunch at the hotel. <...> After consultation among the Iranians with Mr. Adl, who had arrived from Washington, and a sharp exchange between Messrs Entezam and Saleh, we went in the afternoon to Professor Pope's institute. <...>

TUESDAY 24 APRIL 1945

Around 3:00 P.M. the train arrived in San Francisco where Dr. Ali Akbar Daftari, who had gone ahead, was at the station to meet us. After completing the welcoming ceremonies for arriving delegates, which included an honor guard and a band, we went by automobiles belonging to the U.S. Navy to our hotel, the St. Francis. <...>

Among the well-known libraries of the city and the region is the University Library at Berkeley, whose public collection contains 1,250,000 volumes, including some seven Persian manuscripts all of which I examined carefully. One of them was a *Masnavi* written in the thirteenth century, which in the catalog was called "Collection of Religious Tales by J. Rumi."

I commented that some novice had written this description, on the basis of what a bookdealer had said, and not having an Orientalist on staff, they had not been able to amend it. Better to have written "*Masnavi* of the greatest Iranian mystic Jalal al-Din Rumi, thirteenth century." They corrected the catalog and two days later a note of thanks from the library director arrived. [A discussion of other universities and libraries in the region follows.] <...>

The teaching of Oriental languages in U.S. colleges is very rare and flawed, and one meets few Americans who can speak any foreign language well. Comparatively speaking, Spanish is spoken more than any other language owing to the commercial and political relations with South America; however, even that is not done competently or well. Of course this great nation, with no need of the Old World, never had to learn foreign languages and, as a result, American tourists are rarely successful in understanding other nations. However, the new state of affairs in the world and the need to establish relations with the countries of the Old World, like it or not, will force them to study languages and learn about the conditions and attitudes of people in those countries.

The people of the city are healthy, good-looking and good-natured, always content and smiling. It is actually rare to find an ugly face or misshapen body, and perhaps rarer still to meet a frown. One finds nothing but loveliness, good cheer and satisfaction. They are a kind, candid and trusting people. Almost never does one hear anything but the truth from them.

Americans are also known for naïveté, even ignorance. The reason for their seeming simplicity and artlessness is that they do not expect anyone to lie—there is freedom and openness and candor. They are extraordinarily fond of enjoying themselves. Women's freedom is at its apex and relations between men and women have reached their most uncomplicated state, functioning like any other physical need—just as the thirsty are not admonished for drinking water, so neither are women and men belittled or castigated for having relations.

Women are involved in all walks of life, from working in business and commerce, as secretaries, teaching school, being in politics, to being drivers. The question of women's freedom and equality is not even raised because there is no need to—in effect there is no difference in status between the sexes; it is missing even in the realm of thought for no one is capable of conceiving any other way. For a man to express interest in a woman is natural and normal, and the woman accepts the man or rejects him with the same simplicity within the bounds of good manners and respect—as a rule they are not offensive. Ethically speaking as well, relationships have reached the point where there is no difference between what is allowed and what is not. The things I have heard and seen in Paris are not even mentioned here. In Paris the phrases "good and bad," "allowed and proscribed," "permitted and prohibited" and "indecency and chastity" were current, while here they are hardly used. It is said about girls that they are free, and they consider themselves naturally independent in spirit, thought and body. Of course a married woman sees herself bound by propriety and most people are possessed of a sense of responsibility. This same sense is palpable on all levels of society—toward, for example, the state, government organizations, and to democracy and freedom where it is at its height.

No one fears the government, there is no sense of paranoia; rather they all respect the state and are bound by duty to carry out their responsibilities. Defrauding or cheating when it comes to pay-ing taxes and the other duties are rare.

Americans at first glance may seem to be a disparate nation. Because they comprise many different and contrary elements, lacking national unity, one would think that patriotism is not that important; but, to the contrary, Americans are the most patriotic people in the world, extraordinarily fond of their country—without pretense or protest they are devoted to it body and soul. <...>

[There are discussions of UN sessions and some social occasions are mentioned.]

WEDNESDAY 16 MAY 1945

<...> Family gatherings in America, which include a number of peo-ple, men and women together, are cordial affairs with everyone talking and laughing long and loud over little things. Topics of conversation are ordinarily very simple and superficial. The images that Americans have of other parts of the world are generally more like a child's fan-tasies. <...> At their many parties they tend to invite a foreigner whom they consider interesting. This much they do know: across the seas are many different countries with their own special customs, practices, cultures and crafts; however, they have no idea of the nature of those particular things. The awareness of their own ignorance itself causes Americans to accept meekly what they are told, never doubting it and raising questions only to clarify or learn more. This sense of inferiority also holds true in their foreign policy, especially in their attitude toward the British who they think have the last word on everything. <...> The scientific community in this state hosts a great many distinguished people. The few that I have met several times include Dr. Evans,[1] professor of anatomy at Berkeley, who heads a team of researchers in endocrinology and biochemistry. He is the dis-coverer of vitamin E. Dr. Ernest Lawrence,[2] winner of the Nobel Prize in physics, and Dr. Esther Rosencrantz, an outstanding 69-year-old lady who is now retired from her post as professor of lung diseases. She had been one of the early women students of the famed Dr. Osler. She has shown great kindness toward me.

SUNDAY 20 MAY 1945

Tonight we were the guests of Mirza Mehdi Hamadani, a Jewish Iranian from Hamadan who came to this city in 1913 and currently is the owner of a pharmacy. We dined on a variety of Persian foods. This man, who came here thirty-two years ago at the age of twenty-three, is an extremely fine individual, good-natured and kind. By his own account, he was an apprentice to an apothecary in Kermanshah. With thoughts of doing business, he went to Japan via India. He remained there for a time, but not being able to find gainful work, he came to San Francisco. At that time Zahir al-Mamalek Owbehi, now head of the telegraph in Birjand, owned a restaurant where Mirza Mehdi earned a living as a waiter. <…> The young Mirza Mehdi began to study the language and pharmacy, and, with his background, succeeded in getting a license that allowed him to practice in 1915. <…> Gradually he became established and married a fine and kind woman, who is still his wife. He also became the father of a son who is in the army. <…> Mirza Mehdi then became an American citizen. He speaks Persian with a foreign accent and often thinks as a Westerner. <…>

MONDAY 25 JUNE 1945

This morning, at the invitation of Dr. Ernest Lawrence[3] and having obtained military clearance, we went to Berkeley and visited the Cyclotron Laboratory. We had lunch at the Fairmont Hotel where we were specifically invited to meet President Truman.

First the delegates of all nations went to a waiting area called the "Red Room." For each country there was a specific area indicated by a placard. After about twenty minutes we went to an adjacent room. We entered in alphabetical order, beginning with Argentina and ending with Yugoslavia—the American delegation came last. President Truman was at the center of the room and Secretary of State Stettinius[3] was to his right. To his left were two generals and an admiral, his military attaché, and behind him were two Secret Service men standing on guard back to back. In front of him and throughout the room were many other Secret Service men. First the secretary of state shook the delegates' hands and introduced them to the president who also greeted them. Then we shook hands with the generals and the admiral (aides to President Truman). Cocktails and food were served in this room and the adjoining one, and there was also a band. <...>

FRIDAY 29 JUNE 1945

<...> We had dinner at the Omar Khayyam restaurant. The owner, who is called Mister Omar or Mister Khayyam, is an Armenian from Turkey named Mardikian. His restaurant is very good and successful. One has to wait up to half an hour for a table. He has become wealthy and says that Khayyam's blessings have made him a millionaire. A decent man, he would like to go to Iran someday and build something in Khayyam's memory: a tomb or a library. <...>

SATURDAY 30 JUNE 1945

Today Dr. Esther Rosencrantz invited me and Sattareh Farman Farmaian[4] for a drive to see some sights outside of San Francisco. <...> We left the hotel at 1:00 P.M., picking up the lady who owned the car along the way, crossed the Golden Gate Bridge and passed through San Rafael. In St. Anselmo we went to the home of one of her friends that is atop a hill; overlooking very beautiful country. The owner of the house is an older woman of seventy who along with her fifty-year-old daughter could not have been warmer in their welcome. Their garden was decorated with a number of fine pieces of woodwork, among them were birdcages hanging from the trees. They had placed birdseed and bowls of water at the bottom of the cages that were simple frames open on four sides allowing small birds like nightingales and sparrows to enter, eat the seeds, sing, court the flowers beside the cages and fly away.

I was reminded of one of Hafez's lyrical poems:

At dawn the meadow bird said to a newly wakened flower:
Don't flaunt your beauty, for many a rose here has bloomed like you.
The flower smiled and said: The truth does not trouble me—but,
Never would a lover speak to his beloved so harshly.

When I translated the two verses, it produced such an effect on them that it defies description and it actually stirred two things in me. One was the effect of the poem itself and how aptly it fit the situation; the second was how profoundly it moved everyone present, as if we all had been intoxicated by it. Americans are so engrossed in the world of appearances, in work, the material life, and the technicalities of their jobs that they are starving for the nonmaterial and spirituality. It is as if nature has revealed to them that they are lacking a certain blessing—they just have to experience some spiritual yearning and they are rapt with pleasure. One of them said to me, "You are a great poet." "I am a simple doctor, the greatness belongs to our famed poet not me," I said. "But you have made this poem accord to the moment with such enthusiasm and grace and have translated it with such joy and abandonment, that is itself sublime poetry." I said, "Still the art belongs to our great poet who produced this effect in me." I spoke at length about the importance of Persian literature, poetry, aesthetics. The only example of which their great nation knows is the work of our Omar Khayyam—deprived as they are of hundreds of our other great writers. <...>

TUESDAY 3 JULY 1945

At 9:00 P.M. Mr. Mohammad Shayesteh called from Washington to say that there was a telegram from Sepahbodi, the Minister of Foreign Affairs, in Tehran saying, "Inform Doctor Ghani to stay in America so that new instructions can arrive from the Foreign Ministry" and with it extended congratulations. It is clear that Tehran had decided definitely that I remain in Washington as the Iranian ambassador.

WEDNESDAY 4 JULY 1945

Today, American Independence Day, is the most important national holiday and all the stores and government offices are closed. Most people have left the city and there is no other sign of celebration. They say that before the war there were fireworks, but now they are suspended. I had lunch with Dr. Karl Mayo at a restaurant and presented him with an Esfahan vase, which his wife later acknowledged with a card. At the restaurant Dr. Mayo spoke about medicine and the field of microbiology. Some minor naval officer, who was having lunch near us with two others and was blind drunk, turned to the doctor and in a sharp voice, apropos of nothing, said, "You talk too much! Out with it now—what's your point?" So we left the restaurant. This was the first slight breach of manners I have seen; but all he was saying was: What do the words mean? As the poet says:

Wine does not work the same mischief in all;
It only brings out more the type one truly is.

One night I was walking with Dr. Ahmad Farhad down a deserted street when we ran into two drunken sailors who first asked us if we knew of a bar. Then they invited us to join them and later one of the two drunks asked, "Where are you from?" "Iran," I said. "Very well," he said, "you know this is a free country. You see people coming and going in the streets, and everybody minds their own business." "Yes," I agreed. "Is that freedom bad?" he asked. "No," I said. "Then why don't they live like this in Europe? Why does Hitler do those things in Germany?" he asked. <...> In short I never saw a mean drunk. The sailors as a group are very chipper, and people love to spoil them, for they know that they spend months at sea in the face of many dangers—so, when they have a few days leave now and then, anything goes. They are also peerless clowns, playful and witty. They have money coming to them for shore leave, and the girls, apart from the attractions of the sailors' youth and good looks, consider it their patriotic duty to entertain them. <...>

FRIDAY JULY 27 1945

Several days ago I was reminded of Anatole France's *Penguin Island*,[5] an allegorical novel about the evolution of the mores, customs and laws among the nations of Europe, especially France. I thought of how much the chapter on the simple and natural existence of male and female penguins applies to the lives of San Francisco's current inhabitants. The obvious trappings of civilized life aside, one would think that mankind had truly returned to an original state of being, when life was governed by primary instincts.

Among the male and female penguins, one satisfied basic urges with the speed of their occurrence without a thought for logic or etiquette; as if there were no morality or social constraint, as if custom did not exist. No one cared whether or not these emotions had a poetic or lyric bent. Repressed feelings and unrequited love were unheard of. Sexual urges were quickly and easily satisfied. This is nearly what we see among the San Franciscans. Sundays on the beaches, in the gardens and forests, one sees thousands of couples sleeping together in one another's arms. They wear spare apparel covering their private parts. It is as if no one has anything to hide, and, more interestingly, everyone minds his or her own business. At the groceries one sees crowds having emerged from the beaches and parks, both men and women, but especially women, shopping in that same near-naked state. The more I think about it the more I am reminded of male and female penguins, and some of my non-American friends know that when I say "penguin" I mean a male San Franciscan and when I say "penguine," I mean a female.

Another thing worth seeing here is the dancing that is found everywhere, in almost all hotels. In the afternoons and evenings, one often sees sailors and soldiers approach the Red Cross people or the information desks at the hotels asking for a dance partner. They give them the names and addresses of girls, and the amazing thing is how easily this is done. The dances often border on a sexual activity, not at all like the refined movements one sees in Germany or England, which have a classical grandeur. Here dance is about sex, while today in Europe there is still the patina of the eighteenth century.

After all is said and done, no feeling that might be called poetic lingers in the penguin mind for a day besides the burning desire for sexual satisfaction. <...> However, when the tryst is over, whether they continue or not depends on circumstances, not on moral or ethical principles or on matters of responsibility or conscience. There is little poetry to be found here; they neither read nor understand it. In effect, poetry and lyricism are practical matters. A beautiful woman herself embodies a lyrical poem; her behavior is a kind of composition. There is no need for imagination and fancy, reality takes their places. This is because poetry is repressed feeling, the voice of desires denied. Romantic or erotic verse compensates the poetic sensibility for the suffering created by unrequited or unappeased love. Here there is no call for it, everything is about satisfying natural desires and inclinations.

Poetry is born of feeling, and here there is no feeling. For this reason, they all know Khayyam, who encourages hedonism. But all they understand from him is the message "be happy." No one grasps his suffering, nor wants to.

SUNDAY 5 AUGUST 1945

Today a letter came from Ali Akbar Daftari, the first secretary at the Iranian Embassy in Washington. It asks for a formal acceptance [from the U.S. government] for the ambassadorship of Ala. Mr. Shayesteh, the minister plenipotentiary, is not in Washington. This is good news to me, because at least now I know where I stand and the waiting is over. To be fair it is a good appointment; Mr. Hoseyn Ala is preferable to me as he is among the best and most noble of present-day Iranians. He has been sincere, honest and well meaning during his entire career as a public servant. <...>

At noon Mirza Mehdi came by. His mother-in-law, Rabia Martin, had been away, but is now in Fairfax where she lives and heads a Sufi shrine. She has invited us to have lunch and then visit the shrine. Two months ago her son-in-law had written about my work on mysticism (*The History of Sufism in Islam*). This woman, who has visited Iran and met with several dervishes there, is under the impression that I am a Sufi as well. I spoke with her for more than an hour trying to disabuse her of this notion. I explained that rather than being a mystic on the path to God, I was merely a historian who studied the nature of Sufi practices and beliefs because of their profound effect on many of the great figures of Iran and on Persian literature. But she persisted, asking why I did not join the order. I said that everyone has certain inclinations; however, mine was not for mysticism, though I was happy to study the many Sufi orders and had the highest regard for the great masters and their works. I mentioned Iranian masters like Sana'i, Ghazzali, Attar, Jalal al-Din Rumi, Sheikh Eraqi, etc., but the more I equivocated, the more insistent she became. During the course of the conversation I learned that Rabia Martin was the partner of Princess Norina Matchabelli in their Sufism venture. Originally from Florence, she became a princess by marriage to a Georgian prince, whom she later divorced. Now she is a naturalized American living in New York. Several years ago the princess became infatuated with a Sufi known as Mehr Baba who is of Iranian ancestry but now lives in India. The man has given her license, as the dervishes say, to guide others.

Mrs. Martin explained that she had been devoted to God since childhood (she is now seventy), praying for guidance from Him and meditating. She has a daughter, Mirza Mehdi's wife, but spends most of her time on charitable work and has always felt the need for a spiritual guide. In 1910 Mirza Enayat Khan came to San Francisco. From the moment she saw him, she knew that he was the one to whom she must turn for guidance. First he tested her by giving her various tasks to perform, and, after a year, she joined the order. Later he wrote from London suggesting that she represent him in America. They corresponded regularly. She saw him again in the United States in 1926, but the next year he died in India of influenza. Since then she has spent all her time in heartfelt propagation of Sufi beliefs. Her parents originally named her Ada. Enayat Khan later renamed her Rabia. While meditating she often feels the presence of Enayat Khan and speaks with him. She says he has become one with God, etc. These days the divine is manifest in Mehr Baba, who is represented by Princess Matchabelli. Tonight at seven he will give a talk, or, rather, he will speak through the princess, who acts as a kind of wireless receiver for him.

At four the princess comes downstairs and one has his audience with her. She is a woman of about fifty who gives the impression of a hysteric, her eyes moving frantically this way and that. In her younger days she must have been quite captivating. She speaks English and French well, also German, and her native Italian. She explained that in all of human history, fifty-six people have found God, and one of these is Mehr Baba. She spoke rapidly without pausing for breath. She said that the moment her mind tuned in to the voice of the master and the connection was made, she saw and felt him as though he were actually there.

<...>

America is a land of wonders. Americans value everything from the old world: its objects and manufactured things; its ideas and religious beliefs; its mysteries. They are certainly aware that—even though they might not express it—they are young. The city of San Francisco itself is less than a hundred years old and forty years ago was burned to the ground. What is remarkable is that it does not take long for recent immigrants here to completely Americanize, that is to blend in wholly with the environment. The perfect example is Mirza Mehdi who came here in 1913 at the age of twenty-four. He is American both in spirit and thinking, having virtually forgotten his Persian. When he speaks the language—his bilingualism notwithstanding—half of what he says is in English. The attractions of American culture, its power to assimilate, are noteworthy. I have seen many Armenians here who have undergone complete changes of identity.

At this point Dr. Ghani describes a visit to the Buena Vista home of Samuel Hume, whose wife, a psychiatrist, invited him for dinner. Dr. Ghani was particularly impressed by the Humes' residence, from which one could see the lush vegetation on the Berkeley hills, San Francisco Bay and the lights of the city. He also praises the home's neoclassical style and its cloistered garden.

My hostess is a woman of about thirty-six, very beautiful and charming, and in addition to being a specialist in psychiatric disorders is an accomplished sculptor. The décor of the home is the best testament to her good taste. During the party, Mr. Hume mentioned his wife's specialty and asked me whether Iranian physicians of the medieval period like Avicenna had done research on psychological disorders. I replied that Avicenna devotes an entire chapter of his *Qanun* (Canon) to such diseases of the mind as insomnia, fatigue, melancholia, insanity, etc. He classified "love" among mental disorders; that is, as the cause of a number of illnesses. He presented several treatments and related case histories that resemble today's clinical practice. They also had other methods of treatment that are not unlike those of today's psychotherapy like free association of ideas. Avicenna wrote a separate treatise on "love" as well. Razi and others also grappled with this problem. Many psychological issues have found their way into popular Persian literature and writers and poets speak of them.

Mr. Hume was quite interested in what I had to say, and I promised to send him any book I might find on the topic. About a month ago, one of the professors learned from Mr. Hume about what I had said and related it at a faculty meeting at the medical school. One of those present thought it was exaggerated. This forced me to write Mr. Hume—without acknowledging that individual's doubts—explaining in simple terms that though I did not have access to sources I could give an overview of the subject that would help his wife pursue it. I compiled a kind of detailed article, mentioning works like E. G. Browne's[6] *Arabian Medicine* and two works on Avicenna. I also referred to the story from the *Masnavi*, tales from *The Four Discourses*, and showed the chapter of the *Canon* (Latin translation) devoted to psychological disorders and love. This piqued Dr. Hume's interest greatly, and she sent a long letter imploring me to teach and guide her so that she could pursue her interest in a scholarly way. <...>

Tonight I spoke with her and learned that she had gathered a great number of sources and was reading them avidly. I encouraged her because until now there has been no study devoted to the writings of Iranian physicians on psychology. If she were to produce such a study, it would be something original. She insisted that I be her guide. I promised to send her sources as soon as I found them.

MONDAY 6 AUGUST 1945

Today I looked at the calendar and saw that yesterday, the fourteenth of Mordad, was the anniversary of the founding of constitutional government in Iran. This was one of those coincidences that lead one to worlds of endless possibilities—especially in the United States where there is real democracy as opposed to Iran where it is a dream. These thoughts kept me so preoccupied that I didn't notice time pass.

FRIDAY 10 AUGUST 1945

<...> Japan has declared it will accept the Potsdam Declaration. <...>

TUESDAY 14 AUGUST 1945

<...> Japan has surrendered.

At this point Dr. Ghani begins a car trip across the United States.

THURSDAY 16 AUGUST 1945

At 11:30 Dr. Sheedy and I left the city [San Francisco]. When we reached San Raphael, Dr. Sheedy's radiator boiled over. We were delayed for a time, but in fits and starts eventually reached the small town of Petaluma. In peacetime the population is 8,000, but now 10,000 live in the small town, which is about thirty-nine miles from San Francisco. We brought the car to a garage and around four in the afternoon went to a hotel. After resting a while, we ate at the hotel restaurant and then went for a walk around the town. These small towns naturally are as clean and have all the conveniences of large cities. For example, we visited the town library, which has nearly 20,000 volumes. There is a public park and playground for children, a cinema and an amusement area, cafés and restaurants, and attractive shops with the same goods and services found in the cities. There are also banks and commercial establishments and a telephone exchange. People have all the facilities that are in San Francisco, only on a smaller scale. After returning to the hotel I spoke with Dr. Sheedy until ten. <...>

FRIDAY 17 AUGUST 1945

My traveling companion, Dr Sheedy [introduced to me by a mutual friend], is an unemotional, rustic young man. He received his medical degree five years ago, has been in general practice since and, as he says, toured all of America by car <...>, he is like a machine, incapable of smiling or laughter, having absolutely no sense of humor. A good story has no effect on him. He does not understand poetry and figurative language is beyond him. <...>

MONDAY 20 AUGUST 1945

Olympia, Washington. Descriptions of the natural beauty of the area.

I have been in a strange mood lately, traveling three hundred to three hundred and thirty miles a day—I stop wherever I like, eat whenever I am hungry, sleep wherever I please, bathe whenever I feel tired, and the minute I am thirsty I drink some lemonade or orange juice or have some ice cream at a café. Wherever the dervish stops is home. But it is preferable to be a dervish in this country that has all the amenities. Today I passed through a village where near a bridge on the outskirts there was a sign saying it had a population of some five hundred people. I calculated about a hundred families, which made it like one of the miserable little holes in my country where people perch on refuse piles, and there are donkeys surrounded by thousands of flies, mosquitoes, and filth. Where soap is unknown and bathing foreign. Five hundred people, sick, no hair, trachomatous, pale, hungry, jaundiced, malarial, scarred, and hopeless. All malcontent, depressed, everyone encircling the newly arrived traveler, hungry, asking for something. Hospitality is found in the dark, dank coffeehouse full of filth. A soiled samovar and china teapot, its cracks pasted together, and tea glasses stained black and yellow and dirty, bent spoons—no one that hasn't seen it can imagine it. The owner is a miserable, opium addict who serves foul tea, and sometimes a glass of milk and a few eggs. He perfectly embodies the miserable prehistoric caveman.

When I was once speaking with [the late Ali Akbar] Davar about the past, I said that no one understands history as well as the Iranian. Imagining that this was boasting, he said, "Your patriotism is showing again. You mean to say that the Iranian is more intelligent and more perceptive than the rest of humanity?" "No," I said, "people fully understand what is written in history when it conforms to their reality, when they can compare it to their own experiences. How can a European child or an American student understand what prehistoric times were like, imagine some unclothed creature huddling in a cave or at the foot of a mountain or burrowing or crouching in a mudhole trying to keep safe from savage animals? How he patched together the skin of the animal he had eaten into some covering. Nature's pawn, he was born by accident and by accident he would die. He had neither remedies nor medicine, unconscious of the sky, the stars and the planets <...>, all nature a mystery to him. Humble before any natural force, captive to the two basic instincts of self-preservation: hunger and procreation, and passing day and night plagued by thousands of frights and terrors. Feeling is the path to understanding every detailed historical account. [The average American] has no such experience, and what he does understand is ambiguous and clouded <...>. But you and I have seen this kind of life. Now we can go twelve kilometers outside of Tehran and see it. <...>

"The European studies how ancient Roman and Egyptian prisoners lived, but there is a vast difference between studying the topic and experiencing it. He studies the Middle Ages and they explain Scholasticism to him, but what does he grasp? But because I have been the student of such and such a man from Sabzevar, I have observed and heard how he thinks, reasons, the quality of his arguments, and so I know about the period of the Middle Ages, its scholarship and its leading intellectual lights <...>. [The European] studies about the classes of societies but does not experience them. Stranger still is that in our country we have examples of all social strata, historical periods and ages. In some places including Tehran, we see Renaissance times. A certain special group of people thinks the way they did in the eighteenth and nineteenth centuries, some other group engages in twentieth-century debates, while another weaves dreams of the future. For these reasons, then, we digest and assimilate history better."

Whatever the case, one of the unfortunate things about being Iranian is that we cannot just be happy traveling. With each step along the way, I brood about my own life, my father's and ancestors', my children's, neighbors' and fellow countrymen's, and something that should bring pleasure just causes grief. <...> That morning at 8:00, after having breakfast in the restaurant, we emerged from the hotel and were on our way. <...>

THURSDAY 23 AUGUST 1945

Idaho and Montana. Several pages on the beauty of the scenery.
    <...>

Our journey was perfect for introspection. My doctor companion, though a good man, was very taciturn, one of those people who knows nothing, or, perhaps, notices nothing. Conversation with him is impossible. He is a good driver, however, and neither smokes nor drinks. At each stop he buys a newspaper and reads it in the restaurant. He is a prolific writer of postcards to his home, sisters and friends <...>. No matter what I say it has no effect on him. He has no stories to tell, nor does he have a sense of humor. Figurative language is lost on him, and he is immune to the charms of the deserts, forests, rivers, flowers and people.

This type of automaton is common in America. The important thing to understand is that they are no smarter than the people of the East—probably somewhat inferior as individuals—but their social structures allow their limited capacities to unify into a powerful force. In the East the mode of thought is individualistic, and the sense of community is weak. <...> Among ourselves we say that the individual parts are fine, but to hell with trying to assemble them into something larger. Here, though the individual parts may not be superior, collectively they form a fine society. In short, the good doctor proved to be the ideal traveling companion for allowing one's mind to run free. Today I recalled friends from the past and felt grateful to the lot of them, as each taught me something. With some, conversation was so engrossing that it could last hours. It occurred to me then what a good idea it would be to write what I recalled in the form of a memoir. At the very least, it would lift my spirits to know that dear friends were well remembered. In addition, it would be a welcome memento for my two children, Nahid and Cyrus. The other deciding factor was the encouragement of Mohammad Qazvini, who during our long association often heard me speak of the past.

Today the route was all uphill and mountainous, and we arrived in a town called Kalispell (population perhaps 10,000) at around three o'clock. It was past lunchtime, so Dr. Sheedy and I went to a restaurant for coffee and a sandwich or whatever was available. As soon as he sat down, he began reading the newspaper and we ordered. And I, as I ordinarily do in these places, went over to the old proprietor of the restaurant to learn as much as possible about the town. While we spoke, I noticed a girl soaping down the floor and mopping it. She was a picture of beauty, the type who makes the masterpieces of the Raphaels and the Rembrandts pale in my mind. Of course, this natural beauty is the source of all human aesthetic inspiration. The Raphaels, Rembrandts, Michelangelos, Ingres, Sa'dis, Hafezes, etc. were imitators of nature—all of their efforts were aimed at representing their ideas through the beauty of nature. This girl was nature's masterpiece, not a product of the creative brush of the Raphaels or the pen of Sa'dis. I watched her as she concentrated wholly on the task of mopping the floor. They say that on Judgment Day when all of humankind gathers, the Almighty will look upon some and declare that they are no part of His Creation, rather they are the inferior works of the angels. This girl surely was one of those in whom the Majestic Creator would take a pride of authorship.

<...>

SATURDAY 25 AUGUST 1945

Idaho and Montana. Lengthy description of the beauties of nature.

    This morning Dr. Sheedy went to Canada, as it is only twenty-five miles away. Since I had no visa, I remained behind.

    Yesterday and today I was entirely alone. I have not been so alone for years. I was in Paris in 1928 when the clamor and the press of appointments became so great that I grew tired of them. As a result, I longed for peace and quiet, an out-of-the-way place on a mountaintop, for example, far from the noise, where there was no telephone nor café nor post office. Several days later I traveled to Deauville with Mr. Ali Akbar Bahman, at the time minister plenipotentiary in Belgium, who had come to Paris to see the late Teimurtash, who was touring Europe. After staying two days in Deauville, I chose a sanitarium along the Côte de Grace in Normandy, which met all my qualifications. Mr. Bahman returned to Brussels, and I rented a room for ten days, paying in advance. That afternoon I saw several chaises longues in the garden each occupied by a tired or worn-out old man or woman. Not a sound nor whisper could be heard. After dining alone I returned to my room and regretted my choice. Why did a person like me who is neither old nor worn out go against his natural bent for company and conversation? For hours I tried to justify the choice by arguing the merits of the fine weather, the natural peace and quiet, and the opportunity these afforded for study and contemplation. One advantage was that I could work on the Persian translation of Anatole France's *Thaïs* that Mr. Qazvini had been insisting for ages I do. I had already completed a portion of the book while touring Switzerland, the Tyrol, Vienna, Budapest, Prague, Dresden and Berlin. The next morning I went to Honfleur to put the money I had with me in a bank. I told the bank to hold any mail from Paris for me until I came round to collect it. Then I returned and became involved in translating. I managed to force out a few pages and somehow passed the afternoon and the evening; but in the morning I realized that solitude was not for me. Also that if I wanted to write or translate, I could not do it alone. By nature I am gregarious; I have to have people around, conversation, even while studying. I cannot force myself to be otherwise. So it was with this insight I went to Honfleur, which is a few miles from the sanatorium, to retrieve my money and give the bank a forwarding address for my mail. I returned to the place and said goodbye to the old woman proprietor. I traveled to Lisieux, a small town where St. Helen is buried, which makes it the destination of thousands of pilgrims. Visiting several places along the way, I returned to Paris.

So yesterday and today, for the first time in seventeen years, I am alone, that is in a cabin surrounded by others occupied by groups of people, a restaurant and a café. The rest of the people are with their families. They are the types who spend their few days of yearly vacation in such places. They are genuine specimens of Americans, people who can wear whatever their hearts desire and sit down and whistle wherever they like. My neighbors are a couple of about forty-five, two of whose children are in the military and another in school. Last night as I sat outside of my cabin, they stopped by and we spoke for a while. But now, I notice that my mentality has changed a bit since 1928; I no longer feel the burden of loneliness as I did then. This is only natural after seventeen years; however, my basic disposition remains the same. All in all, I still take no pleasure in being alone. Yesterday and today I went for walks and read for the rest of the time. My current reading consists of the history of America and a book with statistics on its population, workforce, localities, laws and infrastructure.

Last night I had a conversation with the cook in the restaurant, who is a Native American woman, but not pure Native American; her father was Irish and her mother was Blackfoot. She spoke of the customs of the tribe, who live six miles away. <...> Tomorrow I intend to go to one of the Indian agents' offices and research these matters further. The Native Americans have their own spoken languages but lack written forms of communication. They do appear to have some form of symbolic notation, which, if my investigations allow, I will record. The women around here wear men's clothing, long pants and jackets, a practice that is not restricted to young girls but widespread among the older women. <...>

Another thing worth noting about Americans is that they are a conceited nation, meaning that they consider the rest of the world beneath them; but this conceit is of a particular kind—they sense that the Old World has the privilege of precedence. They are very much like the nouveaux riches or like those in very humble stations who suddenly achieve prominence <...>. The war was especially nurturing of this sense in them, making them realize the enormity of their global importance, allowing them to imagine that they did not need the rest of the world. In their eyes the only nation with a certain majesty is England, as they feel the British to be more adroit and more skilled in running an empire. All in all the primary element of American society has a British tinge; that is, just as their language is English, so too do the rest of British qualities overshadow all others. <...>

SATURDAY 1 SEPTEMBER 1945

<...> Today around 8:30 A.M. Dr. Sheedy and I reached Rochester, Minnesota, to visit the Mayo Clinic and Museum. Dr. Mayo established the clinic in the late nineteenth century, and he became known for his good character and skill. Soon the clinic became famous and attracted patients from all over. He died in 1915 around the age of ninety. His two sons, also doctors, expanded the clinic and in 1927 had its signature tower built. They died a few years ago and the clinic became part of the University of Minnesota medical school. It is now a teaching hospital where doctors come for their specialties. The municipality, which is known as hospital city, is wall-to-wall flowers, greenery and quiet pleasure. The entire state, through which we are passing this morning, is so beautiful. It is not the immoderate beauty of the forests of Oregon and Washington or of places in California. Those are attractive on a mammoth scale; one is humbled before them. But in this state there are no huge mountains, its forests are not as full, but there are so many enchanting, green fields. It is the type of beauty that

soothes the spirit, the sort most familiar to me. The charms of Oregon, Washington and California are epic, fitting scenes for Ferdowsi, while Minnesota's are the sublime lyrics of Sa'di and Hafez. God spared nothing when He favored these people.

After Rochester the famous Mississippi River valley came into view. On the right bank is Minnesota and on the left is the state of Wisconsin. With its thousands of wooded islands, and hills and meadows, the scenery along this river valley defies description; it must be seen. While seeing this gave me great pleasure, today my spirits are low just the same. God, what good are we? Where are we? What does our past amount to? Our present? Our future? Nothing but anguish, misfortune, pain, helplessness, ignorance, disease, degradation, hunger and depravity. Worse than all are our uncommon indifference to truth and baseless pretense. <...>

The distance to Madison, Wisconsin's state capital, is sixty-three miles and nearly two hundred to Chicago. We arrived in Madison two hours before noon and had breakfast on the outskirts of the city. At eleven o'clock I went to look for Alidad Farmanfarmaian,[7] but he was not at home. I walked for a while on the broad university campus, which is located on the shores of a beautiful lake. Then I went to the capital building and returned to Alidad's home. He pays four dollars weekly in rent and spends two dollars a day on food. Along the way I ran into Alinaqi Farmanfarmaian[8] who lives in a similar building and studies journalism. I had lunch with the two gentlemen, both of whom are very good students. Then we went to the student union and spoke for two or three hours along the lake shore until Dr. Sheedy came around 4:30 and we left. At about 9:30 we reached Chicago and stayed at the Palmer House Hotel. <...>

MONDAY 3 SEPTEMBER 1945

This morning around eleven o'clock I left the hotel and walked around. Today is a public holiday and the streets are comparatively empty. As soon as there is a holiday, Americans leave town, which of course is made easier with the availability of automobiles, thousands of other means of transportation and recreational facilities in the parks outside of the cities. <...>. Apparently they learn from nature to escape the wearying clamor of the city. This country is one of hurry and unrest, especially the large cities, where the expressions on people's faces and the movements of their bodies speak of haste and impatience. At the information counters in hotels, before a question is completed, they hurriedly give the answer. They abbreviate many words, fracturing them, and abhor anything that takes time. God, what extremes there are in this world! It is a good thing I am only passing through; these people are sheer automatons and there are times when I become so mechanistic that I begin to see the world through their eyes. In the restaurants, cafés, and salons of the hotels I often overhear people's conversations—all of them are about work, money, making a living or possessions. Talking is another of their pastimes, like the daily conversations among women friends: uncomplicated, conventional, day to day. Today two women in a restaurant were having lunch next to me and talking, saying things like "How was your trip?" "Great." "Good, I'm happy." "I didn't have film in my camera so I went to such-and-such place and bought some and so-and-so's child got on the horse and I took a photo. So-and-so's daughter's going to middle school this year." "How was your party?" "Fantastic, lunch was great." They smoke cigarette after cigarette, and then each pays her share of the bill and leaves. A bunch of money-worshiping, automatons who happen to be situated in the world's best country, whose society and institutions have performed and perform so responsively to their desires that one cannot conceive of anything better. Nothing touches them but gorging, self-gratification and forging ahead. The feelings and nonmaterial instincts of the East are not to be found here, or are very rare, as a kind of specific type of exercise or meditation. Individuals are not exceptional. It is their collective whole and institutions that are paramount.

TUESDAY 4 SEPTEMBER 1945

This morning I went to the central post office for the mail. There were letters from Dr. Farhad and Mr. Navab. <...> Conditions in Iran are what they were before. The Sadr government has not been introduced yet and the majority and the minority have not reached an agreement. A letter from Dr. Ali Akbar Daftari dated 25 August arrived. A telegram from Tehran, which Shayesteh had not sent, was as follows:

> Esteemed Dr. Ghani, as you are apprised, Mr. Ala has been appointed to the post of imperial ambassador to Washington. The intention is to make use of your presence in the Iranian delegation that we will send to the upcoming United Nations General Assembly. If you prefer to remain in America until that time, Mr. Ala would be happy to profit from your services in the public relations section. If you are in agreement with this proposal, telegraph. Sepahbodi.

I will have to wait until I reach Washington to find out what this is about. <...>

THURSDAY 6 TO TUESDAY 18 SEPTEMBER 1945

Washington, D.C.

TUESDAY 18 SEPTEMBER 1945

At 1:00 P.M. I traveled to New York from Washington D.C. with Dr. Daftari. We arrived at five and went to the home of Mr. Hoseyn Navab, the consul general. After tea and a Persian dinner, Dr. Ahmad Farhad and I went to the Essex House where we shared a room.

Dr. Ahmad Farhad is the son of Abdolhoseyn Khan Moshir Akram, himself the son of Mirza Musa Vazir-e Lashgar (died 1919). After the death of Mirza Mohammad Qavvam al-Dowleh, Vazir-e Lashgar married his wife Esmat al-Dowleh, the daughter of Prince Farhad Mirza Mo'tamed al-Dowleh (whose mother was the daughter of Mohammad Ali Mirza Dowlatshah and one of the beauties of her time). That marriage produced Moshir Akram, who today is an elderly man of seventy. Dr. Ahmad Farhad is a young man of about thirty-seven, who completed his medical studies in Germany and is the leading radiologist in Tehran. He also teaches anatomy at the medical school. We have been friends for several years. On this trip to America we have been together often. He is very even-tempered, well educated, rational, patient, and a man of taste and refinement. One of the blessings of this trip to the United States has been the opportunity to become more familiar with this exceptional man. As our acquaintance matures, we have grown closer and closer in mind and spirit.

Several pages on the Princeton Library.

SUNDAY 7 OCTOBER 1945

At 9:20 A.M. Dr. Ahmad Farhad, my dear friend and trusted companion, and I left by train for Montreal. Mr. Hoseyn Navab saw us off. We had breakfast on the train and arrived in Montreal at 7:25 P.M. The Montreal is a fine hotel with spacious lounges.

MONDAY 8 OCTOBER 1945

Because today is Thanksgiving in Canada everything is closed. We walked around from 9:00 A.M. to 1:00 in the afternoon. Montreal is a very pleasant city similar to places in France without the crowds and the congestion. More than one million people live here. Among the places we visited was McGill University, which is an English-language institution. At the University of Montreal French is the language of instruction. We spoke with an elderly man about the French. He said that there were four million in Quebec, but most of the business and trade was in the hands of the English. I asked him about what the French did for a living. He said sarcastically that they either become lawyers or priests, which actually did summarize the situation nicely.

The Canadians have their own ways of speaking French and English.

TUESDAY 9 OCTOBER 1945

Having set out at 9:15 A.M., we entered Quebec City by 1:35 that afternoon. We stayed at the Frontenac, the finest hotel in the city. While in New York Mr. Pour Reza had invited us to dinner and two nights before our departure arranged a meeting with a Canadian woman, Cécile Bélisle. From the moment we met her, this young lady was a model of graciousness and goodness, and later proved to be our closest friend in Canada.

Upon our arrival in Montreal we went to the hotel and they gave Dr. Farhad and me the rooms that had been reserved for us. Less than a half an hour later there was a call from Cécile, saying that she was on her way to Quebec. She only had wanted to ask about us and make sure that we had a room there. She also promised to meet us in Quebec. When we reached the city and didn't see her, it was clear that she thought we were arriving at 5:00 (as had been planned). Later she came to the hotel and telephoned. The moment we came down, we noticed that she was with a lady, Madame Tourjeune. Madame Tourjeune was about forty-five and rarely in my life have I met a woman with such enthusiasm, energy and personality. She has a large laundry business with three hundred employees and modern equipment. She is also the mother of eight, one twenty-one-year-old daughter named Suzanne and seven sons, the oldest of whom is twenty-five. She has made her eldest son manager of the laundry. Her husband is also there, but, unlike his wife, he is not a real worker. This woman is a familiar figure in all of Quebec's prominent places. She is a magical speaker, unmatched for her repartee, eloquence, and wit. She possesses all the qualities of a man, but her femininity is unsurpassed. Often one sees a manlike woman, but she has no feminine charm; they are similar to effeminate men, who are wholly like women having lost all their masculine traits. But this lady for all her energy, intelligence and imagination still has all the charms and refinement of an upper-class French woman. Though in her forties, she possesses the beauty of a woman fifteen years her junior and her twenty-one-year-old daughter is more like her younger sister.

Added to all these charms is a talent for writing. She gave me an account of one of her trips, which I read. She also has an ear for poetry. The evening we arrived Dr. Farhad and I had dinner with her and Cécile. At nine the next morning she came with her car and chauffeured us around to all the sites in the city. We saw several churches, other famous buildings and the university. We traveled by ferry to the adjacent town of St. Louis. Later we had lunch at a restaurant at the Hôtel de Ville plaza. That afternoon we visited her laundry and then traveled several miles outside of town. Through her acquaintance with a Dominican priest named Levesque, the head of the university's faculty of social sciences and a distinguished man, we were invited to visit and dine at the school. Later we would cap off the evening together at her home. <...>

At six Dr. Farhad and I went to the university. Levesque is a man of forty-two, extremely intelligent and learned. His appointment as dean of the faculty at such an age attests to that intelligence. He dresses like a Dominican friar. He spoke for an hour about the various departments at the university. He explained that in 1760 when the British took possession of Canada, all of the French men of distinction and academicians returned to France, leaving behind a group of peasants and tradesmen.

The clergy remained to protect the people and founded schools and other institutions that resisted Anglicization in a variety of ways. They preserved French arts and crafts, institutions and the French language. There was also some discussion of the issues facing the university and its institutions. With us was Bruno Lafleur, a graduate of Laval University and a journalist. He is an intelligent young writer with connections in the government. Also joining us for dinner at the faculty club was Madame Tourjeune's second son, the twenty-four-year-old Marcel, a graduate of the law faculty. The club was elegant. In the lounge the priest ordered drinks, and we had cocktails, as the Americans say. We then went to the restaurant and had an excellent meal with particularly fine wine. The waitresses who served in the club were striking, and the priest—whatever one might have thought—proved to be both broad-minded and quite the bon vivant.

Conversation around the table covered many topics: the various beliefs and ideas of people from nations all over the world; church history, especially the views of Ernest Renan.[9] I asked why the church excommunicated him and characterized his writings as blasphemous. His *Vie de Jésus* (Life of Christ) presents the Messiah as the greatest and most faithful friend mankind ever had. There was no way, I said, that one could read that book and not feel Renan's love and affection for Christ. As a non-Christian, had I not even heard of Christ, this one book by Renan would be enough to create in me a world of love and respect for the Messiah. If this were the case, why was he excommunicated? The priest said that he was in complete agreement. Renan was very useful to non-Christians, he explained, because nothing is expected of them. But for believers his book is out of bounds, because Renan uses psychological and humanistic standards to judge Christ. This kind of analysis defies accepted religious belief, which rests on a set of shared intuitions and mysteries and without which there would be no faith. He personally considered Renan to be a great scholar, but for the community of Christian devout he thought his book harmful, as it brings Christ down from heaven and portrays him as a great human, not the God and His son of Catholic teaching.

We also spoke of the books of Anatole France and Stendahl.[10] The enlightened point of view of this priest knows no limits. He is also rather good-looking. After dinner he, M. Bruno, Dr. Farhad and I got into Marcel's car and went to the home of Madame Tourjeune. There we met a young lady, a secretary to a lawyer and Marcel's friend, Suzanne, a handsome nineteen-year-old, and Madame Tourjeune's fifteen-year-old son, an accomplished pianist. With the gathering now musical, the full extent of the priest's profound hold on life became apparent. He clearly had a good voice and was a skilled violinist. As the piano played he was in ecstasy, transported to another world. He strummed the violin with two hands, humming a tune and joking all the while.

To cap off the evening Madame Tourjeune served cakes with coffee and tea. When we came to the table, she teased the priest. She showed me my seat and placed her son's girlfriend and Cécile on either side of me. She sat next to Dr. Farhad and said that sitting beside the priest was out of bounds for the ladies. The priest retorted, "That's what you say, but what would happen if one of them decided to sit by me?" Madame. Tourjeune's daughter in the sweetest way possible then sat down next to him. We stayed until one in the morning and then returned to the hotel by car.

WEDNESDAY 17 OCTOBER 1945

<...> Yesterday, I discussed a range of things with Madame Tourjeune, from psychological and sociological issues, the afterlife and religion, to poetry and emotions, etc. Then with typical candor and intelligence she told me that she would dearly like to visit my country, which she graciously described as a seat of wisdom and learning. "Of course," she added, "in addition to the culture of your own country you are steeped in Western sciences and literature, you have traveled and mixed with every sort of person. But there is one aspect of your national makeup that from what I can tell is very important: their mentality being what it is, how could your people accept Islam?" <...> I replied that I was not a narrow-minded zealot, but supposing that the good opinion she had of my country when she praised it for its taste and open-mindedness was true, what contradiction was there between all that and Islam? I asked, "Are you well read in the religion or have you ever encountered a learned Moslem? Have you studied the history of science and the evolution of civilization closely or comparatively?" She said that she hadn't. "So," I said, "the sum total of what you know comes via a handful of either biased or ignorant clerics, who themselves often have no firm basis for judgment and depend solely on rumors spread by their predecessors. One can trace their views back from generation to generation until we reach the first centuries of Islam, when Christians considered the religion the greatest threat to their own faith. Because they had no logical way of combating it, they resorted to all sorts of insulting nonsense."

Until the last years of the nineteenth century, there were two types of interpreters of Islam and Moslems in the nations of Europe. The ignorant or prejudiced clerics formed one group, while politicians, and the agents of imperialism and commerce, who come from the lowest and foulest ranks of society, the other. The latter are people who brazenly use any means required to advance their material interests. Toward the end of the nineteenth century Carlyle[11] showed the rarest courage by praising Mohammad as one of the heroic figures of human history. At the same time and early in the twentieth century, open-minded people from various nations began to study Moslem beliefs, sciences, history and literature using modern methodologies. These efforts have progressed gradually, and day by day lift the curtain on the rumors and falsehoods.

I told Madame Tourjeune that her view would be exactly the same as my forming my understanding of Christianity, the person of Jesus Christ, Mary, and the Apostles solely based on the ravings of some partisan and uninformed rabbis living along the shores of Lake Tiberias. At one gathering where Father Levesque was present with Madame Tourjeune, her daughter and several others, I steered the discussion with the father in such a way as to eliminate any doubts in her mind. And in case she sensed collusion, the encyclopedically learned divine with that clerical robe draped on his shoulders would not brook any laxness or excessive shows of courtesy. I explained that during the Dark Ages when ignorance had spread throughout the ancient world and Greek learning and science were in danger of disappearing, the Moslems took up the torch of knowledge. Not only did they preserve Greek, Roman and other nations' intellectual heritages, but they also augmented those traditions considerably. They worked in the fields of medicine, mathematics, philosophy, literature, chemistry, natural science, astronomy, etc. Diverse peoples from the shores of the Atlantic to the China Sea, from the heart of India to beyond the Caucasus, became acquainted with those fields. They created a religious society that put racial and gender biases aside. The one thing that united the society was the Islamic faith and the fact that all were engaged in learning and teaching. Later Europeans became aware of those sciences, especially in Andalusian seminaries, and from Hebrew and Latin translations. This was how the teachings of thousands of great thinkers like Khwarazmi, Biruni, Razi, Ebn Sina (Avicenna), Ghazzali, Ebn Beytar, Ebn Rushd (Averroes) and Abu al-Qasem Zahrawi circulated. St. Dominic, the founder of the order (to which the priest belongs), was a student of Ebn Rushd's philosophy. <...> Dante considers Ebn Rushd the commentator on Aristotle. In Osler's[12] words, Avicenna's *Canon* was "for centuries the Bible of medicine." For ages universities in Naples, Bologna, Paris, Salerno, and Montpellier were engaged in translating the works of Moslem writers. Thousands of scientific terms were absorbed directly from Arabic into European languages. Many learned works from Greece and Rome, the originals of which were lost, existed only in Arabic and Syriac translations. Much was said along these lines and the fathers supported every word and even occasionally facilitated the talk by providing fresh evidence. <...> I was very gratified to see Madame Tourjeune completely convinced and relieved of any misconceptions. During the discussion, it was also said that all of the writings by Western clerics on Mohammad and Islam essentially boil down to two points:

1. That Mohammad was an ambitious man greedy for power and position, one who climbed so high that he called himself Prophet of God.
2. That Mohammad was addicted to the pleasures of the banquet and the bedroom, had many wives and even fashioned a heaven filled with the mouth-watering fruits of this world, with its delicacies and drinks, and with beautiful women. <...>

At another session, they asked about Moslem beliefs about Christians. These poor souls thought that Islam knew nothing of Jesus and considered Christians their enemies. They were astonished to learn that the three faiths, Judaism, Christianity and Islam, are like sisters, derived from one religious substratum. The Qur'an considers Jesus the "spirit of God" or the "holy spirit," and Mary the supreme manifestation of piety, chastity, innocence and purity. And if

Moslems object to anything, it is to the hyperbole of Christians, not to the fundamentals of their faith. I said jokingly that they didn't have to try to convert me, as the only difference between us was in the manner of belief rather than its substance. <...>

Then there was a discussion of the four Gospels, the Acts of the Apostles, Letters of Paul and John, etc. I asked which was the oldest and most trustworthy manuscripts of these texts and whether Renan and others, who are doubtful about the existence of Christ, are justified in their perplexity. <...>

On Tuesday 23 October 1945, Dr. Ghani left Canada and traveled by train to Washington, D.C.

SUNDAY 11 NOVEMBER 1945

Dr. Ghani saw former Minister of Court and now Ambassador to the U.S. Hoseyn Ala, who told him that Queen Fawzia suffered a recent bout of malaria.

<...> The shah proposed that she travel to Egypt, which means that Fawzia had resisted the idea. But at the same time the king of Egypt invited her to spend the summer in Alexandria with him (Tabet Pasha, who had been informed of her condition, may have proposed this). In any case Fawzia along with Lieutenant General Morteza Yazdanpanah and his wife, Colonel Amini and his wife, Mohsen Qaraguzlu, and the wife of General Arfa' were going to stay at the Antoniades Palace in Alexandria. Soon thereafter Farouq summoned Mr. Jam to tell him that Fawzia will not return to Iran. Queen Nazli is against divorce, but Farouq reiterates that Fawzia will not return.

I know the story of this marriage better than anyone. On the first trip (June 1938) I spent fifteen days in Alexandria, to bring the Qur'an, the wedding ring, etc. The next time (February 1939) I accompanied His Majesty to the wedding, which took place at the Abedin Palace. I personally witnessed everything that happened on the return trip to Iran on the ship *Mohammad Ali Pasha*. Queen

Nazli, her daughters, a group of other Egyptians, and Minister Zulfiqar Pasha were on board. The Iranian queen and her daughters were at Bandar-e Shah to greet the ship. If I have the opportunity I will record everything I witnessed on those trips. It will make something worth keeping. Though the shah and Fawzia are fine people, the problem is that the court is corrupt and is bound to have a negative effect on them.

THURSDAY 15 NOVEMBER 1945

Traveled to Baltimore and spent the entire day at the Johns Hopkins Library, which houses nearly 600,000 volumes. <...> Spent several hours looking at their books on Islamic medicine. There were a few misidentifications that I pointed out and that were rectified. <...> Brief visit to New York. <...>

MONDAY 31 DECEMBER 1945

Left for Princeton early because I have a 3:30 meeting with Dr. Albert Einstein. <...> Some time ago the Iranian Embassy had invited Dr. Ernest Herzfeld,[13] one of the leading archeologists of ancient Iran, for lunch. As he teaches at Princeton, I expressed an interest in meeting Einstein, and he said he would arrange it. On 16 December he wrote in French that Einstein would meet me on a day of my choosing.

Herzfeld was at the station. We went to his home and we spoke about the excavation of certain sites in Iran. Later I met Dr. Wolfgang Pauli,[14] the Nobel laureate in physics. This very humble man, who is not even forty, teaches at Princeton's Institute of Advanced Studies. He had heard about me from Herzfeld and, because of an interest in neo-Platonic theory, wanted to meet me. We spoke for more than an hour. At 3:30 we entered Einstein's small, two-story home. His secretary and caretaker greeted us and led us up the small stairs to Einstein's study. There was the old man radiant and immaculate; to quote Rumi,

He saw an aged man of perfection
A sun among the shades in reflection.

He was of medium height and clean-shaven. On his head was a halo of white hair, long and a bit unkempt.

Einstein welcomed us warmly to a modest study that contained some 200 books and two cases with notes and papers. There was a simple desk covered by a few papers and, in the middle of the room, an old table with a crystal jar for his tobacco and pipe. We sat and he said how happy he was to meet me. Before our meeting, I had asked Herzfeld which language one should speak with him, English or French. Herzfeld asked Einstein who said that he spoke neither language well, but out of necessity it would have to be English. I suggested that he

Dr. Albert Einstein signed the back of this photograph "To my learned friend, Dr. Ghasem Ghani"

had more important things to do than learn languages. He observed that translating scientific writing did not present a problem, but literary works were another matter. They were untranslatable. I said that in a biography of Anatole France, I had read that the writer had met Einstein in Berlin in 1921. Thus I thought he would have preferred French. He said that his French was more fluent in those days, and Anatole France knew no other languages. Einstein felt that a writer should not learn a foreign language, because it would disrupt the elegance of his mother tongue. I told him that I had heard that France considered Goethe the greatest thinker. Einstein confirmed that France admired Goethe very much. He then described France. When he met him, France was very old, but knew his mind was clear. I told him that I seemed to recall that France also spoke very highly of another individual whose name I could not recall. Looking back, Einstein recalled that three things gave France some consolation in the chaotic world we inhabit: Greek art and science, Racine's poetry and the depth of Goethe's thought. I asked him whether France discussed science with him. He said that they just talked generally. <...>

He then asked me about my own interests. I said that I was primarily a physician. The thing that interested me the most was the history of civilization and learning. I told him about the transfer of Greek, Roman, Assyrian and Persian science through Arabic translations. How this led to the rise of the great thinkers of Islamic civilization: Avicenna in philosophy, Razi in medicine, Abu Reyhan in mathematics. He was so taken with this that no matter how hard I tried to pose a question, he kept probing me for more information. I told him that Hippocrates thought that a physician had to have two wings—one experiential, the other theoretical—otherwise he could not fly. The two aspects of medicine, the intellectual and the practical had to guide and mediate one another. This interested him. He said that nowadays they placed too much stock in positivism. There are problems that cannot be approached through experimentation alone. I concluded that he was not well disposed to the American version of the scientific method. He smiled and said that science in this country had been reduced to practicality, had become too result-oriented. He mentioned the pragmatism of William James and gave the following example. When one asks Americans what a fork is, they will say, "Something that facilitates eating." But this does not define the fork.

Einstein quickly went right to the heart of every issue that I would raise in a general sort of way, which is the sign of a seasoned scientist. He said that one had to consider reasoning, logic and other human faculties before resorting to experience. He emphasized the role of intuition in scientific discovery and invention. <...>

I admitted that when I was anticipating our meeting, I remembered a poem by Hatef Esfahani (died late eighteenth century), which I translated for him:

Open the heart's eye to view the soul;
See what is invisible;
Hear what is inaudible;
Eye that which is unseeable.
In the kernel of every atom you split
See the sun that resides therein.

He immediately grasped the allusion and, to my delight, explained the poem simply and concisely. He said that the ancients, specifically Democritus, had intuited the smallest particle of nature and imagined that a sun was nestled inside of it. This elegant idea lies outside the realm of experience. <…>

I asked Einstein about Rabindranath Tagore,[15] whom he had also met. He said that Tagore in *The World and the Home* attacked Indian nationalists, especially Gandhi. According to Einstein, Tagore thought the European nationalist model wrong for India. I also mentioned I had read the works of Henri Poincaré,[16] the French mathematician. At this his eyes lit up and he said that Poincaré was without peer. The only trouble with the mathematician was that he was very much the positivist. I asked whether he, like Poincaré, had ever written anything about his work for general audiences. He said he had not. I then brought up a recently published article of his in which he advocated world government. I asked him to explain what he meant. He said that the three leading powers should form judicial and governmental organizations for solving problems. I asked whether this was feasible. He replied that without such an organization war was inevitable and the next war would differ from all previous ones in its destructiveness. <…>

All in all I spent two and a half hours in the presence of this great man. He speaks with a German accent, but his English is fluent and educated, if deliberate. He dresses very plainly but is dignified like the great teacher he is. He is extraordinarily good-looking with a broad forehead and enchanting eyes. I apologized for taking so much of his time, but he dismissed this and invited me to call on him again. In turn, I invited him to Iran where all Iranians would be honored by his presence. The conversation then turned to the weather in Iran. He asked whether it was dry there. When I told him it was, he said that he would like to visit the country. I added that we had a beautiful, clear sky that allows one to think. When the secretary brought tea, he lit his pipe and I had a cigarette. He insisted on showing me out of his home, and as I left I thought of how fortunate it was to have spent time with one of the greatest minds in science. His discoveries put him on a par with—or perhaps above—figures like Kepler, Galileo and Newton. Despite this, the simplicity of his life and his utter unpretentiousness make Einstein the rarest of humans.

At 6:00 Herzfeld's car drove me to the station and I reached Washington around 11:30 P.M. A memorable day.

TUESDAY 1 JANUARY 1946

Yesterday while waiting for the train a gust of wind took my hat. This evening, having obtained a hat more suitable to my head, I dined with Dr. Daftari and his wife and told them all about my trip to Princeton. Wrote a letter to Herzfeld. <...>

THURSDAY 3 JANUARY 1946

Wrote a letter to Einstein thanking him for the visit. <...>

THURSDAY 10 JANUARY 1946

Went to Harvard University. Saw the museum and library. Had lunch with several professors. <...>

SUNDAY 10 FEBRUARY 1946

7:00 A.M. departed by car to the West Coast, traveled relatively quickly covering 440 miles. <...> Reached North Carolina by lunchtime, Columbia, South Carolina, by 4:00 P.M. [Dr. Ghani's travels also took him through Florida, Louisiana, Texas, New Mexico, Arizona, and California, some 4,500 miles. From 20 February to 9 March 1946, Dr.

Ghani spent his time in Los Angeles and the San Francisco area, Berkeley and Palo Alto. Sees Dr. Rosencrantz, Maryam Mehran… Taqinia, Jamshid Amuzegar, Hafez Farmanfarmaian, Mirza Mehdi, among others.]

FRIDAY 8 MARCH 1946

Saw Dr. Rosencrantz and presented her with an Esfahani embroidered kerchief. Retired now for two years, she was a pulmonary specialist, the product of Johns Hopkins celebrated medical school. Despite this she is as naïve as a ten-year-old, though entirely personable and warm-hearted. The subject of Italy and the Catholic Church came up, and I cannot describe how childish her judgments and generalizations were. The pressures of everyday life do not allow these people to examine anything in depth. For example, the other night she said that she did not like Anatole France. When I asked what she had read of his, she said, "Nothing." I asked her that as a person of science, on what basis she came to such a conclusion, not having read any of his works. "His morals," she said. She condemned him for divorcing his wife and marrying his thirty-five-year-old maid when he was in his seventies. I replied that this was a good thing, as it enabled the maid to become Mrs. France and entitled to her husband's legacy. Besides, I asked, what does his morality have to do with his art? Because da Vinci was lame, should we say that his paintings are bad? She also judged the physician Sir William Osler superior to Shakespeare on moral grounds. <…>

The doctor is a perfect example of middle-class Americans, a group of people who speak mechanically about their own narrow specialties. They are wholly creatures of immediate sensation, satisfied with emotions of the moment rather than abstractions. She read me the program for the retirement dinner her students held and commented how wonderful it was. One of the big differences between Easterners and these people is that our minds are in constant motion and flux, always seeking some distant object. Surface sensations and realities do not engage us. Our minds seek the unknown, the illusory, transcendent matters that defy facile description. This certainly is better than the immediate and the actual. Our minds do not stop to enjoy the happiness we find, but race ahead trying to intuit some other reality. Americans are superb at details. Their minds act as cameras capturing what they see with photographic fidelity. Delighted by these details, they do not prize discovering their "general patterns" nor do they look into what is behind them. Easterners are forever in pursuit of ultimate causes because their minds are at once subtle and fugitive. This is both good and bad, just as is Americans' exaggerated sense of reality.

After growing confident behind the wheel, Dr. Ghani began to drive himself on the trip back to the East Coast.

SUNDAY 10 MARCH 1946

The natives in this part of the United States differ from those in other parts. They are simpler and more natural. Stayed for a while in Las Vegas and then traveled on. At five left Nevada and entered Utah.

Americans are afraid to think. Nevertheless most of them are prosperous, their material needs taken care of. There are very few impoverished Americans. I am reminded of the story Rumi tells about the Arab who put a heavy stone on one side of his camel to balance its load. An indigent man tells him to divide the load into two equal parts; this way the camel would not have to carry so much weight and there would be room for the Arab to ride. Taken aback by this advice, the dim-witted Arab asked the poor man how he figured that out. Using my mind, said the man. The Arab asked him how many camels he had. None, replied the man. He then asked, how many sheep? How much land? The answer was always the same: none. The Arab finally concluded, To hell with the "mind"; the only thing it's good for is poverty. I'll take prosperity over having a mind any day. He then made his camel kneel and loaded it the way he had previously done.

FRIDAY 15 MARCH 1946

Left early this morning and had breakfast along the way. After about a hundred miles, my tires ran over some broken glass. At the service station, I asked them to inspect the tires, and they said they were fine. I continued going toward the Mexican border. About a hundred miles outside of Laredo on a clear stretch of highway, the tire suddenly blew and I lost control of the wheel. The next thing I knew I was lying on the ground fifteen feet from the car. For a moment I hovered between life and death, but soon I regained my senses, started to breathe, and had no internal pain. But then I noticed that my left leg had begun to contort at an angle and the pain became so intense that I realized that my thigh was broken. I managed to straighten the left leg with the right, and the pain decreased. I also lit a cigarette, all the while keeping the pressure on the broken leg. No cigarette in my life has given me the solace, nor tasted as good as that one. It was perhaps about twenty-five minutes before another vehicle came by. Eventually the local sheriff came with an ambulance—a hearse really. They injected me with morphine. A very kind Mexican priest, who later visited me several times in the hospital, appeared and asked if I were Catholic. Though I said no, he prayed to Jesus for my recovery. A shabby-looking old man also came by and allowed them to tear up his field in order to transfer me to the hearse. Once I was in the hospital, they gave me more painkillers and I spent most of the night unconscious. They also injected me with penicillin every three hours. I was to be in surgery at eleven the next morning. The possibility that I would die under the anesthetic was very real, as my heart was weak and I was overweight. During that difficult night, before drifting into unconsciousness, I wrote several friends.

SATURDAY 16 MARCH 1946

They patched my leg with metal pins. When I awoke at five, the Mexican father and some nurses were at my bedside. The pain and the drugs put me in an indescribable state.<...>

MONDAY 18 MARCH 1946

The young insurance agent and his wife visited. The company will repair the car or provide a replacement. All hospital costs are covered.

TUESDAY 19 MARCH 1946

Friends have sent their good wishes, flowers, my favorite foods, an electric razor, etc. <...>

THURSDAY 18 APRIL 1946

Have been in the hospital for five weeks. My knee and leg muscles have responded to treatment and I can walk slowly. <...> By next week I will be able to walk with crutches. <...>

THURSDAY 25 APRIL 1946

This afternoon, while reading the *New York Times* dated the 23 April, I came across a photo of Dr. Daftari. The article said that on the twenty-first, Easter Sunday, he had lunch at the home of Mr. Nemazi with his wife and Ambassador and Mrs. Ala. After lunch Dr. Daftari went to rest and died in his sleep, a victim of a heart attack at the age of forty-six. I was so angry I could have screamed! In the blink of an eye, a young man of such energy, quality and promise died with all the hopes he had for his two children: Jamshid (seventeen) and Shahnaz (fourteen).

My friendship with Dr. Ali Akbar Daftari began in 1939 in Tehran. We renewed our acquaintance in San Francisco in 1945, when he was advisor to the mission to the United Nations. He was of average height, a little overweight, with a ruddy face and very prominent eyebrows. He was extremely intelligent, experienced in the ways of the world and very sociable. After graduating from the German school in Tehran, he went into the Foreign Service, becoming for a time a counsellor at the Iranian Embassy in Kabul. There he married Zahra, the kind and accomplished daughter of Ambassador E'tela al-Molk Khal'atbari. He was the second son of Eyn al-Mamalek, two years younger than his brother Dr. Matin Daftari. After Kabul he was assigned to the Ministry of Foreign Affairs. He later worked at the Ministry of Justice with Davar. In Germany he obtained a doctorate of law. He was a fine writer, particularly of administrative reports. One of his special traits was to take the measure of people quickly and keenly. He had no use for mediocre people but acted with exemplary modesty toward superior individuals.

Around 1939 Dr. Daftari was summoned from Washington to Tehran. At that time his brother, Dr. Matin Daftari, was minister of justice and shortly thereafter was to become prime minister. Six months later Reza Shah imprisoned the two, but after the shah's abdication and exile, Dr. Daftari, the younger, was again serving in Washington, becoming chargé d'affaires at the Iranian Embassy.

Though my close friendship with Dr. Daftari only blossomed during this last year, we were so familiar that it is as if we had known one another for at least ten years. In San Francisco besides our daily work meetings, he would come to my hotel room around 10:00 P.M., and we would talk until 2:00 the next morning. When separated, we corresponded regularly. When in Washington I was, in effect, his houseguest for three months. On April 14, one week before his death, he called me at the hospital to ask when I would be out of bed. I jokingly told him that it would take months of recuperation and walking on crutches, and he responded in kind by telling me to hurry because he missed me.

The late Dr. Daftari was an amalgam of the choice characteristics and habits of Westerners and the best features of an Iranian personality. While he had traveled the world widely on numerous long missions and associated with all sorts of Europeans and Americans, he never indulged in a slavish imitation of the West. He fully understood the negative aspects of Western culture and was able to glean the good things from it and graft them onto traditional Iranian virtues. He was religious in an enlightened way, said his prayers, read the Qur'an and honored the principles of Islam; however, he was not a zealot. <...>

SATURDAY 27 APRIL 1946

Beginning yesterday I was moved from the bed. With the help of two nurses and a cane I walked a few steps. I had no sense of direction or balance and nearly fell several times. I was extremely exhausted by the few steps I took. <...>

THURSDAY 23 MAY 1946

<...> Traveled to Washington by train. <...>

MONDAY 21 OCTOBER 1946

<...> To New York. I am a delegate to the General Assembly of the United Nations. Mr. Ala has duties in Washington. Mr. Qavam, the prime minister, who was to head the delegation, cannot attend. I don't know whether I can carry out my duties. <...>

TUESDAY 29 OCTOBER 1946

Back to Washington. <...>

THURSDAY 31 OCTOBER 1946

I submitted my resignation from the UN post.

WEDNESDAY 4 DECEMBER 1946

<...> Saw a specialist twice. I generally pass the time reading in bed and spending time with Iranian visitors. There is a regular stream here at the home of Hajj Mohammad Nemazi. Sundays he holds an open-invitation at home that men and women, young and old, attend. These are friendly gatherings with Persian and European food, children playing, people talking or playing backgammon or chess. The place has the air of a delightful, informal club.

The host, Hajj Mohammad Nemazi, the son of the late Mohammad Hasan Nemazi, <...> is around fifty, very well-educated and traveled, clever, and dependable. He speaks English extremely well. Though his post as a commercial attaché at the embassy is honorary, he conducts almost all of its important business.

MONDAY 17 MARCH 1947

To Los Angeles by train. <...>

THURSDAY 27 MARCH 1947

Traveled by train to San Francisco. Mirza Mehdi greeted me at the station and took me to the hotel where he had made a reservation.

MONDAY 7 APRIL 1947

Was at the home of Dr. Rosencrantz tonight with the renowned biochemists Professors Herbert Evans and Karl Meyer, and others. Despite the august company, the evening passed in typically American conversations—trivial and rushed. At these gatherings, even with renowned scientists present, whenever a serious subject comes up there may be some discussion, but the talk soon turns mundane—food, travel, the weather, etc. Americans regardless of age or gender are generally cold-blooded; they never go to extremes whether they love or whether they hate. If an Easterner, for example, meets someone he is fond of after an absence of six months, he cannot contain his enthusiasm. For an American in such a situation it is as if he had seen the friend just an hour before—his face masks all feeling and warmth. A simple hello suffices and he moves on.

WEDNESDAY 16 APRIL 1947

<...> I heard that Gholamhoseyn Ghaffari Saheb Ekhtiar has died in Tehran. I was greatly saddened. He was a close friend.

SUNDAY 20 APRIL 1947

Nothing is more intriguing than the amateur study of human behavior. Each individual is a world unto himself. Each is at the center of a universe looking out at the surroundings and considering anyone beside himself superfluous. Of course, we all have certain things in common and fall into identifiable categories. But on closer inspection, one finds that each person is unique, foreign to the rest of humanity.

My travels here have shown me how different Iranians are from one another. In Los Angeles, Abbas Masoudi, Farmi, Pur Reza, Dr. Afshar, Dr. Sohrabi, Prince Mahmud Reza and several students—they are all unique in their own ways. A few weeks ago, on the second day of the Persian New Year celebrations, the talk was of Sa'di and advice to leave the house to find one's heart's desire in nature. To discover God's hand in the marvels of the mountains, seas, trees. Someone recited Sa'di's verse:

How long like the violet will your head nod in disregard
The shame is that while you sleep, the narcissus is wide awake.

One of the Iranians, a mathematics professor, asked in all candor, "what do 'the violet asleep and the narcissus being awake' have to do with one another?" I tried to explain the figurative language in the poem and gave him examples of metaphors from everyday speech, but no matter what I said it did not penetrate. In the end the beauty of Persian poetry that everyone acclaims remained mysterious to him. I thought to myself, his opinion would be the same no matter the topic: politics, sociology, morality, good and evil, aesthetics. God forbid he rise to some position of authority where this opinion could influence public affairs. History provides many examples especially in the East where people are prone to be fatalistic. They accept catastrophes caused by warped minds and their crooked policies the same way they bow to natural disasters like storms and epidemics.

People often dismiss leaders of bloody revolutions like Robespierre[17] and Marat[18] as "monsters," but science does not believe in monsters. One must examine these people closely to understand the reasons for their actions. Robespierre was a man with absolute faith in piety, while Marat was one who believed in justice. As followers of Jean Jacques Rousseau,[19] they thought society corrupted human nature. By annihilating the corrupt they felt that they would purify a corrupt society. With the best of intentions they had thousands killed. Their dogmatism is like our mathematicians blind faith in his solitary science. He recognized no truth other than mathematical truth. This intellectual myopia has demeaned him and made him proud of his own ignorance at the same time. Having rejected all forms of reasoning and logic, other than his own, he could not have the slightest inkling of aesthetic beauty.

People are indeed odd, and the oddest thing is to find people of moderate temperament. One of the chronic evils of our time is the doctorate in philosophy. The degree so intoxicates mediocrities with doctorates that they imagine they have scaled the heights of human understanding. <...>

WEDNESDAY 23 APRIL 1947

It is the first day of Ordibehesht, the second month of the Iranian year, and everywhere in America looks like everywhere else. A young country, it does not have to shoulder the heavy historical and cultural burdens that nations of the ancient world bear. The vast networks connecting every branch of industry and the uniformity of state and cultural institutions have homogenized America. Of course there is variation in the landscape, but when it comes to human habitation, one always sees the same shops, department stores, clothing, downtowns, streets, neo-Gothic cathedrals, etc. Having spent six years in America, André Maurois[20] wrote that the first thing a European notices about it is its "unity."

He was referring to the superficial sameness of American life. Wherever one travels from Tampa to Seattle and from New York to San Francisco, the language is English, and the magazines—the standards of living, the philosophy of life, the role of public opinion—likewise the same. This outward sameness represents an inward intellectual and spiritual uniformity. By contrast, in Europe one finds tremendous variation in languages, food, clothing and manners. Similarly in Iran there is a world of difference between someone from

Yazd and someone from Qazvin, for example. Even within one province people's languages, food and drink, thinking and tastes vary greatly from town to town and neighborhood to neighborhood.

Another difference between a European country like France and America is that one rarely sees land that is not under cultivation in Europe; while in the United States, along the Missouri River for example, there is virtually a "continent" of vacant territory. This is in part why one does not encounter in America the old-world form of jealousy and envy of others' property. In Europe, for centuries and even today, one's neighbors were and are potential competitors for land and water. The major part of litigation and criminal activity among neighbors revolves around property rights in Europe. In America this is not the case. Though the world's languages contain thousands of maxims advising neighborliness—and in some places the advice may be taken—it is only in America that we see the reality. In rural areas Americans gather at clubs and cultivate friendships. Of course, the kind of friendship they practice, tepid and unassuming, is quite unlike the extravagant and acute Eastern variety. But the important thing here is respect for the rights of others. America is democratic in the fullest sense of the term. Democracy is second nature to average Americans, though they are unconscious of how innately democratic they are. Those who are honest by nature or kind and generous are unaware of their goodness, and therein lies all their moral charm.

Of course there are social strata in America—professional, merchant, farmer, worker classes, etc., but one does not find the kind of imperious elites found in older countries. The classes in America are like the limbs of a body, each acting in concert without special distinction accorded to one limb over another. When queuing for tickets or waiting for a table at a restaurant, the upper classes must wait their turn just like everyone else. On a train, for example, with limited seating in the dining car, a senator or cabinet secretary will stand in line with the rest of humanity. The other important thing is that any breach of these rules is considered a "social flaw." In New York, when having lunch in the United Nations cafeteria, I observed how naturally Mrs. Roosevelt would stand in line with her tray. She was once involved in an automobile accident and freely admitted that she caused it by falling asleep at the wheel. As a result they took away her driver's license for a certain period.

America is one of those rare countries where democracy goes hand in hand with discipline. In many places there is democracy but no discipline and vice versa. Elections proceed as freely and orderly as possible, and even in times of war people have the right to criticize the government and the military so long as their criticism is responsible. People can tell the authorities what to do without fear of retribution.

Another thing that characterizes America is its scientific establishment. American pragmatism causes everything to conform to the exacting standards of science. Of course, there are great scientists and scientific foundations in Europe, however, nowhere is science more valued for its practical applications than in the United States. The disadvantage of this is the excessive uniformity one finds in American society. The same merchandise from buttons to canned goods are sold from one end of the country to the other. Likewise customers who deviate from the standard path fluster Americans. In a restaurant, for example, so long as one orders from the menu the waitress is bright and cheerful, but as soon as one strays from the normal choices, she is perplexed.

The abundance of consumer goods in America and its lifestyle, which tends to maximize convenience, have led to certain misconceptions. For example, people often say in exaggeration that there is no intellectual life in America, that its civilization is purely materialistic. Americans' attachment to their vast industrial infrastructure is not entirely based on worshipping the dollar. Rather, Americans take a genuinely nonmaterial pleasure in work, in producing "bigger and better" things. American culture has linked theory and practice to a remarkable extent. Education of the young is so important here that it has become a kind of religion. Far more Americans attend college than do their European counterparts, and American universities have lost their reputations as party and sports schools and become places of serious scholarship. <...>

MONDAY 5 MAY 1947

This afternoon the following telegram from Abdolhoseyn Dehqan arrived: "Congratulations on your appointment as ambassador to Egypt." Clearly they have received word and want to keep me informed.

TUESDAY 6 MAY 1947

I left Los Angeles by train at midnight and arrived in New York on May 9. Went to see Dehqan and his wife. There was a letter from Mr. Ala with a telegram from Prime Minister Qavam al-Saltaneh, which said, "Please indicate your willingness to assume the post of Iranian ambassador to Egypt. If you accept, travel to Iran and receive instructions from HIM the shah." Mr. Ala phoned insisting that I respond as soon as possible because the answer had been delayed. Since the offer has been on the table now for almost two years, I thought it the height of self-regard to refuse. I accepted. <…>

FRIDAY 20 JUNE 1947

The intestinal hemorrhaging has started again, and this time I feel very weak.

FRIDAY 4 JULY 1947

Entered the hospital. The day is auspicious; not only is it American Independence Day, it is also the Prophet's birthday. Amin, Firouz, and Cyrus, who had arrived from London on 26 June, are in New York. They stayed three or four days in a hotel and visited me. Gave several books to Cyrus. Books by Dostoyevsky,[21] Thomas Mann,[22] a one-volume Toynbee's history[23] and several others. <…>

TUESDAY 12 AUGUST 1947

<…> Left the U.S. for Cairo. <…>

NOTES

FIRST TRIP TO THE UNITED STATES

1. Dr. Herbert Mclean Evans (1882–1971). Anatomist and embryologist. Professor at University of California, Berkeley. Discovered hormone that promotes human growth. Discovered vitamin E. Nominated for the Nobel Prize in chemistry.

2. Dr. Ernest Orlando Lawrence (1901–58). Physicist; taught at the University of California, Berkeley. Inventor of the cyclotron. Winner of the Nobel Prize in physics, 1939.

3. Edward R. Stettinius, Jr. (1900–49). Industrialist from Chicago; secretary of state under Roosevelt and Truman. Attended the Yalta Conference.

4. Sattareh Farman Farmaian (1921–). Sociologist. Founder of the Tehran School of Social Work in 1958. Author of *Daughter of Persia* (NY, 1992).

5. A severely near-sighted cleric is marooned on a remote island inhabited only by penguins. He mistakes the penguins for human beings and attempts to convert them to Christianity.

6. Edward G. Browne (1862–1925). Studied medicine. The foremost Western scholar of Persian literature.

7. Alidad Farmanfarmaian (1924–). B.S. University of Wisconsin, M.S.University of Colorado. Became a successful entrepreneur in Iran with involvement in far-sighted industrial enterprises.

8. Alinaqi Farmanfarmaian (1922–). B.A.University of Wisconsin, Doctor of Public Administration, University of Southern California. Served several terms as Managing Director of the Industrial Credit Bank.

9 Ernest Renan (1823–92). Historian of religion. Best known for his secular study of the life of Jesus.

10. Marie Henri Beyle Stendhal (1783–1842). French novelist. Author of *The Red and the Black* and *The Charterhouse of Parma.*

11. Thomas Carlisle (1795–1881). Scottish historian, author of a study of the French Revolution and numerous other books and essays.

12. Sir William Osler (1849–1919). Canadian physician. Made important contributions to preventive medicine and medical research on internal organs.

13. Ernest F. Herzfeld (1879–1948). Archeologist of Mesopotamia and Iran. Made important discoveries in Assyrian sites and Pasargad.

14. Wolfgang Pauli (1900–58). Austrian-born physicist. Winner of the Nobel Prize in physics, 1945.

15. Rabindranath Tagore (1861–1941). Poet and prose writer born in India. Nobel Prize for literature, 1913.

16. Jules Henri Poincaré (1854–1912). French mathematician. His work on function theory contributed to physics and astronomy.

17. Maximilien Francois Marie Isidore de Robespierre (1758–94). Important figure in the early French Revolution. Responsible for the guillotining of more than 1,200 people.

18. Jean Paul Marat (born Switzerland, 1743–93). In the French Revolution, charismatic leader of radicals. Assassinated for his zealous attacks on the moderate Girondists.

19. Jean Jacques Rousseau (born Geneva, 1712–78). French political theorist; considered humans essentially good in their natural state. Author of *The Social Contract* and the autobiographical *Confessions*.

20. André Maurois (pen name of Èmile Salomon Wilhelm Herzog, 1885–1967). French author of biographies, including, Shelley, Byron, Voltaire and George Sand.

21. Fyodor Mikhailovich Dostoyevsky (1821–81). Russian novelist best known for *Crime and Punishment, The Idiot* and *The Brothers Karamazov.*

22. Thomas Mann (1875–1955). German novelist. Author of *Buddenbrooks, The Magic Mountain, Joseph and his Brothers.* Also wrote the short stories "Tonio Kroger" and "Death in Venice."

23. Arnold Joseph Toynbee (1889–1975). Historian. Wrote the multi-volume *A Study of History.*

AMBASSADOR TO EGYPT

The following notes, reports and telegrams, pertaining to Dr. Ghani's tenure as Iranian ambassador to Egypt consist of three sections:

1. A short history of the engagement of Crown Prince Mohammad Reza to Princess Fawzia of Egypt;

2. Reports related to Fawzia's 1945 trip to Egypt; and

3. Matters related to Dr. Ghani's ambassadorship itself.

Supplementing these are a few selected entries from Dr. Ghani's daily diaries, which form a separate volume of some 400 pages in the original. They are more personal and amplify many of his official reports.

The notes begin with a short biography of the young crown prince.

MOHAMMAD REZA PAHLAVI, the son of Reza Shah, was born on 27 October 1919. At the age of six he began his primary education at the Nezam (military) elementary school in Tehran. He graduated on 6 June 1931 and in September of that year was sent off to Europe to continue his studies. He first entered middle school in Lausanne, Switzerland. A year later he enrolled at Le Rosey boarding school in Rolle on the shores of Lake Léman. One of the most exclusive educational institutions in the world, Le Rosey is known for the beauty of its campus and the high quality of its instruction. After completing his studies at Le Rosey, the crown prince returned to Iran on 7 May

1936. For higher education he attended Officer's Training School, from which he graduated on 12 June 1938. Afterward he served in the Imperial Infantry.

Dr. Ghani wrote the following account of the betrothal of Crown Prince Mohammad Reza Pahlavi and Princess Fawzia of Egypt when he served as ambassador in Cairo.

After the crown prince's return from Switzerland, his father, the late Reza Shah, began to think seriously about selecting a wife for him. Even before that time there had been talk both in and out of Iran that Reza Shah had been considering the question while the Crown Prince was still at school. For example, when the crown prince of Sweden visited Iran with his wife and daughter, the nineteen-year-old princess Ingrid, Reza Shah said that she would have been a good wife for the crown prince. She later married the Danish crown prince and is now queen.

Many prominent families with ties to the court were speculating that the shah had the daughter of the late Qajar king Ahmad Shah in mind for his son. But then—exactly when is not known—he began to favor a union with the Egyptian royal family. It is likely from what was said at the time that the idea came to the Shah after he visited Atatürk. Mr. Mozaffar Alam [later foreign minister] told me that when he was Iranian plenipotentiary in Baghdad (1936–38), Rushdi Örs, the Turkish foreign minister, told him confidentially that considering the good relations between Iran and Turkey and Atatürk's personal regard for the shah, he thought a union between the two royal families would be in both Iran's and Egypt's best interests. <...>

Apparently what drew the attention of some of the shah's confidants to the matter was a picture taken at the wedding of the eighteen-year-old Prince Farouq to Safi Naz (20 January 1938). The Egyptian press published pictures of Farouq's sisters and provided biographies of each. At that point Fawzia, the eldest daughter of the late King Fuad, became the talk of the Pahlavi court. The late shah was a man of vision who considered every factor when making decisions; but once

Reza Shah with Kemal Atatürk

he was decided his resolve was unshakable. He also was an uncanny judge of character. <…>

At this time Mr. Ahmad Rad, a venerable official at the Ministry of Foreign Affairs, was serving as plenipotentiary in Cairo. Enayatollah Sami'i, then the foreign minister, sent Rad the following telegram (dated 14 July 1937):

> HIM intends to find a wife for the crown prince. It appears that Princess Fawzia is appropriate in every way. Without anyone learning of it, you are to inquire whether the Egyptian court would favor such a union. If their response is positive, make an official proposal. Also please send a photograph of the princess to me.

Farouq, then eighteen, was completely innocent of the ways of the world. His mother, Queen Nazli, had kept him virtually imprisoned in the palace as long as his father was alive. As soon as he achieved his freedom, he went on a pleasure trip to Europe. Consequently, the court was incapable of deciding about the marriage of Princess Fawzia to Crown Mohammad Reza. The governing council consisting of the new Crown Prince Mohammad Ali, Aziz

Princess Fawzia, Crown Prince Mohammad Reza, and Queen Nazli

Ezzat Pasha (the former foreign minister), and Sharif Sabri Pasha (Nazli's brother and vice-Minister of Foreign Affairs) could not act because Mohammad Ali had gone to Europe for medical treatment. <...>

Another party that had to be heard from was Mostafa Nahas Pasha, head of the Wafd Party. He was a man of considerable government experience and influence. Generally speaking his intention was to take the inexperienced new king under his wing and become the power behind the throne. It was not in his interests to "allow" the king's sister to marry the Iranian Crown Prince.

The British at the time also wielded considerable influence in Egypt. They had excellent relations with Prince Mohammad Ali, on one hand, and were not fond of Reza Shah on the other. They were thus not pleased with the prospect of a match between the Iranian Crown Prince and the new king's sister. They also wanted at all costs to stay on the good side of Prince Mohammad Ali.

One can justly accuse Mr. Rad of being uninformed about these political intricacies. Moreover, without first receiving the permission of Reza Shah, he rushed ahead and raised the issue of the marriage with Nahas Pasha. On the surface the wily politician was very enthusiastic, but advised Rad to keep the matter confidential until he could find the proper time to raise it.

RAD SENT THE FOLLOWING TELEGRAM DATED 20 JULY 1937 TO SAMI'I:

> Deciding the marriage question will necessarily be delayed as His Majesty King Farouq along with Her Majesty the Queen Mother, Princess Fawzia and her younger sister are presently on tour in Europe. His Highness Prince Mohammad Ali, who is pivotal as the head of the three-member regency council, is undergoing medical treatment in Lausanne. But they will return in fifteen days. The opinion of the Queen Mother and that of the minister of court Hasanayn Pasha will be crucial as the young king is obedient to his mother and the court. But as I know that Nahas Pasha's views will also carry a great deal of weight, I have confidentially broached the subject with him. He was extremely grateful that I spoke to him first. After his questions on how Iran and Egypt differed in climate, geography, and religion and about the Iranian Crown Prince's age and education were answered, he promised me he would do his utmost politically to help carry out the mission assigned to me. I suggested to him that after the Sa'dabad Pact, this match would be the best way to cement relations between the Islamic nations of the Middle East and our country.

Reza Shah was so impatient to learn the results of Rad's consultations that he sent the following message:

> Embassy of Iran
> Rad
> No word from you concerning the Princess. Report
> immediately.

The shah was so dissatisfied with Rad's handling of the situation that he ordered him back to Tehran. Instead of returning, however, Rad went on a leave that had been promised him; but he was told not to return to Egypt.

Coincidentally at this time cinemas throughout the Arab world were showing a film set in the second century B.C.E. called *Leyla, Daughter of the Desert*. Since parts of the film seemed deliberately disparaging to Iran, it had some bearing on the impending marriage.

While the Iranian consuls in Palestine and Beirut ignored the film, Seyyed Baqer Kazemi, Iranian plenipotentiary in Baghdad, objected to its distribution and informed Tehran of the matter. On 18 June Tehran had ordered Mr. Rad to take steps to stop the film from being shown in Egypt. But because he had neglected to act in a timely way, Rad was recalled to Tehran as were the consuls in Palestine and Beirut.

The film was a deliberate insult to the Iranian government. Coming at such a critical time in the negotiations, it was especially galling to Reza Shah. But despite this, it was just a pretext for recalling Rad. The real reason was his incompetence in handling the matter of the betrothal. Reza Shah always had reasons for what he did, but when he replaced officials or had them imprisoned, the stated reason was often a pretext for public consumption. He used the same tactic in his foreign policy.

Rad's replacement was Javad Sinaki (the son of Majd al-Molk II), who was an experienced diplomat. He had many things in his favor. Not only did he have experience in Egypt, but Reza Shah thought highly of his intelligence and his foreign language proficiency. The shah thought that the women of the Egyptian court would be very influential in the decision about the marriage. Sinaki's very personable and cultured wife was therefore also an asset. Having grown up in the Caucasus, she was fluent in French, English, Russian and Turkish. The Sinakis set out for Egypt on 16 October 1937.

In Egypt the possible engagement of Princess Fawzia and the crown prince was the talk of the town. Hostile rumors were rife, and it was clear that agents of Mostafa Nahas Pasha and perhaps Mohammad Ali had been busy. In particular the differences between Shiites and Sunnis and common religious prejudices about Iranian heresies were revived.

<...>

<...> Given his suspicion of foreigners and his firm belief in their hostility toward the people of the Middle East, Reza Shah saw the hand of outside agents in the campaign to stop the union of the two royal families. To neutralize these agents and prevent any possible insult to himself and his country, he decided to let the matter rest and instructed Sinaki to that effect.

In order to make it appear that Reza Shah had changed his mind about the marriage, the court spread rumors in Iran about the crown prince's union with women from various Iranian families. The queen and princesses also invited the marriageable daughters of respectable Tehran families to palace gatherings, teas and receptions. So in Tehran it became common knowledge that the crown prince had actually decided to choose an Iranian wife. In the meantime Reza Shah was waiting for an appropriate moment.

As mentioned before Rushdi Örs, former Turkish foreign minister, was very active in the entire affair. He made great efforts to neutralize the kind of nonsense about Iran and the crown prince printed in the Egyptian press. He also spoke of the benefits of such a marriage to respected and important members of Egyptian society. He gradually became convinced that foreign elements had no part in the affair and that the problem was directly related to the unsettled state of Egyptian politics. He informed Reza Shah of this and added that some Egyptian men of consequence were against the union, but there was no insurmountable obstacle to its ultimate success.

After learning the facts, Reza Shah ordered the following telegram (dated 6 April 1939) sent to Sinaki:

Pursuant to telegram 23 dated 25 March, for your
information there has been no change of mind on the matter [of

the marriage] in principle. I am not disinclined to have the union take place, but I also do not want the matter to take on political overtones. Because I felt that were they to reject the proposal at the instigation of foreign interests, then this would be a great insult to us. I preferred that you become certain in your own mind that the proposal would be welcomed at court, that the marriage was possible…if not, however, my first inclination would hold. I also want to know how the minister of Turkey and others became informed of the matter.

<…>

Mr. and Mrs. Sinaki very discreetly worked their way into the inner circles of the Egyptian court becoming close to Queen Nazli. Gradually they opened the eyes of the court to the advantages of the match. The result was that Sabri Pasha, the queen's brother, and Ali Maher Pasha, who at the time were the two closest people to King Farouq, announced the court's official approval of the marriage. [Sinaki telegraphed the news to Tehran.]

<…>

On 21 May 1938 Sinaki informed Tehran that the Egyptian court wanted Mahmud Jam, the then prime minister, to travel to Egypt and head the delegation responsible for arranging the betrothal. <…>

<…>

On Sunday May 29 Jam announced his mission and spoke at length to Parliament. <…>

<…>

The delegation charged with arranging the betrothal consisted of Prime Minister Mahmud Jam, Dr. Mo'addab Nafisi, Ebrahim Dadmarz (the head of the Cabinet), Professor Rashid Yasemi of the University of Tehran and HIM's Special Office, and myself (at that time a member of Parliament). On Saturday 3 June 1938 we set out for Egypt traveling via Syria and Lebanon and entered Alexandria a week later. We stayed at the Antoniades Palace and, according to the schedule worked out in advance by the Egyptians, had lunch at the al-Montazah Palace with King Farouq the next day.

During the time that preparations for the betrothal were being finalized, both the foreign and domestic press publicized it everywhere. A number of those who were hostile to the match began to write all sorts of nonsense about the crown prince. <...>

<...>

In the wake of the impending marriage, officials of the Egyptian government and members of Parliament held talks. On 22 July 1938 during parliamentary discussions on foreign relations, the foreign minister said that the betrothal of the prince and the princess would strengthen the friendly ties between Iran and Egypt. To foster more cordial binational relations the Iranian government decided to upgrade its Cairo ministry to full embassy status. <...> The first ambassador was Mr. Bahman, who had entered Egypt a few days before the marriage was to take place.

As a result of his tireless efforts in preparing the ground for the marriage, the already weakened Javad Sinaki became even more ill. He was one of the high-ranking and intelligent officials at the foreign ministry whose hard work bore fruit. His wife also proved to be an asset in this work. In September 1938, the unwell Sinaki obtained leave, which he spent with his wife recuperating at Vichy.

Around this time through the efforts of Reza Shah, the Iranian Railway was making significant progress. By auspicious coincidence 30 August 1938, the day the two halves of the north-south, Trans-Iranian railway were connected, came during the time when the two royal families were being joined by marriage. As a wedding present to his daughter-in-law to be, Reza Shah ordered the name Sefid Cheshmeh, the site of the north-south rail juncture, to be changed to "Fawzia."

<...>

At this time also an inauspicious event occurred. Early in September 1938 there was an attempt on King Farouq's life. He was leaving his sports club when someone fired several shots at him. The bullets missed the king and struck a bystander. The Egyptian court immediately issued a statement denying the incident; however,

King Farouq, Princess Fawzia and Crown Prince Mohammad Reza Pahlavi

Iranian First Secretary Javad Qadimi, acting in place of the absent Sinaki, was informed that the incident did in fact take place.

<...>

Sinaki returned from his leave in early September and met with the foreign minister and King Farouq, who was in Alexandria at the time. On 25 September Tehran telegraphed Sinaki that his appointment had ended. <...> He was replaced by Hasan Pirnazar, the chargé, who arrived in Cairo on 12 October 1938. From then onward, the two governments worked out the details of the betrothal and marriage through their respective embassies. At the same time the Egyptian press circulated reports originating in Tehran that the wedding would take place in the spring of the following year (1939).

<...>

In October 1938, Abd al-Fattah Yahya Pasha, the Egyptian prime minister, met with Prime Minister Jam to discuss the princess's nationality and the status of the couple's future children. It was decided that on his return to Tehran Jam would take the matter up with the government and Parliament.

In response to Reza Shah's wishes, Parliament passed two bills amending the Constitution requiring any potential spouse of the crown prince to be of Iranian origin. They also conferred Iranian nationality on Fawzia. It appeared a happy marriage. The royal couple had a child named Shahnaz. When in June 1945 Queen Fawzia decided to visit Egypt, which had been impossible during the war years, it appeared that she was to return after a brief stay.

REPORTS RELATING TO QUEEN FAWZIA'S TRIP TO EGYPT IN 1945

On 16 June 1945 the Ministry of Court informed the Iranian Embassy in Cairo that Her Majesty Fawzia Pahlavi intended to visit her family in Egypt. She was scheduled to arrive by airplane in Alexandria on Wednesday 20 June. <...> Her entourage included General Yazdanpanah and his wife, Mohsen Qaraguzlu, Colonel Amini and his wife, and Mrs. Arfa.

On 26 June HIM's Special Office telegraphed saying that Her Majesty wanted newspapers sent to her regularly from Tehran. She also wished to have samples of currency bearing HIM's picture and newly minted gold and silver coins. The Melli Bank was instructed to prepare an album of this currency and send it immediately with the coins requested.

<...>

In response to the Iranian Ministry of Court's request for regular reports on Her Majesty's activities, Jam, now ambassador to Cairo, sent several telegrams. On 19 July 1946 he telegraphed the following.

<...>

Queen Fawzia is very concerned that HIM has not responded to her telegrams and has asked me about the situation in Tehran. I told her that everything is fine with His Majesty and the royal family, and that the pressure of important affairs of state has kept HIM from answering…If it is not an impertinence, I would suggest that HIM speed up the answers to Her Majesty's telegrams. Jam.

ON 22 JULY THERE WAS THE FOLLOWING RESPONSE TO THE TELEGRAM:

Embassy of Iran. Your telegram arrived and HIM was surprised, because he has written letters or telegraphed always asking after Her Majesty's well-being.

The special office then asks the embassy to trace two telegrams and one letter. They find two telegrams but no letter and suggest that if the special office sent letters in care of the American or British Embassy, they would have a better chance of arriving.

ON 30 JULY THE FOLLOWING TELEGRAM ARRIVED FROM TEHRAN:

HIM has asked when the queen will return to Iran. If she intends to stay beyond two more months, would she allow General Yazdanpanah to return to Tehran. Of course, he will soon come back to Cairo to be in her retinue. Shokuh.

IN RESPONSE TO THAT TELEGRAM JAM TELEGRAPHED THE FOLLOWING THE NEXT DAY:

HIM's Special Office. Her Majesty intends to stay in Alexandria another month and has given General Yazdanpanah permission to return to Tehran temporarily. <…>
<…>

ON 3 AUGUST JAM TELEGRAPHED THE FOLLOWING REPORT
TO HIM'S SPECIAL OFFICE:

> This week there is no news about Her Majesty's departure
> from Alexandria. She has spent nearly the entire week in her
> bedroom at the Antoniades Palace, saying she was fatigued. <...>
> The doctors say that this may be a recurrence of the malarial fever
> she contracted in Tehran and have prescribed more rest.

ON 3 AUGUST JAM TELEGRAPHED THE FOLLOWING REPORT
TO HIM'S SPECIAL OFFICE:

> Her Majesty's health seems to have improved; no signs of her
> recent fever since 7 August. This week she has left the Antoniades
> Palace infrequently. Since the beginning of Ramadan King Farouq
> often visits, spending the night there. When I had an audience on
> 8 August, she seemed well and said that she missed HIM and Her
> Highness Princess Shahnaz very much. The doctors have
> determined that the malaria had recurred and must be treated
> until it is fully cured.
>
>   <...>

ON 13 AUGUST 1945 JAM TELEGRAPHED HIM'S SPECIAL OFFICE
THE FOLLOWING:

> This is a coded message for HIM's eyes only. Today King
> Farouq summoned me and said he had very bad news. He said
> that Queen Fawzia did not intend to return to Iran ever. He
> detailed the hardships she had suffered and suggested that I fly to
> Tehran and tell the shah personally. I said that such differences
> often occur in the lives of married couples and hoped that the
> king might think of a way to ameliorate them. Her Majesty
> moved from the Antoniades Palace to the king's palace.
>
>   <...>

ON 26 AUGUST IN RESPONSE TO THE ABOVE HIM'S SPECIAL OFFICE
TELEGRAPHED THE FOLLOWING:

> HIM is greatly perplexed. He said that at one point Her
> Majesty wanted to be constantly informed about us by telegram,
> but now there has been a complete turnabout. Her Majesty's
> remarks that you have reported make us think that there is some
> plot at work. This being the case, there is no need for you to come
> to Tehran. You are to speak to King Farouq and in any way you
> think fit ask him to reconsider the matter.
>
> General Yazdanpanah and Colonel Amini are to return
> immediately. You are to write everything in detail and send it
> sealed with General Yazdanpanah. <...> Shokuh.
>
> <...>

Later Jam went to Tehran but returned to Cairo on 6 September
and arrived in Alexandria on Saturday the eighth. He was to have an
audience with the king and Her Majesty but learned that after the end
of Ramadan, they had gone on a twenty-day pleasure cruise on the
Red Sea.

Since there was nothing more to keep Jam in Alexandria, he
returned to Cairo to wait for Ala. After Ala arrived, Jam explained
what was happening by telephone. Given Ala's previous friendship
with Hasanayn in Washington, Jam asked him to set up a meeting for
them at the Ras al-Tin Palace on 12 September. After the customary
preliminaries, Ala began, "I am sorry that Her Majesty is not in
Alexandria and that I won't be able to have an audience with her to
explain the situation. However, I think it necessary to state that
despite the extraordinary affection that everyone has for her, she has
not performed her duties as queen. Instead of taking an interest in
improving Iranian society and the condition of the people by visiting
hospitals, kindergartens, and working in charitable affairs, she prefers
to sleep until noon. Afterward she either stays in her room or goes
out alone. She not only shows no interest in anything Iranian, she has
also been remiss in carrying out her marital duties. <...> HIM even

repeatedly suggested that Her Majesty have her own retinue so that she could busy herself with people she liked, but she rejected the offer." Hasanayn assured them that as soon as Her Majesty and the king returned from their trip, Queen Nazli would do all she could to correct the situation. They tried to have an audience with Queen Nazli the next day, but she was ill and could not meet with them. She assured them that she would perform her role as a mother and a mother-in-law. <...>

ON 10 OCTOBER SHOKUH OF HIM'S SPECIAL OFFICE TELEGRAPHED THE FOLLOWING:

> After Her Majesty arrives in Alexandria, you are to visit her immediately and offer HIM's salutations on her return. <...>

The next day Jam reported that Her Majesty had not arrived in Alexandria yet and was spending some time in Esmailiyah.

The journal *Majallat al-Ethneyn* (1 October 1945) reported that Cecil Beaton, the famous British photographer, declared Her Majesty to be the most beautiful woman that he had ever seen. <...>

ON 16 OCTOBER 1945 JAM TELEGRAPHED THE FOLLOWING:

> The king and Queen Fawzia arrived in Alexandria on the fourteenth. I had an audience with the king at the al-Montazah Palace and faithfully relayed HIM's remarks. He was deeply moved. <...> I then advised him to direct Her Majesty to return to Iran quickly and put an end to the foolish rumors that are circulating about the two royal families. He said that he could not act on this himself and had to consult with his sister. <...>

On 5 November 1945 the shah congratulates the queen on her birthday and sends flowers.

ON 11 NOVEMBER 1945 JAM SENT THE FOLLOWING REPORT TO TEHRAN:

Nothing to report in Her Majesty's life. No one has visited her since she took up residence at the king's palace. Tried unsuccessfully on two occasions for an audience. <...>

There seems to be no change in her stubborn resistance to returning to Tehran. My advice is that HIM come to Cairo and bring her back. Please advise if HIM intends to visit.

ON 20 NOVEMBER 1945 JAM TELEGRAPHED THE FOLLOWING TO THE SPECIAL OFFICE:

Mohsen Murad Pasha met with me on behalf of Queen Fawzia. He said that King Farouq has informed Her Majesty of the shah's message. She has told the king to tell me that her decision is final and that she has no intention of returning to Iran. She said that the inattention and hardships were more than she could bear and thus was not prepared to renew her life in Iran. I believe that any further steps would be fruitless. It must be said that she intends to spend the winter in Cairo. Perhaps her feeling will change with time. <...>

ON 16 MARCH 1946 HIM'S SPECIAL OFFICE TELEGRAPHED THE FOLLOWING:

HIM has commanded that an appropriately magnificent bouquet of flowers be presented to Her Majesty on the twenty-fourth of Esfand to mark the anniversary of their engagement. Also that this note from HIM in both Persian and French be attached: "On this day that reminds me of a day seven years ago, I cannot refrain from expressing my love and affection. The pleasant memories of that day are still fresh in my mind." Shokuh.

<...>

On 30 December 1946 HIM's Special Office telegraphed the embassy, "Have you obtained an appointment with King Farouq?" In response Jam telegraphed, "On 26 December I met with the King. He

sent his congratulations on the successful settlement of the Azerbaijan affair. He said he would answer HIM's letter in full and send it via Mohsen Murad Pasha. I await King Farouq's response so I can send a full account via Qaraguzlu who will travel to Tehran on 5 January 1947. There is no change in the status quo.

DR. GHANI'S AMBASSADORSHIP TO EGYPT: SEPTEMBER 1947 TO SEPTEMBER 1948

DIARY ENTRY REGARDING BEIRUT STOP EN RÓUTE TO CAIRO.
12 OCTOBER 1947

<...>

I had been in Beirut from summer 1913 to July 1919; thus I am familiar with conditions in the city and in Lebanon. In general I have deduced the harmful French Colonial influence of French culture on the Lebanese, particularly among the upper classes, the rich and the merchants (especially among the Christians). They have adopted the loose lifestyle and manners of the French, their dancing and their debauchery. Almost all aspects of Arab and Eastern culture have disappeared.

The Christians laugh at the Arab League in private. They are uncommonly proud, claiming that Lebanese civilization and literary culture is superior to all other Arab countries. They consider themselves Aryans and go through all sorts of acrobatics to prove that the Phoenicians belonged to the Aryan tribes, not to the Semites.

Arabic is practically defunct among the upper classes. They speak French as though it were their mother tongue, especially when in conversation with foreigners. It is as though they are ashamed of their own language. The women, who are especially affected, are forever speaking of Lamartine, Alfred de Musset and other mediocre writers; but they never say a word about extraordinary Arab poets like Abu al-Ala al-Ma'arri and Mutanabbi, whose greatness puts those French writers to shame. Many of these women say Arabic is difficult. They ask, "What good is it, anyway?" <...>

TELEGRAM TO HIM'S SPECIAL OFFICE DATED 13 OCTOBER 1947:

> After a delay of one week in Beirut, I reached Cairo on 12 October and was greeted by the Foreign Ministry's head of protocol and members of the embassy staff. An hour after my arrival, I went to the Abedin Palace and signed the guest books of King Farouq, Queen Farida and Queen Mother Nazli. <...> Also visited the tomb of the late King Fuad and the temporary gravesite of HIM Reza Shah Pahlavi. Presented two bouquets that I had arranged to be there.

Busy schedule with diplomatic corp, visits and visits to various Egyptian ministries.

CORRESPONDENCE AND TELEGRAMS RELATING TO THE DIVORCE OF HIM MOHAMMAD REZA SHAH AND QUEEN FAWZIA

TELEGRAM TO HIM'S SPECIAL OFFICE DATED 15 OCTOBER 1947:

> Met with the prime minister and the head of King Farouq's Special Office. Results later. In the meantime request several copies of the latest photographs of Princess Shahnaz. Ghani.

CODED TELEGRAM TO HIM'S SPECIAL OFFICE:

> Each year the embassy holds a tea in honor of HIM's birthday. This costs about a hundred pounds. Given the present cholera outbreak, I request that the tea be cancelled and that the money be given to the Egyptian Foreign Ministry for the feeding of the indigent. If this meets with HIM's approval, request additional 100 pounds for the purpose.

CODED TELEGRAM FROM HIM'S SPECIAL OFFICE:

> Dr. Ghani, HIM has approved your suggestion. <...> He also ordered that another hundred pounds be given to the Egyptian Ministry of Health to help in combating the cholera outbreak. Shokuh.

Tuesday 14 October met with Mahmud Fahmi Nuqrashi Pasha, the Egyptian prime minister and foreign minister. I presented him with my credentials and asked for an audience with King Farouq. As Nuqrashi holds two important Cabinet posts and is a trusted advisor to King Farouq, I thought it right to dispense with formalities and speak frankly. He has, after all, a reputation for honesty and selflessness. So at our first meeting I raised the issue of Queen Fawzia, which would have to be negotiated in the near future in any case. <...>

I addressed him as a fellow Moslem, relying on a common amity that exists among people of the Middle East. I said, "Because it has gone on so long, the issue of Queen Fawzia has become a problem not merely for the two royal families, a question that in itself is important, but also for the two nations, Egypt and Iran, and as such may even affect Islamic societies throughout the Middle East. Especially in these days when safeguarding our mutual interests is of paramount importance, all the Islamic countries from Casablanca to Pakistan must present a united front to the rest of the world. As single nations we are weak, but were we to reach a common understanding of what is in our interests as a region, then we can be an abiding force. Given the bonds between the two royal families of Egypt and Iran, if statesmen from the two nations can achieve a meeting of the minds, they could enlarge the circle of goodwill generated by such an agreement to encompass the rest of the Moslem countries. At the present time Queen Fawzia has shunned her exalted position as the queen of the country to everyone's disappointment.

<...>

"Today the standing of the two nations and the two royal families is in jeopardy. Our enemies mock us, while our friends are disenchanted. Those who dislike us consider the rift a sign of the two countries' lack of social progress. I told the prime minister that it was our social, moral and religious duty to collaborate and try to find a solution to the problem. <...> I also pointed out that Her Majesty is the parent of a precious daughter, Princess Shahnaz, who is in need of her mother's love. With each passing day the girl is more aware of her absence. One can imagine the psychological effect this has on the child." <...>

I also told him that apart from these considerations, the misunderstandings between the royal couple would be a simple matter for His Majesty the Shah to put right. He is prepared to take into consideration any suggestion Her Majesty has about their life. The important thing is that Her Majesty resume her positions as queen, wife and mother. I also reminded him that King Farouq is not merely Her Majesty's brother, but also is in the position of her father and of brother to the shah, who holds him in high regard.

The expression on Nuqrashi's face and his quavering voice indicated how much what I said had moved him. He congratulated me on my sincerity and remarked on how adroitly I played on his Easterner's heartstrings. With equal sincerity he assured me that as long as we were able to maintain contact we would collaborate in a spirit of brotherhood and selflessness. He warned me that on first broaching the subject with the king, I might meet with resistance. But I was not to be disheartened and should persist in the matter. He advised me to broach the subject first with Mr. Ebrahim Abd al-Hadi Pasha, the head of the King's Special Office. He is an understanding and kind man and has considerable influence over Farouq. <...>

I also told him that one of my missions as ambassador was to speak with Her Majesty. He advised me to go through Abd al-Hadi Pasha. <...>

At the end of our conversation, Nuqrashi Pasha asked whether I had current photographs of Princess Shahnaz. I told him I did not, but I had requested them from Tehran.

At 3:00 P.M. I met with Ibrahim Abd al-Hadi Pasha at the Abedin Palace and asked him officially to convey my respects to Her Majesty. We then discussed the necessity of solidarity among the Islamic nations and the general state of the world. I also called

Yusef Zulfiqar Pasha, who presently resides in Alexandria. <…>
He is very favorable to Iran and HIM. On 19 October we spoke of
Queen Fawzia and he advised me to maintain friendships with
Nuqrashi Pasha and Abd al-Hadi Pasha, stressing that both were
fine men with influence over the king. The next day I met with
Yusef Zulfiqar Pasha at the embassy. During our conversation he
expressed regret that the king [Farouq] and Queen Farida were
irreconcilable and on the verge of divorce. <…> His Majesty King
Farouq is recuperating from a minor operation and will return to
Cairo in a few days. Queen Nazli is presently at the Mayo Clinic in
Rochester, Minnesota. She suffers from kidney stones. They
operated on one of her kidneys and she is reportedly better. Sabri
Pasha has gone to America to visit his ailing sister. <…>.

TELEGRAM TO HIM'S SPECIAL OFFICE DATED 18 OCTOBER 1947:

At this time the cholera epidemic in Egypt is becoming
progressively worse. It would be highly appropriate for HIM to
telegraph Her Majesty, asking about her health, expressing his
concern. A similar telegram from Princess Shahnaz along these
lines would be useful. Dr. Ghani.

CODED TELEGRAM FROM HIM'S SPECIAL OFFICE IN RESPONSE TO
DR. GHANI'S TELEGRAM NO. 4. TO BE DECODED
AND TRANSMITTED TO QUEEN FAWZIA:

Queen Fawzia, my dear mother, your absence is very hard on
me, especially now that the cholera epidemic is worse. I implore
you to tell me how you are feeling. God keep you in good health.
Shahnaz.

TELEGRAM TO HIM'S SPECIAL OFFICE:

In complete agreement with HIM's opinion that on 5
November, Queen Fawzia's birthday, a telegram expressing HIM's
affection be sent. I also recommend that Princess Shahnaz send a
congratulatory telegram. Dr. Ghasem Ghani.

<…>

Both telegrams were sent.

DIARY ENTRY 29 OCTOBER 1947:

Had a long conversation with Mrs. Qaraguzlu whose husband, Mohsen, is the head of the Protocol Office at the Ministry of Court. Before her departure from Tehran, HIM had asked her to tell Fawzia that he would be willing to send his sister, Princess Ashraf, and the Queen Mother out of the country if that would satisfy her. She gave the message to Fawzia who said it was too late. HIM had also stated that under no circumstances would he agree to a divorce. <...> Mrs. Qaraguzlu related that Fawzia, a few weeks after her arrival, had received a letter, which made her cry. Thereafter she refused to see any member of her entourage. She only sees her brother, King Farouq. <...>

Dr. Ghani makes further enquiries about the alleged letter but is unable to shed any light on the matter and begins to doubt its existence. He laments HIM's predicament and believes HIM is sincere and guileless.

DIARY ENTRY 10 NOVEMBER 1947

King Farouq's Declining Popularity

He is acting more dictatorially. He has removed the respected Dean of Al-Azhar University and replaced him with a mediocre, obedient substitute. According to Crown Prince Mohammad Ali Pasha, Farouq is surrounded by procurers; frequents nightclubs and places of ill repute; is not attending to his mother, wife and sister; and is separating from his wife who is the mother of their three children. He is wasting the assets of a poor country and is becoming increasingly arrogant.

TO HIM'S SPECIAL OFFICE:

On Tuesday 11 November 1947 had an appointment at the Abedin Palace at 4:00 P.M. Talat Pasha was waiting at the entrance

to greet me. He immediately escorted me upstairs where I had an
audience with the king. Here are some details of our
conversation.

<...>

*The diary entry for this date provides details about King Farouq's physical
appearance and the language in which he and Dr. Ghani conversed
(French).*

<...> King Farouq is a tall young man, about six feet, stocky in
build, dark complexioned with turquoise-colored eyes. His mustache
resembles Wilhelm II's of Germany. When I entered he rose from his
desk and approached me with all the bearing of a proper monarch.
<...>

When I described how the separation of Queen Fawzia and HIM
affected poor Princess Shahnaz, he replied, "C'est ce qu'est bien
regrettable." [This is lamentable.]

I gave him the confidential letter I bore from HIM. He opened it
and looked briefly at the contents. He asked whether this was my first
time in Egypt. I told him that I had visited in 1938 in the company of
Mr. Jam and had had the opportunity of meeting him then. <...> He
said he had heard many good things about me and about my time in
the U.S. He also said that achieving success in the U.S. was especially
crucial, because coming to terms with the young nation was a problem. He expounded on the difficulties between Egypt and the U.S.
over the Arab-Jewish question and the background behind Egypt's
complaint to the United Nations. I told him that I was aware of it
from the press and hoped that the combined wisdom of His Majesty
and the Egyptian statesmen could solve the problem. I added that
Americans are generally good people, who listen to reason. One can
deal with them. They have an orderly government. He agreed but
added, "The problem in this case is the inordinate influence of Jews
in American society. The press, the radio, and the movie industry are
in their hands." I said such was the case but added that the Jews had

also made great contributions to the sciences and mentioned Einstein and Oppenheimer.

He said he had heard a lot about me and that I had written many books. He asked for a complete set of my writings. <...> He remarked how wonderful it would be to have some of my books translated into Arabic. I told him that Dr. Abd al-Wahhab Azzam, the head of the Faculty of Literature who knows Persian well, had already selected one of my writings for this purpose.

He then asked about the late Mr. Foroughi. I told him that we were friends and that when Foroughi was the head of the Persian Academy of Culture, we collaborated on an edition of the poetry of Omar Khayyam. <...>

After a pause, he said that it was unfortunate that my mission in Egypt had to begin on a disagreeable note. He had hoped that the matter could have been resolved during Mr. Jam's tenure as ambassador. <...>

The purpose of this introduction was to steer the conversation toward the topic he had now raised. I asked him for permission to speak about the matter. He agreed. But before I did so, I said, "There are two requests. One is that you permit me to speak with complete candor. The other is that after considering my comments, you realize that I have only the best interests of Iran as well as Your Majesty, the royal family and the Egyptian nation at heart." <...>

I continued, "In 1938 Mr. Jam and I came to Egypt for the engagement ceremonies of Her Majesty Queen Fawzia. A year later I accompanied HIM on his trip to Egypt for the actual wedding and was privy to all that occurred. I was not only overjoyed that the then crown prince of Iran was to wed such a suitable wife, the daughter of King Fuad and the sister of Your Majesty, I was also extremely pleased at the prospect that the joining of the royal families would ensure the future welfare of the peoples of the two great Islamic nations. I was certain that the marriage would foster good relations between Iran and Egypt as well as among the other Islamic countries. Having spoken with people from the upper levels of Egyptian society, I concluded that they shared my feelings in regard to the union. But not long after it took place, a war began that plunged my own country and the rest of the world into misery. Now [that the war is over], it is time to make the hopes raised by the royal marriage a reality. The global situation makes it imperative that we join hands and accomplish what is vital to our mutual interests. We must show that our two societies have matured enough to solve what is actually not a very profound difference between two young people.

"Your Majesty realizes the important position Egypt holds in the world, its great prestige among nations of the Middle East. Given how much you value this national prestige, it is in your best interests to strengthen it with every means at your disposal. Thus you must contrive a solution for this superficial disagreement as soon as possible, and not let it mar the dignity of the royal families of Egypt and Iran or the national interests of the two great Islamic nations. <...>

"All Iranians are especially attached to their beloved queen and expect her imminent return to the country." I then described the plight of Princess Shahnaz, who is the innocent victim of all this uncertainty. The king interjected, agreeing that the Princess' situation was indeed unfortunate.

<...>

He then said, "I am in accord with everything you say—you know that I have tried to arrange the reconciliation you speak of—but most of the statesmen and members of the royal family are against it. Even my mother is not enthusiastic. I have tried my best to reestablish the bond, but sadly nothing worked. I love my sister and she loves me;however, when she returned from Iran, she was very weak and ill. She is in somewhat better spirits now, but under no circumstances does she want to return to Iran. I cannot do anything as her decision is final."

I told him that I had heard that the malaria that coincided with Her Majesty's return to Egypt had weakened her. But, I said, Tehran does not have a bad climate and, besides, a temporary illness is a perfectly natural thing. I assured him that HIM would spare no effort to ensure the empress' health and happiness. <...> Despite my assurances and declarations of the shah's undying love and concern for Her Majesty's welfare, the king said that his hands were tied.

<...>

I then asked if I could speak with Queen Fawzia in person, hoping an explanation of the facts would change her mind. After pausing, he said, "Mr. Ambassador, you are the kind of person that everyone would love to talk to, but since the matter is closed Her Royal Highness does not desire to reopen it. Seeing you would only unsettle her." I told him that despite this, I was not discouraged. He declared me an optimist. I replied, "A realist, actually. I see the facts clearly, and I speak in all sincerity." He said, "You are overly optimistic, and I fear that one day you will be sorely disappointed because of it."

After the audience had gone on for fifty minutes, I asked permission to leave. I told the king that I was not going away disheartened, for that would not please him. He assured me that the good relations between our countries would continue and this personal matter, which must be kept separate, would not impair them. <...>

I personally feel that he does not want to solve the problem, otherwise he could have done so easily. All the kindness he showed me was an apparent attempt to placate me. It was only a display of powerlessness. One look at the king's life shows that there are not thoughtful or influential people around him with any concern for his or the country's best interests. His nights are spent drinking and carousing with nonentities and his disreputable cronies. Steadfast and honest figures like Mostafa al-Maraghi, Sheikh of al-Azhar, Hasanayn Pasha, etc. are not close to the king. <...> The royal princes and the nobility are as a group wealthy sybarites who have no influence on the king nor among the people. The king secretly despises Crown Prince Mohammad Ali. <...>

Nuqrashi Pasha and Abd al-Hadi Pasha, who head the King's Special Office, have some dignity, but they are terrified [of losing their positions]. Though they are aware of what is going on, they lack the nerve to make the king understand that what I had deduced is right. They have divined that the king is not inclined to do anything about the marriage so do not intrude. Farouq has thus become somewhat the tyrant and autocrat. This is why the Wafdists, who have considerable influence among the people, and the clergy did not participate in the elections held two years ago. The royal egotism has also spurred him to lofty gestures like his protest to the UN, <...> his public shows of opposition to the British, his claims to some of the former Italian colonies and lands along the Red Sea that rightfully belong to Ethiopia. He also claims to stand at the head of North Africa among the Arab states. His moral authority and popularity among the people is declining.

<...>

My advice is to allow the matter to remain dormant for two days. I will continue my discussions with Nuqrashi Pasha and Abd al-Hadi Pasha. I am also passing photos of Princess Shahnaz via Naguib Salem, special administrator of the royal lands. <...> Dr. Ghani.

TELEGRAM TO THE SPECIAL OFFICE 22 NOVEMBER 1947:

<...>

16 November met with Abd al-Hadi Pasha and again went over the Fawzia issue in general and in detail. <...> I said that it was the responsibility of a few well-meaning people, including himself, with access to the royal family to impress upon the queen that it is her sacred duty as a mother and a wife, as well as vital to the prestige of the two families [that she return]. Abd al-Hadi Pasha, who has daily audiences with the king, completely agrees that were the situation to continue it would endanger the reputation of the royal family. I deduce that the people are now blaming the king for the dilemma and the disruption in the royal household it has caused.

<...>

At the same time the king's own irregular habits at hotels and cabarets have fueled criticism. He is surrounded by a group of unsavory people. This contrasts with Farida's forbearance and her care of the children. <...> The king's mother has been traveling for the past two years and thus is removed from her children. Princess Faiza has married a Turk called Mohammad Ali Rauf, a man of no reputation. <...>

The same day at 1:00 P.M. I met with Nuqrashi Pasha at the prime minister's office. <...> He counseled me to wait until the king had had more time to know me better. The king, he said, was especially interested in elegant Oriental handicrafts like miniatures, gilded manuscripts, fine calligraphy, etc. He suggested I try to engage him in conversation about these things. He also solemnly promised to raise the matter of Fawzia with the king himself.

TO HIM SPECIAL OFFICE 25 NOVEMBER 1947

I met with Mr. Naguib Salem Pasha, the head of royal properties and special advisor to the king. I gave him the photographs of Princess Shahnaz and asked that he present them to the king and Queen Fawzia. He told me that he would immediately give them to His Majesty and the queen. In the meantime, he said, he had presented telegrams from the princess and HIM to them and that these would necessarily lead to a discussion of Fawzia's prolonged stay in Egypt. <…> Dr. Ghasem Ghani.

<…>

TO HIM'S SPECIAL OFFICE 9 DECEMBER 1947:

<…> I have decided that it is best not to revive the Fawzia question. Regretfully it is becoming clearer and clearer to me that no one in the king's immediate circle has the backbone to say to him what is in his and the family's best interests. And the strange thing is that they all share my feelings on the matter, but they do not have the moral courage to go against the king's desires. Dr. Ghasem Ghani.

TO HIM'S SPECIAL OFFICE 11 DECEMBER 1947:

As I stated in a previous report (26 November), Queen Fawzia has communicated through Naguib Salem Pasha <…> that she is adamant in her decision not to return to Iran. She requests that the matter be settled expediently through divorce. I in no way considered this an official response and chided Naguib Salem in a friendly way about how he is an intimate of the royal family and must therefore think of preserving their dignity. <…> I asked him for an audience with Queen Fawzia.

Four days ago Naguib Salem Pasha telephoned to ask whether I still wanted to see Queen Fawzia. I told him that I did. <…> He again telephoned to say that the audience would take place at 1:00 P.M. on 17 December <…> .

I arrived at the palace and Naguib Salem Pasha immediately led me to the entrance of her parlor where two of her companions were waiting. <…> Her Majesty admitted me graciously and asked me to be seated. She ordered coffee to be served. I told her how much of an honor it was to be in her presence. I said that I had the privilege of communicating HIM's and Princess Shahnaz's deep love and affection for her. I also told her that I conveyed the loving admiration and respect of the Iranian people.

"Given this," I said, "Your Majesty's stay in Egypt, which has gone on for quite a long time, has caused everyone involved some distress. Though I do not know the reasons behind the delay, I do know that it has caused a mutual misunderstanding that must be rectified. It is in Your Majesty's power to restore peace to the imperial household."

She remained completely still, saying nothing. Her features did not betray what she felt. I described Princess Shahnaz again, her cleverness, her conversations with her teacher and governess at the home of General Yazdanpanah and later at Princess Shams's palace at Sa'dabad. She smiled at this point and asked how her daughter was. I said that she was well but continually asked about her mother. She made a scrapbook of pictures of Her Majesty that have appeared in the press. I told her that it was quite natural for a ten-year-old girl to need her mother and that no governess could take a mother's place. After a pause, she said that she had decided never to return to Iran. <…>

I told her that every decision had positive and negative consequences. She must weigh the consequences of her decision and also be assured that in everything I was about to say I only had her best interests at heart. I begged her not to be silent, but express anything that was on her mind. I said that the issue had to be examined from three different viewpoints, each one important in its own way.

"First, Your Majesty is the queen, beloved and esteemed by the entire Iranian nation. I am terribly sorry that the war and the state of the world prevented Your Majesty from getting to know them well. Otherwise you would have known how much they were attached to you. Now with all they have heard of your character, their longing for your return grows greater daily. Yours is a profound duty to settle the misunderstanding that has troubled a nation to such an extent. <...> You also have a duty as a mother. If you could only know how much your daughter misses you. The country has passed a law that declares you Iranian in origin so that as the potential mother of a crown prince, your son will inherit the throne.

Second, you are the wife of a great sovereign whose affection and concern for you knows no bounds. I am certain that no matter how much I speak of this love I will never do it justice." <...>

She said she was certain that what I said was true: HIM has these feelings but my own have changed. "But why?" I asked. "Doesn't everything I have said argue for another change of mind?" I reminded her of her nobility, her lineage and the prestige of the royal family. "Reason dictates," I felt conscience-bound to say, "that you think of the future and not allow things to continue, to become, God forbid, cause for sorrow later on."

"No," she said, "I have considered everything and want the matter to end amicably in separation and divorce. If not, I will be forced to take action."

<...> I asked her why she had made such a decision. <...>

"People change sometimes," she said.

"Change does not happen without a reason. Now you can change your mind again," I replied, but she merely repeated what she had said.

I said, "If I am being impertinent in my curiosity, it is only out of concern for your welfare and my devotion to you. From what I understand, when you first left Iran for Egypt, it was to be a temporary absence, a change of scenery and a visit to your august family. You said that it would last two months, and during this period there was constant communication between you and HIM and Princess Shahnaz. <...> General Yazdanpanah sought your permission several times to return to Tehran. You told him to leave and come back to Cairo in twelve days time at the end-of-Ramadan, when you would be ready to return with him. My question is what happened during those twelve days to change your mind?" <...>

"Instead of my going on at length the way I have on this matter, if only a meeting with His Majesty the Shah himself could be arranged. I am sure that the feelings in your pure heart would remove all the misunderstandings and the two of you could resume your life together in happiness and prosper. <....>" I went on like this, mustering as much candor and feeling as I could, but she remained silent and with that same flat tone said, "No, my feelings have not changed. What I would like you to do is tell His Majesty to part amicably, otherwise I will have to act."

I begged her not to ask this of me and reminded her of the consequences to her child and to the two nations, and her duties as queen. But I also thanked her for the audience, which lasted one hour and twenty minutes. The only thing she said that was cause for optimism came at the last moment when she asked me not to communicate any demands for now. Dr. Ghasem Ghani.

REPORT TO HIM'S SPECIAL OFFICE 20 DECEMBER 1947:

As I indicated by telegram, Naguib Salem Pasha came to the embassy and said that nothing he did was to any avail and that Her Majesty was adamant that the marriage end in an "amicable" divorce. I said nothing, but I am amazed at their stubborn insistence. <...> It seems that no matter how many times I urge her to reconsider the matter, in the end the response is the same formula: "Feelings not changed—decision made—too late—there is no hope of a change of mind and return is impossible—separation must be accomplished amicably..." From my private audience with King Farouq (reported on 15 November 1947), I surmised that he was not being candid with me. He pretended to have said all he could to Her Majesty, but he could not impose his will on her. Therefore, he said, it was better to settle things in an amicable manner. If not, he would be forced to refer the matter to a special royal commission.

During my audience with Her Majesty, she used the same expression. Likewise Naguib Salem Pasha. Every message ended by requesting an "amicable" settlement.

From what I have been able to determine, Egyptian public opinion has turned against Her Majesty and the king in this matter. Egyptians ask themselves how could she have abandoned her country and child? Why doesn't the king settle the matter? <...> In addition they see the Egyptian princess's renunciation of her position as queen of an ancient country like Iran a blow to national pride. <...> The king himself is more or less aware of how the public feels but remains steadfast in his arrogant insistence on an amicable divorce. He knows that if the matter goes to a royal commission, it will disgrace him even further. <...>

The issue of a royal commission that he keeps waving in our faces is not as simple as he imagines. Islamic jurisprudence is very clear on the subject of divorce: it is the man's prerogative. There are many exceptions such as when the man is afflicted with an incurable and contagious disease that might infect the woman through conjugal contact. Or when the man is incapable of providing a household for the woman. <...> The upshot is that some cleric on a royal commission would not be able to issue a divorce decree just to please his monarch. <...>

Another consideration is that Her Majesty is a citizen of Iran by virtue of a special law that was adopted before the marriage. She herself has accepted this status. <...> In my opinion the best course for now is that we respond by stalling and equivocating until they become tired. In the interim there may be a change of mind.

<...>

In the meantime I have been contacting anyone who can be of service in this matter both directly and indirectly. Just today I met with Mr. Ahmad Khashabeh Pasha, the new minister of foreign affairs. <...> We spoke for an hour and a half about various things that are the talk of Egyptians these days: the issue of Palestine, the League of Arab States, etc. When the conversation turned to Iran, he said that the country had always been an important center of innovation and great intellectual movements. I agreed and said that today the Moslems of Iran are among the most enlightened in Islamic society. <...> I also mentioned the vital importance of cooperation among the Islamic nations and emphasized the role of the elite and enlightened members of those societies in turning words into action. <...> This introduction allowed me to steer our discussion toward the subject of Queen Fawzia. <...> I appealed to his sense of duty to his country and to the royal family. He said that he would do everything in his power to help solve the problem. Dr. Ghasem Ghani.

<...>

TO HIM'S SPECIAL OFFICE 23 DECEMBER 1947:

Last night Crown Prince Mohammad Ali telephoned to say he wished to see me. I met with him at ten the next morning at the palace. He asked about the Cabinet crisis in Iran. One question was whether the Russians had nominated anyone for the Iranian prime minister's position, a person who would do their bidding. I told him no such thing happened. The man chosen, Mr. Hakimi, is a patriot through and through, an honorable person. He then asked, Aren't most of the merchants of Tehran Russian and most trading houses in their hands? Likewise most cafés, nightclubs, and restaurants. I said that this was totally false. He asked if we were worried about the Russians. I answered that we are not overly concerned, but the whole world is in a chaotic state these days. <...> Two years ago there was something that worried us, but that is gone now. Under the enlightened leadership of HIM, Iran has prepared the way for its progress and advancement.

<...> He said that his purpose in raising the topic was something else. He asked, Why Her Majesty Fawzia doesn't return to the country where she is the Queen? I said how good it would

be for him to raise this question with Her Majesty herself. He said he wanted to hear my answer because the only reason he could think of was that the political situation in Iran was dangerous and that she was afraid of becoming caught in a revolution. I assured him that such was not the case. He then suggested that Tehran's great elevation above sea level did not agree with her. I said that the city was not that high above sea level, some 1,200 meters. Her Majesty had spent several years in Iran and her health was always good. <...>

He then spoke about himself. He said that he was nearly seventy and had traveled a great deal. Craving nothing for himself, he was above all bound by Islamic law and his conscience. His only interest was the welfare of his country. He was devoted to his paternal cousins the king and Her Majesty Fawzia. <...> In 1914 the British forced his brother Khedive Abbas Hilmi to resign from the Egyptian government, then offered to place him on the throne if he agreed to declare war against the Ottoman government. He refused. <...>

<...>

Crown Prince Mohammad Ali ordinarily has no moral sway with King Farouq. From the beginning of Farouq's reign, there were misunderstandings between the two that Mohammad Ali made no attempt to resolve. Rather, because he was critical and candid, he never became a favorite. <...> Currently the crown prince's relationship with the king seems to have improved to the extent that he wants to play the role of the grey eminence of the family. Whatever the case, if his involvement fails to produce anything, it cannot damage our position either. Dr. Ghasem Ghani.

TO HIM'S SPECIAL OFFICE 28 DECEMBER 1947:

Last night I met with Nuqrashi Pasha and continued to expand upon previous discussions. <...> I told him that if he were to take a matter of such importance lightly, he would have to answer to history and the Egyptian people.

<...>

At the end of our talk I arranged to meet with Nuqrashi
Pasha again so that he could keep me informed. Last night I also
met with Abd al-Hadi Pasha.

<...>

There is an advantage to these meetings and repeated caveats.
These men come from the top echelons of society. One could
hope that their input will carry some weight with the king;
however, as I have said before, Farouq rules in such an autocratic
way that even though these figures have their own ideas they still
defer to a large degree to the king's wishes.

<...> Let me here also request several pictures of Princess
Shahnaz be sent so that they can be presented to her grandmother
as soon as possible. Ghasem Ghani.

<...>

TO HIM'S SPECIAL OFFICE 8 JANUARY 1948:

<...> Early Monday morning (5 January) Naguib Pasha
telephoned to renew his request for an answer on the issue (i.e.,
the demand for an amicable divorce). I said that there was
nothing new.

To prepare myself on the subject of the "royal commission"
that the king, Fawzia and Salem Pasha have repeatedly mentioned,
I consulted Egyptian law. I have extracted the exact statutes and
am sending a copy for HIM's perusal. According to the statute, the
commission will consist of several people headed by the prince
most proximate to the royal family, who is at the present time
Mohammad Ali. As I had surmised in an earlier report, the crown
prince has spoken to the king on the matter and strenuously
objected to the commission on the grounds that it violates the
clear dictates of Islamic law. He also added that it is detrimental
for political, social and moral reasons.

<...>

Dr. Ghasem Ghani.

<...>

The Egyptian prime minister suggested that gifts, preferably Iranian, be presented to Her Majesty Fawzia at an appropriate time. Later a fine Persian carpet was chosen.

TO HIM'S SPECIAL OFFICE 10 JANUARY 1948:

As previously reported I met with Ahmad Khashaba Pasha (20 December 1947). On 5 January 1948 Khashaba Pasha came to the embassy for lunch, but he said that his busy schedule did not allow him to make any contacts. We agreed to meet again at the Foreign Ministry three days later.

He said that he used the occasion of a meeting of the king with Egypt's new ambassador to Iran to broach the subject of Fawzia. The king said:

1. Her Majesty's return to Iran was out of the question. He could do nothing as her decision was final.

2. Were the matter of the separation and the divorce accomplished amicably, there would be absolutely no change in the close social and political relations between the two countries.

3. Were the matter of the separation and the divorce accomplished amicably, there would be absolutely no alteration in the brotherly ties between the two monarchs themselves.
   <...>

I responded to the three points one by one. First, merely to assert that return was impossible and that the decision was final was not enough to justify the divorce. Even if these were two anonymous people, one would have to be more specific about the grounds. <...> This was especially true in the case of Moslems, under whose law a woman cannot request a divorce unless there are exceptional circumstances. <...>

On the second point: How could one say that a demand for divorce with no stated reason or justification will have no ill effects on relations between the two countries? Unless, God forbid, you believe that Iran is a paper tiger whose people are indifferent to its fate or who are incapable of reacting to an insult to their national dignity.

The third point about the continuation of brotherly relations between the two monarchs is an obvious inconsistency. The words "divorce" and "separation" have nothing to do with friendly personal relations.

<...>

A few weeks ago the American ambassador to Egypt Mr. Tuck, a close friend, told me confidentially, "Our relationship compels me <...> to tell you that I have heard several times that the reason Queen Fawzia is not returning to Iran is that she fears the shah will never permit her to come back to Egypt." I have made it very clear to King Farouq on behalf of HIM that such was not the case and that Her Majesty would have complete freedom to do whatever she wishes. <...> Dr. Ghasem Ghani.

TO HIM'S SPECIAL OFFICE 25 JANUARY 1948:

Several entries on a fine Tabriz carpet to be sent from Iran to Queen Fawzia. King Farouq communicated through Naguib Salem Pasha that she could not accept the gift personally, but he would do so on her behalf. Dr. Ghani said that he found little difference between Her Majesty and her brother, so he suggested that the carpet be presented to him on the occasion of the Prophet's birthday.

I asked Naguib Salem Pasha how Her Majesty could refuse to accept the gift. It was not the monetary value of the carpet itself, but what it represented: the love and affection of a husband and a daughter. He said that his instruction was to deliver King Farouq's message but confided, "I am absolutely certain that the relationship between Fawzia and HIM will never improve and that she will never return to Iran." He asked me why I was pursuing a lost cause so stubbornly. I told him that I had only the best intentions not only toward Iran but to the Egyptian royal family. <...>
Dr. Ghasem Ghani.

<...>

TELEGRAM FROM SHOKUH, HEAD OF HIM'S SPECIAL OFFICE
2 FEBRUARY 1948:

> HIM has read your letter and asks: How long are we to
> observe these diplomatic niceties? To this point we have done
> everything possible, unfortunately to no effect. Instead [of
> civility], our telegrams go unanswered and our gifts are spurned,
> behavior that is cause for insult. Under these circumstances do
> you still think it advisable to pursue the matter in a friendly way?
> <...>

In a long report to the Special Office dated 7 February 1948, Dr. Ghani
goes into more detail about his conversation with Asal Beyg, the new
Egyptian ambassador to Iran.

DIARY ENTRY 19 FEBRUARY 1948:

Witnessing the general state of Middle Eastern nations—the deep,
extraordinary corruption that has taken hold of the whole region and
its inhabitants—has depressed me. In recent years one has heard
much about national and individual rights, and the words "independence" and "liberty" are on everyone's lips, but intellectual and
spiritual freedom have declined.

The people have a slavish mentality, their minds are captive to the
basest desires. They falsely believe that freedom is something gained
from the outside, rather than the intrinsic, spiritual thing it truly is.
<...> When they do desire freedom, it is the freedom to enslave oth-
ers. <...> From morning to night they commit crimes in the name of
freedom. <...> The basest elements govern these societies using the
most deplorable means. What is worse, self-importance and tyranny
have become universal. Every seed of virtue and decency has fallen on
barren ground. As Hafez says:

> *There is not one man to be found in this mortal world,*
> *The world must be made anew and likewise man.*

TO HIM'S SPECIAL OFFICE 21 FEBRUARY 1948:

On 18 February I met with Crown Prince Mohammad Ali, who expressed his frustration. He has no power or influence but continues to criticize the political, economic and social conditions in the country. These days antiroyalist and antistate movements are growing and the government is helpless to stop them. The peasants live in deprivation and poverty. Revolutionaries and those connected to foreign powers are on the move. King Farouq is greatly troubled but does nothing.

He still speaks pessimistically about the Fawzia matter. The royals are out of touch with society and no one around them appreciates or understands the situation. <...>
Dr. Ghasem Ghani.

DIARY ENTRY THURSDAY 4 MARCH 1948:

Professor [Arthur Upham] Pope, who has arrived from India, telephoned. I asked him to lunch here [at the embassy]. He wants to scrounge money from HIM, who has promised to help his foundation. This man is all about money and truly will stop at nothing to obtain it. He went to Mashhad about seventeen years ago as the guest of Mr. Jam and took photographs of historical sights. He has also taken a series of photographs of Shiraz, Esfahan and other places. Pope was active later at the London Exposition, which may have been in 1938, and gained a reputation. He wrote a six-volume work composed of descriptions of historical monuments called Survey of Persian Art. Later he established the Iranian Institute in New York and became known as a specialist in Iranian artwork. Pope collected a number of Iranian manuscripts, plates, water jars, carpets, weavings, and paintings. He bought and sold things. He set up classes in Iranian languages and Arabic, and for meager compensation assembled a group of Iranians and Eastern European Jews driven from Europe who were specialists in Middle Eastern art. He then renamed his foundation The Asia Institute. He also had dealings with India and the Arab countries. His wife, Phyllis Ackerman, is well known. She is also no scholar. Now that he has become friendly with the Russians, Pope has become their advocate. He has written articles for them, interpreting the weakening of Iran in their favor, all the while mixing socially with Iranians. In the United States he visits Washington often, staying at the Russian Embassy. When Mr. Ala arrived [in Washington], Pope was his guest at the embassy. <...>

TO HIM's SPECIAL OFFICE 13 MARCH 1948:

> Your latest letter asks, "Whether there is any indication of foreign elements in the matter of the separation of Her Majesty and HIM." After conducting an investigation, I can say that no such elements are involved. <...>

Dr. Ghani gives the details of his investigation and then repeats his view that Her Majesty's decision is not based on reason but on her immaturity and vulnerability to others' opinions.

> So long as Her Majesty stays in Egypt she will remain adamant, but were she to go to Iran, her feelings would change. I place most of the blame for this on Farouq. He could easily have put an end to the misunderstandings, but now that things have gone this far, he insists that he is powerless to alter them. The king has completely lost direction not only in this matter, but in all aspects of his public and private lives. There is little rhyme or reason to his behavior, which is why he has alienated large segments of the population. <...>
> One of his traits is a strange stubbornness that borders on intransigence. He is perhaps encouraged in this obstinacy when those short-sighted courtiers label it "moral firmness" and "decisiveness." <...> The king is also an exceptionally jealous person. If, for example, the crowd at some event applauds an actor or athlete, he is not pleased. As a specific example, I can mention the way he changed the program for Queen Farida's public appearances. Normally at the opening of Parliament, she

would precede him to the royal observation box, but when the deputies and others in attendance showered their affection on the beloved queen, the king arranged it so that they entered simultaneously. It is no exaggeration to say that one of the things that soured the royal couple's relations is her great popularity among the people. It would also not be far from the truth to suggest that Her Majesty's (Fawzia's) title "queen" also incurred Farouq's jealousy. <...>

The way the common people revile the king grows more palpable daily. At his public audiences there is absolutely none of the old verve and expressions of popular support. Only a few of those in attendance seem genuinely happy. On the city walls one often finds graffiti that reflects what is being said among the people, who have dubbed Farouq "the king of women." Taxi drivers openly regale their passengers with jokes insulting to him, and students protest his actions. <...> The purpose of these details is to provide a backdrop of the general tenor of the times here, from which a clear picture of the Fawzia issue can emerge by itself.

<...>

DIARY ENTRY 13 MARCH 1948:

<...> 5:30 P.M. Mr. Taha Husayn visited accompanied by Farid Shamatah, his private secretary and aid—in reality his guide [Taha Husayn was blind]. We spoke for a time on academic matters. He has promised to study Persian. He said that Mutanabbi, a few months before his suicide, visited Shiraz. His Shiraz verses possess a certain freshness because he was speaking of nature. After Mutanabbi returned to Iraq with the intention of going back to Shiraz permanently, the poor man died. I asked him to compare Mutanabbi and Abu al-'Ala. He said that it was chalk

Taha Husayn

and cheese; Abu al-'Ala was a world writer, while Mutanabbi was one of a number of good and clever Arab poets.

We spoke a great deal about the eighth century in the Islamic era, (fourteenth century C.E.). He agreed to draw up an agenda. I invited him for lunch on the twentieth of March, saying that at that point our Iranian year would come to an end. I recalled that the end of the Christian year was the time I had met Einstein.

Dr. Ghani developed a close friendship with Taha Husayn, an Egyptian author and scholar. Blind from a young age, and from modest circumstances, Taha Husayn studied in Paris and became one of the most gifted writers of Arabic prose in the twentieth century. Dr. Ghani was the witness at the marriage of Taha Husayn's daughter to Muhammad Husayn Zayat, who later became Egypt's foreign minister.

TO HIM'S SPECIAL OFFICE 1 MAY 1948:

Dr. Ghani reports on conversations with Nuqrashi Pasha and other high-ranking Egyptians that reflect the general pessimism about Fawzia's return to Iran. Finally he admits his own conclusion that nothing more can be done and recommends divorce as the only option. He then lists three conditions governing the nature of the divorce process.

1. It must not put HIM in a bad light. We cannot effectively admit that Her Majesty became fed up, demanded a divorce, and that we, having taken her demands at face value, merely acceded to them. She must acknowledge in writing that she has absolutely no complaints about the behavior of her esteemed husband the shah or about the affections of the Iranian people. She will blame the divorce on the poor weather of Iran or some other factor that you might suggest.

2. The precious jewels HIM brought to Egypt and presented to (the then Princess Fawzia) must be returned. <...>

3. After these conditions are adopted, it must be agreed that the Egyptians will meet with me promptly. I must not be forced to

seek them and continually renew the issue. <...> The reason for this is, as I have indicated a number of times, official negotiations between high-ranking Egyptians and me have broken off during the last few months. To effect this it is necessary to instruct Asal Beyg, the Egyptian ambassador to Iran, that HIM has complete faith and trust in Ghasem Ghani, Iranian ambassador to Egypt. He must refer to Dr. Ghani who will determine what is advisable. <...> Of course King Farouq has an inordinate fondness for jewels, and I am certain that he will do his utmost not to return them. Failing that, he may try to give at least some of them back. <...> Dr. Ghasem Ghani.

HIM's special office telegraphed on 9 May 1948 to say that the bulk of the jewels given to Fawzia were in a safe in Tehran. On 23 May 1948 Dr. Ghani responded in a long letter detailing the bad faith on the part of the Egyptians, on one hand, and the shah's patience and magnanimity, on the other. He calls for the return of valuable items sent with the body of Reza Shah and of the fine carpet rejected by Fawzia.

TELEGRAM FROM HIM'S SPECIAL OFFICE. 27 MAY 1948:

1. On the matter of where the divorce procedure will take place, HIM agrees that it should be in Tehran.

2. On the return of the jewels, your opinion is correct. But given the greed of the other side, which has become so sordid and distasteful, HIM has decided that only the two rings be returned and that we forgo the rest of the jewels.

3. On the matter of the sword, medals and other valuables that accompanied the late shah's body, HIM says that this be kept separate from the matter of the divorce. Since the new tomb site in Iran is near completion, the items should be returned with the body. <...> Shokuh.

<...>

DIARY ENTRY 29 MAY 1948:

Asal Beyg (ambassador of Egypt to Tehran) called on me at 11 A.M.
He had five audiences with the shah. He told me HIM had been kind,
etc. <...> Concerning the matter of the divorce, His Majesty had said
that the terms must meet Dr. Ghani's approval:
1. Fawzia to write to the Shah and give the reason(s) for the
divorce.
2. A press release giving the reasons for the divorce.
3. Return of two pieces of jewelry, preferably some to be given
to Princess Shahnaz, but she can keep the rest.
4. Relations between the two countries will be unaffected.

*The matter of the divorce drags on into September 1948. Dr. Ghani
returns from Geneva, where he was the Iranian delegate to the UN conference on world health, and has an audience with King Farouq. While
in Geneva Dr. Ghani saw a good deal of the great Iranian writer
Mohammad Ali Jamalzadeh. He also sees the shah. With His Majesty
behind the wheel, the two drive to a secluded inn outside Geneva and
have a long talk.*

TO HIM'S SPECIAL OFFICE 8-9 SEPTEMBER 1948:

In the audience with King Farouq, the king stressed that the
issue of the divorce be kept apart from all other matters. The
good relations between the two states should not be influenced
nor should the king's close personal ties with HIM. <...> He also
confided in me that his sister had not been cut out to play the role
of a queen. He said that I had no idea how anxious she is for the
divorce to take place. When he was away for twenty days involved
in military movements in Palestine, not a day passed that she did
not call or telegraph asking when it would take place. <...> Dr.
Ghasem Ghani.

DIARY ENTRY 16 SEPTEMBER 1948:

Various issues: Egyptian reluctance to return the medals and sword that accompanied the body of Reza Shah. HIM asks whether Dr. Ghani wished to stay at his post after the divorce. Dr. Ghani informs him that his continuing to stay in Egypt is not appropriate.

FROM HIM'S SPECIAL OFFICE 23 SEPTEMBER 1948:

Dr. Ghani. According to HIM's edict, given our upcoming dealings with the Egyptian royal family, your mission in Cairo is no longer advisable. HIM has asked the Foreign Ministry to seek your acceptance of the post of Iranian ambassador in Ankara. Shokuh.

FROM HIM'S SPECIAL OFFICE. SEPTEMBER 1948.

Dr. Ghani. According to the royal decree, Ali Dashti is to replace you as ambassador in Cairo. <...> Pirnazar.
<...>

DIARY ENTRY FRIDAY 15 OCTOBER 1948:

<...>
Dr. Taha Husayn has written from Paris that his daughter had told him that my [Dr. Ghani's] departure from Cairo was imminent. In a letter well worth reading he expressed his brotherly regard for me. Dr. Husayn has recently written a work called *Rehlat al-Rabi'* [Journey of Spring]. He devotes the entire fourth chapter of this work to my unalloyed friendship with him without mentioning me by name. <...>

CODED TELEGRAM FROM HIM'S SPECIAL OFFICE. 19 OCTOBER 1948.

The divorce took place in Cairo two days ago, therefore your presence in Cairo is not appropriate. As soon as word of the new ambassador's acceptance is received, proceed to Ankara immediately. Shokuh.

The following are excerpts from political reports on Egypt that Dr. Ghani prepared for the Special Office.

<...>

THE GENERAL SITUATION IN EGYPT. 22 NOVEMBER 1948.

Situated midway between the East and the West, Egypt's vast size, population and natural resources have accorded it a leadership position among Arab nations.

Given the current world situation and Egypt's experienced diplomatic corps, the country could have played an important role in political affairs from Morocco to India. Unfortunately, because most Egyptian statesmen are products of the colonial system, tools of foreign powers, without natural talents, or marginalized as a result of domestic or foreign politics, it has been unable to fulfill that role.

<...>

[Dr. Ghani then briefly summarizes King Farouq's life beginning with his birth in 1921 and ending, after the death of his father, King Fuad, with his sudden accession to the throne on 6 May 1936. Dr. Ghani also mentions Farouq's marriage in 1938 to Safi Naz (later called Farida), a popular choice because she was not related to the royal family.]

FAROUQ'S VARIOUS ROLES

1. After World War II when the people of Syria and Lebanon rose against France, the British, acting in their own political interests, promised to aid them. To intimidate the Lebanese, the French imprisoned two of their leaders. At the time King Farouq telegraphed his support for these Lebanese leaders. When they finally were released from prison, the Egyptian press was full of articles about how decisive the king's actions were in effecting their release.

2. When the League of Arab States was first established, differences between the House of Saud and the Hashemites of Jordan kept the Saudis from participating. Taking the Saudi lead, Yemen also did not attend. King Farouq visited Saudi Arabia with his ministers and managed to reconcile the feuding parties. <...>

3. <...> In addition to hosting a number of leaders attending the League meeting at his farm near Cairo, Farouq also gave sanctuary to a number of other Arab leaders. Among them were Seyyed Mohammad Idrisi Sanusi (the former emir of Libya); and Mohammad Amin al-Hosayni the mufti of Jerusalem. Thus the king made Egypt the center of Arab nationalist aspirations. Several independence leaders from Algeria, Habib Bourghiba from Tunisia, Mohammad Ali Fasi from Morocco, etc. made the country their headquarters. <...>

THE KING'S INTEREST IN RELIGIOUS MATTERS

Because of the deeply religious nature of the Egyptian masses, Farouq attached a great deal of importance to Islamic ritual from the outset of his reign. During the Friday prayer services, many of which were published in the press and broadcast on the radio, preachers praise his piety. Pictures of him exiting from the mosque are also published in magazines that are popular throughout the Arab Middle East.

During Ramadan, he makes a great show of fasting. At night his palaces host famous Qur'an reciters, ministers, representatives of Islamic countries and students from al-Azhar. Food from these gatherings is also distributed among the indigent. <...> During other Islamic holy days and festivals, he also invites religious leaders and students from abroad to Egypt, thereby winning adherents among the foreign religious classes.

CHANGE IN THE KING'S BEHAVIOR AND
HIS CONSTITUTIONAL AUTHORITY

In the last several years a youthful pride has combined with the extraordinary constitutional powers granted to the monarch to inflate Farouq's importance. The king's authority is far greater than a constitutional monarch; he can approve or veto legislation, appoint and dismiss ministers, he has complete authority over the military and can declare war.

Added to all of this is that due to retirement or death, there have been no people of substance around the king for some time. A group of corrupt and disreputable figures has taken their place. These people have wormed their way into Farouq's circle with flattery and have been his regular companions at Cairo's notorious cabarets and clubs. Their nightly excursions have become common knowledge and appear to be the reason for the queen's (Farida's) estrangement from her husband. Things have reached such a state that she has asked for a divorce. This request coincided with Fawzia's return to Cairo, which has caused people to speculate that Fawzia had come back to try to reconcile the royal couple. <...>

<...>

THE KING'S CHARACTER AND HABITS

Lately Farouq's demeanor has taken on an arrogance and rudeness. Gone is that special warmth that he had shown the people, his courtiers and ministers who accompany him to Friday prayers. The way he treats the peasants on the royal lands leaves a great deal to be desired. They are prey to the same poverty, ignorance and disease that the rest of the country's peasantry endures. This is in spite of the fact that the royal holdings are among the most important and fertile in the country. Though Farouq had no need for more land, he has followed in his father's footsteps in coveting any choice property that happens to abut his. If the owner is unwilling to sell for the bargain price the king determines, he resorts to coercion or allows the royal sheep and cattle to graze on the land, thereby ruining it.

<...>

THE COURT BUDGET

Until 1946 the yearly court budget was 771,731 Egyptian pounds, <...> which was raised this year (1947) to 807,961 pounds. In addition to this, the royal family has extensive land holdings that produce a large income. Despite this, their charitable contributions are hardly commensurate with their wealth. <...>

THE KING'S RELATIONS WITH THE BRITISH

Since the late King Fuad was placed on the throne as a result of British efforts, he considered himself beholden to them. His son's relations with the British proceeded on the same friendly basis. However, after Italy's entrance into the war and the many successes enjoyed by the Axis powers, Anglo-Egyptian relations became clouded. At the time, Prime Minister Ali Maher Pasha did not think declaring war on the Axis to be in the best interest of the country. Since the king trusted him completely he followed his prime minister's advice. Farouq also feared alienating the 70,000 Italian residents of Egypt who, it was thought, would join the Axis cause. This, of course, did not sit well with the British, so in 1942, when their situation was precarious, the British forced the king to accept Nahas Pasha, who was wholly obedient to them, as the new prime minister. On 4 February of that year (1942), they surrounded the Abedin Palace with tanks and armored cars. The British ambassador Sir Miles Lampson (Lord Killearn), accompanied by a number of officers, entered the palace and forced the king to accept the change. From that time relations grew worse. <...>

This is followed by a six-page summary of the history of Morocco; a thirteen-page report on the prospects of a union of Arab countries. There is also a twenty-one-page report on the history of the rule of King Farouq, his father, mother and sister.

THE KING'S RELATIONS WITH THE POLITICAL PARTIES

THE WAFD PARTY

Farouq does not have good relations with this party, which is backed by an extraordinarily large segment of the public, for several reasons. The head of the party, Nahas Pasha, an arrogant and fearless man, does not treat the king with the proper respect. Emboldened by his new-found national status, Nahas Pasha is as indifferent to Farouq as the other party leaders. After the events of 4 February described earlier, the king's relations with the Wafd Party worsened, and attempts to better them were unsuccessful. <...> As long as Nahas Pasha is the head of the party, the situation will remain unaltered.

THE HAY'AH SA'DIAH AND AHRAR DASTURIYUN PARTIES

By contrast, the king's relations with these two parties, which are obedient to him, are good. The respective heads of the parties, Nuqrashi Pasha and Haykal Pasha, are on good terms with him.

THE WAFD KUTLAH INDEPENDENT PARTY

When the head of the Kutlah Party, Makram Ebeid Pasha, first broke with the Wafdists, he was one of the most active enemies of Nahas Pasha (Wafd Party head). Because of this, the king, operating on the principle of "the enemy of my enemy is my friend," showed special favor toward Makram Ebeid Pasha. The king ordered his release from prison and appointed him minister of the treasury. The court also provided exceptional assistance in the publication of Makram Ebeid's *Black Book* against Nahas Pasha. Recently, however, the king has become disaffected with Makram Ebeid and the Kutlah Party. This has driven Makram Ebeid and his former Wafdist colleagues closer together, as they share the goal of bringing down the present Cabinet.

<...>

AL-AZHAR

At the beginning of his reign, Farouq was particularly attentive to religious matters. He was especially attached to the al-Azhar Complex [the main religious institution in Egypt]. He held the head of al-Azhar, the late Sheikh Mohammad Mostafa al-Maraghi, in high esteem. He was one of Farouq's close companions and advisors. <...> After al-Maraghi's death the king appointed Sheikh Mostafa Abd al-Razzaq, who was outside of the circle of al-Azhar divines, to replace him. Because this went against the wishes of the leading clerics, the king's relationship with al-Azhar changed. <...> Dr. Ghasem Ghani.

Dr. Ghani devotes the next twenty pages of the memoir to short histories and descriptions of the political parties of Egypt. These include the National Party (Hezb al-Watanin), the Wafd Party, the Ahrar Dasturiyun Party, The Hay'ah Sa'diah or Sa'd Party, the Wafd Kutlah Independent Party, the Egyptian Front Party (Jebheh Mesr), the Young Egyptian Party (Hezb Mesr al-Fatat) and the Workers Party (Hezb al-Ommal). He also describes important religious groups that, though not political parties per se, played a role in Egyptian politics. One was the Moslem Youth League (al-Shobban al-Moslemun), the other the Moslem Brotherhood (Akhwan al-Moslemun). Dr. Ghani's remarks on the latter are a contemporary picture of Sheikh Hasan al-Banna, the group's controversial founder, that contrasts with many present-day views of him.

THE MOSLEM BROTHERHOOD

<...> Although the Moslem Brotherhood was founded in 1928, one year after the Moslem Youth organization, it has now eclipsed that party in importance and infrastructure.

The founder and head of the Brotherhood is Sheikh Hasan al-Banna, who for several years taught Arabic grammar and calligraphy in the Egyptian public schools. In 1928 he and some like-minded people banded together to form the organization with the purpose of reviving the glory and grandeur of Islam. At first the group was of little importance, but gradually its principles and program gained a following among al-Azhar and university students. They also have established branches in the provinces as well as in the Sudan, Palestine, Syria, Lebanon and Transjordan. They now have a following of about two million people.

The Brotherhood's religious purpose is to proselytize Islam and interpret the Qur'an in keeping with the spirit of modern times. They disseminate these teachings among diverse strata of Egyptian society and other Islamic nations to unify the various Moslem sects. The phrases "God is our sacred aim, the Prophet is our leader, the Qur'an is our platform and the struggle in God's path is our fondest desire" sums up their religious agenda. The political goal of the Brotherhood is to free Egypt and the other Arab and Islamic nations in the region from foreign domination. Thus, from a political point of view they share the aims of the Unity Party; but, because their anti-British feelings are combined with religious fervor, one can say that the members of the Brotherhood are more extreme than the Unity Party adherents.

The head of the Brotherhood, Sheikh Hasan al-Banna, is a very intelligent man and a good orator. He leads a very simple and moral life. He is humble, reliable, and is well versed in the Arabic language and qur'anic studies. Because the Brotherhood's organizations are so well run, many imagine that foreigners had a hand in its founding; but this is baseless. One could say, however, that the political conditions and nationalist sentiments that arose in the wake of the two world wars abetted peoples' willingness to accept the type of religious and patriotic messages the Brotherhood spread.

Sheikh al-Banna had wanted to participate in the last round of elections for the Egyptian Consultative Assembly, and it had been predicted that he would have been successful. However, the British, who felt his presence in the assembly would be a threat, objected. As the war was still going on, the state forced al-Banna to refrain from running for office. Now, however, with the number of his followers greatly increased, al-Banna will participate in the elections and is assured of very positive results.

<...>

AL-AZHAR MOSQUE COMPLEX

In this entry, Dr. Ghani gives a brief history of the al-Azhar mosque complex and has valuable and detailed comments on its inner politics.

<...>

In 1928 the late Sheikh Maraghi became the head of al-Azhar and proposed to former King Fuad that the institution be divided into a number of independent colleges, each with its own discipline. However, since Maraghi's tenure as Chief Sheikh ended, reform fell to his successor, Sheikh Ahmad al-Zawaheri.

The reform and modernization of al-Azhar's institutions led to greater political influence in its affairs, in the appointing and dismissing of clerics. <...> Sheikh Ahmad al-Zawaheri, who was a zealot and a reactionary, opposed the reforms. However, since the late Fuad was in favor of them, al-Zawaheri was forced to comply with his predecessor's wishes.

Sheikh al-Zawaheri remained in office until 1934. His intransigent opposition to every proposed change to al-Azhar induced a corresponding obstinacy in the anticonservative movement. This obstinacy manifested itself in demonstrations against Sheikh al-Zawaheri. The Sheikh, on his part, adopted a very hard line. He dismissed a number of al-Azhar clerics and expelled some of the seminary students, claiming that they had left the faith and therefore had no legitimate place in the complex.

<...> Eventually things reached such a state that King Fuad was forced to intervene and appoint Sheikh Maraghi again as head. They say that owing to Sheikh Maraghi's good relations with the British when he was chief justice in the Sudan, their representative approved his reappointment to lead al-Azhar.

Sheikh Maraghi's policy during his second term differed completely from that of his first. In contrast to Sheikh Zawaheri, who rigidly enforced academic and moral standards, Sheikh Maraghi this time was very lax. He allowed politics to influence the running of al-Azhar. After the death of King Fuad in 1936, the Sheikh's contacts with people at court and, later, with King Farouq became more extensive. Sheikh Maraghi had considerable influence with Farouq in political matters; he was instrumental in the rise and fall of his Cabinets, and in schemes to boost the new monarch's popularity.

The late King Fuad saw al-Azhar as instrumental in propagating his ideas regarding the caliphate. He therefore thought that it was necessary to strengthen the institution and to maintain the standing of its sheikhs in the Islamic (Sunni) world. However, under King Farouq, al-Azhar devolved into an extension of the court, a device for increasing its influence vis-à-vis the political parties. The late Maraghi tried very hard to implement Farouq's plans. He made extensive changes to al-Azhar's rules and regulations, and placed the decision as to who would occupy positions at the institution in Farouq's hands.

<...>

Fawzia obtained her divorce on 16 October 1948. Some five or six months later she married Ismael Shirin, an Egyptian with close ties to the Egyptian court.

Prior to assuming his new post as ambassador to Turkey, Dr. Ghani departed for Tehran on 27 October 1948. The following excerpts are from a lengthy diary entry of some fifty pages written between 28 October 1948 and 5 January 1949, which covers his stay of about two months in Tehran.

I met the Turkish ambassador to Tehran on two occasions and had several audiences with HIM. Almost every day I called on several aged friends: Mohammad Qazvini, Amir Arfa, Mokhber al-Saltaneh Hedayat; the family of Nasrollah Taqavi; and other close friends including General Yazdanpanah, Abbas Arya, Hoseyn Shaybani, Mohammad Jam and Vosuq. <...> I had several invitations to the U.S. Embassy. <...> The new foreign minister is Ali Asghar Hekmat with Dr. Aliqoli Ardalan as undersecretary for political affairs and Qods

Nakhai as administrative undersecretary. <...> The ministry is staffed with incompetent individuals. These recent changes will be beneficial.

On 7 October I took the flight to Mashhad accompanied by my brother Hoseyn. I was met at the airport by city officials and close friends, including Shams al-Din Nakhai, Dr. Qavam, Dr. Sheikh, Hasan Ameli, Dr. Hasan Fazel, Dr. Mahmud Zia'i, Dr. Hasan Eftekhari, Mahmud Farrokh, Mohammad Qoreishi and Ali Golkani. Several people from Nishapur and Sabzevar had come to greet me: Ebrahim Sa'idi, sons of the late Salar Mo'tamed, Drs. Rajabali and Abbas Jarahi, Hasan Nabavi, Dr. Motavali, Mirza Badi', Aqa Reza Ebrahimi. Later I traveled to Nishapur to pay my respects at the grave of Kamal al-Molk, who is buried near Sheikh Attar's grave.

RETURN TO TEHRAN

Had several audiences with His Majesty. We talked about Egypt and Turkey, but most of the conversation was about Iran. Unfortunately His Majesty is surrounded by nonentities, some of whom are even ill intentioned. <...> The Minister of Court Mr. Mahmud Jam is a loyal and dedicated public servant, but he is powerless. Others such as Yusef Shokra'i, the chief of protocol at court, carry more weight. He sets up audiences for His Majesty. <...> He has allowed incompetents to staff key positions at court. <...> Lieutenant General Yazdanpanah has been marginalized. Mr. Adib al-Saltaneh (Hoseyn Sami'i), a noble and virtuous public servant, is not taken seriously.

Princess Ashraf is the most influential of all members of the royal family. The influence she has on her sovereign brother is unusual. Her intervention in the appointment of ambassadors, Cabinet ministers and other high officials is decisive. Through her appointees she also influences the choice of undersecretaries at various ministries. She is in contact with proprietors of several publications and other notables. Her close entourage includes Abdolhoseyn Hazhir; Shokra'i; Movaffaq Nuri Esfandiari; Khosrow Hedayat; Ahmad Dehqan, publisher and member of Parliament; Sardar Fakher Hekmat, speaker of Parliament; and Dr. Javad Ashtiani, member of parliament. <...>

Princess Shams, on the other hand, lives a quiet life. She has a small group around her, hosts a literary tea every Tuesday and is honorary head of the Red Lion and Sun Society. She has a two-year-old son. <...> People close to her are Mr. Mahmud Jam and General Yazdanpanah. <...> The Queen Mother leads a subdued existence, never mixing socially.

Prince Abdolreza, a graduate of Harvard University, is honorary head of the Seven Year Plan Organization. Prince Alireza also lives in Tehran but is not active socially. Prince Hamidreza lives with his mother, Esmat Pahlavi. <...> Prince Gholamreza lives with his wife, Homa (Amir Alam), and their son.

One cannot help but feel sorry for His Majesty who has to support and supervise his large number of brothers and sisters. He pays their expenses and provides them with palaces, offices and a number of aides, functionaries, etc. <...> Unfortunately they are not of great help to HIM. <...>

His Majesty's time is often wasted. Shokra'i arranges useless audiences. <...> The shah's popularity is his greatest asset, but it is being squandered. <...> It peaked after the resolution of the Azerbaijan Crisis, the withdrawal of Soviet forces and HIM's trip to Tabriz; but soon afterward came the unpopular government of Hazhir. <...> Several newspapers criticized the shah for his support of Hazhir.

Then there was HIM's visit to England. It assumed importance as it was his first state visit, and greater effort should also have gone into its preparation both in Tehran and London...Above all, it should have been an official state visit. Greater care also should have been exercised in determining who accompanied HIM. <...> Other than Mr. Mahmud Jam, minister of court, who had experience and dignity, the rest of HIM's entourage were not people of much weight or substance. It consisted of individuals like Hormoz Pirnia, Hoseynqoli Qaraguzlu, Brigadiers Hejazi and Ayadi, and Colonels Ansari and Fardust. <...>

From discussions I have had with HIM, I know that he has been contemplating some changes in the constitution that would bring moderation to the extreme positions that the Ministry of Court and Parliament have adopted.

Among the amendments HIM is considering are:

1. The right of veto by the shah of any legislation passed by Parliament, which requires the signature of the shah. <…> In case of a veto, the bill would be sent back to Parliament for reconsideration. <…> If Parliament chooses to override the veto and once again ratify the legislation with or without revision, the bill would be deemed as approved without the Shah having a veto power over its ratification.

2. Creation of a second chamber (the Senate), which had been foreseen and provided for in the constitution but never implemented.

3. The shah to have the power to dissolve Parliament if evidence shows that the members elected are not the true representatives of the electorate. <…> However, the shah would be bound to call for a new parliamentary election within two or three months. Irrespective of who is elected to the new Parliament, the shah would not be able to dissolve that term of the Parliament again. <…>

4. Amendment of the bylaws of Parliament with respect to quorum and voting, which would prevent a small minority from tying up the consideration and approval of a bill.

5. Placing a time limit of two or three months on parliamentary deliberation on the approval of the budget. If deliberations exceed the period, the government would have the right to proceed on the previous year's budget.

6. Providing for the procedure and mechanism to amend the Constitution if the need should arise.

HIM raised these topics with me several times. (At HIM's urging) Mr. Abolhasan Ebtehaj called, wanting to see me. I went to the Bank and spent some two hours with him. Ebtehaj is a man of 45 or 46. His entire working life has been spent in banking and economic affairs. He worked for years at the British-run Imperial Bank. He then transferred to Bank Melli (National Bank). During HIM's reign, Mr.

Ebtehaj finally became managing director of Bank Melli. He speaks excellent English and is knowledgeable about finance and economics. He is thoroughly honest, meticulous in his work and has managed the bank well. He has assembled an excellent staff. He is hard-working, emotional and loses his temper often, but he has good intentions. He is passionate in his beliefs.

Mr. Ebtehaj stated that His Majesty has had talks with him on the near paralysis of the country and had suggested that he consult me on the matter. <...> Mr. Ebtehaj reiterated the matters I have previously outlined. <...>

HIM has set out a very difficult agenda. <...> The present Parliament may balk every step of the way and may not be willing to yield any of its powers. There may be vested foreign interests that are inimical to what HIM has in mind. <...> I told Mr. Ebtehaj that the matter needs to be studied further and we must consult some of the so-called elders (fathers of the Constitution), such as Messrs. Hakim al-Molk, Taqizadeh, Ala and Seyyed Mohammad Sadeq Tabataba'i. I had four meetings with Mr. Taqizadeh and sought his advice and met with HIM several more times.

The difficulty we face is that the number of trustworthy people has dwindled. Those in power are mainly superficial and selfish people who only wish to protect their own positions and financial interests. There is a great shortage of people with courage.

The diary goes on to describe the literary salons hosted by Princess Shams, Dr. Ghani's meeting with Princess Ashraf and the Queen Mother, and the shortcomings of the Cabinet. It then turns to evils of contemporary Iranian society.

<...>

The newspapers are as a whole degraded and without content. They pander to the lowest tastes, stopping at nothing in the pursuit of larger circulation. Gambling is rife and some term it "a sign of civilization." Opium use is also more common than ever, as everyone is inwardly depressed but outwardly carefree and clownish.

The schools and university are in ruins and the love of learning is gone. The general level of information is in decline. Politics has poisoned the intellectual climate as teachers scheme and vie for position. Some disruptive elements have gained professorships at the university and are corrupting their students. It all amounts to the passionate pursuit of the B.A., which is the ticket to government service and further careerism.

Popular fiction has become wholly lethal. It amounts to romantic literature couched in the most obscene language, which poisons the minds of school children. The motive behind these publications is profit. Rarely is a useful book published. <...>

Dr. Ghani's notes on his tenure as ambassador end with various reports to the Iranian Foreign Ministry and HIM's Special Office. He writes eight pages on the political repercussions in Egypt of the UN proposal to partition Palestine. He also discusses the Saudi reaction. In another report he details attempted and successful assassinations of Egyptian officials and British military personnel that occurred during the period 1941–46. Finally, he writes in detail on the history of the Egyptian struggle for independence from the British. He includes the roles the various political parties, including the Communists, played in this movement.

AMBASSADOR TO TURKEY

AMBASSADOR TO TURKEY: JANUARY 1949 TO 31 MAY 1950

All attempts to heal the rift between HIM and Queen Fawzia failed. When Fawzia officially asked for a divorce, Dr. Ghani felt his presence in Egypt would be inimical to the interests of Iran, and asked to be recalled as ambassador to Cairo. The shah appointed him ambassador to Turkey. He returned to Tehran for a brief stay.

WEDNESDAY 5 JANUARY 1949

An extremely cold day. I was to fly to Turkey on 28 December, but heavy snowfall closed the Tehran airport. After a delay of eight days a KLM flight arrived in Tehran and I left for Istanbul, arriving at 12:30 P.M. local time. <...> I was greeted by Mr. Bahman Zand, the Iranian consul general, consulate employees, leaders of the Iranian community, and newspaper reporters. After having tea at the Consulate and viewing the library there, I went out to see some sights including the Aya Sofya. <...> At five there was a reception for Iranians residing in Istanbul. The consulate had formerly served as the Iranian Embassy, which had been built by Mirza Hoseyn Khan Sepahsalar. It is a three-story building of some importance. There are photographs of former ambassadors such as Sepahsalar himself, Hasan Ali Khan Garrusi, Mohsen Khan Moshir al-Dowleh, Ala al-Molk, Sadeq

Mosteshar al-Dowleh, Mohammad Ali Khan Zoka al-Molk Foroughi, Seyyed Baqer Kazemi. <...>

THURSDAY 6 JANUARY 1949

9:30 A.M. visited the Valide Abd al-Aziz Mosque with Mr. Zand. <...> Afternoon visited the Dolmabahçe Sarayi Palace with Mr. Zand and the deputy director of historical buildings of Istanbul. <...> Reza Shah stayed at this palace during his visit. Atatürk was also residing here when he became ill and died. <...>

FRIDAY 7 JANUARY 1949

Left early by train for Ankara. Arrived at the station at 8:50 A.M. and was met by Turkish protocol officials and Iranian Embassy staff. The members of the embassy staff are Mr. Jamshid Qarib, first secretary who is presently the counsellor; Dr. Reza Esfahani, press attaché; Mr. Mashhun, second secretary; Mr. Sobhani, filing officer; Mr. Yahyavi who helps in translation of newspaper articles; and Madame Amirabi, typist. Mr. Qarib is the son of the late Mirza Abbasqoli Khan Qarib who was a French teacher and an official translator. He died eight years ago and was survived by five children: the eldest Jamshid; Hormoz Qarib, the head of Princess Shams's office; and three daughters.

    <...>

MONDAY 10 JANUARY 1949

Busy with correspondence. I wrote a long letter to Cyrus. <...> Mr. Mashhun, the second secretary who is an emotional young man, had had a misunderstanding with Mr. Qarib. I smoothed over their differences. I am alone and read a great deal. After my hectic days in Tehran, this is a blessing. <...>

TUESDAY 11 JANUARY 1949

<...>

Made a formal call on Foreign Minister Nejmuddin Sadek and submitted my credentials. Sadek is a pleasant man and we spent close to twenty minutes in routine conversation.

Invited to the home of Mr. Sobhani for dinner. The rest of the embassy staff were there. Some of them do not know any foreign languages and are deficient in their own, but they are good people all the same. How our Foreign Ministry is able to operate is a mystery.

WEDNESDAY 12 JANUARY 1949

Attended to embassy business. <...> I am not feeling well. My liver disorder is giving me great trouble. <...>

<...>

SATURDAY 15 JANUARY 1949

<...> Still not feeling well. <...>

SUNDAY 16 JANUARY 1949

Feeling better. I wrote many letters: Ardalan, Navab, Amir Arfa', Mo'ayyed Sabeti, Farrokh, Khazra'i, Mrs. [Batul] Farmanfarmaian, Nahid [Ghani], Shaybani, Jam, Sami'i, Yazdanpanah, Seyyed Ahmad Farhang, Mr. Azodi, Dr. Mohammad Gilani, Hoseyn Ghani, Dr. E'tebar, Shokuh, Saljuq, Ala and Abbi [Dehqan]. I also wrote a detailed report on Palestine and Turkish foreign policy. <...> Invited the entire Embassy staff and wives for dinner. <...>

MONDAY 17 JANUARY 1949

As had been previously arranged, I went with senior embassy staff for an audience with President Ismet Inönü. Streets covered in snow and motoring difficult. <...> Inönü is sixty-seven years old, short, handsome, and resembles the late Dr. Benes, president of Czechoslovakia.

Delivered a prepared speech extending the warm greetings of HIM and presented my credentials. <...> He responded to HIM's greetings with a short but very warm reply. <...> He spoke of the bond between the two nations. I then asked permission to introduce the embassy staff. He took my arm and asked the foreign minister to bring the staff in. <...> We had champagne in the adjoining dining room. <...> The audience lasted about thirty minutes. <...> Tomorrow at 10:00 A.M. will lay a wreath on Atatürk's grave.

TUESDAY 18 JANUARY 1949

<...> Atatürk's grave. <...>

The Turks have their own particular view of Iranian Azerbaijanis. Pan-Turkism is deeply ingrained here. They regard the Azerbaijanis as Turks, members of their own people. Fortunately most Azerbaijanis find this idea laughable. <...>

Beginning this afternoon I am to meet some of the foreign emissaries to Turkey below the rank of ambassador. <...> The representative of Saudi Arabia called at 4:00 P.M. <...> 4:30 P.M. Met with the Norwegian minister, Krug Hansen, who had at one time served in Iran as third secretary. He is about fifty-two or fifty-three and had served at the Norwegian Embassy in Turkey as chargé when he had been invited to the reception Atatürk hosted for Reza Shah in 1934. He had also been invited to the Iranian Embassy for the occasion. He related the story that the British ambassador Percy Loraine[1] (who spoke some Persian) had approached Reza Shah and carried on a conversation. The Soviet ambassador became uncomfortable and began pacing the room. Finally he went over to where Atatürk was standing and said something to him. Atatürk walked over to Reza Shah and interrupted Loraine's conversation. He said that the Iranian Embassy has one of the loveliest views and guided Reza Shah to the windows thus halting the conversation with Loraine that had so distressed the Soviet envoy. At 5:00 P.M. the Danish minister and at 6:00 P.M. the Egyptian chargé came. <...>

WEDNESDAY 19 JANUARY 1949

Today began the traditional protocol calls on ambassadors. At ten I called on Sir Davis Kelly, the British ambassador. <...> He is a seasoned diplomat, who had served in the late thirties in Egypt. <...> He was fairly optimistic about the world. He said, "From 1934, I had known war was coming, but I don't have that feeling now." <...> At 3:30 P.M. called on General Victor Odlum, the Canadian ambassador. He speaks English only. He has served in Japan, China, and the US. He knows South Africa and Europe well. <...> He is a good conversationalist. At 4:00 P.M. I called on the U.S. ambassador, Mr. Wadsworth. He has served in several Eastern countries; at 5:00 I called on the Chinese ambassador, Mr. Lee Tee San. <...> At 6:00 P.M. I called on Mr. Fuad Jarem, the secretary general of the Turkish Ministry of Foreign Affairs. He had traveled to Iran in 1936 and had fond recollections of his meeting with Reza Shah. He considers himself a friend of Iran. <...> He spoke a great deal about the inexhaustible energy and long working hours of the sixty-seven-year-old Ismet Inönü.

Today heard on the radio sad news of the death of Seyyed Hasan Tabasi Meshkan, who was a good writer well versed in Western and Eastern philosophy and literature. He was a decent person and excellent company. He had also been a judge on the Supreme Court for several years. <...>

THURSDAY 20 JANUARY 1949

10:00 A.M. called on Soviet Ambassador Alexander L. Chechov, a young man of about thirty-eight who speaks his own particular brand of French with cheeks puffed out. They have a very grand embassy with some fine Tabriz and Turkman carpets. <...>

At 11:30 called on Mr. Seraj Oglu, the president of the Turkish Parliament, the number two man in Turkey. He has been prime minister several times and is a candidate for the presidency in the next election. <...> It was a warm meeting.

<...> At 12:30 P.M. I visited the ambassador from Brazil. <...> At 4:00 called on French Ambassador M. Jean Lecouye, a man of about

fifty-five. He visited Iran in 1941 and had served in Egypt. He is a refined and learned individual. We spoke of Egypt. He believes the kingdom will fall. He called Farouq a "fool." <...> The French Embassy is a sumptuous mansion, well decorated. The walls are adorned with very fine Gobelin tapestries.

At 4:30 P.M. I called on Mr. Chaman Laal, the Indian ambassador. Around the same time Nehru was addressing a conference of Asian nations. Turkey had decided to boycott the conference. The Turks are desperate to identify themselves as Europeans and thereby benefit from the Marshal Plan. <...> We had a warm meeting.

At 5:30 P.M. the envoy from Syria, Ehsan Sharif, who has the rank of minister, called on me. He was well versed in the status of the Arab countries and British policy in the area. He was very dispirited about Palestine. He admitted that part of the responsibility for the situation lies with the Arab countries. We had little knowledge of the Zionist movement and we underestimated it. He was especially critical of the Mufti who has been involved in the problem for the past twenty-five years. He also blamed disunity among the Arabs and their ignorance of the role of outside powers in their politics. He said that the British withdrew their forces from Palestine but reentered through the back door via Transjordan. <...>

<...>

SUNDAY 23 JANUARY 1949

Read the entire Qur'an and selected passages that were appropriate [to the matter of the shah's divorce]. At eleven Mr. Chaman Laal, the Indian ambassador, a knowledgeable man, called on me. He is greatly disturbed by what is happening in China; especially now that India has a common border with the communist nation. He related that yesterday he had seen the Canadian and U.S. ambassadors and told them India must ready itself to resist the Chinese and the Soviets. He asked for help from the U.S. <...>

MONDAY 24 JANUARY 1949

10:00 A.M. the Soviet ambassador called on me to repay my visit. He stayed for half an hour and we had the usual superficial conversation. At 11:00 I called on the Saudi ambassador. He was completely disheartened by the situation in Palestine. He unequivocally said the partition of Palestine and creation of a Jewish state is a fait accompli. There was no going back. The only thing subject to change is the configuration of the boundaries and no more. <…> He also stated that [the Arabs] should not have listened to Amir Abdullah.[2] <…>

At 11:30 I called on the Norwegian minister. He said that they are being pressured to join the Western block, the Atlantic Pact. If they refuse, they will not be given any outside help. Norway is willing to join the Pact but Sweden is against it and believes that it can remain neutral as in the last war. Denmark is neutral and wants to play the role of broker between Sweden and other European countries. <…>

At noon called on the Danish minister. He is a well-read and learned man. We talked about Anatole France, Voltaire and English literature: Shakespeare and Milton.

At 1:00 P.M. had a liver enzyme injection. <…> At 4:00 P.M. the U.S. ambassador came by and stayed for an hour and fifteen minutes. <…> He spoke of the U.S. budget for 1949, set at $40 billion and an additional $2 billion to the NATO countries. <…> He said that the U.S. wants Sweden, Norway, Denmark, and Portugal to join the Pact. Spain is a problem. The Labor Party in Britain is against the addition of Spain, but sooner or later it will become part of the Pact; soon both Italy and Turkey will join. <…> Greece will join in the next stage. <…> He praised the Turkish army, which is capable of engaging the more than 750,000 Soviet troops. <…> We spoke a great deal about Iran and I asked why the U.S. doesn't help Iran. <…> I said Turkey has a great strategic position. Iran in addition to its strategic position has another asset, oil. The Soviets have a fifth column in Iran and it is possible they will become predominant in the country. Then the U.S. will be faced with a fait accompli. The best way to neutralize the Soviets is to extend financial, economic and military aid to Iran—

the same help it has offered to Turkey. We suffered greatly during World War II; now we have a seven-year economic recovery plan and we need the U.S. <...> I ended by suggesting that we have further talks after the ambassador returns from Istanbul. <...> At 5:20 I received the minister of Spain. <...> At 6:00 P.M. the ambassador from Afghanistan. <...>

TUESDAY 25 JANUARY 1949

At 10:00 A.M. the Belgian chargé d'affaires came by. <...> At 11:00 I repaid the visit of the Syrian minister. <...> Again there was talk of Palestine. <...> At 11:30 I called on the minister of foreign affairs. <...> At noon, I called on the Egyptian chargé. <...> [Most of the conversation was on internal news of Egypt.] <...> In the afternoon the representative of United Press came for an interview. <...> At 5:00 P.M. the ambassador of "Nationalist" China paid a visit. He is very pessimistic about events and believes the Communists will seize power in Southeast Asia followed by Korea and India. <...> At 5:30 the minister for Jordan paid a visit. <...>

WEDNESDAY 26 JANUARY 1949

At 10:15 the British ambassador Sir Davis Kelly paid a return visit. He was interested in talking about Egypt. <...> He was very critical of Farouq saying that he never had a proper education and when he became king, he surrounded himself with disreputable people. <...> We also discussed Turkish history. He is a very sociable person. <...> At 11:30 A.M. I called on Semseddin Günaltay [the prime minister]. He speaks no foreign languages, and we had a translator. He has written books on Turkish and Iranian history. <...> He spoke a great deal about maintaining close relations with Iran and expanding cultural ties. <...> The Turks often say these things, but the test will be what they do once the common threat of Communism is gone. They deeply believe that anyone who speaks Turkish is a Turk and therefore must be part of the Pan-Turkist movement. What do they have in mind for our Azerbaijan? <...> Anyone living in Turkish-speaking Russia, e.g.,

Turkmenistan, which had been part of the old territory known as Greater Khorasan, is considered a Turk. They consider Avicenna both Turkish and Iranian. In any event my replies were commensurate with the childishness of his positions. <…>

THURSDAY 27 JANUARY 1949

The minister of Iraq came by at 11:00 A.M. He considered the issue of Palestine closed with the Arab defeat. At noon the minister of Lebanon came. The same conversation about the Arab countries. <…> The people of Beirut are undoubtedly more advanced and better educated. <…> At 4:00 P.M. the Polish ambassador called. <…> We talked about the devastation and human casualties that Poland suffered during World War II. <…> At 5:00 P.M. the minister of Finland to Turkey, who is also accredited to Iran. <…> We spoke about the political situation in Finland. <…> At 6:00 P.M. I called on the minister for Spain. He is an intelligent, well-traveled man and speaks French well. We spoke of the Prado Museum, which is named for the Spanish word for "field," as it was built on an area that in the seventeenth century had been a pasture outside of the city. The ambassador admitted that Spain has contributed little to music and architecture, but it has always had great painters. At 6:30 I called on Amir Hoseyn Nasr, the Jordanian minister. <…> He said that he has always been a Shiite but under Ottoman rule [the family] pretended to be Sunni.

FRIDAY 28 JANUARY 1949

11:00 A.M. the Italian ambassador came. The conversation was mostly about philosophy and literature. At noon the French ambassador visited. Most of our conversation was about Egypt. He said that the British are becoming close to Nahas Pasha and the Wafd Party. If Nahas becomes prime minister, there is a strong likelihood that Farouq will leave and Mohammad Ali or someone else will become king. It would, however, be a mistake if Nahas decided to become president in a republic. He added that the Egyptian princesses are transferring their funds to Brazil via the Brazilian minister. Farouq is also preparing for his escape. He believes Farouq is a degenerate cow-ard and most of the elite are incompetent. If there is a revolution, the lives of Jews, Europeans, especially the French, and the Pashas will be in danger. Egypt resembles Russia of 1905. <…> There is great poverty. <…>

I wrote a detailed report about relations between Turkey and its neighbors and Turkish foreign policy. I also wrote a report on Lebanon. <…>

SATURDAY 29 JANUARY 1949

Readied three reports for HIM's Special Office for the morning mail to Tehran:

1. HIM's letter to Mr. Inönü and his reply.

2. The situation in Egypt.

3. Turkey's political relations with its neighbors and the Anglo-Saxon countries.

At 10:30 A.M. the chargé of Hungary called on me. <…> Lunch at the Norwegian Embassy <…> with several other ambassadors. <…>

SUNDAY 30 JANUARY 1949

Wrote another report to the Special Office about friendship with Turkey. <…> Visited the water reservoir that is about twelve miles from the city. <…>

MONDAY 31 JANUARY 1949

Called on the Lebanese minister, later Belgian and Finnish ministers.

TUESDAY 1 FEBRUARY 1949

<…> I am completing a report about the changes that have taken place in Turkey.

WEDNESDAY 2 FEBRUARY 1949

<…> Have my ordinary headache, my eyes ache. Slept in the afternoon. I was uncomfortable during the night.

THURSDAY 3 FEBRUARY 1949

Four members of the Iranian Parliament are visiting Turkey. I was with them all afternoon. I am hosting a dinner for them tonight. The entire embassy staff will attend.

FRIDAY 4 FEBRUARY 1949 (15 BAHMAN 1327)

Completing two reports. <…> At 10:00 A.M. the Spanish minister came by. He is seeking our help at the United Nations in establishing a relationship. <…> At noon the minister from Holland visited and we spoke about Indonesia. <…> The Iranian guests came for lunch.

At 5:00 P.M. Radio Tehran reported that the shah has been shot. It appears that when the shah went to the University of Tehran [to celebrate the 15 Bahman founding of the institution in 1935], a person named [Naser] Fakhraraei fired five shots at him. One entered his cheek and came out the other cheek without damaging the jawbone. Another bullet grazed his back. People on the scene fatally beat the assailant. Martial law was declared. <…>

SATURDAY 5 FEBRUARY 1949

Wrote a letter to HIM's Special Office. At 11:30 A.M. the minister of Argentina came by. He was worried about his country under Peron. <…> Later a special representative of President Inönü visited to express the president's great happiness over the shah's miraculous escape. <…>

Dr. Manuchehr Eqbal reported [the details of the assassination] to Parliament. The shah exited the car at 3:00 P.M. After reviewing the ceremonial guard and greeting the ministers, he went toward the entrance of the Law Faculty building. <…> The assailant ran toward him and fired five shots. Three of the shots hit the shah's hat; next a bullet hit his right cheek and came out of his upper lip without damaging any bones. The next bullet hit the right shoulder. The shah acted calmly. Dr. Eqbal and Colonel Daftari took him to the nearest hospital to treat the wounds. After they were bandaged, the shah went back to his palace. <...> The assailant died at Sina hospital. He was twenty-eight years old and carried a card that identified him as a reporter for the newspaper Banner of Islam; he also had membership cards for the Union of Printers, the newspaper *Cry of the Nation,* and the Tudeh Party. <...> He carried a diary begun ten years ago that said he had been imprisoned in Qasr Prison. It also revealed that he had served in the military. <...> He had made a list of books that the public must read. These books concerned revolution, the meaning of communism, armed uprising, Karl Marx, and the policies and aims of the Tudeh Party. <...>

The military government announced the arrest of the following people: Seyyed Abu al-Qasem Kashani, the Emami brothers, Dr. Jodat, Dr. Yazdi, Dr. Seyyed Baqer Hejazi, Ahmad Qasemi (son-in-law of Abu al-Qasem Kashani). <...>

Last night the centers of the Tudeh Party throughout the country were overrun and closed. Membership in the party was outlawed. <...>

Several pages on the assassination attempt.

TUESDAY 8 FEBRUARY 1949

The Swiss ambassador came by at 10:00 A.M. He is very knowledgeable about the Far East, having been ambassador to Japan and the Far East. He had also worked with the League of Nations for some twelve years. He explained that MacArthur's strategy in Japan is to lift the standard of living of the laborers so as to forestall the growth of communism. <...>

Dinner at the U.S. ambassador's residence. <...> Several other members of the diplomatic corps were invited. After dinner we saw a film about the experimental atomic bomb on Bikini Atoll.

THURSDAY 10 FEBRUARY TO WEDNESDAY 16 FEBRUARY 1949

Summary of the aftermath of the attempts on the shah's life, visits of members of the Iranian community.

<...> Telegraphs to and from the shah and the Queen Mother. <...>

THURSDAY 17 FEBRUARY 1949

<...>

The loose talk of a member of the embassy staff, who revealed confidential information to another staff member, has upset me greatly. <...> Corruption and decay has permeated the very fiber of the younger generation. <...> Worse still is their ignorance. <...> Their knowledge is confined to their clothing, the various types of alcoholic beverages, bridge and poker, and a few words of café French. <...> How can one admit to a foreigner that there is no way to safeguard a secret in the Ministry of Foreign Affairs? Or that an employee does not dare confide in his superior for fear that the superior may be serving the interests of a foreign power? <...>

I spent nearly two and half years in the United States and traveled by car through most of the states. I met people from various strata of society: secretaries of state, professors, writers, businessmen, shopkeepers, typists, salesmen, waiters and drivers. One of the great and exemplary assets of this nation is the mutual trust they have in one another. <...> Within half an hour of meeting an American, he will tell you of his entire background and his present situation. He will reveal his thoughts and plans for the future. No matter what you may tell him, he will readily believe it. Some visitors to the U.S. have described the Americans as "gullible" and "too simple," by which they mean "stupid" and "superficial." This is not so. What these visitors judge as reasons to taunt Americans, are truly grounds for admiring them. Giving the matter a little thought one realizes that their behavior shows there is little falsehood in America, <...> freedom of thought is such that there is no reason to hide one's beliefs. <...> The nature of the social order precludes the need to withhold one's future plans, source of income, or wealth. <...>

In America the Iranian formula "Keep these three hidden: your faith, the direction you are going and your wealth" is not in effect. We think wise anyone who makes this his motto. The Iranian must keep his wealth from public view, at times going so far as to bury it under the ground. He must also complain about the misery of his life and his poverty. Why? So that the ruler, government official, cleric, khan, busybody, all of whom have but one occupation—pillaging—don't get wind of what he owns.

The Iranian must keep his beliefs, whether religious, political, social or intellectual, hidden. Why? So that he won't be excommunicated or branded as corrupt, heretical or half-witted. The intellectual environment in Iran is not one in which ideas can be exchanged freely. No tyrant, cleric, zealot, nor corrupted person can brook the slightest opposition to his own ideas, ways of doing things or religious beliefs. They would curse any critic, attack him, declare him an apostate or even kill him. The cautious, thinking person has no choice but to beware of what he says, go along with the majority, in effect to live a lie. He falsely honors long-practiced rites and customs, and makes a pretense of praying, fasting, crying at passion recitals, going on pilgrimages to Karbala, Mecca, etc. <...>

<...> I should state at the outset that Iran is a land of contradictions. There are many exceptions. <...> One is amazed at how exceptional people can survive in that environment of lying, cheating and begging. People like Mohammad Qazvini, Kamal al-Molk (Mohammad Ghaffari), Seyyed Nasrollah Akhavi (Taqavi), Abbas Eqbal Ashtiani, Aqabala Khan Salar Mo'tamed Ganji (originally from Qazvin, but residing in Nishapur), Colonel Alinaqi Vaziri, Dr. Meer, Mirza Ali Akbar Khan Davar, Abdolhoseyn Dehqan, Ali Mohammad and Mahmud Dehqan and all members of their family, Seyyed Hasan Taqizadeh, Mirza Ali Akbar Dehkhoda, ... Mohammad Ali Farzin, ..., Kamal al-Vozara...Mehdiqoli Hedayat...and many others of equal measure whom I have not mentioned. I know their mentalities, human qualities and natures well enough to understand that they are exceptions, credits to the human race.

<...>

SATURDAY 19 FEBRUARY 1949

<...> Dinner at the French Embassy. Some of the guests were Mr. and Mrs. Qarib, Mr. Qarib's sister Maryam, Serajoglu and Fereydun Fekri Doshonsi, respectively the head and deputy head of the Turkish Parliament, who forcefully advocated a union of Iran and Turkey. <...> There were several other guests.

   <...>

Aqabala Ganji, Dr. Ghani and Kamal al-Molk (ca. 1930)

WEDNESDAY 23 FEBRUARY 1949

The University of Tehran has proposed that a statue of HIM be erected at University Square. <...> The number of telegrams sent to the Shah congratulating him on his miraculous escape has reached a point where most telegraph offices across the country have to stay open twenty-four hours a day. <...> I am afraid that all the tricks and false adulation will only make HIM vulnerable to more flattery. <...> The university will erect a statue, the chancellor of the university will sing the praises of the shah and speak of the heartfelt emotions of the students, <...> and everything will revert to the status quo ante. <...>

Today is the thirty-first anniversary of the formation of the Red Army, and the Russian military attaché has invited the diplomatic corps, senior Turkish military officials, and members of the Turkish Ministry of Foreign Affairs. <...> Most of the Russians at the embassy are under forty years old. They are products of the present regime. <...> They have the look of religious zealots, like fanaticism compounded with a desire for revenge.

<...>

SUNDAY 27 FEBRUARY 1949

Yesterday and today worked on a glossary and index of words from the *Divan* of Hafez. This project has the gratifying effect of allowing me once again to delve into the depths of this sublime work. Once one has thoroughly tasted the exquisite joys of Hafez's lyrics, the poetry of Sa'di can no longer have the same claim on the heart; they appear merely superficial and repetitive. <...>

TUESDAY 1 MARCH 1949

<...> Lunch with a few embassy staff; dinner with the entire staff. My spirits are very low. Our country is in seriously bad shape. The ministries are poorly run; it is all favoritism and corruption, <...> most seem oblivious and self-satisfied. <...>

WEDNESDAY 2 MARCH 1949

I work longer hours in Ankara. From early morning I am involved in routine embassy demands. Then I work on the Hafez glossary. For the past several days I feel alone. There is no joy in my work. <...>

THURSDAY 3 MARCH 1949

<...> Radio Moscow has made three defamatory statements about Iran: (1) Iran is officially under American influence and the War (Defense) Department determines Iranian policy; (2) the Iranian government works for the benefit of foreign powers and to the detriment of Iran; and (3) the government should not have outlawed the Tudeh Party. Iranian Ministry of Foreign Affairs has lodged an official protest. <...> Was invited to dinner at Qarib's, but could not eat. I don't feel well. <...>

FRIDAY 4 MARCH 1949

<...> Letters to Tehran. <...> A team from the World Bank is in Ankara on its way to Tehran. <...>

SATURDAY 5 MARCH 1949

Still very ill, cannot eat anything. Liver not functioning well. Mrs. Amini (Fakhr al-Dowleh) has built an elementary school in Tehran for 250 students. She has invited the entire government to attend the opening ceremony, after which she will donate the school to the state. It will be named the Amin al-Dowleh Elementary School. She is a remarkable lady. Reza Shah [referring to her] is purported to have said, "The Qajar family is comprised of nonentities. Only one of them is worthy of note, and if she were a man, I would have been very careful when dealing with her."

SUNDAY 6 MARCH 1949

I stayed in all day and have no appetite. I came across a book <…> written by a Frenchman who has traveled to Iran. He appears to be ill-educated and uninformed <…>; however, he has one interesting tale. He says that while he was in Esfahan, he had intended to find the grave of Jean Jacques Rousseau's uncle who had gone there in the first half of the eighteenth century to sell clocks. This uncle married an Iranian woman and became close to the Safavid court. It is possible that his descendants can be found in Julfa. <…>

MONDAY 7 MARCH 1949

Still not well but busy with work. 11:00 A.M. the Bulgarian minister called. He is a strange-looking man with fallen eyelids. At 8:30 P.M. I am hosting a dinner. The ambassadors of the U.S., Italy, the ministers of Austria and Chile, General McBride and his wife, two Turkish ladies, and the Counselors from the Italian and French embassies are also invited. <…> Despite my illness, the evening went well.
    <…>

WEDNESDAY 9 MARCH 1949

My health has not improved and I have no appetite. At 3:00 P.M. Dr. Fereydun Nafez, a descendent of Jalal al-Din Rumi and professor of medical history and ethics, came by. He has published works of Rumi. He is a very well-educated and polished individual. I had also invited Professor Lukal Necati who teaches Persian and Arabic at the university here. He is presently translating the works of Ferdowsi into Turkish prose. Both know Farsi very well. I was very pleased to have met them. Tonight the ambassadors of China, France, Denmark, and Argentina together with Messrs. Zurlu and Qadri Razan and their wives are invited here.

THURSDAY 10 MARCH 1949

Feeling better. The best measure of my health is when I can work.
<…>

TUESDAY 15 MARCH 1949

Three years ago to the day I had broken my leg in America. Still suffer pain. Wrote letters. <...> At noon repaid the visit of the Yugoslav ambassador. 4:30 returned the visit of the minister from Bulgaria. At 5:00 P.M. had a press conference regarding Iran and the law establishing a senate and constituent assembly. At 7:00 P.M. went to the Hungarian embassy on the occasion of their independence day. <...>
<...>

SATURDAY 19 MARCH 1949

<...> Yesterday sent Now Ruz gifts for the entire embassy staff. <...>

SUNDAY 20 MARCH 1949

<...> A year has passed. One gets used to misfortune and pain. <...> Dante says that after seeing the various circles of hell, he came across a group, which saddened him even more. One wonders what could have been worse than hell. <...> Dante continues, saying he encountered a group on whose foreheads the word "despair" was written in bold letters. These people were most unfortunate because they had no hope or future. Dante is right. No matter what the adversity, as long as there is hope, there is life. Despair means death. <...>

SUNDAY 20 TO MONDAY 21 MARCH 1949

The [Iranian] New Year will arrive about 8:30 P.M. on 20 March, which is also my birthday. The embassy is hosting a dinner party. Over 600 people were invited: the entire diplomatic corps with their families; the entire Turkish cabinet and notables; members of Parliament; university professors; bankers, journalists. The celebration lasted until 3:30 A.M. The president of Turkey sent his eldest son.
<...>

SATURDAY 26 MARCH 1949

<...> The old infighting among embassy staff has broken out again. <...> I have to mediate. <...> My time is wasted in listening to their feuds. <...> There is too much lying. <...> I hope God will protect us. I do not know where we are headed as a nation. I am an optimist by nature, but I am losing hope. <...> The late Gholamhoseyn Ghaffari (Saheb Ekhtiar), an exceptionally fine person who died in 1947 at age ninety-one, once related the following incident. <...> "During the early months after Reza Shah's coronation [1925], he sent for me. <...> In those days Mirza Hasan Khan Mostowfi al-Mamalek was very popular with the people, and Reza Shah had great respect for him. Reza Shah knew I was very close to Mostowfi and wanted me to influence him [to accept the post of prime minister]. Reza Shah spoke for more than an hour and analyzed how and why he came to power. <...> At the end he told me to tell Mostowfi that it is not enough to be merely popular. We have to build a new Iran. There is no Iranian nation as such. We have to create a sense of nationhood." <...>

There is a lengthy account of a lunch Dr. Ghani had with Hasan Vosouq (Vosouq al-Dowleh) in London in 1924, when they spoke for more than five hours. Vosouq gives his family background, the positions he had held, and justifies his endorsement of the 1919 Anglo-Iranian Treaty, which gave England virtual control of Iran's finances and its military. Vosouq also speaks of the endemic corruption in Iran and his belief that Iran under British rule could become a U.S., Canada, Australia or New Zealand.

<...>

I am not in agreement with Vosouq's thesis, and I am not as pessimistic as he. I still entertain hopes that someone will rise up and implement plans for the revival of Iran. But I am doubtful, because given the strategic position Iran enjoys, we will not be permitted to act independently. <...> Can several Iranians work together?

<...>

SATURDAY 2 APRIL 1949 (13 FARVARDIN 1328)

Today is the thirteenth and last day of Now Ruz. Tradition says that it is unlucky to do work or stay at home. It is doubly unlucky because it coincides with the day Fatemeh, the wife of Imam Ali, died.

Nothing in this world is contingent upon any other thing. Our dividing of time into years, months, weeks, and days and our association of events with these divisions are artificial. As Rumi says,

Where were Christ and Moses,
When God strung His bow?
Where were Moses and Christ,
When the sun began to nurture life?

In any event this thirteenth of Farvardin, which is an unlucky day for most, is auspicious for me. Everyone at the embassy has left Ankara for the day to picnic near a dam. I could not go and besides it is cold.

The mail came at noon to complete the happiness of my day. There were letters from very dear friends: Hajj Mokhber al-Saltaneh Hedayat, Abbas Eqbal, Hoseyn'ali Qezelayagh, Rokn al-Molk Sadri, Abdolhoseyn Khan Dehqan, Dr. Ghasemzadeh, Mas'ud Mo'azed, Dr. Mahmud Afshar, Ahmad Meshgan (the son of the late Seyyed Hasan Tabasi), Mohsen Gonabadi, Rahi Moayyeri. At 4:00 P.M. called on the French ambassador who has just returned from a trip to Paris.

Dr. Fereydun Nafez has sent me four apples grown in the garden where Rumi is buried. I gave three of them as gifts and shared the fourth with three others. With the memory of Rumi fresh in my mind, I enjoyed the apple as though it had been grown in heaven.

SUNDAY 3 APRIL 1949

Preparing for a trip to Istanbul. Received a telegram that Mr. Reza Moshiri has been instructed to move from Cairo to Ankara. At 5:00 P.M. Dr. Nafez and I went to the home of Veled Çelebi Efendi. ("Çelebi" in Turkish means "godlike" and is a name given to the direct descendants of Jalal al-Din Rumi). This eighty-five-year-old man is the elder of the Rumi mystics and the nineteenth generation of descendants of the great master. He served for a time as a member of Parliament from Kastamonu but is now retired. With his handsome long, thin nose he has an attractive profile. It was pleasant for me to look at him and try to imagine what Rumi may have looked like. His son-in-law, daughter and grandchildren were also there. He promised to come to the embassy. His Persian is very good, and he has translated a substantial part of Rumi's *Divan-e Shams* into Turkish. He has also written a book on mysticism. Dr. Nafez is his brother's son. <...>

WEDNESDAY 6 APRIL 1949

<...> Full schedule in Istanbul. Meetings with Iranian businessmen, the mayor, etc. Cocktails at U.S. ambassador's Istanbul residence. Visit to the university, met several professors. <...> Returned to the hotel exhausted.

THURSDAY 7 APRIL 1949

<...> 9:00 A.M. visited the Consulate. This afternoon I attended a gathering of devotees of Persian literature. <...>

10:00 went to the library of the University of Istanbul, where they have about seventeen thousand Persian manuscripts, but no catalog. There is nothing particularly interesting or rare. Mr. Abdülbâki Gölpinarli, a hard-working Persianist, is preparing an edition of Khayyam. <...> Dr. Helmut Ritter's Oriental Institute is also here.

The mayor paid a courtesy call early in the afternoon. <...> I went to the old bazaar, still the center of the traditional trades, but now the destination of many foreigners. It has everything in the way of Oriental antiques. I went to several shops. Davud Musazadeh, who is from a Jewish family of Mashhad that had recently converted to Islam, was my guide. Bought several souvenirs.

At 5:00 P.M. there was a reception at the consulate. Among the invitees were the philosopher Reza Tewfik, an eighty-five-year-old man with long white hair, a large beard, and very red cheeks. He has penetrating eyes, looks much younger and is highly articulate. He reminds me of Khezr [the prophet Elias who is said to have drunk from the fountain of youth]. He has become a mystic and has written a book on mysticism. I also met Professor Ritter, the German Orientalist who knows Persian, Arabic and Turkish very well. There were several other professors. <…> It was a good gathering. <…>

FRIDAY 8 APRIL 1949

9:00 A.M. went with Abdülbâki Gölpinarli and others to the Aya Sofya Library, a former church that has been made into a museum. <…> The library has about 15,000 volumes, most of which are manuscripts. There is a Hafez manuscript dated 1411 and several other very rare books, but no catalog. <…> An impressive collection. <…>

SATURDAY 9 APRIL 1949

Visited the Iranian elementary school, a coeducational institution. The children sang several songs, which was highly enjoyable. <…> Later I went to the gravesite of Ayyub Ansari, a contemporary of the Prophet Mohammad. <…> There is a library next to the cemetery, which houses some 3,000 to 4,000 manuscripts. I also visited the city museum, which has some rare manuscripts. <…> Had lunch with Abbé Qanawati, an Egyptian Dominican monk whom I had known in Cairo. He is in Turkey to prepare a catalog of rare books. I should convince Iranian authorities to undertake similar projects. <…>

Dr. Ghani's main interests were in manuscripts of Avicenna's works. There is a listing of other libraries in Istanbul. An Iranian charitable foundation is mentioned. A list of some 100 prominent Iranian residents of Istanbul. A list of Iranian graduates of Turkish colleges and their fields of study. <…> A visit to Topkapi Saray Museum. Cocktails at the Iranian Consulate attended by Istanbul dignitaries, including the governor, heads of the army and navy, journalists and Iranian residents.

TUESDAY 12 APRIL 1949

Left late for Ankara; will arrive tomorrow. <...> In the morning met several Iranian students attending colleges in Istanbul. <...>

<...>

SATURDAY 16 APRIL 1949

<...> 5:00 p.m., Austrian Embassy <...> After dinner I went to Mr. Sobhani's house. They told me that Mr. -, the second secretary at the Iranian Embassy, with a B.A. in law and an employee of the Iranian Ministry of Foreign Affairs for the past eight years, was spreading the rumor that the Soviets have attacked Iran at several points along the border. [Knowing nothing of this] from reading the newspaper or listening to the 8:30 P.M. news or from the proceedings of Parliament. Soon afterward Mr. - arrived. I asked him for his source. He said, "Excellency, let me go and ask Mohammad Ali, the janitor." (Mohammad Ali is about seventy years old, is hard of hearing and has been with the embassy for more than fifty years.) I asked him how he could rely on Mohammad Ali as a source. Mr. - responded in a tone common to simpletons that these Russians are dangerous; <...> one has to placate them. I said, "As the second secretary, what you say, people believe. How could you say such things? If the Russians attack, it would be the beginning of World War III." <...> One wonders how he was admitted to the ministry. He is useless. <...> He is the son of a middle-ranking mollah <...> He does not belong in the diplomatic service and is more suited to manual labor or reading verses of the Qur'an over the dead. <...> This is so depressing.

SUNDAY 17 APRIL 1949

Guest of the U.S. ambassador at the golf club. We spoke for more than three hours. He briefed me on the situation in Syria and later on Iraq and Palestine. <...> About Nuri Said Pasha he said that the Iraqi leader followed two principles for twenty-five years. He never did anything to violate, first, the trust of the British and, second, the trust of the Hashemites.

On Palestine he predicted that even the Arab part would be eliminated and definitely taken by the Israelis although the United Nations recommended that it be divided. <...>

Toward the end he talked about Iran. <...> He said that in the view of some army officers, Turkey is Iran's potential enemy, and they were afraid of an attack. He said in effect that such was not the case.

<...>

MONDAY 9 MAY 1949

In the morning I was involved in embassy work, both the minutiae and the consequential, which is very taxing. At 5:00 P.M. Memduh Sevket (former Turkish ambassador to Iran) and Dr. Rabi'i, both now members of Parliament, called on me. Sevket is a handsome man, over sixty. In 1920 he served in Moscow. In 1925 he was appointed ambassador to Tehran, where he was accredited to the court of Ahmad Shah [the last Qajar king]. He called on Reza Khan, the prime minister, at his home and also had a long meeting with Teimurtash, who was minister of public works. When the Qajars were deposed, his accreditation was transferred to Reza Shah. <...> In 1930 he returned to Turkey and was later appointed to Kabul. In 1941, on his return from Afghanistan via Mashhad, Reza Shah asked to see him at the Sa'dabad Palace [in Tehran]. Reza Shah received him graciously and complained about his own circumstances. He spoke of his difficulties with Germany, Russia and England, and especially about the oppression and corruption of Europeans. He sent a private message to Esmet Inönü who responded with a message by special courier. Sevket said that he spoke a great deal with Reza Shah. <...> Both he and Dr. Rabi'i are highly regarded in cultural circles and speak Persian well. They remained until 7:30 P.M. <...>

<...>

FRIDAY 13 MAY 1949

9:00 P.M. attended a performance of Jean Cocteau's[3] *Les Parents terribles.*

SATURDAY 14 TO SUNDAY 15 MAY 1949

Attended performances of Jean Cocteau's *Les Enfants terribles* and *La Machine infernale.* Met and spoke to Cocteau at a reception held for him.

<...>

TUESDAY 17 MAY 1949

<...>

All reforms in Iran are at a standstill. Corrupt elements are the principal obstacles. <...> Still the same opportunists and incompetents occupy sensitive positions. Still the same acts of larceny and malfeasance. To implement the Seven Year Plan, one needs some honest and decent, learned, and exceptional people, <...>

<...>

SATURDAY 21 MAY 1949

<...> Called on the American ambassador. During our discussion, he said that Iranians are envious of Turks. I said that there is no jealousy. Since we have a common foe, we are most pleased that Turkey is emerging as a powerful country. It was agreed that we would have lunch at the Country Club. Americans are generally deliberate and cautious; so it takes time for them to enter upon the right course. But once they choose, it is very difficult to deter them. It is akin to a childish obstinacy.

<...>

THURSDAY 26 MAY 1949

<...>

Read the newspapers from Tehran. The leadership of the Tudeh Party has been sentenced to several years of imprisonment for sedition. Sentenced to ten years is Dr. Nur al-Din Kianuri, the son of Sheikh Nuri and grandson of Sheikh Fazlollah Nuri. Dr. Kianuri studied architecture in Europe, where he became active in communist circles. <…> Two or three years ago he married Maryam Firuz, daughter of the late Farmanfarma. Maryam is presently in hiding and has been sentenced in absentia to five years' imprisonment.

<…>

MONDAY 30 MAY 1949

Crushing news announced on radio Tehran: two days ago the distinguished scholar and revered teacher Mirza Mohammad Qazvini died. The death of this man who was on a par with the very greatest of scholars of Islam is a tragic loss for the world of learning and for all humanity. He stood at the apex of those singular scholars, whose emergence is by chance and who coincidentally combine all the requisite qualities of greatness: <…> vast and profound knowledge with impeccable ethics and morality. Such people honor the human race with their existence. <…>

I believe he was born in 1877 in Tehran. His father was Abd al-Vahhab Qazvini, known as "Molla Aqa," a learned man of his day who was one of four authors of *Nameh-ye Daneshvaran,* an encyclopedia of the eminent scholars of the Islamic world. Molla Aqa had two sons and a daughter. <…> Mirza Mohammad was the eldest of the three. <…> When barely an adolescent, his father died, whereupon the late Shams al-'Olema Abd al-Rabbabadi became his guardian. Molla Aqa had been poor. His heirs received a nominal sum from the government in the form of proceeds from publications on which he had worked. Mirza Mohammad's early education began when he entered the Mo'ayyer Seminary, which was to prepare him for the clergy. His extraordinary native intelligence, his phenomenal memory, and his uncompromising perseverance and labor were hallmarks of his academic career. <…> He studied with two of the most learned clergymen of the day, Mirza

From left to right: Dr. Ghani, Mohammadali Foroughi,
Mohammad Qazvini, Mohammadali Farzin (ca. 1940)

Hasan Ashtiani and Sheikh Fazlollah Nuri, as well as the poet Adib
Pishavari. <…> [After the seminary,] he enrolled in the Alliance
[Israelite Universelle] School to learn French. Since in those days it was
unusual for a cleric to learn French he devised ways to go unnoticed.
According to Mr. Hoseyn Shokuh (Shokuh al-Molk), Qazvini would
go to school early in the morning and not leave until early evening.
Mirza Mohammad's brother, Sheikh Ahmad, who had learned English,
was employed by the Hajj Kazem Malek Tojjar Company and sent to
their London offices. After completing his studies, Mirza Mohammad
Khan worked in government publishing offices translating articles
from Arabic to Persian. Then Sheikh Ahmad wrote to his brother that
in several months he would be returning to Iran. He suggested that giv-
en his love of rare books and manuscripts, Mirza Mohammad might
want to come to London and, after a few months, they could return
together. Mirza Mohammad, nearly thirty at the time, traveled to
England in 1904, but instead of staying two months he was to live in

Europe thirty-six years. When he reached London, [the Persian scholar] Edward G. Browne and some of his fellow Orientalists immediately grasped Qazvini's importance and began to make use of his learning. With his help and guidance they edited and annotated many seminal, medieval Persian texts. <…> Qazvini was the Iranian forerunner of painstaking and scientific textual editing, research and literary criticism, which he taught to his contemporaries.

<…> After his stay in London, Qazvini went to Switzerland and later to Berlin, spending the entire period of WWI there. <…> He became the leading light in a group of luminaries that included Hajj Mirza Fazl'ali Tabrizi, Seyyed Hasan Taqizadeh, Kazemzadeh Iranshahr and Seyyed Mohammad Jamalzadeh. In 1920 he went to Paris where he stayed until 1939. In Paris he purchased with his savings a modest four-room apartment near Porte d'Orleans. <…> Several colleges and universities offered him professorships if he would become a French citizen. In response he would simply say, "How could I, I'm not French?" <…> He made a living by lecturing at universities and annotating rare manuscripts. <…> Around 1920 he married a French woman named Rosa and had a daughter named Suzanne (Nahid). His wife proved to be the perfect companion, devoting her life to maintaining a comfortable household conducive to her husband's scholarly pursuits. Qazvini, in turn, was devoted to his family, eating lunch and dinner exclusively with them and also spending his Sundays with them. If occasionally he accepted an invitation, his wife and daughter were included. He also escorted his daughter to school and back every day. <…>

Qazvini's personal library consisted of some four thousand volumes in many languages. Thus he had no need to borrow books from others. In addition he personally annotated his books with corrections, glosses, and his own special indexes. Occasionally his comments in the margins of works could be very harsh criticisms of the authors' efforts.

Qazvini's scholarly zeal was matchless. He never paid the slightest attention to personalities; his attention was fixed on one thing: the truth. He doggedly pursued the smallest details from one reference to another whenever he was in doubt. He raised the bar of scientific certainty as high as possible. I don't think that any scholar had Qazvini's command of the corpus of works that comprise oriental studies. He knew the details of every book and manuscript. <...> He was also a world-class authority on Arabic literature. His knowledge of Iranian literature was incomparably broad and deep, as he knew the works of all the poets and prose writers from the most accomplished to the mediocre and even the inferior. <...>

Qazvini's vast learning was solely devoted to research and the pursuit of truth. He was astonishingly modest and unaffected. Though people with Qazvini's mind and accomplishments rarely say "I don't know" or "possibly," these and other admissions of doubt were regular parts of his conversation. He spoke with the precision of a mathematician, always choosing the word that exactly fit the meaning he intended. He would question any erroneous statement and demand to know the reasoning behind it.

Above all Qazvini was a very, very serious person; the kind of wit and off-color humor that is common in Persian had no place in his life. When he did make jokes, they always had a serious, veiled edge. He seemed to have thought extraordinarily long and hard about the basic questions that confront humanity and come to his own conclusions. On moral questions he was adamantly independent. <...> But he would never try to force his opinions on others. <...>

Qazvini was an excellent and witty companion, but he had no use for the incompetent and dishonest. He did not fault anyone for ignorance and would gladly enlighten people who genuinely did not know something. But he would not tolerate the twisted, hypocritical and affected. <...> He would spend hours with someone who he believed was gifted but would not waste two minutes on a fool. <...> His religious beliefs were ecumenical; i.e., he would accept any logical and well-thought-out proposition regardless of the source. He would reject any superstition or sophistry. This fidelity to the truth exemplifies what Rumi says:

> The rose blossoms no matter where the vine,
> Where brewing vat is frothing there is wine.

And were the sun to appear from the west,
It would still be the sun, no more no less.

<...>

Late in 1939 when life in Paris became difficult, Qazvini, his wife and daughter, traveled by train through the Balkans to Istanbul. He entered Iran from Iraq to Kermanshah and then on to Karaj outside of Tehran. Greeting him there were Mohammad Ali Foroughi, Foroughi's brother Mirza Abolhasan, Seyyed Nasrollah Taqavi and his son Jamal al-Din Akhavi, Esma'il Mer'at (then minister of education) and me. <...> At first he lived in a rented house in Tehran. In 1946 he purchased a home for 36,000 tomans with a grant of 20,000 tomans from HIM and loans from the Mortgage Bank. <...>

After the occupation of Iran in 1941, HIM, who had heard a great deal about Qazvini, expressed a desire to meet him. He had raised the matter with successive ministers of court, Farzin, Foroughi and the current minister, Ala. The matter had been repeatedly raised with me in order that I persuade Qazvini to seek an audience. Qazvini had refused, arguing that he, as an ordinary citizen, should not overstep his bounds. <...> Finally, he was prevailed upon and presented himself to HIM.

HIM was aware that Qazvini had his circle of intimate friends. On his own initiative he told Ala that he wanted to spend half a day weekly with Mr. Qazvini and his associates. The group assembled on HIM's order were, besides Qazvini, Hajj Seyyed Nasrollah Taqavi, Hasan Esfandiari (Hajj Mohtashem al-Saltaneh), Ali Akbar Dehkhoda, Hoseyn Shokuh and me. Some time later, General Yazdanpanah, HIM's adjutant, suggested that Dr. Shafaq join the circle. Ala, Adib al-Saltaneh Sami'i and Yazdanpanah, who were all connected to the court, also attended these sessions. On Tuesday afternoons automobiles sent by the court transported us to the palace. The first meeting was during the month of Ramadan at Sa'dabad. With characteristic humility and politeness HIM said, "I have been aware that you people meet regularly and discuss literary, philosophical and other matters. I do not have the knowledge to

Mohammad Qazvini with Dr. Ghani

become a member of the group, but I do wish to become a listener. This is why I requested that you hold your gatherings at my home. Please regard it as yours. I will be a mere auditor. I wish our gatherings to be free of any formalities." The first meeting lasted until sunset, when HIM ordered a fast-breaking meal to be served. <...> Thereafter meetings began every Tuesday at 3:00 P.M. either in the city or at Sa'dabad. HIM would sit down and immediately tea and sweets were served. HIM offered cigarettes to everyone.

In a chamber on the lower level of the Marble Palace, we sat around a long rectangular table. HIM sat at the head of the table. To his right was Qazvini and then Dehkhoda. On HIM's left were Taqavi and then me. Across from HIM were Mohtashem al-Saltaneh and several others. <...> The meetings would end at seven or eight and a few times lasted until 9:00 P.M.

The conversations ran like this: HIM would ask a question, always directed to Qazvini. For example, once HIM asked about

Avicenna. Qazvini <...> passed the question to me. HIM turned to me and asked jokingly why I had never sent him any of my publications. I said I shall obey your order and had the bindery at Melli Bank bind a series of books in beautiful red leather and sent them to him. I gave a detailed answer on Avicenna. <...> At the very beginning of the following week's session, HIM had a series of questions on Avicenna, which indicated that he had paid careful attention to the details of the discussions of the previous week. <...> Qazvini was quite taken by the attention HIM paid. In private he told me that he was impressed by the young shah's intelligence and by how amidst all his other preoccupations and difficulties he could focus on literature and history. I remember once in Sa'dabad, Hoseyn Shokuh recited a line from Hafez, which I believe to be:

Though it's Ramadan, bring a cup of wine so pure
That it ripens novices into the wholly mature.

Mr. Shokuh said that he could not recall the remainder of the ode, but he was sure that I would remember. The shah asked for the rest, and I recited it. I cannot remember which line visibly moved HIM. He admitted that he was not very familiar with our literature, but he appreciated the depth of thought of the great poets. HIM's inner disquiet was apparent. When we were leaving that evening, Qazvini confided in me, "I have been very touched by this young man. Any person unmoved by good poetry must be made of wood or stone, not among the living. Today I noticed a spark in the shah's eyes and one could see agitation on his face. I realized that the young man has a great reserve of emotions." <...>

Once HIM asked about Ferdowsi, and Qazvini gave a detailed explanation of the epic poet's importance. He spoke at length about the satirical attack on Ferdowsi's patron Sultan Mahmud in the introduction to the *Shahnameh*. On other occasions Dehkhoda would read from his poetry; Seyyed Nasrollah would read from his treatises; at times there were general conversations on a variety of things, but the sessions were always warm and engaging.

On one occasion HIM asked Qazvini to discuss Mirza Taqi Khan Amir Kabir. He informed the shah that I had done research on him. I spoke at length on many aspects of Amir Kabir's life: the policy of his predecessor Qa'em Maqam, the events of the period, and the death of Mohammad Shah [1848]. I also discussed the rule of Mohammad Shah's successor, the seventeen or eighteen-year-old Naser al-Din Shah, his program of reform, the political influence of foreign powers during his reign, his adversaries in Iran and the attendant fear and suspicion that caused the king to have Amir Kabir exiled and murdered in the Fin Gardens (in Kashan). I also touched briefly on Amir Kabir's letters to the shah. As we were leaving the session, Qazvini was eager to know whether I had been prepared for that long talk and whether I had intended the implied parallels between Amir Kabir's time and the present situation in Iran. I told him that it hadn't occurred to me at first, but as I spoke I realized that certain events had to be mentioned.

At one point Hajj Seyyed Nasrollah suggested that we arrange to formalize the program for each session. I said that the gatherings would then lose their spontaneity and become tiresome seminars. Letting the young shah be himself I thought would be best; that way he would feel free to raise whatever topic struck him and speak unselfconsciously. In short these sessions, which all found useful and relished, continued until I left for America. <...>

There was a loftiness in Qazvini that compelled him to the pinnacle of his field. He was entirely preoccupied with knowledge and truth. <...> He coveted no earthly possessions. He woke early and had one or two cups of tea with some bread and cheese or a spoonful of jam. For lunch and dinner he had vegetable soup and boiled vegetables. <...> Cold weather put him in agony. When he came to Tehran I provided him with a lined cloak, and Mr. Mahmud Jam gave him a sheepskin coat made in Kabul. He was as happy as a child with these gifts. <...>

During the Reza Shah era, Foroughi and General Habibollah Shaybani, both of whom held Qazvini in the highest regard, were instrumental in securing for him a monthly stipend of 100 tomans from the Ministry of Education. This was later raised to 200 tomans when the economic situation in Iran soured. In return for this Qazvini wrote introductions and annotated editions of old manuscripts published by the ministry. For the Ferdowsi millennium celebration, Qazvini wrote a valuable article on the prose introduction to the *Shahnameh*. <...> He also wrote an important article on Sa'di's patrons for the 700th anniversary of the poet's birth. <...>

I first met Qazvini at the French National Library in 1924, when I went to Paris for specialized training in internal medicine. I was with Ali Bozorgnia (Sadr al-Ashraf), a fellow Khorasani, who was in Paris at the time. After an introduction, we went to a café on Rue Rivoli and had tea. I did not see Mohammad Khan for almost four months. I traveled to Germany, Holland, England and Belgium. <...> In these countries I met some of the leading Orientalists, including Edward G. Browne. I realized that they all viewed Qazvini as the foremost Iranian scholar of the day. <...> He was regarded a modern-day Aristotle. <...> His opinion, which was often solicited, was the last word on any aspect of Iranian scholarship. <...> After I returned to Paris in the fall, I wrote Qazvini saying that I would like to see him again. <...> He suggested a Monday, <...> which later became our regular meeting day during which we would talk for some five hours. <...> Qazvini rarely accepted a lunch or dinner invitation. He religiously spent these with his family. <...> Even when in Tehran, he only accepted invitations from four people: Dehkhoda, Hajj Seyyed Nasrollah, Farzin and me.

From our very first Monday meeting (later Friday was added), I had decided to prepare questions for Qazvini. After the meeting, I jotted down notes of what he had said. These meetings lasted two years, after which I returned to Iran. In late 1926 I was in Paris again and stayed until November 1928. On my arrival I wrote to Qazvini about resuming our twice-weekly meetings. Abbas Eqbal Ashtiani, who was in Paris at the time studying for his degree, also attended. <...> Soon it was decided that others be included. Thus Vladimir Minorski[4] became a regular member of our group on Mondays. Sometimes Iranians who happened to be passing through Paris were invited.

However, Friday meetings were exclusively Qazvini, Eqbal and me.
<...>

In my entire life I have never experienced more useful, nurturing
and spiritual, yet spontaneous gatherings as those. <...> Qazvini's
interests were amazingly varied. <...> He was a good storyteller.
Sometimes he would have a glass of wine. He was most interested in
European classical music. Two or three times a month, he would go
with his wife to the cinema, concerts and the theatre. He had read most
of the world's classic literature. <...> I doubt whether anyone read and
knew Arabic as well as he. <...> Qazvini's annotations of books were
often written in Arabic. His Persian and French were equally good.
<...> He knew the roots and origins of words and their usage in
French; he also knew some German and English as well as Chagatai
Turkish and Mongolian. <...> He liked Anatole France and encouraged me to translate the works of the French writer into Persian. <...>

Qazvini was of medium height, very thin and pale. His digestive
system was very sensitive. He worked very hard <...> and wasted no
time. <...> He read two newspapers daily, a practice which he picked
up in Paris and continued in Tehran. <...> He also loved flowers.
When Farzin was alive we would spend one or two nights a week at
his home. Colonel Alinaqi Vaziri, an accomplished tar [traditional
six-stringed instrument] player, always joined us. He would play and
sing Hafez. Dr. Meer was also there, mostly remaining silent. Qazvini
was very fond of him. <...>

Qazvini died in 1949 at the age of seventy-four. On the face of it
his death was the demise of one individual, but in reality it is the loss
of much more. Everyone dies, but few truly live. <...> An astute man,
Qazvini observed that human life has three dimensions: length,
breadth and depth. Most people are unaware of the latter two, which
are the most important. Length is not that significant. For most the
breadth and depth of their lives do not count. Even if they were to live
a thousand years, they would feel that they have not lived long
enough. <...> People like Qazvini are very rare.

According to the radio, the University of Tehran will be closed on
Sunday. The funeral services were held at the Sepahsalar Mosque and

were attended by a large number of distinguished people including [Ebrahim] Hakimi and Seyyed Hasan Taqizadeh. <...> Foremost among the scholars Qazvini had trained was Abbas Eqbal Ashtiani. Qazvini respected certain contemporary scholars like Taqizadeh (who in a way he trained) and Badi' al-Zaman Foruzanfar's work on Rumi. <...> He also trusted Dehkhoda's lexical knowledge and ety-mological intuition. <...> I hope that I will have an opportunity in the future to write a fuller account of this extraordinary man.

Tonight I am invited to the Syrian Embassy at 9:30, and despite my fragile emotional state, I must make an appearance.

TUESDAY 31 MAY 1949

<...> Sent a telegram concerning Qazvini's death to Shokuh al-Molk with the intention that the shah read it. <...>
  <...>

SUNDAY 19 JUNE 1949

Rested in the morning. At 2:00 P.M. went to the American golf club. Several people were playing bridge, a hallmark of Western civiliza-tion. More of a bane, actually, a game in which a group of silly men and women sit around wasting hours.

Today the Canadian ambassador, General Odlum, a seasoned and perceptive diplomat outlined U.S. ambassador Wadsworth's three functions: (1) golf, (2) bridge, (3) spinning political fantasies. Odlum says that Wadsworth is entirely superficial, uninformed, doubly igno-rant, in fact, because he believes he knows something. Since he is the ambassador from a country with money and clout, he can talk non-sense and people will agree. <...> General Odlum also told me that Sumer, the Turkish minister of economy, resigned because of clashes with Wadsworth. Sumer's replacement is a lackey of the United States.

I asked Odlum about U.S. policy in the Middle East. He thought for a while and then asked, "Do you imagine an eight-year-old boy is capable of having a policy? This is a country that acts on impulse, and its mood varies with the time of day." I asked whether the British agree with their U.S. counterparts. He said, "On the broad issues there is little difference. Where they do differ is in the details." Odlum believes that the British bring more experience and planning to the process. We also spoke about U.S. policy in general. He said that four principles are involved:

    1. The Truman policy: Odlum believes that Truman is not experienced in foreign policy. He relies heavily on his advisors. The difference between Truman and Roosevelt is that Roosevelt himself initiated policy with the help of his advisors.

    2. The armed forces: There are factions. One group relies heavily on air power, while another places its faith in land forces. The air force group is gaining ascendancy. <…> They are working on a plan to win any future war with bombs, planes, and technology. The navy does not have the power of the other two branches but is strong in the Pacific theatre.

    3. The State Department, he says, is a place packed with careerists. They are also divided into several factions. Odlum believes that the State Department has improved and will continue to do so, but it will be a while before it can match the expertise of the British Foreign Office.

    4. The media has great influence, but their primary interest is commercial. Thus they exaggerate threats and broadcast sensational news only. Americans are good people but gullible.

I again asked him about U.S. policy in the East, but he did not have a clear answer. The conversation then turned to the recent Paris conference. He said that the Soviets have raised the issue of trade and commerce with the West. They want to barter their own products like wheat and lumber, which the U.S. can resell elsewhere, for American manufactured goods. The Americans are amenable to the arrangement as they fear unemployment. There is also the precedent of their giving foodstuffs to England in exchange for woolen fabric, silver, etc. Moreover the industrialists, who are influential in policy-making, are in favor of it. <…>

There is, however, a group in America that is opposed to any commercial transactions with the Soviets, because it would strengthen them and allow them to wage war in three or four years. <...> Odlum believes that there will be no agreement with the Russians. <...>
<...>

WEDNESDAY 22-FRIDAY 24 JUNE 1949

<...>

In some early entries, Dr. Ghani describes how he fulfills a long-held hope to visit Konya, where Jalal al-Din Rumi is buried. He also devotes many pages to Konya's geography, history, important mosques, seminaries and cultural institutions.

<...> The world is a tangle of feelings, emotions and non-material inclinations; those very things that people label fanciful and illusory. But if we were to eliminate those spiritual refinements, nothing but the banes of existence would remain. [As Sa'di says,]

> *Eating, sleeping, coveting, lusting after devilry*
> *and [living in] ignorance and savagery, the*
> *animal has no idea of the world of humankind.*

All of life's beauty, the enjoyment of friendship, music, art, love, etc. is based on those things that people call dreamlike and ethereal. However, they are unmindful that the value of life lies in these very dreams; for if we were to abandon them, what remains would appear terrifying and horrible. That which we call attractive and well proportioned is composed of a series of lines, shapes, curves, high and low points, convexities and concavities, which stimulate our sense of beauty. The purely down-to-earth rationalist, reared solely in the laboratory, calls this thinking unreal, wishful and daydreaming. <...> Of course, scientific truths and principles can have their own beauty, so long as they do not displace our aesthetic sensibility. <...>

<...>

We set out at 4:00 A.M. with Habib the driver and the attendant Reza Shafi'i. We picked up Mr. As'ad Otuner, former Turkish ambassador to Spain, who is about fifty years old, a good companion, and a knowledgeable person. <...> Konya is 264 kilometers southwest of Ankara. <...>

<...>

We reached Konya at 3:00 P.M. and stayed at the Hotel Salamat. <...> Mr. Otuner and I immediately went to the Rumi Museum. As we were leaving the hotel, the chief of police of the city called on us and extended his welcome. He told us that the mayor was not in town, but the museum curator had been told to accompany us the entire time and act as our tour guide. We first went to the gravesite, which may have been used as a place of meditation for Rumi devotees. Beside it is the grave of Rumi's father. The grave of Salah al-Din Zarkub, one of Rumi's students and confidants, is also there.

Another place known as a retreat offers musical sessions [that brought devotees into an ecstatic state] and houses a large collection of musical instruments. Next to it was a mosque, which has now been converted into a museum. <...> In the entry hall of the former mosque are the kaftans and headgear of the dervishes and prayer carpets. In a large room opposite the hall there are a number of subterranean graves as well as a collection of calligraphic pieces, various manuscripts of Rumi's great *Divan* and Qur'ans. <...>

As I said, Rumi's father, Baha al-Din Mohammad Valad, is buried at the mausoleum. Baha Valad went to Mecca early in the thirteenth century and ultimately settled in Konya. He died in 1230, when Rumi was about twenty-six. <...> Next to Rumi's grave is a slab of stone in honor of another of his close companions, Shams al-Din of Tabriz. There is also the grave of Rumi's son Soltan Valad. <...> There are a number of other graves including that of Hosam al-Din Çalabi, Rumi's student and successor. The *Masnavi* was written at the pleading and insistence of Çalabi between the years 1261 and 1272. Rumi dictated the epic poem and Çalabi recorded it. <...>

<...>

THURSDAY 23 JUNE 1949

Last night I was extremely tired having been on my feet until 8:30 P.M. <...> Woke early and went to the local bazaar. <...> Nothing worth buying. Went again to the gravesites. Making an extraordinary exception, they allowed me to stand next to Rumi's grave. I took the opportunity to solicit blessings for all my friends. <...>

Next I went to the library and examined the rare books and manuscripts. <...>

FRIDAY 24 JUNE 1949

Started back to Ankara at 3:30 A.M. and arrived at 11:30 A.M. <...>
    <...>

SUNDAY 26 JUNE 1949

Picnic lunch at the golf club sponsored by the diplomatic corps. The same crowd was there playing golf and bridge. It was not enjoyable. Returned at 5:00 P.M. and so another day in life's limited supply ended. <...> Read mail and newspapers from Tehran. <...> Dr. Meer—a devoted friend and worshiper of Qazvini—who is himself an exceptional human being and one of the best surgeons in Tehran, writes in a letter dated 17 June 1949:

> <...> The strange thing is that when he [Qazvini] died there was no doctor in attendance. <...> We all have to go, but it was tragic for Mohammad Khan Qazvini to have died without a physician in attendance. This has depressed me greatly.

MONDAY 27 JUNE 1949

<...> News from Iran indicates that the government follows the same old policy of vacillating between being too forceful and too weak. <...> Now they have imposed martial law; Parliament is hastily passing legislation; opposition newspapers have been shut down. <...> Nothing

basic or constructive is being done. The government holds all the cards, when there should be more give and take and moderation. But moderation can come only with reasonable and wise leadership; they would be able to inculcate moderation in the people until it becomes second nature. Those who are not in positions of responsibility have too much influence. The elections, as usual, will be mishandled.

<...>

TUESDAY 28 JUNE 1949

Today is the first day of Ramadan, the month during which the Qur'an was revealed. But there is no sign of it here, except for lights in the unused minarets of mosques. The Turks are being indulgent in this case because they don't want it said that there is no freedom of belief here.

<...>

Dr. Meer writes from Tehran:

> You asked about what I am doing. My surgery is an infirmary without equipment and real beds. Patients are fed food that is not edible. The state of the hospital grows worse daily; it would be better not to accept patients and to shut the doors. <...> Despite this, several empty heads have gathered in a meeting with the intention of establishing five universities in cities around the country. Considering the way the university in the capital is run, woe betide a college in Ahvaz. One should ask the gentlemen where all the students will come from? The faculty? The funds?
>
> <...>

WEDNESDAY 29 JUNE 1949

I am reading through the embassy archives. Reached the 1860s and found correspondence between Mirza Sa'id Mo'tamen al-Molk, the foreign minister and Mirza Hoseyn Khan (later Moshir al-Dowleh and still later Sepahsalar). <...>

THURSDAY 30 JUNE 1949

Calls on members of the diplomatic corps and continues to read correspondence in the archives from the 1860s.

<...>

WEDNESDAY 13 JULY 1949

<...>

Reviewing embassy archives, which begin in 1857 with Mirza Aqa Khan Nuri as first minister [the term prime minister was adopted later]. Sa'id Khan Mo'tamen al-Molk as foreign minister and Mirza Hoseyn Khan Qazvini as minister and later ambassador, followed by Hasan Ali Khan Garrusi, followed by Sheikh Mohsen Khan Moshir al-Dowleh, Mahmud Khan Ala al-Molk <...>. Correspondence between the embassy in Istanbul and Tehran concerns the following matters:

1. Incidents that occurred at border crossings: robberies, assaults by Turkish highwaymen including murders.
2. Transportation of the bodies of deceased Iranians from Turkey to Iran and the overcharging for such services on the part of Turkish officials.
3. Issues related to outbreaks of cholera and quarantines.
4. Treatment of Iranian pilgrims by Turkish [Ottoman] authorities in the Shia shrines of Iraq, Syria, Saudi Arabia; deaths of pilgrims and attacks on them.
5. Disputes among Iranian and Turkish merchants.
6. The absurd number of letters of recommendation for Iranians traveling in Turkey, beginning with the reign of Mozaffar al-Din Shah.
7. Awarding of medals and citations to Turkish nationals, promised by people close to the Iranian throne (more than 150 medals had been promised at one time). <...>

The correspondence makes it clear that during the reign of Mozaffar al-Din Shah, courtiers saw the awarding of medals as a way to enrich themselves. During Naser al-Din Shah's time there had been more discipline. Mirza Sa'id Khan took his duties more seriously than the people around Mozaffar al-Din Shah, such as Mahmud Khan Ala al-Molk, Prince Arfa' al-Dowleh, etc.

Though taken separately, the letters are each about something mundane, routine, but one learns something from the totality of the correspondence. They show the sloppiness, weakness and stupidity in the everyday workings of the embassy; the decline of Iran. The present is a child of the past. During the past century when the West was making great strides in every field, scientific discoveries and inventions, Iran remained stagnant, passing its days and nights powerless in the face of events. Kings and leaders of the country, consumed by lust, fell asleep and ultimately died, to be replaced in time by successors who were even worse. It is terrible to wonder whether the thousands of years of our history have always been like this, and now we are in this sorry state. We have to wait and see what the future will bring.

<...>

THURSDAY 14 JULY 1949

<...>

At 6:30 A.M. we reached Samsun. We were met by the Turkish civilian police who escorted us to the hotel. <...> I met several Iranian businessmen who live in Samsun. They were very kind. The Iranian residents of Turkey that I have met on these trips have expressed special affection for their fellow countrymen. A motorboat took us to the ship, which is to bring us to Trabzon. We stopped at several ports before reaching it at 4:00 P.M. These regions are abundantly green and beautiful. I met several of the passengers including a professor of French at the University of Ankara. We were met at Trabzon by our consul general <...> and went to the consulate. Toured the city for some time. <...>

<...>

SUNDAY 17 JULY 1949

In the morning visited the Iranian school, mosque and Iranian cemetery. At 3:00 P.M. met with the mayor. I dissuaded him from hosting any social functions as I must leave by car to Erzurum. The population of Trabzon is 35,000; it has piped water and a recently built 500-bed hospital. There are also other civilian and military hospitals. <...>

MONDAY 18 TO WEDNESDAY 20 JULY 1949

Visits to Erzurum, Erzincan, Sivas and Kayseri with descriptions and comments, then return to Ankara.

THURSDAY 4 AUGUST 1949

4:00 A.M. with Reza Moshiri and Habib the driver set out for Eskishahr, one of the secondary towns of Anatolia, 279 kilometers from Ankara. Arrived at 9:00 A.M. Its importance stems from the airbase situated near the town. <...> Arrived in Bursa at 1:30 P.M. <...> and entered the Çelik Palace Hotel, which is superior to the best hotels in Ankara. Surrounded by rolling green hills with mountains as a backdrop and blessed with an abundance of mineral springs and many waterfalls, Bursa is a lovely place. The weather is far superior to Istanbul as the sea is about thirty kilometers away. <...> It is one of those towns that a person wishes to visit again and again. <...> A traveler once said that it is impossible to know Turkey without seeing Bursa. <...>

Bursa (originally Prousa) was built in 200 B.C.E. by Prusias I of Bythinia. There is little left of Prusias's age. <...> When the Byzantines ruled the town, which they named Bursa, it was a luxury resort. The Romans knew of its mineral waters. <...> It fell to the Ottomans in C.E. 1327 and became their capital until 1453, the year they conquered Constantinople [Istanbul]. The mosques in the city that were built before 1453 owe a great deal to Iranian and Byzantine architecture, but the Turks do not accept this and call the style the

"Turkish" school of architecture. The Bursa Museum has some stonework from the Greek and Roman eras. It also houses apparel worn by the dervishes and a small library. <...> We visited the tomb of Mohammad Çelebi, the son of Sultan Bayazit Ilderum, who ascended to the throne by having his brother killed. It is from this period that fratricide and the killing of offspring became practiced by Ottoman sultans. <...>

We visited the Yesil (Green) Mosque that has beautiful tile work and the Ulu (Great) Mosque. <...> Returned at 8:30 P.M., had a bite and fell asleep. Seldom have I been so tired. <...>

FRIDAY 5 AUGUST 1949

Visited the Murat I Mosque <...> the Muradiye Mosque complex, and graves [of many Sultans and other historical figures].

SATURDAY 6 AUGUST 1949

Left Bursa at 4:00 A.M. for Çanakkale, which we reached at 3:00 P.M.<...> Staying at a very dirty, inferior hotel. <...> With a member of the civil police as our guide we started out for Troy, which is thirty-five kilometers southeast of Çanakkale. Heinrich Schliemann[5] began excavating this area in 1871. In 1882 he was assisted by [William] Dörpfeld, who continued the work until 1891 a year after Schliemann's death. Their finding confirmed that the Homeric city of Troy was located on this site. They also confirmed that the city had been destroyed and rebuilt on several occasions. Their findings showed that the first city, parts of which were discovered, dated back to the Stone Age, twenty-five to thirty centuries B.C.E. The next structures, the third, fourth and fifth layers, were from the Bronze Age, 2500 to 2000 B.C.E. The next, also Bronze Age, dated from 2000 to 1500 B.C.E. The sixth layer was the Troy of Homer, 1500 to 1000 B.C.E. <...>

Travel to Eskishahr. <...>

SUNDAY 7 AUGUST 1949

Started out at 3:45 A.M. and reached Balikesir. <...>

MONDAY 8 AUGUST 1949

Traveled to Iznik (Nicea). *[Greek background of the city, its name, Byzantine structures, etc.]* Visited the sites, met local dignitaries, exhausted, slept early.

TUESDAY 9 AUGUST 1949

Returned to Ankara. <...>
    <...>

THURSDAY 18 AUGUST 1949

Last night had a conversation with the American General McBride about my trips around Turkey, to Çanakkale and Troy. He asked why people from the East are so concerned with the past. He said that Americans only look forward, to the future. I answered in various ways, including a quote from Anatole France who said, "'Life is very short, so we have no choice but to extend it in two ways: first, by studying the past, and second, by conjuring the future in our dreams and poetic fantasies.' Easterners have taken his advice. We are greatly interested in the past and have also cultivated our poetic imagination. Besides, it is our own history. You are fortunate not to have an extensive history; but, of course, you are interested in the little you have. We have a history that goes back several thousand years, so it is natural that we find the past compelling." I gave ready answers, but the real reason is that as one becomes older there is little to look forward to. One is preoccupied with the road he has taken and the difficulties experienced along the way. Nations are similar in outlook. We Easterners have become old. Like any young person, General McBride's nation would naturally think principally of its future. <...>

FRIDAY 19 AUGUST 1949

A while ago I wrote to Istanbul asking them to buy and send me the book *Textes persans relatifs à la secte des Horoufis* (ed. Clément Huart, Leiden: E. J. Brill, 1909). The book was unavailable, so I borrowed it from the library. I have read it and will summarize part of its contents.

<…> It includes several treatises and a very scholarly and insightful afterword on Hurufi thinking by Dr. Reza Towfiq:

The conquest of Iran proved to be tragic for Islam. First, the Semitic religion did not conform to Aryan sensibilities. Second, with a 1,500-year history of independence and grandeur, Iranians in their hearts and souls did not submit to the Arabs. Thus began a resistance movement that continues to this day. Shiism and all of its diverse offshoots arise from this.

Hoseyn, the son of Ali, married Shahrbanu [daughter of the last Sasanian king Yazdagird] and named their son Zeyn al-Abedin [literally "Ornament of the Believers"]. The half-Persian Zeyn al-Abedin was the lone representative of the Iranian people, and Iranians' devotion to him was considered a form of protest [against the Arab conquest of their land]. The Iranians with their Shiism and their <…> many sects have effaced the original simplicity of Islam <…>.

After the great conquests, it was as though Islam succumbed to fatigue and became diluted. This gave rise to conflicting political factions that eroded the spiritual hegemony of Islam. After the Islamic sciences and seminaries were established, the dissent took the form of scholastic disputes and arguments, during which each faction would cite the Qur'an in support of its own position. Dialectical theology came into being and the attributes of God were debated. <…> Some theologians were so afraid of declaring the createdness of the Qur'an (lest the sultans and caliphs try to change it), they accepted its eternal nature as dogma. <…>

Hurufi theology is a hodgepodge of Neoplatonism, and Jewish, Shiite, Sufi, <…> and Druze beliefs. <…> All in all, when juxtaposed to the world's great religions, Hurufism is a caricature. But one should not be surprised to find that there are several thousand Hurufi devotees, especially in Turkey. Generally the unthinking find superstition especially attractive.

<...>

TUESDAY 23 AUGUST 1949

Preparing for a trip to Izmir to attend the exhibition of Iranian goods and products. At 10:30 A.M. I went to the Ministry of Foreign Affairs for the opening session of the commission on the transit of goods between Iran and Turkey. The members of the commission were selected and approved. <...> In the afternoon I paid a call on the members of the Iranian delegation. Went to bed at 10:00 P.M. and started out for Izmir at 3:30 A.M.

WEDNESDAY 24 AUGUST 1949

<...> Reached Bursa at 2:00 P.M. and spent the night. <...> I felt that the people accompanying me were not interested in seeing the town. <...> We therefore set out for Izmir early the next day and arrived at 3:00 P.M.

THURSDAY 25 AUGUST 1949

<...>

Visited the Iranian and Turkish pavilions. The Trade Exposition is in a large park in the middle of the city. It has spacious avenues, a casino, cafés and restaurants, and other diversions.

THE IRANIAN PAVILION

More than ninety percent of the objects are from the collection of two Iranian Jewish brothers named Mehdizadeh, who are antique dealers in Tehran. There were fine carpets from Tabriz, Tehran, Mashhad, Esfahan, Na'in, Yazd and other parts. There were also tribal Turkmen and Qashqa'i carpets. Some of the items on display were masterpieces of the Iranian carpet industry; one was a woven portrait of Reza Shah, which was hard to distinguish from a painting. There were very good examples of wood inlay pieces, Esfahan silverwork, mosaics, ivory, pins, bracelets, necklaces and silk brocades. <...> Also on display were fine miniatures by the Emami family. There was a small booth devoted to the oil industry and the geology of southern Iran. <...>

The Ministry of Trade and Commerce's exhibit was a letdown, however. There were a few boxes of sample gum tragacanth, raisins, dried apricots and some packets of cigarettes. I was shocked. What was the ministry thinking of? Why not display karakul sheepskins, a collection of various types of marble, wood from Mazandaran, Gilan, etc. Why not agricultural products like pistachios, filberts, almonds, or caviar and precious minerals?

<...>

FRIDAY 26 AUGUST 1949

<...> Spent the morning sightseeing. At 1:00 P.M. a reporter from a trade and economy magazine came by for an interview. I met with Dr. Hu, a professor of history and geography, and asked about Ephesus and Sardes, the capital of Lydia. At night I returned to the trade fair, visiting the Iranian, German, Czech, Hungarian, British and U.S. exhibits. <...>

SATURDAY 27 AUGUST 1949

8:00 A.M. accompanied by Professor Hu, Mrs. Qarib and [Mr. Qarib's sister] Maryam, went seventy-four kilometers south of Izmir to Ephesus, which at one time had been the most important city in Asia Minor. It is now a village with a population of some three or four thousand. The ancient city has been destroyed but recent excavations attest to its greatness. The temple of Diana (Artemis), one of the Seven Wonders of the World, was at Ephesus. The city was destroyed by the Goths in 262 C.E. . <...> It was rebuilt, but from the fifteenth century it declined. <...> There was a cocktail party at the Iranian exhibition attended by the mayor and foreign consuls general. <...>

SUNDAY 28 AUGUST 1949

Left Izmir at 7:30 A.M.; stopped at Bursa and arrived in Ankara the following day at 6:00 P.M. <...>
<...>

SATURDAY 3 SEPTEMBER 1949

At nine, Colonel -, the new military attaché, is arriving from Tehran with his wife and three children. Qarib and Moshiri went to the train station and invited them for lunch and to meet the staff at the embassy. Colonel...is about thirty-five. At lunch and later he said some things that taken together seem strange.

1. The Turks are our enemies and will be a threat to our security in the future.
2. The Turks are ahead of us in everything.
3. Our border police are all opium addicts.
4. The Americans see us as pro-British and that is why they don't give aid to Iran; whereas they do assist Greece and Turkey.

For an official representative of Iran to say such things may at times have serious and distressing consequences for the government. He appeared unseasoned to me, but I'll have to wait and see.

MONDAY 5 SEPTEMBER 1949

<...>

I reminded Colonel...to be more careful in what he said and not to make such statements as "The Turks pose a threat to Iran in the future" <...> or "The Turks are ahead of us in every respect" or otherwise imply that there is no hope of reform in Iran. He must listen and say little and observe the utmost civility in his dealings with his Turkish counterparts. I told him to learn the basics, first by reading a short history of Turkey up to 1919 and, second, a detailed account of Turkey from 1919 onward, including the creation of a republic. He needed also to become familiar with the geography of the country, especially regions that bordered Iran. <...>
<...>

THURSDAY 8 SEPTEMBER 1949

<...> Not feeling well. Newspapers from Tehran arrived. Whenever I read about government authorities sympathizing with the plight of the poor in Iran, I become depressed. It is not because commenting on poverty is wrong, but because it is the same old lip service those in power have always paid to the suffering. <...> Expressing sympathy for the poor will not by itself cure what ails them. Liberating them from their misery and despair must begin with the fundamentals. The standard of living and the purchasing power of the people must be raised. <...> It is now more than three years that there is some talk of a seven-year plan and more than $750,000 has been spent on consultants without practical results. There is no single decisive person, rather a bunch of lackeys, their eyes fixed on the British. <...> The country will go nowhere as long as these people are in charge. <...>
<...>

THURSDAY 15 SEPTEMBER 1949

<...> It appears now that the new military attaché and his subordinate, Major -, know no foreign languages. I am greatly upset. Some nine months ago I had a long talk with General Razmara about the choice of a military attaché. I said that I am in principle in agreement with having a military attaché, but in practice the wrong person is sometimes chosen for the post. Because we share a long history and border with the Turks, we have to be completely conversant with their military status. Once the Soviet threat is gone, it is possible that old notions of Turanism and Pan-Turkism will revive. The Turks have always had their eyes on Azerbaijan in particular. The long borders that we share are constantly being traversed by tribal peoples like the Kurds. <...> As I said to him, in principle I am in total agreement that there must be a military attaché, but I have seen that the man chosen for the post is not qualified and can cause problems. If someone is to be appointed, he must be a graduate of a military academy and someone with a command of military affairs. He must be sufficiently well informed in general matters, to the extent that he will be

a credit in any public gathering. <...> He also must at least know either English or French. He must have a good physical appearance as he is representing the Iranian armed forces. His pay should permit a good standard of living. General Razmara replied that he had no one in particular in mind. He said that HIM knows the officer class, so it would be best that I discussed the matter with him. A few days later I had an audience with HIM and repeated what I had said to Razmara. At the end I mentioned that as HIM was wearing a military uniform, I thought of him as a soldier. Whoever is sent <...> must represent HIM. He agreed with what I said. <...> A few days later, General Razmara came to my house and spoke about the cost of living in Ankara. I told him that I would report on this as soon as I reached there. <...> But now, after almost nine months, they have sent someone who is totally inadequate. <...> His only recommendation is that he is the nephew of -. He knows neither Turkish nor any European languages. I don't understand why they have sent him. <...>

FRIDAY 16 SEPTEMBER 1949

Plato identifies seven forms of government: monarchy, aristocracy, theocracy, oligarchy, democracy, despotism and absolutism. <...> He concludes that all these forms are transitory. <...> The reason they do not last for long periods is that each of them is carried to excess and exaggeration, which results in its degeneration and overthrow. Furthermore, the degeneration is accompanied by a decline in the virtue of those who are ruled. There can be no separation between the ruler and the ruled.

Though we Iranians have not experienced all of Plato's forms of government, we have had just and equitable kings and dictators. In recent years we have had an unbridled pseudodemocracy; we have been ruled by a foolish and ignorant king, or a well-meaning monarch who, however, was slave to his passions, followed by a dictator. Anarchy produced Reza Shah, who at first was a good man at the right time, but then there was excess followed by a strange type of democracy. <...>

I have been elected to the Iranian Senate from Sabzevar during the first round of elections. Received congratulatory telegrams and a letter from the Ministry of Foreign Affairs <…> asking me to be present in Mashhad for the second round of elections. I replied thanking the voters but <…> unfortunately I could not be present. <…> I received another telegram from Mr. Nabavi, the deputy from Nishapur, stating, "HIM has said that there is no need for you to resign and return to Iran." I answered that I had already declined, and apologized for not returning to Mashhad.

SATURDAY 17 SEPTEMBER 1949

<…> Attended a gathering hosted by Mr. Webster of the U.S. Embassy for Mrs. Joan Rosita Forbes, a world traveler and lecturer. She has been to the African Sahara, Ethiopia, covered WWII, and has written books. Her knowledge of the East is superficial, but like many American ladies she bursts with energy and life, something one finds often in the U.S.

SUNDAY 18 SEPTEMBER 1949

Spent the entire day reading the *Visit to Mecca* of Mehdiqoli Khan Hedayat (Mokhber al-Saltaneh), which the author personally sent to me. He writes with the same simplicity that he uses when he speaks. Every event is presented as commonplace. There is no artificiality to his style. He was accompanied by Atabak, who had been dismissed as first minister. Their journey took them through Russia, China, Port Arthur, Japan, Honolulu, and on to San Francisco. They spent six days in the U.S. Then they went to Alexandria, Cairo, Suez, Jedda, Mecca and Medina, Damascus, Beirut and Austria. Mehdiqoli Khan then returned to Iran, and Atabak went to Tunisia but returned to Iran at the request of Mohammad Ali Shah. He was assassinated in Tehran.

Canadian Embassy for dinner.

MONDAY 19 SEPTEMBER 1949

Routine embassy work. Read Anatole France's *The Gods Are Athirst*, a truly amazing masterpiece. The man has delineated every aspect of the human soul.

<...>

THURSDAY 22 SEPTEMBER 1949

I have wasted much of my life on fruitless pursuits. Depressed. <...> Read in bed until around noon. Lunch at the Pakistani Embassy. Several guests. <...>

FRIDAY 23 SEPTEMBER 1949

5:00 P.M. the new Turkish ambassador to Tehran called wishing to see me. He is an intelligent man. Several topics were raised including the strengthening of relations between the two countries and strengthening our mutual defenses. He referred to our past relationship and how Turkey and Iran exercised great influence in the East. <...>

SATURDAY 24 SEPTEMBER 1949

I have begun liver injections.

At 10:00 A.M. the Indian ambassador, Chaman Laal, who is returning to his country, came by. He is fed up with the diplomatic service and wants to return to India to become active in politics. Chaman Laal is an emotional, sincere and good man. He recalled that Nehru believed if the Communists had won the election in Italy, there would have been war. Nehru emphasized the importance of Turkey and suggested that Chaman Laal accept the ambassadorship for one year and then return to enter politics. <...> In any case his view is that the threat of war has passed. The crucial acts occurred when the Russians sent Albanian aviation advisors and troops to help the insurgents in Greece. In response to this the U.S. was prepared to invade Albania. Tito, who had become disillusioned with the Russians, held secret meetings with the Americans. <...> Chaman

Laal still believes that there may be clashes between the two forces. He said his wife would like to meet me and we arranged this for 11:00 A.M. tomorrow. In the afternoon paid a courtesy call on the new Turkish ambassador to Tehran. <…>

    <…>

MONDAY 26 SEPTEMBER 1949

At 10:00 A.M. I was called upon by the former ambassador of Turkey to Iran, Köprülü, who had served in Tehran for four and half years and had been there several times before his ambassadorship. <…> During the time he was ambassador, Köprülü was a keen observer of events in a very difficult period in Iran's history. He spent two full hours with me. He was very knowledgeable and was familiar with all the key players in Iran. In sum he said that after the assassination attempt on HIM (4 February 1949), the shah became very popular. This enabled him to gain firm control over the political scene. However, as usual a group gathered around the shah and gradually eroded his moral authority and popularity. He spoke at length about one of his sisters who exercises great influence on the government…This influence was responsible for the appointment of one of her protégés as minister of labor <…> Dr. Nasr was fired. <…> Jam was removed for the same reasons while Hazhir became minister. <…> He believes Hazhir is very unpopular and his presence will affect the shah's popularity.

[Köprülü mentioned that] on the proposed trip of the shah to the U.S., the Americans have insisted that only nine people accompany him. <…> Sa'ed is not well and may want to go to Europe. <…> There is talk of the prime ministerships of Hakimi and Hazhir. <…> Taqizadeh has become very unpopular for several reasons. He thought Reza Shah responsible for the extension of the oil agreement. <…> At the urging of the Court, Golshayan published papers that indicated Taqizadeh had paved the way for the oil agreement extension. <…> Köprülü believes that all power rests with the shah. As he spoke about everyone with such authority, I became embarrassed that what went on in Iran was so transparent. <…> I invited him to have dinner with me tonight as the new

Turkish ambassador is also to be a guest. Had to attend a cocktail party, but returned to greet my guests. <...>

<...>

SATURDAY 8 OCTOBER 1949

Had dinner at the U.S. Embassy. Mr. Eric Johnson, senior administrator of the Marshal Plan, and his wife were there. Also attending were General Odlum and his wife and Colonel Sterling, who is an official with British Intelligence. The U.S. ambassador has invited me to go to Cyprus on 10 October. Accepted and will return [to Istanbul] on 12 October. <...>

WEDNESDAY 19 OCTOBER 1949

Returned to Ankara. There was a telegram waiting for me from HIM's Special Office:

Ankara. Iranian Embassy.
His Excellency Dr. Ghasem Ghani.
Pursuant to an invitation from the president of the United States, HIM will travel to the U.S. HIM has decided that your excellency will be a member of the retinue. Delegate all embassy affairs to any member of your staff as you see fit and return to Tehran on 6 November. <...> Shokuh, Head of HIM's Special Office.

<...>

WEDNESDAY 26 OCTOBER 1949

HIM's birthday. There was a reception at the embassy between six and nine. More than 700 guests were invited. <...> It was well organized. <...> Am extremely tired.

FRIDAY 4 NOVEMBER 1949

Left the airport for Istanbul at 9:30 A.M. Then on to Tehran and, later, the U.S.

NOTES
AMBASSADOR TO TURKEY

1. Sir Percy Loraine (1880–1969). An experienced British diplomat. Minister to Tehran 1921–26; high commissioner to Egypt 1929–34; ambassador to Turkey 1934-39; ambassador to Italy 1939–40.

2. Abdullah ibn Husein (1882–1951). Amir of Transjordan from 1921 and king from 1946 until he was assassinated.

3. Jean Cocteau (1889–1963). French poet, dramatist, artist, director of plays and films.

4. Vladimir Minorski (1877–1966). Born in Russia. Began career as a diplomat. One of the great scholars of Iranian literature and history. After the Russian Revolution, lived mostly in Paris and London.

5. Heinrich Schliemann (1822–90). A businessman and amateur archeologist who spent his retirement searching for the site of Homer's Troy. His discoveries there and at Mycenai, Ithaca, etc. encouraged other archeologists, both amateur and professional, to explore other sites in Turkey.

SECOND TRIP TO THE UNITED STATES

The following telegram had been sent from HIM's Special Office on October 16:

> His Excellency Dr. Ghasem Ghani, Iranian Embassy, Ankara. Pursuant to an invitation from President Truman, HIM will travel to the U.S. HIM has decided that your excellency be a member of the official party. Return to Tehran by 15 Aban to accompany HIM. <…>

The background to this invitation is as follows. In 1943 when President Roosevelt, Prime Minister Churchill and Marshal Stalin met in Tehran, the late president invited HIM to visit the U.S. President Roosevelt reiterated the invitation by telegram on his return to the U.S. When Princess Ashraf was visiting the US last year, President Truman repeated the invitation. US ambassador John Wiley extended a formal invitation on the president's behalf.

Due to the internal situation in Iran, HIM was unable to accept the previous invitations. However the latest invitation was accepted and the presidential plane, *The Independence,* will arrive in Tehran on 15 November 1949 to convey HIM and an entourage of nine to the

U.S. We are due to arrive on the sixteenth and will be met by President Truman and senior government officials. There will be a formal military review. Because of repairs being done at the White House, HIM will stay at Blair House. HIM will visit agricultural and academic centers in several states. He will also deliver fourteen speeches, including one to a joint session of Congress. <...>

THURSDAY 20 OCTOBER 1949

I telegraphed my acceptance of HIM's instructions to the Special Office.

I hope the visit is beneficial. From the time of the occupation of Iran by the British and the Soviets in August 1941 until the end of the war nothing had been accomplished in the country. In the chaos resulting from the machinations of the occupying powers, Iran was never able to have a coherent foreign policy. A semblance of stability came about only in 1946, after the Azerbaijan Affair. I hope the trip will result in finding a way to relieve the Iranian people of their poverty, hunger and insecurity. <...>
<...> Paid a call on the Canadian ambassador and had a lengthy talk about Iran. He said that [in the U.S.] we must speak with General Bradley, the chairman of the Joint Chiefs of Staff. <...> He said that we must avoid any talk of philanthropy and instead emphasize that Iran is important in its own right. <...> Stayed for dinner at his insistence. <...>

SATURDAY 22 OCTOBER 1949

I spent some time with the Canadian and U.S. ambassadors to Turkey. To update my knowledge of Washington we spoke of current affairs in the U.S. Specifically asked about Dean Acheson,[1] Generals George Marshal[2] and Omar Bradley,[3] and the leaders of the Senate and the House of Representatives. <...>

THURSDAY 27 OCTOBER 1949

At noon called on Najm al-Din Sadek at the Ministry of Foreign Affairs and talked for an hour. Most of the conversation was about US aid to Iran. The Turks consider any weakness in Iran as a weakness in their sphere of interest. The Turks are promoting an eastern Mediterranean pact with Iran alone, i.e., without the Arab countries. The U.S. may consider such a pact as provocative, but even the Americans have become aware of the strategic position of Iran and of the value of the Persian Gulf to the Indian Ocean area and Southeast Asia. <…> Equally important is the country's oil. It was a very friendly exchange of opinions.

Lengthy telegram from Mr. Ala in Washington explaining the schedule of HIM's visit, attire for various functions, and asking Dr. Ghani to make sure that HIM rehearses his speeches.

WEDNESDAY 2 NOVEMBER 1949

Received a letter from Gholam Abbas Aram. The people accompanying HIM are: Lieutenant General Yazdanpanah, Brigadier General Hejazi, Brig. General Ayadi, Minister of Court Hazhir, Dr. Shafaq, Dr. Yahya Adl, Hormoz Pirnia, Hoseyn'ali Qaraguzlu and Major Hoseyn Fardust.

SATURDAY 5 NOVEMBER 1949

Arrived in Tehran via KLM at 3:30 P.M. Mr. Hamid Sayyah informed me on landing that Minister of Court Abdolhoseyn Hazhir was assassinated at the Sepahsalar Mosque. The assailant, a broker in the Esfahan bazaar, was a certain Emami, who two years earlier had assassinated the secular scholar and jurist Ahmad Kasravi but was never prosecuted. Emami was a member of the Mojahedin al-Eslam and even had printed a card identifying himself as Kasravi's assassin.

I reached home at 5:00 P.M. Together with Mr. Yunes Vahabzadeh went to the home of the late Mohammad Qazvini to see his wife and his daughter, Suzanne. I next called on Mr. Hadi Amir Farrokh and later visited General Yazdanpanah's home. Returned around 11:00 P.M. and learned that the Court had telephoned to inform me that the audience with HIM was set for 10:30 A.M. at the Marmar Palace.

SUNDAY 6 NOVEMBER 1949

7:45 A.M. called on Mr. Mohammad Sa'ed, the Prime Minister, who is a sincere and decent person and a friend of many years. I next called on Mr. Hoseyn Shokuh, the head of HIM's Special Office. My audience with HIM ended at noon. Most of the conversation was about Turkey and related matters. HIM said he wished to see me every day before the trip. Lunched with Mr. Sa'ed.

MONDAY 7 NOVEMBER 1949

Had an audience with HIM for ninety minutes. He asked me to come by tomorrow and the day after to review speeches that have been prepared or that are in the process of being completed. The Ministry of Foreign Affairs was next, for work related to Turkey. I saw Mr. Golshayan in the afternoon; at night I visited Colonel Vaziri and later Mrs. (Abdolhoseyn) Dehqan.

TUESDAY 8 NOVEMBER 1949

Devoted the early morning to seeing friends. Around noon I went to the Ministry of Foreign Affairs for work; later I called on the ministers of health and interior to reciprocate their visits to me. 4:00 P.M. called on Prince Abd al-Reza. At 7:00 P.M. saw General Razmara. Then I saw Doctors Loqman al-Dowleh, Hakim al-Dowleh and Loqman al-Molk. In the evening I saw several other friends.

WEDNESDAY 9 NOVEMBER 1949

In the morning, audience with HIM; in the afternoon I called on Mr. Qavam al-Saltaneh. I was invited to dinner at the U.S. Embassy. I began to feel unwell and could not attend.

THURSDAY 10 NOVEMBER 1949

I have an abdominal hemorrhage again. Professor Adl came and injected vitamins C and K.

FRIDAY 11 NOVEMBER 1949

Spent the day in bed. Several friends came by.

SATURDAY 12 NOVEMBER 1949

Messrs. Ardalan, Qods, Mas'ud Mo'azed and Navab visited. Later my dear friend Dr. Meer came by.

SUNDAY 13 NOVEMBER 1949

I rested the entire day. Messrs. Hormoz Qarib, Yunes Vahabzadeh, Khazra'i, Mrs. Vosouq, Kashef, Ali Vakili, and Ali Asghar Hekmat came by. Mr. Izadi, representing Princess Ashraf, visited.

MONDAY 14 NOVEMBER 1949

Had breakfast early in the morning with Mr. Sa'ed. Later Mr. Mohammad Mehdi Nemazi, General Yazdanpanah, Colonel Baharmast, General Matbu'i, Hormoz Qarib, Yunes Vahabzadeh and Rashid Aqa called on me. 4:00 P.M. Mr. Golshayan came for a while. 5:15 P.M. I paid a visit to Prince Abd al-Reza. <...>

TUESDAY 15 NOVEMBER 1949

We boarded *The Independence,* a luxurious plane with ample accommodation. <...> Stopped briefly in Rome, where Mr. Mahmud Jam (former prime minister, presently ambassador to Italy) met us with a large reception committee. HIM told me to look after the U.S. ambassador (Mr. Dunn). Jam, Yazdanpanah, and I had a lengthy talk with him. During a wide-ranging conversation, Dunn praised HIM, and then we discussed antiquities, ancient dynasties, the terms "Iran" and "Persia." After a delay of four hours, we reboarded the plane.

Professor Ádl, General Ayadi, Colonel Ansari and Major Fardust played cards during the entire flight. Pirnia, General Hejazi, and, later, I napped. <…> We stopped overnight in the Azores. <…>

WEDNESDAY 16 NOVEMBER 1949

We landed in Washington at exactly 4:00 P.M. Smiling broadly, President Truman shook HIM's hand, they took photographs, and each leader spoke briefly. A band played the national anthems of the two countries and HIM reviewed the honor guard. The president and HIM traveled in an open carriage, while the rest of us traveled by car. I rode with Messrs. George Allen, former U.S. ambassador to Tehran, and Dean Rusk,[4] assistant secretary of state. HIM along with his valet, Mr. Sharifi, Generals Yazdanpanah and Ayadi will spend the first night at Blair House, but because it, as well as the White House, is under repair, they will move to Prospect House tomorrow. The rest of us will be at the Shoreham Hotel.

Tonight the president will host a dinner at the Carlton Hotel (as the White House is undergoing repairs). It is a formal dinner attended by members of the Cabinet, Supreme Court, and senior military officers. At the dinner I was seated next to Mrs. Acheson. (There were speeches by HIM and the president.) During my brief conversation with the president, I said that it was the fourth time that I had had the honor to shake his hand. The last time had been two and a half years ago. I thanked God to find him in good health. Given all the problems he faced, I said, only an inner moral strength and serenity could have kept him so fit. He thanked me and asked about my own health, adding that HIM was concerned. He said that HIM had impressed him and that he would do everything in his power to help. He then took me to meet Acheson and others.

THURSDAY 17 NOVEMBER 1949

I went to Prospect House and attended HIM's press conference, which went well. After the conference, he voiced his concern about my health and said that after the New York portion of the trip, I

Mohammad Reza Shah and President Harry S. Truman shake hands. Lieutenant General Morteza Yazdanpanah stands behind them with Dr Ghani on the right.

should rest and see my doctors. He had expressed similar concerns in Rome. HIM then left for Annapolis. I had lunch with Mr. Ala. It appears Mrs. Ala has quarreled with him and refuses to attend any of the functions. Later I had a long talk with Mrs. Ala but failed to influence her. <...> She objects to the presence at the embassy of Aram and Gudarzi, whom her husband supports. Tonight Mr.

Acheson hosted a dinner at which HIM and the secretary of state gave short addresses.

FRIDAY 18 NOVEMBER 1949

Mr. Nemazi stopped by. I gave him a manuscript of the Qur'an in which to record the birth of a child he and his wife are expecting. Tonight at 7:30 HIM hosted a dinner after which he and the president spoke. At 10:30 there will be an elaborate party, which I will not attend.

SUNDAY 20 NOVEMBER 1949

Had breakfast with Mr. Nemazi; then went to Prospect House for a short audience. At 11:00 we began our train journey to New York City. Had lunch on the train with HIM, Mr. Ala and General Powell, special assistant to the president. The conversation was on various subjects. The mayor of New York welcomed us. We stayed at the Waldorf Astoria.

The next three days were taken up with official functions, receptions and lunches.

THURSDAY 24 NOVEMBER 1949

HIM's schedule included a visit to Hyde Park to pay his respects at the grave of President Roosevelt. Mr. Ala had forgotten to tell Dr. Ghani that it would be useful if Dr. Ghani accompanied HIM. Mr. Ala telephoned after HIM's entourage had departed.

The American group in charge of HIM's visit have performed their tasks flawlessly. Everything is on time, nothing is left to chance. (The same cannot be said of events under Iranian supervision.) The functions and duties of those in HIM's retinue are undefined. Had I been in Ala's place, I would have chosen the nine people to accompany HIM this way: two with backgrounds in economics and finance; two military advisors, graduates of military academies; and two knowledgeable about U.S. affairs. These six people would review HIM's speeches daily and consult with him on their contents. The other three members of the official delegation could have been chosen purely for companionship; but as it is, the retinue consists of:

1. Lieutenant General Yazdanpanah, the one distinguished member of the party. His potential contribution has been wasted as there is no organized program.

2. Brigadier General Hejazi who is about forty. He has a French military education and knows some English. Presently he is head of the military academy in Iran and serves as HIM's adjutant. He has courage and is devoted to HIM.

3. Brigadier General Abd al-Rahim Ayadi is a military doctor and private physician to HIM.

4. Professor Yahya Adl is a member of the delegation solely because he is HIM's close companion.

5. Hormoz Pirnia is the son of Mirza Hasan Khan Moshir al-Dowleh and the husband of (his cousin) the daughter of the late Mo'tamen al-Molk Pirnia. He is about forty and has been functioning at court as "master of ceremonies"—a decent but limited young man.

6. Hoseyn'ali Qaraguzlu, the second son of Abolqasem Khan Naser al-Molk, about the same age as Hormoz Pirnia. He speaks English quite well and has some of his father's qualities. He keeps to himself, and receives no salary from the court. He goes to the court once every several weeks. His sister Fatemeh is the wife of Mr. Hoseyn Ala. His mother has lived in Washington, D.C. for the past three years.

7. Dr. Rezazadeh Shafaq is about sixty and comes from Tabriz. In his youth he had been active in the Constitutionalist cause. He studied at Roberts College in Istanbul and later went to Germany where he received a doctorate in philosophy. He has been a member of Parliament for some six years. He expects to be appointed to the Senate by HIM and already calls himself "senator." He is extremely conceited and constantly complains of being underappreciated. His absurd logic leads

him to draw absurd conclusions and to say absurd things. <...> He is close to Mrs. Ala and her mother, through whose influence he became part of HIM's retinue. <...>

8. Major Hoseyn Fardust, who has known HIM since childhood. At HIM's insistence he was sent to Switzerland to be his classmate at Le Rosey School. He is now a kind of domestic servant.

9. Air Force Colonel Gilanshah, who is not an official member of the delegation.

10. Colonel Ansari, the son of the late Amir Eqtedar, who is in charge of transmitting coded telegrams. Not an official member of the delegation, he is hard-working and useful.

11. I was in Ankara when HIM recalled me to Tehran and asked that I accompany him. I am only a spectator. There is no rhyme or reason to anything that goes on in Iran.

Four journalists have also come from Tehran at their own expense: Messrs. Majid Movaqqar, Javad Mas'udi, Dr. Mesbahzadeh and a representative of *Tehran Illustrated.* <...>

FRIDAY 25 NOVEMBER 1949

Audience with HIM during which I said farewell. I entered New York Hospital. *[Medical history of Dr. Ghani.]*

SATURDAY 26 NOVEMBER 1949

Extensive blood tests. Mr. Nemazi called from Washington and informed me Hakim al-Molk has been appointed minister of court.

The U.S. government through one of its agencies has loaned $21 million to Afghanistan. Part of the loan is to be used for a dam project on the Helmand River. Neither Afghanistan nor the U.S. has deigned to notice that this river runs through both Afghanistan and Iran. This means that Iran must be apprised of any work on the system. Unfortunately, we have no foreign policy nor government agency to look after our interests.

*From left to right: Nezam al-Din Hekmat, Hasan Esfandiari, Mahmoud Jam,
Ali Akbar Davar, Amanallah Jahanbani, Dr. Ghani (Gorgan, spring of 1935)*

Slept for fifteen minutes after lunch. People talking in the hallway woke me. Hospitals are a world of their own, while life is simply a farce. We spend the first half of it feckless and naïve, chasing this fugitive goal or that; the second half for various psychological reasons we spend reliving the past and regretting it. If God had only decreed otherwise—given us several years of youth to spend at the end, after which we would die. As Khayyam says,

> *Alas, the letter of youth has run its course,*
> *And that flush spring of life has wintered.*
> *That bird of joy whose name was boyhood,*
> *I know not when it came nor when it went.*

One has to wonder at times how even a limited number of sane and saintly Iranians have managed to survive their bizarre surroundings: people like Abdolhoseyn Dehqan, the late Mohammad Qazvini, Mirza Ali Akbar Davar, Colonel Vaziri, Abbas Eqbal, Dr. Meer, Ali Akbar Dehkhoda, Kamal al-Molk, Hajj Seyyed Nasrollah Taqavi. The general intellectual and social climate in Iran is so repugnant as to defy description. Obscenity has exceeded the obscene. People make no pretense of hiding their repulsive acts; they flaunt them. Larceny is now deemed "cunning," treachery "good sense," lawlessness "freedom." It depresses me to see how they justify themselves by commuting these crimes to virtues.

The day before yesterday, prior to his departure for Detroit, HIM asked for my assessment of the visit thus far. I offered that it has been successful and assured him it would continue to be so. I added that I am still apprehensive about conditions in Iran. <...> Then there was a lengthy discussion, and I added that out of a population of fifteen million, the twelve million in the provincial towns and villages were decent and hard-working. If local authorities treated them fairly, they would follow HIM's every step. They are by nature generous and possess good will. <...> But the local authorities treat them harshly. They live in poverty. A petit bourgeoisie is also emerging in these small towns. They are traditional and religious. Even in Tehran the majority are not much different. What is needed to begin deep-rooted reform is a dedicated, courageous government that enjoys HIM's support. The outside world would also be willing to extend aid. HIM was moved and said that we would talk further on his return. <...>

WEDNESDAY 30 NOVEMBER 1949

Extensive x-rays. Victor Hugo[5] has said there are two blessings that are priceless: ignorance and hope, and when I weigh them I feel that ignorance is the better of the two. Dr. Forkner[6] believes that the source of the hemorrhage is esophageal varicose veins. The origin of the disease, a hypertrophy of the liver, may have taken place twelve years ago, or probably much earlier when the hemorrhaging first began. According to Dr. Forkner, the liver has remarkable self-restorative properties. My liver has scars and liquid around it. He prescribed a strict diet—no oil, salt, pepper or alcohol.

Returning to Victor Hugo's maxim that ignorance is a great blessing, I say because I am a physician that the words "always" and "never" do not exist in medicine. <...>

The thing now is why should I worry about how long my liver
will work, whether one day this disease or another will kill me. Life is
a book that opens with birth. Its contents are pages of the sound and
fury that we call existence. The final page is inscribed with death. As
Amir Shah Sheikh Abu Eshaq[7] (the Injuid ruler of Shiraz during
Hafez's time, died 1357) awaited execution on "The Square of Good
Fortune" at the hands of his successor Amir Mobarez al-Din
Mozaffar, he is said to have written one of the master quatrains of
Persian literature. The attribution is not certain, but it is probable the
following is his:

> *Contend not with contentious fate—and go.*
> *Don't fight the turning of the wheel—and go.*
> *Welcome the cup of poison they call death,*
> *But save a draft to wet the ground—and go.*

Pouring some wine on the ground was one of the drinking gestures practiced by the *javanmardan* or brave, young and chivalrous
defenders of the oppressed during the medieval period in Iran. Their
indifference to death is expressed in the cup of poison conceit. Shah
Sheikh Abu Eshaq was fairly young— around thirty-five as I recall—
when he was killed.

Dr. Forkner, despite his diagnosis, was guardedly optimistic and
my spirits were buoyed somewhat. The downhill slope of aging is so
slight that one is not aware of nearing the precipice of death. Life is a
slow and gradual descent, a creeping death. <...>

*Thursday 1 December through Monday 5 December were taken up with
further tests and numerous visits from friends.*

TUESDAY 6 DECEMBER 1949

Mr. Nemazi telephoned and told me Esma'il Mer'at is near death and has been kept alive with a respirator. He is slightly better today but still unconscious. Nemazi told me confidentially that Mer'at had been ignored by Ala during HIM's entire visit. He had not been invited to any of the functions and consequently submitted his resignation. Mer'at was extraordinarily upset by this. Two days later he suffered a stroke, for which, Mrs. Mer'at believes, Ala's behavior is partly to blame. Ala is a foolish and ignorant man. By contrast, Esma'il Mer'at, who had become minister of education and out-ranked him, was knowledgeable in his field, having studied at the École Normale, and was a true servant of the people. Damn this miserable country and its lack of discipline. While excluding Mer'at, HIM's party includes the likes of Dr. Shafaq and HIM's close friends Dr. Adl, Fardust and Ayadi. <...>

FRIDAY 9 DECEMBER 1949

Dr. Forkner does not object to my leaving the hospital for a few days. <...> *[Mention of visitors and medical tests.]*

SUNDAY 11 DECEMBER 1949

Left the hospital and took the train to Washington. I stayed at the Roger Smith Hotel. Visited an old dear friend, General Yazdanpanah, who did not accompany HIM on his westward trip. <...> I went to Mr. Nemazi's, where he was hosting a reception for a large number of friends. <...>

MONDAY 12 DECEMBER 1949

<...> Called on General Yazdanpanah, who told me that HIM had said that if the government had not paid my expenses, he (HIM) would pay them personally. <...>

TUESDAY 13 DECEMBER 1949

Made arrangements for HIM's stay at New York Hospital. Lunched at Mr. Nemazi's; called on General Yazdanpanah. Several people called on me. <...>

Mr. Ala had suggested other hospitals for HIM. Dr. Ghani selected New York Hospital.

WEDNESDAY 14 AND THURSDAY 15 DECEMBER 1949

Dr. Ghani spent a considerable amount of time with General Yazdanpanah; called on the unconscious Mr. Mer'at at a local hospital.

FRIDAY 16 DECEMBER 1949

Wrote a number of letters. At 9:00 A.M. Abolbashar Farmanfarmaian called on me. He is intelligent and has become a well-educated person. He has character and I enjoy our conversations. His sister Haideh is well brought up. Took them to dinner. <...>

SATURDAY 17 DECEMBER 1949

To New York.

SUNDAY 18 DECEMBER 1949

HIM returned from his western trip. Accompanied him to his hotel.

MONDAY 19 DECEMBER 1949

Audience with HIM at noon. I explained the nature of my illness and why I needed to be near a medical center. He assured me that he would work something out. I suggested a leave of absence from Ankara and he agreed. He asked me to return at five to discuss a joint statement to be issued by HIM and Truman. At seven I accompanied HIM on a visit to Columbia University. Iranian students were introduced. Then dinner with General Eisenhower [President of

Columbia University at the time] who gave a short but warm speech. As a photograph was being taken, HIM told Eisenhower that I would be the next ambassador to the United States.

TUESDAY 20 DECEMBER 1949

Tonight at seven gathering for HIM at the Overseas Group. Warm and informal.

WEDNESDAY 21 DECEMBER 1949

Called on HIM twice at the hospital. We spoke about his visit to Pakistan, a general policy about the East and reorganization the of the court. HIM said he would think about it. Presented a book to HIM to read while in the hospital. *[Essays of Ralph Waldo Emerson]*

THURSDAY 22 DECEMBER 1949

Morning and afternoon audiences. The conversation was about reform and reorganization of the ministry of court and other ministries.

TUESDAY 27 DECEMBER 1949

Went to the hospital for a blood test. Mr. Nemazi came to New York. There is talk of lavish spending on clothes and furs by people around HIM.

WEDNESDAY 28 DECEMBER 1949

HIM entered the hospital again because of intestinal discomfort. Several specialists have come from Philadelphia and Chicago. <...> They decided that surgery is not necessary <...> but in six months there must be more x-rays. <...>

FRIDAY 30 DECEMBER 1949

Went to the Waldorf and had a short audience and then to the airport for HIM's departure. <...>

From left to right: Mohammad Reza Shah, dean of the School of International Relations, General Dwight D. Eisenhower (President of Columbia University), Dr. Ghani, Prince Mahmud Reza Pahlavi

SATURDAY 31 DECEMBER 1949

Flight to Los Angeles. Cyrus and my nephews Firouz and Amin were at the airport. I am staying at the Georgian Hotel in Santa Monica.

SUNDAY 1 JANUARY 1950

Mr. Yadollah Zafari and Gholamreza Moghaddam, students at Stanford, came by. Dinner at Mr. Farmi's, whose wife is the daughter of Dr. Bozorgmehr. Met Keyumars Bozorgmehr (the youngest of Dr. Bozorgmehr's children and an extremely intelligent eleven-year-old).

MONDAY 2 JANUARY 1950

Cyrus came by at 11:30 A.M. He is a serious and confident student. He leads a simple, decent life. We talked a good while. He has become interested in English and Russian literature and has read some worthwhile books. Sattareh Farman Farmaian stopped by. She has married a student from India, a Brahmin named Arun Chadhuri. They have a seven-month-old daughter Mitra.

Dr. Jessie Marmorston[8] telephoned to say she has a cold and will come by tomorrow. She was born in the Ukraine, was seven years old when her parents immigrated to the United States. She is a well-known physician in Los Angeles and does some research. Her two daughters from her first and second marriages are Elizabeth (nineteen) and Norma (fourteen). Presently she is married to Mr. Laurence Weingarten,[9] an executive producer at MGM. They live in Beverly Hills. She asked whether her daughter Elizabeth, a student at Stanford, could see me today and whether I might persuade her to study medicine.

TUESDAY 3 JANUARY 1950

Changed my hotel to Town House, which is closer to the center of Los Angeles. Lunched with Bahram Farmanfarmaian, son of the late Abbas Mirza Salar Lashkar. In the afternoon I went to see Dr. Marmorston and her husband. Had dinner with Cyrus, Amin and Firouz. I am pleased that they are serious students. May God protect them and may they become useful to society and their country. <...>

WEDNESDAY 4 JANUARY 1950

The newspaper reports a mercy killing in Manchester, New Hampshire. Dr. Herman N. Sander has killed his patient, a fifty-nine-year-old woman, Mrs. Barrato, who was suffering from incurable cancer. The doctor has been arrested and charged with murder. Several years ago I wrote an article on euthanasia for the journal *Iran-e Now*. Doctors for centuries have condemned the practice. The duty of a doctor is to prolong life, not shorten it. Furthermore, we do not know the secrets of life and what is incurable. The idea of mercy killing is advanced by unbalanced people. <...>

Mr. Nemazi called from Washington. He is ill and bedridden. We talked for almost an hour. HIM has returned to Iran. <...> The Soviet hospital in Tehran has announced free medical care, even house calls, by their Russian doctors. The weak central government does nothing to counter their propaganda. <...>

I am more disheartened. HIM comes to the United States on Truman's presidential plane, which is filled with the likes of Adl, Fardust, Ayadi, Hormoz Pirnia and Dr. Shafaq, none of whom speak English. Other than General Yazdanpanah, there is not one distinguished elder present. <...> Mr. Ala who was to have overseen the schedule offered no suggestions. His only contribution was to go over speeches that Mr. Nemazi had written and insert a comma or add a word. <...> No attempt was made to have the shah meet the several hundred Iranian students in other parts of the United States. They are of an impressionable age. Some are communists and HIM must do something to counter their poisonous propaganda. Poor Mer'at (the Iranian student advisor in the U.S.) was ignored. Ala is afraid to invite certain people, among them Aram and Gudarzi, because his wife disapproves of them. <...> HIM, of course, must appear democratic and attractive, but he must not be seen as a puppet and must maintain his dignity. <...> The Americans have handled the visit with their typical efficiency, but the Iranians have bungled everything.

As I was writing letters to various people, Amin came with a telegram from the minister of foreign affairs to Mr. Ala asking him to inform me of the death of my mother. <...> There were also a telegram from the minister of foreign affairs and a letter from Mr. Golshayan, minister of finance, expressing their condolences. <...>

This saddest news has been a great shock. My mother was seventy-six <...>. When my father died she was nearly thirty. After his death, she devoted the rest of her life to raising four orphans, forcing us to study. We, my two brothers, my sister and I, were all minors. She was always a world of love. <...> Many images passed through my mind. I was in a strange mood. <...> I told her grandchildren, Cyrus, Amin and Firouz and answered the telegrams of condolence. <...>

THURSDAY 5 JANUARY 1950

Spent a restless night and, contrary to my normal pattern, dreamt a lot. Parents are the dearest human beings. Though my mother and I aged over the years, I remained her child and she my mother. When Anatole France died at eighty-one in 1924, his last word was "Maman." The emptiness that I feel now is hard to describe. I last saw her thirteen months ago. My uncles called her Baji, meaning "sister," and we, her children, always called her that. As I say the word I revert to my childhood when she would come to my bedside to make sure a quilt was on me. <…> I wrote many letters. <…> I remained in my hotel until 2:30 P.M. Amin, Firouz, and Cyrus came by and we had lunch. <…>

At 8 P.M. Dr. Marmorston came and took me to a concert by Yasha Heifetz.[10] She has invited Will and Ariel Durant[11] and Harold Lamb[12] for dinner Saturday night.

FRIDAY 6 JANUARY 1950

Mr. Weingarten hosted a lunch for me at MGM in Culver City. Met several producers. Later we went to the office of Mr. Louis Mayer,[13] the head of the studio. He is sixty-seven but has the vitality and energy of a thirty-year-old. He never completed his secondary education but is highly intelligent and a very able executive. He is Jewish and we had a long talk in his private dining room about Palestine and other current issues. As a businessman, he expected something of our lunch. He suggested that he would feed my stomach while I would feed his mind. He called one of his assistants and told him to take me on a tour of the studio including the sets, wardrobe department, and the warehouses. <…> Some well-known actors were also introduced. Later at Mr. Mayer's office, I asked whether there was any substance to the rumors of communist influence at the studios. He said that it was exaggerated.

In the late afternoon, Dr. Barber, head of the Engineering Department at USC, came by for tea. Dined at Mr. Shahrokh Firuz's home.

TUESDAY 10 JANUARY 1950

Returned to Washington, staying at the Roger Smith Hotel. <...>

WEDNESDAY 11 JANUARY 1950

Mr. Nemazi came by. I called on Mrs. Mer'at who was not at home. Went to the embassy and saw the Ala family. I had a telegram from Mr. Wiley (U.S. ambassador in Tehran) wishing me a speedy recovery. Telephoned Mr. Wadsworth (U.S. Ambassador in Turkey, who is in Washington) and we agreed to have dinner at the Metropolitan Club. He invited two people from the Council on Foreign Relations, his daughter and her husband, and another American couple from Vermont.

THURSDAY 12 JANUARY 1950

There is turmoil at the embassy. [Mrs. Ala dominates the scene.] She dislikes Aram and Gudarzi [while Mrs. Farzanegan and Ali Reza Heravi are her favorites]. Entezam does not please her because he may one day become ambassador in Washington. Aram in effect runs the embassy. Dr. Parviz Mahdavi performs the consular affairs very well, and Mr. Nemazi does the essential things.

Mr. Aram came to the hotel and picked me up, and we went to Mr. [Abbasqoli] Ardalan's home. Mrs. Ardalan is the daughter of the late Davar. There was a large gathering. Later I went to Mr. Aram's home and met Mrs. Aram.

A call on the Afghan ambassador; lunch at Iranian Embassy, where several U.S. senators had been invited. A call on Mrs. Mer'at and her children. Two interviews with reporters from a French newspaper and the Los Angeles Times.

SATURDAY 14 JANUARY 1950

Woke up at 3:00 A.M. and went to the bathroom. Vomited a great deal of blood. At six I called Mr. Nemazi and asked him to arrange for me to go to New York. Instead, he called for an ambulance, which took me to Doctor's Hospital in Washington. I regained consciousness on the fourth day, after repeated blood transfusions. Dr. Forkner came from New York. I could not see for a few days and thought I had gone blind. My closest friend Mr. Dehqan had called Forkner, and they both traveled down to Washington.

I call Dehqan "Abbi," or "fatherly," a term Sufis use for the consummate ascetic, one who has no need for a guide to reach the highest stations of spirituality. So free of personal ambition and greed is Dehqan that he embodies Hafez's famous line:

Long have I been in the company of the prodigal,
Until with reason's writ I imprisoned greed.

He is unalloyed goodness. While he knows full well the difference between the flower and the thorn, he smiles with equanimity on both. This is not pretense, but he masks his feelings so well that people cannot tell that his acute intelligence sees into their souls.

Rarely in my life have I encountered anyone with more composure, more stoicism, than Dehqan. During those agonizing moments that everyone must endure in life, he smiles thinking that revealing his own suffering might cause others pain. As Hafez says:

Despite your savaged heart, bring a smile to your lips shaped like a cup;
Yours may be the wound of the reed, but you still sing like the harp.

If I were to continue to recite Dehqan's virtues, it would exhaust several volumes. Suffice it to say that this man and his family are among the most exceptional beings in my life.

WEDNESDAY 25 JANUARY 1950

I write this some ten days since I regained consciousness. My condition is wholly better, but I have to stay in the hospital until the twenty-seventh. Mr. Nemazi, who arranged my admittance, has come by twice a day and watched over my recovery. What can one say about him? He is pure goodness. There is not one mean bone in his body. Though one of the wealthiest Iranians, he lives as if cut off from the world. He exemplifies the wisdom that one should own property rather than be owned by it. He has spent nearly $1.5 million to build and equip a modern hospital in Shiraz and install a piped water system in the city. Ironically he made his fortune outside of Iran and is now spending it on the country. He is the exact opposite of [some of my countrymen] who have made money in Iran by deceit and invest their gains abroad. I have seldom seen a person with such decency, warmth and generosity. In addition he is learned, well informed on world economics, trade and banking. He stands out in any international gathering. He expresses a wealth of general knowledge in excellent English. His private secretary, Mr. Tuti, has also looked in on me several times. <...>

Received many letters in the last few days. <...>

FRIDAY 27 JANUARY 1950

Checked out of the hospital. Mr. Nemazi informs me that his wife has given birth to a boy. I was very pleased and took this as a good omen. Nemazi stopped by. At 6 P.M. called Mr. Ala. He told me that the government in Tehran is complaining [about funding] and asks why the U.S. is not helping. Ala said that the World Bank has asked us to submit the details of our development projects, especially the costs, and they would help. Former minister of foreign affairs Hekmat has assured the shah that the U.S. will grant Iran $47 million, which is pure nonsense.

Ala had sent a memo to the State Department on 29 November, about two weeks after the arrival of the shah in the U.S. <...> Here is a summary of the reply. "Mr. Truman and the secretary of state explained to the shah that the U.S. cannot increase its military assistance. <...> As to the question of whether the Truman Doctrine encompasses Iran, on 12 March 1947 President Truman pronounced the Doctrine of Free Nations. Iran, as one of the free nations, is included in the doctrine. <...> On the formation of a Middle Eastern pact of nations on the model of NATO, the secretary of state explained to HIM that the matter rests solely in the hands of the regional countries. The U.S. government neither encourages nor discourages such a pact for the time being. <...> On the question of the Tehran Conference declaration signed by Roosevelt, Churchill and Stalin, the U.S. considers it a binding instrument and respects the independence and territorial integrity of Iran. <...> The State Department believes the Iranian ambassador should be convinced that <...> the U.S. has fulfilled all of its undertakings. <...>"

MONDAY 30 JANUARY 1950

Saw Mr. Aram who complained about the pressures placed on Mr. Ala. HIM has sent the following telegram to Ala: "In answer to your [telegram] 672, which was about a comment by the U.S. that Iran intends to use oil revenues to expand the army <...>, we need to increase the present army and border guards from 150,000 to 186,000. If the U.S. does not increase military assistance, I will no longer be responsible for the independence of Iran. <...> You should remind the U.S. of that."

The last sentence in HIM's telegram puzzles me. There is no one around the shah to ask him, what the independence of Iran has to do with America? We were to receive financial and technical assistance from the U.S. and no more.

TUESDAY 31 JANUARY 1950

Had lunch with Mr. Ala and discussed the latest issue of *The Economist*. Dr. (Taqi) Nasr came by at 7 P.M. and took me to his home. Mr. Aradalan and his wife were also guests.

WEDNESDAY 1 FEBRUARY 1950

Wrote some ten letters to Tehran. <…> Went to the embassy. There is a reception for Dr. Nasr who is going to Tehran tomorrow to assume the post of minister of national economy. <…>

FRIDAY 3 FEBRUARY 1950

Three-paragraph entry on several Qajar-era figures.

<…> Had dinner with General Mo'arefi at the Sheraton Hotel. There was a band, [which caused me to notice] how much pleasure Americans take in dancing. When they dance, they do so with a feverish enthusiasm, an inner fire that contrasts with the European manner, which is more formal. <…> On the whole Americans are good-looking, wear simple, functional clothing and appear satisfied with life. Their future is assured. <…> They work from morning to 5:00 or 6:00 P.M. <…> When I see their joyful faces, I cannot help but contrast them to my own people in Iran, who face poverty, privation, hunger. <…>

SATURDAY 4 FEBRUARY 1950

<…> Mr. Golshayan has written: "From what HIM says, you are to become ambassador in Washington. It will be good for the country and yourself, but friends in Iran will be deprived of your company." Mr. Yadollah Azodi and Dr. Farhad also have written that rumor circulates widely. Mr. Ala still has nine months in his tenure as ambassador. Mr. Aram has told me that the State Department mentions my name as Ala's successor as well. In any event I am on leave of absence until the end of February, and then I will see what happens. <…>

Lengthy entry on several Reza Shah-era military figures, including Generals Ansari and Amir Khosravi; their marriage to ladies of prominence.

SUNDAY 5 FEBRUARY 1950

Mrs. Ala telephoned to say that there was a telegram from HIM. Mr. and Mrs. Ala, her mother, and their son [Fereydun] came to my hotel. The telegram reads:

> c/o Iranian Embassy Washington.
> His Excellency Dr. Ghani.
> Inform us of the state of your health. Shah. <...>

My reply was full of the appropriate responses and added that HIM's telegram itself constituted tidings of my recovery. I hope my treatment would be completed by the end of March. <...>

MONDAY 6 FEBRUARY 1950

Travel to New York.

FRIDAY 10 FEBRUARY 1950

Today, 21 Bahman in the Iranian calendar, brings very sad memories. It is the anniversary of Ali Akbar Davar's suicide, a national disaster. Davar was one of those rare talents comparable to the likes of the great nineteenth-century statesman Mirza Taqi Khan Amir Kabir. Of course, he was a latter-day version and more moderate in character; however, his knowledge of politics, law and literature was just as encyclopedic. He was extremely hard-working and productive. He was determined, steady and never shirked a duty. But the miserable social and political climate of Iran caused him to take his life. <...>

Had lunch with Mr. Mahbod, the consul general in New York. He complained bitterly about Hekmat. He added that people are no longer afraid of the shah and abuse his kindness. Seyyed Zia had an audience and there is talk of his becoming prime minister. Dr. Mosaddeq has also had an audience and the rumor is he, too, has been offered the post of prime minister. Dr. Mosaddeq had said he preferred to remain a deputy in Parliament. <...>

SATURDAY 11 TO MONDAY 13 FEBRUARY 1950

Busy social schedule. Visits from Nasrollah Entezam and others. Letters to individuals in Tehran, including Qavam al-Saltaneh, who is to have a prostate operation. <...>

TUESDAY 14 FEBRUARY 1950

<...> New York. Had a letter from Mr. Jam in Rome. He is greatly distressed by conditions in Iran. There are no worthwhile people at the court. With the exception of Mr. Hakimi who is honest and decent, all are out for themselves. <...> Ala and Nemazi have asked me to give a lecture at Georgetown University about "The Position of Iran in the Middle East" on 29 March. I will have to begin work on the lecture soon. <...>

MONDAY 20 FEBRUARY 1950

To Washington. *[Entries on the state of the oil industry in Iran.]* <...>

MONDAY 27 FEBRUARY 1950

<...> Today the newspapers announced the new cabinet. Sa'ed has been appointed prime minister. They offered the post of minister of foreign affairs to Ala. <...> He called and asked my opinion. I advised him to accept it. He is to leave by the end of March. <...>

TUESDAY 28 FEBRUARY 1950

<...> I sent a telegram to the Ministry of Foreign Affairs asking for an additional forty-five days leave. <...> Mr. Nemazi told me Mohsen Ra'is [ambassador to London] is [lobbying to become ambassador to the U.S.]. Mr. Ala has consulted with Nemazi as to which of us would be the best candidate: Entezam, Ra'is or me. Nemazi told him several things. Ra'is is too cautious, and timid, basically a civil servant. Entezam is active at the United Nations and there is a possibility of his becoming head of the General Assembly this

year. Dr. Ghani is therefore best suited for the job. <...> I should have a talk with Ala tomorrow and tell him that if I am not appointed, I will resign from the embassy in Turkey. In light of the repeated statements by HIM during the last few years and his recent comments, the matter has become a joke. <...>

WEDNESDAY 1 TO SUNDAY 12 MARCH 1950

Called on Mr. Ala to say farewell. Mr. Ala attempted to assure me. I said that I never asked for the appointment to Washington. After all the talk now it is becoming a farce. <...> Trip to New York. Social engagements. Letters from Tehran. Invitation from the Middle East Institute for the screening of the film *Grass* on the seasonal migration of the Bakhtiaris.

MONDAY 13 MARCH 1950

<...> At 1:50 P.M. I took the train from Grand Central Station to Westport, Connecticut, and arrived around 3:00. A car took me to Helen Keller's[14] house. I returned at 5:30 P.M. I will write a detailed account of this remarkable lady, who is to travel to Europe the day after tomorrow and will return in July. <...>

THURSDAY 16 MARCH 1950

Off to Washington. <...>

SUNDAY 19 MARCH 1950

<...> Went to the Shoreham Hotel to call on Brigadier Generals Mozayyeni and Batmangelich, whose wife is the daughter of Mir Fendereski. Colonels Amini and Takesh were there. <...>

MONDAY 20 TO FRIDAY 24 MARCH 1950

Busy social schedule. <...>

Helen Keller, photo inscribed to Dr. Ghani
"Dr. Ghasseme Ghani, whose friendly eye saw in my world
not darkness but unquenchable light. Cordially, Helen Keller."

SATURDAY 25 MARCH 1950

<...> There is change in Tehran. Mr. Mansur al-Molk has become prime minister. He telegraphed Mr. Ala and offered him the post of foreign minister, which he has accepted. <...>

WEDNESDAY 29 MARCH 1950

<...> Completed the lecture that I am to deliver at Georgetown. <...> Dinner with Ala, then to the lecture which lasted from 8:30 to 10:30 P.M. <...>

THURSDAY 30 AND FRIDAY 31 MARCH 1950

Social functions. Meeting with Mr. Ala and recommending Navab and Mahmoud Foroughi.

SATURDAY 1 APRIL 1950

To New York.

TUESDAY 4 APRIL 1950

<...> At 3:15 P.M. went to New York Hospital where Dr. Forkner examined me. At 5:00 P.M. met with Dr. Frank Glen,[15] who has discussed my condition with Dr. Forkner. They have reached the conclusion that surgery is required to link the vena cava with the portal vein to decrease the blood pressure in the liver and esophagus. This will reduce the chances of hemorrhaging. <...>

Dr. Glen said that the operation is dangerous. He has performed it ten times, and six patients have not survived. I asked him if he were in my place, what would he do. No decision was made. Dr. Barr is against the operation; Dr. Forkner is undecided. <...> Returned to my hotel. I am working on an article on Avicenna. <...>

THURSDAY 6 TO THURSDAY 13 APRIL 1950

Social calls. Visits to bookshops; reading.

FRIDAY 14 APRIL 1950

Delivered a speech at Columbia University on Iran's position in the Middle East. There were many questions from the audience. <...>

SATURDAY 15 APRIL 1950

Mr. Hamzavi came for lunch. He devoutly believes that there is no power in the universe other than Great Britain. He feels that the British dislike the shah and consider his government corrupt. They will try to get closer to the Iranian public. Mansur's government, he says, is the last chance. I don't understand why Ala wants such a person to become head of the Iranian propaganda machine in the U.S. He left at 4 P.M. <…>

SUNDAY 16 APRIL 1950

<…> At 5:00 p.m. called on Mrs. Roosevelt[16] whom I had not seen for some time. Her youngest son John was also there. <…>

MONDAY 17 APRIL 1950

<…> To Washington, D.C. <…> Mrs. Ala telephoned and invited me to lunch at the embassy.

FRIDAY 21 APRIL 1950

<…> Mr. Ala has asked me if I could write an article on "reforms in Iran." I began to prepare it.

SATURDAY 22 APRIL 1950

<…> Completed the article and went to Mr. Nemazi's home where it was typed *[it was published posthumously in Tehran]*. Wrote a letter to Mr. Mohammad Vahid, deputy minister of education, to arrange a scholarship for the children of the late Esma'il Mer'at. <…>

MONDAY 24 APRIL 1950

Gave the first nineteen pages of my article, which had been typed, to Mr. Ala. Lunch at Mr. Nemazi's—stayed until the evening. Mrs. Ala, her mother, Mrs. Naser al-Molk and Heravi also came by. <…>

SATURDAY 29 APRIL TO FRIDAY 5 MAY 1950

Social visits. Began work on paper to be delivered on Avicenna. Prepared an address for Mr. Ala to be delivered on *Voice of America* on the occasion of the transfer of the late Reza Shah's body from Egypt to Tehran. *[Text of the speech prepared by Dr. Ghani is quoted.]*

SATURDAY 6 MAY 1950

From what I have seen, there are few cities in the world with trees as crisp and clean and as varied as those in Washington. More candidates for the post of U.S. ambassador: Ebtehaj, Dr. Matin Daftari and Dr. Nasr. <...>

SUNDAY 7 MAY 1950

<...> Mr. Ala left today for Tehran via New York. Few people saw him off: the Turkish ambassador and Heravi (the only Iranian). Mrs. Ala not only did not come to the station, but also ordered embassy staff to stay at their desks. Her motives are unclear to me. <...> She is intensely disliked by the Iranian community. <...>

Ala is sixty-six years old, very short, with a slight build. <...> His secondary education was in England and France. He returned to Iran in 1909 or 1910. His father became minister of foreign affairs, and later prime minister. All his early positions were with his father. He is a decent, honest and conscientious man, but he is also naïve. At times he is a blank slate open to any influence. <...> His English and French are very good, and he is also well versed in the intricacies of protocol. He is incapable of original or independent thinking, but once instructed in a matter he pursues it. He can, however, be influenced easily and thus can change course suddenly. He is courageous and principled. He is close to the shah, who considers him faithful, but superficial. He now has become minister of foreign affairs. I don't believe the Mansur government will last long. Ala, however, will be in subsequent governments and probably form one himself some day. As he is incapable of any bold action, he is not the man for the political scene in Iran. He was a sad figure leaving Washington without an official send-off. <...>

MONDAY 8 MAY 1950

<...> Worked on the Avicenna article.

TUESDAY 9 MAY 1950

Planning for the trip to New York. In the morning Mr. Shahidi, brother of the late Mirza Taher, and his wife called. In the afternoon Mr. Hajj Malek (Aqa Taqi Mahdavi) came by, and I was pleased to see him. <…>

WEDNESDAY 10 MAY 1950

Took the train to New York, arrived at noon, staying at the Drake. Saw Dr. Marmorston. Nafise Shaybani's French instructor has asked her to write an essay on Romanticism. I prepared a three-page summary. <…>

THURSDAY 11 MAY 1950

<…> Dr. Marmorston came by at 10:30 A.M. and we had a snack. She left for Los Angeles. She told me that her daughter Elizabeth has informed her in a letter that she will not study medicine. It was a letter I enjoyed reading. She addresses her mother as "My dear Jessie," explaining that as she is twenty-one she can treat her mother as a friend. <…> Dr. Marmorston wants me to write and encourage her to pursue medicine. <…>

FRIDAY 12 MAY 1950

Telephoned Mr. Nemazi whose sister has recently died. I then called Mrs. Nemazi who is staying at the Waldorf. Met with Dr. Guillemin, the Belgian Orientalist who teaches at Liege. His field is Zoroastrianism. <…>

SATURDAY 13 MAY 1950

Read the whole day. A small book on the nineteenth century English Romantic movement: Byron, Shelly and Keats. Met Habib Sabet and Hoseyn'ali Qaraguzlu. Sabet is a businessman living in New York. He is the son of Mirza Abdollah, a cloth merchant. He is the grandson of the daughter of Mirza Khalil, a self-taught Jewish physician, who converted to the Baha'i faith. Mirza Khalil had several sons and a daughter. His eldest was Rahim Khan Arjomand, who became director general of the Ministry of Post and is now retired. He is a very decent person. His second son was Dr. Masih Arjomand, who studied medicine but became a civil servant at the Department of Post. He is married to General Ayadi's sister. The third son was Ebrahim Arjomand, who died a few years ago. In 1908 after the shelling of Parliament during the reign of Mohammad Ali Shah, my uncle and I came to Tehran from Sabzevar. We were looking for a house to rent and found a place owned by Rahim Arjomand. The owners were very decent people. Rahim Khan's mother, who lived next door, often came by to see whether I needed anything. Once, when I was ill, she looked after me. Mirza Rahim Khan married the daughter of Dr. Mohammad Khan Darvazeh Qazvini, who was also a Baha'i and had several children. The eldest was Khalil who became a very able engineer and did a great deal of community work. He died tragically when he accidentally fell down a well. <...>

[Mirza Khalil's daughter had several children and a grandson, Habib.] Habib Sabet became a truck owner/driver and ferried goods across the country. Later he established a successful carpentry shop. He now lives in the U.S. and is a very wealthy man. He is clever and opportunistic. On this trip he attracted the shah's attention, becoming close to him. <...>

MONDAY 15 MAY 1950

<...> Had a doctor's appointment. Feeling slightly better. 1:30 p.m. Ahmad Vahabzadeh, Yunes's brother, called and had a letter from Amir A'zam [Yadollah Azodi], which saddened me greatly. His wife, Turan, has developed breast cancer. They are to operate. Turi's father, Vosouq al-Dowleh, had breast cancer in 1939 and was successfully operated on in Europe. Around the end of World War II, Qamar, another daughter of Vosouq al-Dowleh and the wife of Dr. Javad

Ashtiani, died of breast cancer. Batul Amini also underwent breast cancer surgery, which was successful. Now poor Turi is ill.

Helen Termegerdichian called. Her husband has suffered a fatal heart attack. I had tea with her and she cried a great deal. She is to come for lunch tomorrow. She is one of the daughters of the well-known Armenian merchant based in Moscow. They lost everything during the Russian Revolution, and the whole family came to Iran settling in Sabzevar. The father had two sons, Shahin and Gurgen, now sixty-five and fifty respectively, and two daughters, twins, Helen and Marguerite. They founded a cotton-cleaning plant in Sabzevar and Nishapur. Most of the family has passed away. Marguerite lives in Moscow, but no one has any news of her. I was very friendly with the family. Before my own marriage, I spent several nights a week with them and was considered a member of the family. I loved Helen very much and decided to marry her. I told her brother who approved, but left it up to his sister. Helen candidly admitted that she loved me but had already been spoken for [this was the husband who just died]. Twenty-five years ago her answer came as a great blow. The memory is even more bitter because Marguerite, a promising painter, one night confided tearfully that she was in love with me and blamed me for ignoring her in favor of her sister. In any event they moved from Sabzevar to Tehran in 1925. I went to Europe the next year and after-ward would see them in Tehran every year—either at Now Ruz or the Christian New Year. For the last five years, I had had no news of Helen. Apparently they moved to the U.S. after World War II. I felt very sorry for her. Arranged to have lunch with her the next day.

THURSDAY 18 MAY 1950

<…> To Washington, staying at the Roger Smith. <…>

FRIDAY 19 MAY 1950

Preparing my remarks for the Princeton seminar and discussion groups on Avicenna. Also went over what I had prepared for Nafise Shaybani. Very tired, went to bed early.

SATURDAY 20 MAY 1950

<...> I have been depressed for several days. <...> Liver disease greatly affects one's perspective and outlook. <...> The entire area from Casablanca to the far reaches of the Middle East is mired in ignorance, superstition, poverty, deceit and hypocrisy. The colonial powers are feeding on countries in the region like ravenous wolves. <...> One of those countries is Iran, which boasts of a glorious past that no longer exists. Once it was a great part of world civilization, but now the world imposes its will upon it. We have a small, corrupt minority with such titles as "member of Parliament," "senator," "minister" and "court-affiliated." <...> Letters from Iran depress me further. Golshayan has added to the gloom. He writes that Mansur, who should be prosecuted, becomes prime minister. <...> There is no economic planning. Generals Zahedi and Razmara have had a falling out and try to undermine one another. The shah is losing popularity. The son of Mohammad Hasan Mirza[17] is in Paris agitating against the shah. Qavam al-Saltaneh wants to establish a "free Iran" in Paris. <...>

FRIDAY MAY 26 1950

<...> Mr. Nemazi came to the hotel and we took the train to Princeton together. <...> [Seven pages on the university, the library, and the names of other guests.] The subject of the conference was "What the Near East Expects from the U.S." Dr. Hitti[18] opened the conference. The first speaker was Dr. Charles Malik, ambassador to the UN from Lebanon. Next came the Egyptian ambassador to the U.S. and then my talk.

SUNDAY 28 MAY 1950

Princeton.

Return to Washington, D.C.

<...> Mr. Aram called to say there was a telegram from Ala, which reads as follows:

> Mr. Aram, please inform His Excellency Dr. Ghani of the following in any way you deem appropriate: In order to economize on expenditures and as it is the practice of most countries, it has been decided that HIM's ambassador to Washington shall also serve as ambassador to the United Nations. It has been decided that His Excellency Mr. Nasrollah Entezam shall serve in this dual capacity. On the other hand, the presence of Dr. Ghani in the United States will serve the important purpose of extending cultural relations between Iran and the United States. Therefore, if Dr. Ghani's health does not allow his returning to Ankara, he may continue to receive the salary and emoluments of an ambassador to the U.S. until such time as he believes appropriate for this purpose. Inform us of his decision as soon as possible.

I immediately sent the following two telegrams, one to the ministry of foreign affairs, the other to His Majesty's office:

1. Ministry of Foreign Affairs. Tehran. His Excellency Mr. Ala. Your views were transmitted to me by Mr. Aram. As your purpose of economizing on expenditures and my receiving the salary and emoluments of an ambassador are contradictory, I hereby request you select someone as ambassador to Ankara and exempt me from your deliberations.

2. His Majesty's Special Office. Tehran. A telegram sent by His Excellency Mr. Ala was received informing me that for

reasons of economy it has been decided to have one person hold the position of ambassador to the United States and the United Nations. It was also proposed that if I decide not to return to Ankara I would receive the salary and emoluments of an ambassador to further cultural ties between Iran and the U.S. The proposal runs counter to the plans to economize and, in any event, as I do not wish to become a burden I hereby request His Imperial Majesty to appoint someone else as ambassador to Ankara and exempt me from service.

I had a telephone conversation with Abbi [Dehqan] and asked whether Mr. Nemazi could come by. I discussed the matter fully with him and benefitted from his views. I also asked Mr. Gudarzi to come by and transmit the two telegrams. He coded and sent them. I had a restful night and am glad it has turned out the way it has. The only matter that gives me pause is that HIM has repeatedly assured me and, for the last several years, has insisted I remain in the U.S. Now he has changed his mind or relented. I cannot understand it. Is it the influence of the Anglophiles? In any event, I am relieved. Since I accepted HIM's assurances, I could not withdraw. Now I can just walk away. I am glad I resigned from Ankara also. <...>

THURSDAY 1 JUNE 1950

Had a letter from Mr. Jamshid Qarib in Ankara. He writes rumor has it in Tehran that because I am known for my friendship with the U.S. and since the shah is surrounded by Anglophiles, I was not appointed as ambassador. <...>

SATURDAY 3 JUNE 1950

Today in Iran there are five types of Anglophiles. Each supports British policies and implements them in his own particular way.

    1. Agents and informers. They are the ones who distribute money to the mobs. While the British look upon them with a wary eye, the people know them for what they are: lackeys

and servants. Examples: Lesan al-Molk Sepehr, Emam Jom'eh, Seyyed Mohammad Tamaddon, Seyyed al-'Eraqeyn, Hajj Moshar Sa'dieh.

2. The people employed by British companies and firms, such as British Petroleum and The Imperial Bank. The very nature of their occupations bonds them with the British: British interests become their interests. The people view them as foreigners. However they do not advertise what they do, preferring to work discreetly. By nature and demeanor they are anglicized. They have even taught their wives how to mix with the British. Sometimes they indulge in British diversions and vices. They copy British mannerisms down to the smallest gestures: shaking hands, showing deference, giving greetings. They celebrate Christmas, and their year begins on the first of January. They often ridicule their countrymen for being "too Iranian." Habits and mores are more consequential than rules. Over the course of time, their foreign habits have become second nature. Some of them in pronouncing Persian words contort their mouths the way the British do when attempting unfamiliar phrases. In many ways they are more British than the British. Actually they are neither fish nor fowl, but some intermediate species. Examples: Mostafa Fateh, Fathollah Nuri Esfandiari, Mosharraf Nafisi, Isa Khan Feyz, Shadman… Emami, Ardeshir…

3. The people who either themselves or several generations of their families have enjoyed British protection—like Qavam Shirazi and Naser al-Molk. They are beholden to the British for their property, positions and titles as khans. These are devoted and faithful British servants. They give a good account of themselves at critical times. Those that try to play both sides against the middle are known and punished by the British. They constitute the most plentiful and important group. Examples: Mansur, Seyyed Zia al-Din Tabataba'i,

Mosharraf Nafisi, Sa'ed, Ali Asghar Hekmat, Sardar Fakher Hekmat, Seyyed Mohammad Taddayon. <...>

4. In this group are newcomers who aspire to gain entry into the other three groups. <...> They will do anything to attract the attention of their masters. <...> Examples: Hormoz Pirnia at court, Shokra'i at court (now a deputy), Nojumi, the vice-minister of post <...>.

5. Members of this group differ from those that fall into the four other categories because they love Iran. They are not foreign agents, nor are they hungry for position. Their sincere political belief is that we cannot control our own destiny. Coming to terms with the Soviets is impossible. The U.S. does not really have interests in Iran; moreover, its foreign policy is often unreliable or isolationist. Apart from the Monroe Doctrine and the insistence on the unity of the Americas, Canada and South America, its foreign policy is based on loose principles. The young nation is inexperienced and impatient and may again become isolationist as after the First World War. These Anglophiles reason that it is therefore essential to come to terms with the British and seek their protection. They firmly believe in the rightness of British . policy, and, being prestigious figures in Iran like Taqizadeh, Hakim al-Molk, and Foroughi, they are the greatest advocates of the efficacy of that policy. <...>

Had a letter from Ankara today saying that the Turks, who had recently commemorated the anniversary of the death of Jalal al-Din Rumi, are now translating and publishing his works. They are also teaching young students that he was a Turk. Apart from decrying the demeaning affiliation of Rumi with a particular nationality when he was a guide and leader to all humanity, especially the Islamic peoples, one should ask, why Turkey? Their reasoning is based on this couplet from his great *Divan*:

Don't take me as foreign to this place;
In your town I seek a home of my own.
I am no enemy, though I may seem one;
I am Turk, though I speak as a Hindu.

All Rumi's contemporaries and historians agree that he was born around 1207 near Balkh [in present-day northern Afghanistan]. When he was six, his father took the family on a pilgrimage to Mecca. While they were in Nishapur, he is said to have met the renowned Sufi poet Attar, who predicted great things of the boy and gave him a copy of his *Elahi-nameh*. Two factors, the Mongol invasion of Iran, which took the life of Attar, and his father's uneasy relationship with the ruler in Khorasan, compelled the family to move westward. They eventually found refuge in Konya, in what is today eastern Turkey. There a mystic named Shams-e Tabrizi kindled an extraordinary fire in Rumi's soul. <...>

Needless to say, we often see place names used metaphorically in Persian literature. "Hindu," for example, often stands for "dark." Hafez says he would gladly trade all of Samarqand and Bokhara for one "Hindu birthmark." <...> "Turk," by contrast, signifies "beautiful" in the sense of being "fair-skinned." Rumi—himself in an ode found in the *Divan* dedicated to Shams-e Tabrizi, the oldest copy of which is housed in Konya—uses "Turk" metaphorically:

O moon-faced Turk what if you one morning
Come to my cell where one would think your face a rose;
You are a Turkish moon, and though I am no Turk,
This much I know of your tongue that water is su. <...>

Finally one should ask: What ailed Rumi that he left behind no poetry or prose in Turkish? His poetry is Persian, and so are his recorded conversations and correspondence. Not one traditional literary chronicle nor any of Rumi's contemporaries mention writings in Turkish. Making such laughable claims [as Rumi was Turkish] that are contrary to the historical and textual evidence causes the rest of the world to dismiss everything Middle Eastern as fiction. <...>

MONDAY 5 TO SATURDAY 10 JUNE 1950

Dr. Ghani refuses to attend a cocktail party at the Iranian Embassy. He sees Nemazi several times. Dr. Rosenkrantz invites Dr. Ghani to attend and give a talk to the annual meeting of the American Medical Association. Several people call on him.

SUNDAY 11 JUNE 1950

<...> Aram telephoned saying he wished to see me. <...> These polite meetings and visits, the pretense upon pretense, the hypocrisy, are all out of personal interest or fear. People think that their flattery is gratifying, but it is doubly foolish because they do not realize that the person they are dealing with sees through it.

Over the years I have concluded that <...> everything the ruling class does in contemporary Iran boils down to three basic things: begging, thieving and lying. Today the minister, the lawyer, the courtier, the merchant, etc. behave like beggars. They have wealth but they do not eat nor dress nor behave appropriately. They hoard like beggars, but even if they become ill, they won't spend a cent on their own medication. <...> Their basic fear is that if people get wind of their wealth, someone will steal it. <...> Stealing is their second vice, stealing in various forms. The merchant who short changes, the thieving lawyer, minister, <...>, rich and poor, all are larcenous. Lying is their third principal activity; even their greeting is a lie. Their politics and elections are a sham, their political parties, their religion, even their Mecca and their Karbala—all lies. <...> These three basic vices give birth to other forms of depravity: <...> bullying subordinates, flattering superiors, selling favors, spying, worshipping Westerners, etc. <...>

TUESDAY 13 JUNE 1950

<...>

Received word today of the death of Seyyed Hadi Khan Amir Arfa'. I became friendly with this honorable man late in 1919 after I had returned from studying medicine in Beirut and he was in actual practice the ruler of Sabzevar. [A five-page biography of Amir Arfa' follows.]

WEDNESDAY 14 TO SATURDAY 17 JUNE 1950

Dr. Ghani spends most of his time in the company of the Dehqan family.

SUNDAY 18 JUNE 1950

<...> Mr. Aram has sent me the following telegram from HIM:

> His Excellency Dr. Ghasem Ghani: your telegram was read by HIM. He stated that your devoted service has always been appreciated by us and received our special attention. We are deeply saddened by your prolonged illness and we know that you have always chosen to labor in our interests. <...> You have never been a burden. If you don't wish to return to Ankara, we believe you should accept the proposal of the Ministry of Foreign Affairs and continue to promote Iranian culture and civilization to American audiences. We hope your health will improve soon so that we can utilize your services in more important positions. Shokuh, Head of HIM's Special Office. <...>

Dr. Ghani replies that he is on the road to recovery, but he declines the shah's recommendation to accept the Ministry of Foreign Affairs' offer to become cultural ambassador. He concludes that it is his patriotic duty to introduce Iranian culture to audiences in the U.S.; therefore he will continue to perform this service without accepting any title or position. A five-page personal letter to Shokuh follows.

TUESDAY 20 JUNE TO FRIDAY 14 JULY 1950

Seeing friends; lengthy correspondence with friends in Tehran, Egypt, and two-page comments on the Korean War. Works on an expanded version of his earlier article on Romanticism.

FRIDAY 14 JULY 1950

<...> To Washington. <...>

TUESDAY 18 JULY 1950

<...> Two letters from Mr. Jam. He has been removed from his post as ambassador to Italy. <...> Mansur al-Molk will replace him. <...>

WEDNESDAY 19 JULY 1950

Further commentary on the Korean War.

FRIDAY 21 JULY 1950

<...> Mr. Golshayan writes to me from Tehran. He is critical of everyone, including the shah. In his last audience he told the shah that if he has any complaints against U.S. or British policy, he should relay them to the respective ambassadors and not to an Iranian newspaper owner or to his courtiers. The shah became very annoyed. On his last day as minister of finance, Mr. Golshayan says he told the shah that with the people around him, the Pahlavi dynasty could be doomed. <...> When Reza Shah came to power, conditions in the country were even worse, but thanks to his firmness and the backing of devoted subordinates, he turned the country around. Golshayan also says that during the recent negotiations with the British on the oil agreement, he begged the shah not to interfere, but he did and promised them he would make sure it passed Parliament. This forced us to sign the agreement. When Parliament refused to ratify it, the shah retreated, making us the targets of the people's abuse. <...>

Golshayan continues and relates that for two-and-a-half millennia the people of Iran considered the shah symbolic of the country's independence. Now the shah shows his weakness by favoring proven traitors. By contrast, when Reza Shah had decided that Ali Asghar Hekmat was to be his ambassador to Germany, the German ambassador objected. He told the Iranian Minister of Foreign Affairs that he had heard that one of Hekmat's ancestor's was Jewish, and therefore Hekmat was not pure Aryan. As soon as Reza Shah learned of this, he appointed Hekmat minister of the interior (the second most important ministry) saying that he was needed more in Iran than abroad. <...> "These days the shah tells everyone that Dr. Ghani will become ambassador to the U.S., then changes his mind because of Ala's or Entezam's influence."

Heard from Mr. Jam who writes, "They needed to reward Mansur for services rendered on 20 Shahrivar (the 1941 invasion of Iran by British and Soviet forces). <...> Nowadays the climate in Iran does not favor sincere and candid people like you and me. <...>"

<...>

WEDNESDAY 26 JULY 1950

Had lunch at the Mayflower Hotel with John Wiley, the U.S. Ambassador to Tehran, and his wife, Irene. The upshot of our conversation was that I had been definitely slated to become the ambassador, but it was rumored later that I was seriously ill and could die in a day or two. When he was in Tehran, Wiley said, he and his wife met with the shah in private and the shah praised my knowledge and character. My illness was unfortunate, but my recovery amazed him. <...> Wiley was optimistic about the Razmara government and seemed to feel that Mansur was a disreputable individual. He also felt that Jam had been treated unjustly. <...>

Mr. Nemazi's name came up. Wiley was critical and said that Nemazi had made a lot of money in Hong Kong—I defended Nemazi, saying that he was a decent, learned, and generous man, who had contributed to charity. The millions he gave to Shiraz, for example. He accepted what I said but felt that it was not inconsistent with what he alleged. I attempted to change his mind as I consider Nemazi a decent person, but I was unable to persuade him. Whatever the case, he said, Nemazi's reputation at the U.S. State Department is not good. <...>

THURSDAY 27 TO SATURDAY 29 JULY 1950

Busy social engagements. Mailed copies of his article on euthanasia to Dr. Rosenkrantz and an article on Anatole France he had written to Will Durant. Letters from Baqer Kazemi and Hoseyn Navab and letter to Mirza Mehdi.

MONDAY 31 JULY 1950

<...> Letter from Abbas Eqbal. A great deal about Ala, most of it unflattering. <...>

WEDNESDAY 2 AUGUST 1950

<...> Answered Professor Cuyler Young's[19] query about the theme of a Gobelin tapestry that hangs in Princeton's Firestone Library. It depicted a story told in Book I of Herodotus's *History:* Cyrus the Great courting Tomyris, Queen of the Massagetae. Knowing that Cyrus did not want her as a wife but had designs on her territory, Tomyris rejected his proposal. Cyrus then attacked her kingdom. <...>

SUNDAY 6 AUGUST 1950

Had lunch with Generals Mahmud Amini and Mozayyeni. Both consider the shah a weakling surrounded by inferior people. General Mozayyeni had accompanied Reza Shah on his state visit to Turkey. He spoke of an incident that I had never heard before. One day Atatürk took Reza Shah, Esmat Inönü and several other high-ranking people to a military installation. Atatürk wanted to demonstrate that he had enlisted illiterates into the army and had taught them to read and write in a short time. He called a soldier to the blackboard.

Atatürk asked him, "Were you illiterate when you were drafted?" The soldier said, "Yes." Atatürk asked, "You can read and write now?" The soldier nodded yes. The soldier was ordered to write, "Long live the king of Iran," which he did. Atatürk then said, "I changed the alphabet to Latin and this facilitated their learning in a short time." He then asked Reza Shah why he did not change the Persian alphabet. Reza Shah answered in Persian and General Koupal translated. Reza Shah said in essence that Iranians are different from Turks. Ninety percent of the Turkish language is Arabic and Persian and its literature is in these two languages. Persians have a literature of their own. If we were to change the alphabet, how would we answer to Sa'di and Ferdowsi? Amazing how a conventional person, but seasoned by time, could give such a learned and definitive answer. Atatürk dropped the subject. This was the best exchange I have heard of in years.

MONDAY 7 AUGUST TO SATURDAY 2 SEPTEMBER 1950

<...> Correspondence and an extremely crowded social schedule.

SUNDAY 3 SEPTEMBER 1950

<...> Traveling by plane to Los Angeles via Chicago. <...>

Went to the less-crowded seats in the back to stretch out for a while. There were two young women sitting there. Both were lovely, one was stunning, a Leda or a Venus, twenty-one or so and the very model of innocent beauty. The reading light over the seat next to her illuminated part of her face. When she moved her head, the lamp revealed another part of her face. At times her head bent forward and a golden light shone on her auburn hair. <...> As I sat there charmed by these shifting images, the delicate pleasures of poetry and music took shape in my mind, the magisterial odes of a Hafez or a Sa'di. I saw her as an ode penned by God. Every painting seemed inadequate and inarticulate now, and the true meaning of the Arabic saying "perceived, but not represented" became clear. In the course of these thoughts, her entire face became visible. Partly owing to the soft reading lamp and partly abetted by my own imagination, with the rest of the world in shadow, for the first time in my life I understood the secret to Rembrandt's brush and colors. His ability to focus the viewers' attention on one particular point—usually the face—and to invite the imagination to delve the mysterious darkness around that point was unsurpassed. <...>

Now a world of discovery was available to me, and I was able to visualize the poet's sensibility and the delicacy of his feelings.

<...>

We landed at 9:00 P.M. local time. Mr. Zafar had come to the airport to meet his wife. Amin and Cyrus were there as well as Qasem Reza'i, the son of the late Hajj Mohammad Reza Salduz, a Sabzevari merchant and one of the world's decent people. Mohammad Reza, known as Salduz, was the most prominent and wealthiest merchant in Sabzevar. <...> He was close to Mirza Mahmud Arabshahi. In my opinion, neither of these men ever told a lie. <...> Qasem was forty days old when his father died. <...>

MONDAY 4 TO THURSDAY 14 SEPTEMBER 1950

Very hectic social schedule, visiting, invitations.

FRIDAY 15 SEPTEMBER 1950

<...> With Amin and Cyrus went to the Huntington Library in San Marino [California] and spent the entire day. <...> Impressive library and important collection of incunabula. There is also a collection of some 25,000 species of cacti. <...>

TUESDAY 19 SEPTEMBER 1950

Called on Mr. Bowren, the mayor of Los Angeles. We talked about the state of the world for forty-five minutes. At 4:00 P.M. called on Dr. Marmorston. Lailee Bakhtiar and her fiancé were there. Stayed for dinner.

WEDNESDAY 20 SEPTEMBER 1950

Called on Dr. Von Kleinschmidt, chancellor of the University of Southern California. He has invited me to lunch next Monday. Dinner at Mr. Melvin Levy's, a screenwriter. His daughter Suzanne is Cyrus's girlfriend. <...>

SATURDAY 23 SEPTEMBER 1950

Went to the airport at 12:30 P.M. to meet Mr. Yunes Vahabzadeh. I was extremely happy to see him. We had lunch at the Miramar Hotel. Yunes believes the situation in Iran has worsened. <...> Razmara has been unable to do anything and his government will fall in three to four weeks. Seyyed Zia will probably be the next prime minister. He has asked Yunes to become the minister of national economy. <...> Mansur is extremely unpopular and the Seven Year Economic Plan has been discarded in effect. Dr. Mosaddeq has become very strong. He derives his power from his national popularity. He towers over others. <...> Dr. Taqi Nasr has proved to be a failure and no one has any faith in him. Everyone is talking about the classification of people into groups labeled A, B, and C.[20] Yunes insists that I return to Iran. Said that the shah hinted at it in several ways. I convinced him that I cannot accept any position. <...> The British continue to have great influence over Iranian affairs. The power of the Tudeh Party is somewhat overrated. There is corruption in the government. <...>

MONDAY 25 SEPTEMBER 1950

Lunch with Kleinschmidt. I suggested that there be an advisor for the Iranian students. He said he would think about it. There are presently about twenty-five Iranians at the university. He asked me to give a talk for the other guests he had invited, mostly university professors. Instead of a formal talk, I answered their questions, which were mostly about the United Nations. <...>

TUESDAY 26 SEPTEMBER 1950

<...> Yunes has left but telegraphed from New York. He was telling me yesterday that scandals are rife in Iran. An American blonde arrives in Tehran. She is seen riding horses with the court insignia. People put two and two together. <...>

I invited Mr. Levy, his wife and two daughters. Levy is the author of more than twenty filmed screenplays. <...>

WEDNESDAY 27 SEPTEMBER 1950

Mr. Weingarten and Lailee came for dinner. <...>

THURSDAY 28 SEPTEMBER 1950

<...> At 4:30 P.M. Dr. Gerhard Gnoser, a forty-year-old member of the Austrian Ministry of Foreign Affairs and graduate of the Sorbonne, called on me. He is intelligent and speaks French well. I met him through Dr. Von Kleinschmidt. At 7:00 P.M. Dr. Barber, the head of the Engineering School, and his wife had dinner with me. He thinks very little of Dr. Fogg, the newly appointed head of USC. He said that the new chancellor is neurotic and does not attend faculty meetings. There is already talk of his removal.

FRIDAY 29 SEPTEMBER 1950

Dinner at Simin Ataba'i's. Am reading several works by Tagore: *The Home* and *The World and Nationalism*. They read well, and he proves to be a mystic yet well versed in most concerns of everyday life. <...>

MONDAY 2 OCTOBER 1950

<...> Sardar Fakher, the perennial Speaker of Parliament, has been classed a "C." He gave a speech in Parliament saying that he served liberty and the country. Though his land holdings had comprised forty villages, he now does not have a home. He concluded with a reference to Christ's crucifixion, and then left the chamber. Dr.

Mosaddeq replied that Sardar Fakher was never a servant of liberty and that he had gambled away his holdings. He asked, "How can one who is unable to control his own property run a country." The minority faction requested that all people classified less than "A" be dismissed. The government does not know what to do.

WEDNESDAY 4 OCTOBER 1950

<…> Had dinner at the Levys. <…> A producer at MGM and a composer and his mother-in-law were there. Levy is working on a script based on a novel by Sir Walter Scott. He said that moviegoers like films about old English heroes. I raised the name of Sir Thomas More as a real English hero.

THURSDAY 5 OCTOBER 1950

<…> Summary of seven articles by Hansen Baldwin, military correspondent of *The New York Times* on the "Mistakes of War." <…> Cyrus has also read the articles and asked questions. We talked for a while, but I said he should read more of the history of science. <…>

SUNDAY 8 OCTOBER 1950

Another four pages on Hanson Baldwin's articles.

<…> At 1:15 traveled to Santa Barbara to see Abdollah Qashqa'i, his mother, twelve-or fourteen-year-old sister Nahid and eleven-year-old brother Kambiz. The family has bought a new house for $22,000 and are now furnishing it. Mr. Naser Qashqa'i will himself come to the U.S. at the beginning of winter. Came back to Los Angeles by 6:15. Had dinner with the children. Cyrus brought some opera records and played them.

MONDAY 9 OCTOBER 1950

To San Francisco. Mrs. Mehdi picked me up at the airport. At 5:00 P.M. I paid a call on Dr. Rosenkrantz and spent the evening with Mirza Mehdi and his family.

TUESDAY 10 OCTOBER 1950

<…> At 5:00 P.M. went to Berkeley for dinner at Evans's in honor of Dr. Ernest Lawrence, the inventor of the cyclotron and winner of the Nobel Prize in physics. <…> Professor Robert G. Aitken, eighty-seven, who has spent his life in astronomy, spoke about double stars. Evans (himself a nominee for the Nobel prize in chemistry) spoke a great deal about me, which was embarrassing. <…>

THURSDAY 12 OCTOBER 1950

 <…> Mr. Nemazi called in the morning and confirmed the engagement of the shah and Soraya Esfandiari. Wrote a letter to Mr. Shokuh al-Molk. <…>

SATURDAY 14 OCTOBER 1950

<…> Afternoon went to Mr. Masoud Mehran's home. Returned at 7:00 P.M. and with Mr. and Mrs. Mehdi went to Fairfax where they have a weekend home. Slept there. <…>

WEDNESDAY 18 OCTOBER 1950

<…> President Truman gave a long speech at the San Francisco opera house. His main thesis was that Western democracies are more revolutionary than the reactionary Soviet Union. <…>

Lengthy entry on the city of San Francisco.

THURSDAY 19 OCTOBER 1950

<...> Dinner at Mr. Rafi' Mayeri, an Esfahani Jewish merchant with family in New York. <...>

SUNDAY 22 OCTOBER 1950

Today is Ashura. <...> Flight from San Francisco to New York. Staying at the Hotel Croydon.

MONDAY 23 OCTOBER 1950

<...> Read until 3:00 A.M. Came across several new facts about the early career of Mirza Taqi Khan Amir Kabir from Western sources. Sent them to Mr. Abbas Eqbal.

TUESDAY 24 OCTOBER 1950

Invited to the American Medical Association Convention. There were several long addresses. The chairman of the Association gave a long speech against socialized medicine, and then he spoke about medical advances in the U.S. He predicted that in the next fifty years medicine will find cures for cancer, infantile paralysis, arthritis, rheumatism, and high blood pressure. He also said that the incidence of infectious disease will decrease and that longevity will increase. As I was listening, all of my thoughts were on the poor people of Iran and their poor prospects for better health. <...> Later wrote letters to Dr. J. Robert Oppenheimer, Dr. Lawrence, John Wiley, Dr. Porter, Professor Evans, Dr. Rosenkrantz, Mr. Samuel Kahn, Amin, Cyrus, Dr. Laplace. <...>

WEDNESDAY 25 OCTOBER 1950

<...> Dinner with Patsy Sidenberg (née Kahn). I met her in San Francisco in 1945. She was one of the volunteers from prominent San Francisco families who helped the delegates to the founding sessions of the UN. Patsy speaks French well. She is a very attractive

woman around thirty. <...> She married a man named Sidenberg, who appears to be unbalanced, and divorced him. She now lives in San Mateo in a house that resembles a palace. <...>

TUESDAY 31 OCTOBER 1950

Last night received a letter from Tehran saying that Aqa Reza Ebrahimi has died. I am grief-stricken. He was the son of Hajj Aqa Ebrahim, one of the respected merchants of Sabzevar. <...> I saw Hajj Aqa Ebrahim during my childhood, when he would occasionally visit our home. He was alive until the start of the Constitutional Revolution. He was a gambler, who always had a game on with drinking and music. He had two sons, the oldest being Aqa Reza, the youngest, Hajj Aqa Ali, died twenty years ago.

Aqa Reza Ebrahimi was extremely bright. He had only a basic education, but no one knew as much about civil and criminal law as he did. He was fearless and always stood up to injustice. He also had a wicked sense of humor. <...> No one knew what was happening in Sabzevar better than Aqa Reza.

<...>

SATURDAY 4 NOVEMBER 1950

<...> 3:00 P.M. felt blood in my stomach. Dressed and went to New York Hospital and called Dr. Forkner, who arranged for me to be admitted. Semiconscious on the fifth, regained consciousness on the sixth. Also attended by Dr. Maryanne Payne,[21] a specialist in liver diseases. <...> Patsy Sidenberg is the only person who knows about my hospitalization. She has visited several times. Others believe I am in Boston. <...>

MONDAY 13 NOVEMBER 1950

<...> On Saturday 11 November, I saw Dehqan and his wife. He has just returned from a three-month inspection tour of factories in Europe. <...>

I never had the honor of meeting Dehqan's father, the late Mirza Mohammad Baqer Khan. He was in every sense of the word a man who typified the best in the Iranian character: sincere, gallant and well-intentioned. <...> His home was a center of traditional hospitality as well as a haven for victims of injustice and oppression. <...>

WEDNESDAY 22 AND THURSDAY 23 NOVEMBER 1950

On 14 November the hemorrhaging began again. I was unconscious for three or four days. When I regained consciousness, Dehqan, of course, was at my side. Patsy had come with flowers before leaving for California. <...> Blood transfusions twice a day and a feeding tube kept me alive. But this time Drs. Forkner, Payne and Glen unanimously decided on surgery and raised the issue with me. They had raised it nine months earlier, when most of the people Glenn had performed this operation on had died. Since then the technique has changed somewhat. There are only three surgeons who perform this operation. One is Glen, a professor of surgery at the university and the senior surgeon at the hospital. Nine months ago I had argued that this was a difficult decision for me. This time Glen bluntly said that there are two ways for me to die: through a hemorrhage or on the operating table. On the operating table there is a chance that the liver will heal, but it is certain that my present condition will destroy me. I decided to have the operation. <...>

The operation is to take place on the twenty-fifth, a day after Thanksgiving. Dr. Forkner closed his offices on Friday and Saturday so he could be with me for three days. The day before the operation my very dear friend Abbas Eqbal sent me a Hafez manuscript from the Royal Library of Akbar Shah dated toward the end of the sixteenth century. It is in a fine hand and illuminated with drawings of birds. I took this as a good omen. I telephoned Mr. Mahmud Foroughi, the consul general in New York, to come to the hospital and prepare a statement to the effect that in case of my death, all my affairs in the U.S. will be in the hands of Mr. Dehqan. I also prepared a will and gave it to Mr. Dehqan. I stated that I was to be buried in New York or wher-

. ever he saw fit (to God, the One, the Almighty, belongs the Kingdom). What I have in the bank should be spent on the education of Cyrus, Amin, and Firouz. <...> I transferred 200,000 French francs to Mr. Abbas Eqbal and 2,000 tomans to Mr. Mohammad Hasan Khazra'i. I also signed a release statement for the hospital. <...> In the last few days the following people came by: Mr. [Mohammad Ali] Varasteh, Mrs. Effat [Esfandiari], Dr. [Mohammad Ali] Hedayati, Mr. Mohsen Esfandiari, Mr. and Mrs. Kia, Mrs. Aalam [Minbashian], Mr. [Azad] Qarabaghi, Mr. and Mrs. Sayfpur Fatemi, Mr. and Mrs. Habib Sabet, Dr. and Mrs. [Aliqoli] Aradalan, Mr. [Mahmud] Ameri, Mr. and Mrs. [Ali Akbar] Kashef, Mr. and Mrs. [Mahmud] Foroughi, Dr. [Ghasem] Ghasemzadeh, Mr. Mohammad Nemazi, Dr. [Taqi] Nasr, Mr. [Hushang] Safinia, [Nasrollah] Entezam, Mrs. Maryam Mehran, Mr. Seyyed Ali Nasr, [Ali] Fotuhi, Dr. [Jalal] Abdoh, Lailee and Haideh Farmanfarmaian, Dr. [Ali] Amini, Mr. and Mrs. Bahman Zand, Dr. [Gholamhoseyn] Khoshbin, Mr. [Manuchehr] Moqaddam. <...>

WEDNESDAY 13 DECEMBER 1950

Released from the hospital. I have rented an apartment for six months, near Abbi's [Dehqan] home. Thus far the Lord has shown only goodness, for which I offer my thanks to His exalted Throne. <...>

THURSDAY 14 TO FRIDAY 29 DECEMBER 1950

Dr. Ghani wrote of preparing a will; Dehqan to be executor. To be buried in the area where he dies. <...> Letters to friends. Active social life.

TUESDAY 26 DECEMBER 1950

Today I heard Dr. Esther Rosenkrantz has died. I was greatly saddened. She was seventy-three. She was a very lively woman and one of the Dr. Osler's best students.

SATURDAY 30 DECEMBER 1950

Spent the morning in bed until ten. Mr. Dehqan came by with Mr. Asgharzadeh, the son-in-law of Mr. Dabir A'zam Bahrami; later Dr. Afrukhteh, Mr. Kia, Dr. Ghasemzadeh, and Mr. Ahmad Dehqan. Dr. Ghasemzadeh reported some disheartening news about Iran. The arrival of Fatemeh Pahlavi and her American husband has caused quite a stir; Ayatollah Kashani has said that the queen of Iran should wear a headscarf. Newspapers have started to ask why women are appearing at gatherings in low-cut gowns. The anarchy in Iran will lead to revolution, encouraged by Dr. Baqai and people like him. He spends the night at his newspaper office, surrounded by about five hundred thugs armed with knives. The oil question is unresolved, the court is weak, and then there is the issue of the fishery rights. <...>

SUNDAY 31 DECEMBER 1950

<...> Had a letter from my brother. <...> He has sent 50,000 tomans. This dear man is always concerned about my welfare. <...>

MONDAY 1 JANUARY 1951

Wrote some letters including condolences to Major General Abdollah Hedayat whose father, Mokhber al-Dowleh, has recently died. <...> Entire day I thought of dear friends who have died.

TUESDAY 2 JANUARY 1951

<...> Had a letter from Shokuh al-Molk, who complains of the spread of graft in Iran and the withdrawal of honest people from government in favor of the corrupt. Navab has written from Holland asking me to stay at the embassy on my way to Tehran. Sa'ed who had been in The Hague had told him that he accepted the post of ambassador to Turkey when he made certain I was not returning. <...>

WEDNESDAY 3 JANUARY 1951

<...> Aliqoli Khan Nabil stopped by. <...> He complained bitterly that at the Ministry of Foreign Affairs they say that Iran does not have an ambassador here. <...>

THURSDAY 4 JANUARY-SATURDAY 10 FEBRUARY 1951

Brief entries mostly about visitors; letters to and from friends.

SUNDAY 11 FEBRUARY 1951

Sent a telegram to HIM congratulating him on his marriage to Soraya Esfandiari (daughter of Khalil Esfandiari, who is the son of Esfandiar Khan, brother of Sardar As'ad). <...>

WEDNESDAY 14 FEBRUARY 1951

<...> Received a letter from Mohammad Qazvini's daughter, Suzanne. She writes that with the help of Ali Akbar Dehkhoda and Dr. Siasi she was able to sell her father's Persian and Arabic books to the University of Tehran for 40,000 tomans. They also had been able to sell the French books for 10,000 tomans. I was distressed to hear that Seyyed Hasan Taqizadeh had been to their house only once after Qazvini's death to purchase his unpublished writings. He wanted to pay for them on the spot, but Suzanne refused. He never returned. <...> In any event Suzanne has taken all of them to Paris with the intention of publishing them later. <...>

THURSDAY 15 FEBRUARY 1951

Back in Washington. Mrs. Nemazi, Mr. Rad and Mr. Eftekhari greeted me at the station. <...>

FRIDAY 16 FEBRUARY 1951

Wrote letters of condolence to the daughters, son and relatives of the late Vosouq al-Dowleh.

<...> General Yazdanpanah called this evening and we talked until 1:30 A.M. Everything he said points to the shah's lack of resolve and his susceptibility to flattery. He also said that in Tehran rumor has it that Razmara had become prime minister at the urging of the Americans. They wanted Mansur to resign, and he insolently said he would provided they made him ambassador to Italy. <...> Razmara began to court the Russians. <...> He had secret meetings with the Soviet military attaché. <...> Aware of how unpopular they were, the British made it appear as though Razmara had been backed by the Americans. Meanwhile the shah thought he would gain more power with Razmara as prime minister. <...> Yazdanpanah said that he told the shah, Razmara's comings and goings reminded him of the latter days of Ahmad Shah, when he [Yazdanpanah] was Reza Shah's [Reza Khan's] adjutant. [Visibly upset], the shah had said: Razmara is no Reza Shah and I am no Ahmad Shah. <...> You need to be less impressionable and influenced by these events. Yazdanpanah replied that he was the shah's loyal servant, but what did his Majesty mean by the term "impressionable"? But HIM would not answer. <...> Yazdanpanah also said that my name came up, when the shah expressed his surprise at my resignation. He told HIM that it was a simple matter and he should not be surprised. He then related a lengthy account of Reza Shah's actions on events surrounding the coup of 1921. <...>

Yazdanpanah spoke more about the shah. He said that HIM is surrounded by a group of informers and spies, and he cannot keep a secret. He tells everyone what is on his mind. About the shah's U.S. visit, Yazdanpanah said the following, "I had spoken to Hazhir (the late minister of court) and later to the shah as to who should be in the entourage." The shah answered, "You definitely would be included." Yazdanpanah told the shah, "Your Majesty, I wasn't thinking of myself." He also said that he had mentioned my name and that the shah said it would be very good and said he would think about the rest of the [members of the entourage]. <...> Later HIM said that Fardust and Dr. Ayadi should also come along. Yazdanpanah, obviously dismayed, added that the shah had not thought much about who should accompany him. <...>

SUNDAY 18 FEBRUARY 1951

<...> Wrote more letters of condolence to the relatives of the late Vosouq al-Dowleh, who was an exceptional individual. Mirza Hasan Khan Vosouq al-Dowleh (Vosouq) was the son of Ebrahim Khan Mo'tamed al-Saltaneh, son of Mirza Mohammad Qavam al-Dowleh. Mirza Mohammad was the principal advisor of Hamzeh Mirza Heshmat al-Dowleh during the time of Naser al-Din Shah in the campaign against the Akhal Turks in Turkmenistan. Qavam al-Dowleh's ancestry goes back to three brothers, each of whom was the head of an Ashtiani clan. *[A detailed genealogy follows.]* <...>

SUNDAY 4 MARCH 1951

Iranian newspapers are full of news about the shah's wedding and the disorder at the reception. Ala has become minister of court, Abdollah Entezam, head of protocol at court. <...> There is the same uproar over the proposed oil agreement. The British are still up to their old tricks sowing confusion, while Iranians remain ignorant as they undermine one another. The only good news amidst the chaos is the appointment of Abdollah Entezam. <...>

THURSDAY 8 MARCH 1951

News of the assassination of Razmara at the Shah Mosque by one of the Islamic Fedayeen, followers of Seyyed Abol Qasem Kashani. Mass demonstrations. <...>

FRIDAY 9 MARCH 1951

<...> No one will accept the post of prime minister. <...>

Ali Izadi related a conversation he had had with Reza Shah when he [the shah] was living in exile in South Africa. Reza Shah rejected Izadi's suggestion to write his memoirs. He told Izadi that it would be shameful to admit how much the Iranian elite had become tools and spies for Iran's enemies. If he were to write his memoirs, he would have to deal with this at every point and name names. <...>

SUNDAY 11 MARCH 1951

Not feeling well again. <...>

Ala, a true Anglophile, has become prime minister. He will not last long and unless he resigns soon, his reputation will be tarnished. <...> People will not tolerate this British yoke. <...> It appears he will only be an interim prime minister until a strong man is found. Revolution in Iran seems more imminent as the days go on. <...>

MONDAY 12 MARCH 1951

<...> Came down with jaundice. Must rest and diet on proteins, high-calorie food, and food with vitamin B. Went to the hospital. <...>

TUESDAY 13 MARCH 1951

Yellowness of the skin and eyes more pronounced. <...> Wish I knew what lies ahead. Liver disease does not end well. In any event what happens makes little difference ultimately. It is part of the natural course of life. <...>

Among the important symptoms of jaundice are irritability, pessimism and depression. But today I have become very sentimental about the world, and I love everyone I have known in life. If I have witnessed unpleasant behavior, it is now forgotten. I have never held grudges. Sometimes I blow up, but that passes instantly and I blame myself for over-reacting. <...> In these diaries I have been very harsh on some people for not being honest. <...> But now I let it go and wish them all well. <...> We cannot always be saints; we are all subject to petty human feelings. <...> Some of the things I have written on these pages are the result of my not being able to control those feelings. I hereby erase all the rancor, as I have nothing but love for everyone. <...>

Have transferred the 50,000 tomans received from my brother to Mr. Dehqan's account. In case of my death, he is to use the money for the education of Cyrus, Nahid, his sister, Amin, and Firouz. <...> Mr. Dehqan will administer the affairs of my children. <...>

There are a number of precious manuscripts and old coins. <...>

Like the rest of humanity I am awaiting the inevitable. Nor have I been unlucky, having never been wanting for anything in life. I have received a good education, traveled, associated with the great and good and, whenever I could, served the people and worked for their happiness. <...> Even now in the best hospital, I am surrounded by doctors and nurses who, with every possible device, devote themselves to my care. Also by my side are people like the Dehqans tendering their love and affection. The hospital has given me the best treatment medicine has to offer. For now it has proved successful, and I will live a little longer. But it has only delayed the inevitable. Sooner or later I must go. My only wish is that my family exercise forbearance, as their grieving will agonize my soul. I expect them to be happy in every sense of the word, to laugh and rejoice so that my soul can do likewise. <...> I have nothing special to add to my will, merely what I have already written. They can bury me wherever I die. <...> *[Condensation of a four-page entry]*

THURSDAY 15 MARCH 1951

Now Ruz gifts for some thirty people. <...>

FRIDAY 16 MARCH 1951

Mr. Nemazi called last night to enquire how I was feeling. He informed me that Parliament had passed a law nationalizing the oil industry with two addenda. There is a grace period of one month before it takes effect. The purpose is to give Britain time to reach a compromise with Iran.

SATURDAY 17 MARCH 1951

Letters to Abolhasan Ebtehaj, Soheyli, Foruhar, Sa'ed and Aram (who has had an operation). Letters from Qavam al-Saltaneh and his wife, Mo'tamed al-Saltaneh, and the Vosouq al-Dowleh family; telegram to the shah for Now Ruz. <...>

Letter from Mr. Nabil. Puri Teimurtash came by with flowers. She is a very kind girl. Puri was nine and her sister Nush Afarin six, when their father was killed. Afsar (a companion of Teimurtash) misappropriated some of Teimurtash's property. He sold some of his rare books. <...> These two daughters are not well off and work very hard to sustain themselves. <...>

TUESDAY 20 MARCH 1951

<...> The situation in Tehran is worse. Martial law has been declared. <...> Ala has announced his Cabinet. He himself is minister of foreign affairs; interior, Afkham Hekmat; economy, Varasteh, minister without portfolio, Ali Dashti; justice, Amir Ala'i; war, Major General Naqdi; agriculture, Farmand; post and telegraph, Ahmad Zanganeh. <...> Apparently they have contacted Yazdanpanah regarding the post of minister of court.

Shuresh, the organ of the parliamentary minority and Ayatollah Kashani, has published articles harshly critical of Ashraf Pahlavi and Fatemeh and their husbands, Ahmad Shafiq and Vincent Hillyer <...>. It claimed a document has come into its possession that says Razmara intended to overthrow the shah, shut down Parliament and execute a number of people. <...>

WEDNESDAY 21 TO MONDAY 26 MARCH 1951

Letters from Iran, visitors.

TUESDAY 27 MARCH 1951

Visitors. Letters from friends, including greetings from Dr. Mosaddeq. Decided to write him a letter emphasizing that he should be careful not to let his agenda be hijacked by ignorant opportunists, thereby allowing the Russians to reap the benefits. Telegraphed my brother and am awaiting his trip abroad. <...>

WEDNESDAY 28 MARCH 1951

Long letter to Dr. Mosaddeq.

THURSDAY 29 MARCH 1951

Don't know what course my illness will take. It is possible that there will be further damage that will end in my death. <...> Terminal ill-ness is always accompanied by a great deal of sorrow and torment. One is apprehensive and depression sets in. But I am not fearful and ready for anything. Were I to live longer, the world that I know would not change. Loggers in Mazandaran have a saying: "Live a few more years and chop a few hundred more trees. Then what?" In my case, assume I would witness a few more heartbreaking events. Then what? <...> May God grant my dear brother Mirza Hoseyn Khan good health and long life so he will be around to bring up the children and see to their education. <...> Omar Khayyam says,

> *My childhood was with teachers for a time;*
> *Soon I was proud of this learning of mine.*
> *But look what happened to me in the end;*
> *From dust I came and now blown by the wind.*

FRIDAY 30 MARCH 1951

<...> Received many letters, but do not feel well enough to answer them. Doctors have encouraging news. They believe the jaundice has run its course and I will be feeling better soon.

SATURDAY 31 MARCH 1951

Dr. Jalal Abdoh, Maryam Pirnia, the daughter of the late Mo'azed al-Saltaneh, and her fiancé Mr. Fotuhi came by; later Dr. and Mrs. Baher and their son visited for tea; still later Abbi and Ahmad Dehqan. During this stay at the hospital, which began before Now Ruz, I must have written more than 200 brief notes and letters.

SUNDAY 1 APRIL 1951

<…> Knowing that these liver diseases are incurable, I began to recall and record all the names of people I have met, chance meetings and casual acquaintances and long-time friends. For example, when I was a delegate to the annual meeting of the International Red Cross, I was called to report to Ahmad Shah who was staying at the Hotel Majestic in Paris; or the chance meeting with Crown Prince Mohammad Hasan Mirza in Paris one night at the famous Shahrezad Cabaret in 1928, when I spent the entire evening talking to him. <…> [Here Dr. Ghani supplies a list of more than 1,100 names of people from every walk of life, high and low, famous and ordinary.] <…>

WEDNESDAY 4 APRIL 1951

The opening day of Parliament in Iran and events will now unfold. [Ayatollah] Kashani and his group will be free to do anything they want. Hazhir is responsible for the power of Kashani. In order to save himself he was willing to do anything. In effect he is responsible for creating a theocracy. <…> There is a great deal of talk about Qavam al-Saltaneh. He has gone to Lahijan [to his tea plantation], but groups of people travel north [from Tehran] to see him. The shah has probably realized his mistakes. He will have to rely on members of his personal circle who are of little use these days. <…>

Some people came by this afternoon. <…>

FRIDAY 6 APRIL 1951

Received some letters and answered Dr. Ali Akbar Fayyaz regarding his article on Chinese Moslems. I wrote a harsh letter to Cyrus [regarding his choice of study]. <…>

SATURDAY 7 APRIL 1951

Slept badly last night. Abbi telephoned, saying that it appears the U.S. has counselled Britain to accept the nationalization of the oil industry. <…> Mr. Nemazi called and said the shah will visit Transjordan. It appears the shah is ill and there is talk of appendicitis.

MONDAY 9 APRIL 1951

<...> 2:30 P.M. Prince Shahpur Mahmud Reza who is temporarily in New York with Mr. Kia, came by. Shahpur is busy writing his thesis, but it is not clear on what subject. <...>

TUESDAY 10 APRIL 1951

<...> Dr. Khoshbin and Dr. Ardalan stopped by. <...> They related that yesterday in the Iranian Parliament, [a deputy named] Ashtianizadeh had accused the British government of keeping Ala in reserve for a day like this [when he could be of service] to them. <...>

SATURDAY 14 APRIL 1951

In this entry of some six pages, Dr. Ghani describes the contents of Dalil al-Sofara *(Guide for Emissaries) and a number of travelogs* (Safar-nameh) *written by Iranian diplomats. Most of these works exist in unique manuscripts held in libraries or in private hands.*

Dalil al-Sofara by Hajj Mirza Abu al-Hasan Khan Shirazi, known as Ilchi-ye Bozorg, covers events in the early nineteenth century, during the reign of Fath Ali Shah. At the time rivalry among the European powers worked in favor of Iran. The Russians were allied with the British in their conflict with the French. For this reason, the tsarist government, which had been warring with Iran, was now interested in rapprochement. The author of *Dalil al-Sofara* was involved in the negotiations. One can consider the book the second volume of Ilchi-ye Bozorg's *Heyrat-nameh* (Book of Wonders).

In addition to the *Heyrat-nameh,* the well-known travelogs *Talibof's Travels,* the *Safar-nameh* of Khosrow Mirza, *Resaleh-ye Sarhaddiyeh* (Boundary Treatise) by Seyyed Ja'far Khan Moshir al-Dowleh, the *Safar-nameh* of Farrokh Khan Amin al-Molk, and two others by Mirza Mohammad Ali Khan Shirazi and Mirza Taqi Khan Amir Kabir. <...>

TUESDAY 17 APRIL 1951

Late in the afternoon Dr. Forkner came and was satisfied with my progress. Around 9:00 P.M. he returned to discuss the shah's illness with me in private. He said he had read in the papers that the shah was ill and on his way to Europe for an appendectomy. He told me confidentially that they had discovered a small tumor in the shah's stomach last year that they had thought required surgery. But they determined that it would be necessary to x-ray the tumor in six months to see if it had enlarged. If that is the case, they must operate. I said I would write to HIM, but I also urged him to write to say that if the operation is necessary, it could be done in Iran or Europe, preferably in Stockholm or Zurich. <…> *[Dr. Ghani then wrote a two-page letter to the shah and sent it via Shokuh al-Molk.]*

<…> Hope to God it all goes well, but I fear that the meddlers will confuse HIM. It would be poison for the shah to go to Britain for it would completely damage his popularity. There are British agents prodding him to have the operation there, but people would think the HIM's trip had something to do with the oil dispute. (I wrote a lengthy letter to HIM.)

WEDNESDAY 18 APRIL 1951

<…> Dr. Ali Amini came by at 9:00 A.M. Mrs. Amini is still in Tehran. He informed me that Turi's (Azodi, sister of Batul Amini) illness is worse. <…> Qavam is well and will become prime minister in another month. The shah is not in a good mood. He had promised the British an agreement on oil, but he was unable to deliver it. The morale of the military is very low. The shah's influence has dwindled, and, as a result, the British have taken a tougher stance in the negotiations. <…>

Dr. Amini believes that Qavam will resolve the dispute as he has prestige; <…> he will form a strong government from the outset, <…> but the shah will oppose Qavam as he believes that a strong government may dethrone him. <…>

<…>

SATURDAY 21 APRIL 1951

This afternoon Mr. (Nasrollah) Entezam, the Iranian ambassador to the U.S., came by and we spoke for two hours. He is an odd person. <...>

MONDAY 23 APRIL 1951

<...> Wrote to Abbas Eqbal who is in Rome but soon to leave for Damascus. I sent two chapters of the proposed book about Amir Kabir. Also wrote to Mr. Qods (Nakhai) at the foreign ministry telling him to pay Eqbal's salary for the first three months of the year as soon as possible. <...>

SATURDAY 28 APRIL 1951

Parliament has voted overwhelmingly for the premiership of Dr. Mosaddeq.

WEDNESDAY 2 MAY 1951

<...> Dr. Mosaddeq's Cabinet is as follows: Economy, Amir Homayun Bushehri; Post and Telegraph, Vosouq Moshar (Moshar-e A'zam); Foreign Affairs, Kazemi; Agriculture, Hasan'ali Hedayat; Interior, General Zahedi; Health, Loqman al-Molk; Finance, Varasteh; War, Naqdi; Justice, Amir Ala'i; Education, Dr. Sanjabi. <...> There has been a large demonstration in Tehran organized by the Tudeh(Communist)Party attacking Dr. Mosaddeq who has said that Iran is only exercising its national sentiment and has explained the aims of nationalization. I sent congratulatory telegrams to Dr. Mosaddeq, Bager Kazemi, foreign minister designate, and Dr. Loqman al Molk, minister of health.

FRIDAY 4 MAY 1951

The U.S. amabassador has called on the shah advising him not to travel abroad for his operation. Any physician or surgeon who is required can come to Tehran. The British ambassador has also called on the shah advising him to travel to London for the operation. <...>

Read in the paper that Mohammad Taqi Bahar (Malek al-Sho'ara) has died. The exact date was Sunday 22 April. <...> The cause was a prolonged bout of tuberculosis. <...> [Here Dr. Ghani gives an account of Bahar's life and work of which the following is a summary translation.] Mohammad Taqi Bahar was born in 1886 in Mashhad. He was the son of the distinguished poet Mirza Mohammad Kazem Saburi Kashani (died 1904) who was the poet laureate of the shrine of Imam Reza in the city. Bahar distinguished himself in a variety of fields: journalism, politics, education, and literature. His career as a journalist began in 1910 when he started the newspaper *Now Bahar* (New Spring) in Mashhad, and a few years later another weekly called *Bahar*. In 1915 he was elected to Parliament and came to Tehran. He was reelected as deputy from Mashhad to the fourth, fifth, and sixth sessions, becoming one of the leaders of the "minority" faction. Bahar was also a gifted educator and writer. In 1917 he began to teach history and geography at the Higher Teacher's College. Under the sponsorship of the Ministry of Education he created scholarly editions of key texts on medieval Iranian history. He also taught a course on Persian stylistics and wrote the basic textbook on the subject. Bahar's most lasting legacy is his poetry. The Qajar king Mozaffar al-Din Shah [reign 1896–1907] dubbed him Malek al-Sho'ara (King of Poets) after the death of his father. Bahar's complete works consist of some 3,000 couplets. In addition to his expertise in Persian and Arabic, he learned to read and write the Pahlavi language of ancient Iran. <...> He was the center of attention at any gathering—elegant, witty, sophisticated and charming. He was a decent human being and extraordinarily bright. I liked him very much. <...>

MONDAY 7 MAY 1951

<...> Received a reply to the telegram I had sent to Dr. Mosaddeq. <...> The *New York Times,* an Anglophile newspaper, has an article

that is basically anti-Mosaddeq. <...> The article will make the U.S. unpopular in Iran. <...> In the past the *Times* has praised Razmara, who was not popular in Iran, as a true friend of the U.S.; in fact the opposite was true. <...> The article does not even mention that Mosaddeq has the backing of the people. It also fails to mention that Dr. Mosaddeq became prime minister with the near unanimous vote of the Parliament. <...>

FRIDAY 11 MAY 1951

Most of my days are spent reading Jalal al-Din Rumi and jotting notes. <...> Several people came by. I had a letter from Mr. Nemazi who informed me that Mrs. Ala has tuberculosis. Ala has telegraphed from Tehran to say that she must go to a sanitarium. Mrs. Ala is greatly upset. I felt sorry for her. Wrote to Nemazi to convey my best wishes to her and to ask whether there is anything I can do. <...>

SATURDAY 12 MAY 1951

Wrote to my brother urging him to come to the U.S. <...>

MONDAY 14 MAY 1951

Mr. Varasteh, the new minister of finance in Dr. Mosaddeq's Cabinet, came by at 4:00 P.M. I mentioned Abbas Eqbal's back pay as well as Jamshid Qarib's, Reza Moshiri's and my own. <...>

TUESDAY 15 MAY 1951

<...> Released from the hospital. <...>

WEDNESDAY 16 MAY 1951

Sent another short segment on Amir Kabir to Mr. Eqbal. <...>

THURSDAY 17 MAY 1951

News from Iran all disquieting. Dr. Mosaddeq will not leave Parliament until he finalizes the oil issue. <…>

SUNDAY 20 MAY 1951

Reading many non-Iranian sources on Amir Kabir. Nothing new in these sources. <…>

WEDNESDAY 23 MAY 1951

Examined by Dr. Forkner. He will go to Tehran next week. Dr. Barr will go first. If [the shah] needs an operation or other specialists are required, he will request that New York Hospital supply them. This is all very confidential. The doctors have been instructed by the State Department. The shah has insisted on complete secrecy. <…>

SATURDAY 26 MAY 1951

Stayed home. Batul and Dr. Ali Amini and Abbi came for tea. Qavam is in Geneva for health reasons. It appears Vosouq al-Dowleh had written his autobiography and left it with Ali (Vosouq). <…>

SATURDAY 2 JUNE 1951

Invited John Wiley (former U.S. ambassador to Iran) and his wife to lunch. I had not seen them for several months. This foolish man still believes Razmara was an Iranian nationalist and a friend to the U.S. He still maintains that U.S. and British policy are exactly the same. I talked a good deal and said that all of Iran's misfortunes can be laid at the door of British Petroleum. They have damaged us over the years. I told him that the Americans were mere spectators and that American friendship was always illusory, never substantial.

Dr. Forkner came by at 10:30 P.M. He and his wife will travel to Tehran early tomorrow morning. From what I gather, he has the task of a good will mission to the shah and country in addition to his medical duties. <…>

TUESDAY 26 JUNE 1951

<...> At noon called on Dr. Glenn who leaves for Tehran tomorrow with an anesthesiologist and a very capable assistant surgeon. He does not know any details other than what the State Department has told him. Dr. Forkner is already in Tehran. He said that the tumor could be one of three kinds: (1) A simple harmless growth. <...> (2) A type of spasm that has developed from overwork or tension. (3) A cancerous growth that may be too late to cure with surgery. We have to wait until he reaches Tehran. I acquainted him with the political situation in Iran and I extended my greetings to the shah. <...>

WEDNESDAY 27 JUNE 1951

Four pages on the Arab League.

FRIDAY 29 JUNE 1951

Mr. Nemazi called to say that Ala has sent his greetings. Last night Dr. Qorban relayed a similar message from Ala. Ala also told Qorban that it appeared to him that I was annoyed with him. "Ghani performed well in Cairo and Ankara. When he recovers, the Iranian government will make use of his services." <...> Mohammad Hoseyn Khan and Khosrow Qashqa'i came by. They are very resentful of the British. Other than Naser Khan, no member of their family is in Tehran. Mohammad Hoseyn Khan told me that when he was on the parliamentary Petroleum Commission, the shah called and told him not to vote for the nationalization of oil. He also said that Dr. Mosaddeq had told him to tell Entezam to put more effort into publicizing Iran's position. In response to this I said it was as if Iran had no representative at the United Nations. He added that someone had told his mother that I [Dr. Ghani] was to be ambassador to the U.S. His mother replied that it was impossible as the ambassador must be a tool of the British. They wanted one of their own people. <...>

TUESDAY 3 JULY 1951

Have had a bad cold for the past few days. This afternoon I had a severe chill with a high fever. Passed out. Ahmad Dehqan called the hospital and I was taken there. <...> Revived.

SATURDAY 7 JULY 1951

The newspapers have reported the story of the shah's operation by Dr. Glenn and his team. <...>

FRIDAY 13 JULY 1951

<...> Dr. Glenn has returned from Iran. He telephoned to say the [shah's] illness was not serious. There was just some old adhesion, which he removed from the appendix. <...>

SATURDAY 14 JULY 1951

At 10:30 Dr. Glenn came by and we had a long talk. <...> Wrote a letter to the shah about what the doctor had said. <...> Glenn told me that the shah had asked about me several times. The shah had said that he always remembers my past services, but that I should not forget him. <...> Glenn also said that he told the shah that he wanted only his own personnel in the operating room. The shah agreed and doctors Radji, Adl and Ayadi stepped outside. <...>

MONDAY 16 JULY 1951

Lengthy entry on the British and Iranian oil agreement and the enormous disparity in their revenues. Dr. Ghani also writes of the moral blight caused by the British policy in Iran.

A fistful of creatures for hire—some going back several generations, others freshly minted—have come onto the scene. These along with other thieves and sycophants have infiltrated the ministries, embassies, banks and other government institutions. This has foiled progress in Iran and instead fostered a servile, colonial mentality.

Everything from drug use, superstition, hypocrisy to ignorance are rife. A government within the government has emerged, and our fiscal disgrace allows a small number of fabulously rich to live among masses of the starving and unclothed, the living dead. Now the British entertain the world with the old tune of the Bolshevik threat. <...>

The bovine Americans understand nothing of this, as they consider what the ravaged British think the last word in political wisdom. I doubt whether they will ever catch on.

TUESDAY 17 JULY 1951

Dr. Glen came by again and told me that the State Department has paid all his and his team's fees. They were told to keep the matter secret. The shah has given the doctors some fine carpets and other gifts to the rest of the medical team. <...>

FRIDAY 20 JULY 1951

<...> The British have mounted a slander campaign against Mosaddeq. The ignorant Americans do not understand and parrot their slander. <...>

THURSDAY 9 AUGUST 1951

<...> Seyyed Mohammad Taddayon <...> has some form of cancer and is being treated at New York Hospital. I visit him almost daily and we have long talks about the early days of Reza Shah. He knows a great deal about the period and about the leading players: Mo'tamen al-Molk, Moshir al-Dowleh, Davar and Modarres. <...>

MONDAY 8 OCTOBER 1951

Dr. Mosaddeq arrived in New York today. I was informed that the plane would land at 9:30 A.M. <...> Had little sleep last night. <...> The plane finally landed. The Iranian ambassador and Dr. Ardalan had gone to the front [of the greeting line]. They took me and several others with them. The rest of the greeters were kept in the rear. I think the [embassy] plan had two purposes: (1) To let it be known in Tehran that we prevented the kind of reverence shown to the shah on his arrival two years ago. (2) The British arranged the segregation of the Iranians at the airport to diminish the effect of the reception.

The ambassador gave Mosaddeq a written speech to for him to deliver. He said that he could speak for himself. <...> The Iranians asked Mohammad Foroughi, the consul, why they were being kept from greeting Mosaddeq. Foroughi said that it was the ambassador's decision. Many people raised their voices to protest not being allowed to greet Mosaddeq. <...>

Mosaddeq went directly from the airport to the hospital. <...>

FRIDAY 12 OCTOBER 1951

Saw Dr. Mosaddeq at the hospital and spent an hour with him. <...> After he leaves the hospital, he will stay at the Ritz Tower. <...>

TUESDAY 16 OCTOBER 1951

Early this morning Mr. Emad Kia came by. It appears that [Baqer] Kazemi is feverishly going after the Washington post (and the removal of Entezam). Mr. Nemazi has told Mr. Dehqan that it is his understanding that I would be appointed as head of the Iranian mission to the UN. Dr. Mosaddeq has also implied that this is his intention. I plan to go to the West Coast in the next few days and will refuse any post. <...> I answered a letter from Mr. Shokuh al-Molk, and I also raised the issue of the pension for Qazvini's wife and daughter. <...>

SATURDAY 20 OCTOBER 1951

Dr. Mosaddeq attended an Iranian sponsored reception at the Columbia University faculty club. <...> In his welcoming address, Abdolhoseyn Dehqan[22] said that it was a great honor to welcome our popular prime minister whose <...> patriotism is evidenced by the fact that despite illness, he has made the long journey to New York to defend the rights of Iran [at the United Nations]. <...> Dr. Mosaddeq gave a very good speech. At his urging I sat next to him during the entire event. He was warm to all the attendees and expressed his gratitude for their coming. People were visibly moved. Those who insisted on kissing his hand, he kissed on the cheek. He gladly autographed numerous cards and photographs, bowed to everyone, and was a calming presence. At the end we went for tea. He remained a while longer and left. I told him indirectly that I could not accept any appointment and that I would be leaving for the West Coast in fifteen days. <...>

FRIDAY 26 OCTOBER 1951

Wrote letters to Qarib, Moshiri and Mehrdad Pahlbod concerning a book on Kamal al-Molk. Letter to Hekmat and recommendations for Moshiri, Baqer Varasteh, Dr. Radji, Nabavi, Professor Shams, Vahid Eshraqi. <...> Had a letter from Suzanne Qazvini asking me about pricing her father's manuscripts. I asked Dr. Baqai and Shayegan to help her. <...> Abbas Eqbal has written to me from Istanbul, where he is attending an Orientalist conference. He has discovered three very rare manuscripts in various libraries. The librarians had been unaware of their existence. <...>

THURSDAY 1 NOVEMBER 1951

To Los Angeles. <...>

FRIDAY 2 NOVEMBER 1951

Found an apartment near Beverly Hills, near the home of Simin Atabai and Dr. Marmorston. Tonight I am invited to the opening of a new UCLA college. Mr. Earl Warren,[23] the governor of California, Dr. Evans, and several other leading scientists and academics were present. They were especially kind and spoke a good while about me at the table. I was forced to give a brief talk. We were there until 1:30 A.M. I had met the governor several times before.

Mr. Weingarten has arranged for me to visit Charlie Chaplin.

MONDAY 5 NOVEMBER 1951

<...> In the afternoon I paid a call on Princess Fatemeh Pahlavi. She has married an American who changed his first name to Ali. Tehran was scandalized because they had been married in Rome without a religious ceremony. The shah had severed her relationship with the court. She had gone to Paris. Aqa Khan Mahalati had interceded with the shah and Mr. Mirza Mohammad Reza Ayatollahzadeh Shirazi married them in a traditional Moslem ceremony. <...> The shah had sent a lengthy reply to my telegram congratulating him on his marriage. <...>

SATURDAY 17 NOVEMBER 1951

Sent notes to Teimurtash's two daughters, General Patrick Hurley,[24] Will Durant, Dr. Oppenheimer[25] and some others.

<...> I am a guest at Dr. Marmorston's. The other guests include:

1. General David Sarnoff[26] who controls the largest television network [NBC]. He is a man of about sixty-five, healthy and full of life. <...> He has three sons, all of whom work in television. Sarnoff is gifted at conversation, entertaining and is well informed.

2. Mr. and Mrs. Dore Schary. Mr. Schary[27] is chief of MGM studios, having replaced L.B. Mayer, who is ill and retired. Mrs. Schary's face is partially paralyzed. <...> He himself is quite robust.

3. Mr. and Mrs. Gabriel Pascal.[28] He is a producer of Hungarian origin. He has the film rights to all of George Bernard Shaw's[29] plays. His wife is around twenty-seven or twenty-eight, very blonde and attractive. Five years ago she was able to leave Hungary and marry Pascal in Paris. She is an actress but currently is not working, as she is taking care of her children.

4. Mr. and Mrs. Burt Friedlob. Mr. Friedlob is another famous producer. His wife is blonde to an extreme degree and sat opposite Dr. Marmorston, our hostess.

5. Mr. and Mrs. David May. Mr. May is a film producer and explorer.

6. Mr. and Mrs. Spencer Tracy, whom I had seen before at Dr. Marmorston's. He is old but apparently a very famous movie actor.

7. Weingarten and his two daughters (Liz and Norma) and Liz's fiancé (Hal Horowitz), a professor of law.

8. Mr. and Mrs. Cornelius Jackson.[30] He is the chairman of the William Morris Agency, which represents most actors. His salary is on a par with movie producers. His wife, (the actress) Gail Patrick,[31] has completely white hair; her natural color is black. She is one of the most beautiful women I have ever seen. <...>

FRIDAY 23 NOVEMBER 1951

Anniversary of my operation. <...> It is really my birthday, and I should date my life from a year ago today. <...>

THURSDAY 29 NOVEMBER 1951

7:30 P.M. invited to dinner at Dr. Marmorston's. The other guests were Dr. Robertson, the deputy chancellor of the University of California; Dr. John Marrel, professor of medicine at Harvard; Dr. Cellars and his wife, a lawyer; Dr. Whitney, a researcher on blood pressure, and his wife, herself a physiologist; Mr. Joseph Levine, a film producer; Mr. and Mrs. Ronald Colman,[32] both actors and well read; James Mason, an actor; and Mr. Weingarten's mother.

SUNDAY 2 DECEMBER 1951

Mr. and Mrs. Ronald Colman came by. We talked a great deal. They recommended that I write stories for the stage and films. I don't know how they reached that conclusion. <...>

SATURDAY 8 DECEMBER 1951

With Amin and Cyrus left at 9:30 A.M. for the Odlum ranch, the home of Jacqueline Cochran Odlum[33] [whose husband's brother Dr. Ghani had known, when he was Canadian ambassador to Turkey]. We arrived at 1:15 P.M. More than a ranch, the place consists of a large house with several guesthouses. It is located in Indio about 170 miles south of Los Angeles. The other guests were:

1. Lt. Col. Evert, an airforce officer, and his wife. Toward the end of World War II, his plane was shot down and he spent the last five months of the war in a German prison camp.

2. Captain Nash, who was a flight instructor during the war. He is married with three children.

3. Captain Charles Yeager.[34] The first person to break the sound barrier. A World War II ace who downed seventeen German planes. He is married with several children.

4. Captain Merotei, also an airforce officer, who was stationed at Pearl Harbor. <...>

5. A woman who was in the government during the presidencies of Calvin Coolidge and Herbert Hoover.

6. Mr. and Mrs. Rache. Mrs. Rache works in the cosmetics industry with Jacqueline Cochran. Jacqueline herself is a very competent pilot and has set several records.

There were also a Miss Walsh, the secretary to Jacqueline and Mrs. Strauss, the housekeeper.

During lunch I told a story about Field Marshal Rundstedt that happened when he was a prisoner of war of the Allies. He said three things surprised him about his captors:

1. the incompetence of their generals;

2. the expertise of the Canadian, American and British pilots; and

3. the bravery of the soldiers of countries under the colonial rule of Britain and France.

There was a great deal of discussion, but the others generally accepted what he had said. My interest was basically in the third proposition. The rest of the conversation at lunch had to do with planes. Jacqueline is now about fifty-five years old. She had been active in World War II. After lunch I played several games of backgammon with her. She had arranged for skeet shooting, which was fun to watch. Everyone, even the wives, was very able with rifles. <...>

TUESDAY 11 DECEMBER 1951

Met the sixty-one-year-old Charlie Chaplin at his studio. We spoke alone for a while before lunch. <...> He is busy making a film called *Limelight*. His wife is twenty-six. They have two children. He has two older sons. The younger, Sydney Chaplin, works primarily in the theatre. His wife is the daughter of Eugene O'Neill,[35] the Nobel Prize winner. O'Neill has written several plays including a version of [Aeschylus's[36] *The Oresteia*] set in modern times as *Mourning Becomes Electra*. Chaplin and I arranged to talk more after he finishes his picture. <...>

MONDAY 17 DECEMBER 1951

<...> The situation in Iran is bad. Differences among various groups is impeding Mosaddeq's work. <...>

FRIDAY 28 DECEMBER 1951

<...> Sent a high-quality miniature to Mrs. Warren and a copy of Morgan Shuster's[37] book on Iran to the governor. I wrote a note to Mrs. Warren: "Handiwork from Esfahan, a Persian miniature carved on ivory, contemporary. With best wishes for the season. Hoping the

First Lady of California becomes interested in Persian art. Happy and prosperous New Year." In [Shuster's] book I inscribed the following: "To my learned and distinguished friend Governor Earl Warren. A book on a brief but important page in the history of my country. Hoping you become interested in Persian history. Sincere wishes for a happy and successful year for you and the state." <...>

MONDAY 31 DECEMBER 1951

Invited by the Evanses for dinner. A small group was there, including Dr. Frederic Koneieg, a professor of chemistry and thermodynamics at Stanford, and his wife; Dr. Pabst and his wife; and Dr. Evans' wife's sister. Wide ranging conversations about science. At midnight they served champagne and the new year began. They brought a notebook in which every guest was to inscribe his name. Dr. Evans insisted that I write some words. I wrote a poem written in Arabic by a Persian and translated:

> I console myself with hopes, things I expect from the future.
> How narrow would life have been, were it not for the breadth of
>   those expectations.
> The days in which we live lack that precious dimension and the
>   consolation that compensates for the narrowness of life.

"I hope earnestly that the coming year will grant mankind the gift of hope and the present company will be reunited under the roof of the Evanses next New Year's Eve and rejoice in the fulfillment of this wish." <...>

MONDAY 21 JANUARY 1952

<...> Cyrus telephoned. <...> It is becoming clear that he is not interested in medicine. He is making a mistake. <...> Wrote a long letter to Mr. Sa'id Nafisi concerning his efforts to change the Persian alphabet. I advised him to cease this harmful campaign. <...>

SUNDAY 27 JANUARY TO THURSDAY 20 MARCH 1952

Voluminous correspondence <...> and a few social calls, mostly Mirza Mehdi, Kamal Khamsi, Mr. Henry Grady (former ambassador to Tehran), Dr. Jahanshah Saleh, Mr. and Mrs. Mas'ud Mehran; Mr. Naser Qashqa'i; and an interview by a Mr. Ellis Walker from a San Francisco newspaper.

The last entry dated 20 March 1952 records an answer to a telegram that same day. On Thursday 20 March, Dr. Ghani spent the evening at a Now Ruz reception held by Iranian students at International House at Berkeley, where he delivered an address on Iranian civilization. From Friday 21 to Tuesday 25 March, he received guests and called on friends. On the twenty-sixth, the maid entered his apartment and found him unconscious on the bathroom floor. After a fairly long delay, she called his nephew Amin Ghani in Los Angeles. The unconscious Dr. Ghani was transferred to a hospital in Oakland. He never regained consciousness and died on 29 March 1952. His son, Cyrus, and two nephews, Amin and Firouz, were at his beside. After a brief service, he was buried at Woodlawn Memorial Park, near San Francisco. Several people spoke at the service. The principal speakers were Dr. Herbert Evans, the late A. H. Dehqan, the late Naser Qashqa'i, and Mr. Hashem Naraqi, whom Dr. Ghani had recently met. Mr. Mirza Mehdi hosted a dinner at his home that evening. He gave a very moving talk about Dr. Ghani.

NOTES
SECOND TRIP TO THE UNITED STATES

1. Dean G. Acheson (1893–1971). American statesman, Secretary of State (1949-53). Played key part in the Marshall Plan and establishing NATO. Author of *Present at the Creation.*

2. General of the Army, George Catlett Marshall (1880–1959). Chief of Staff in World War II; secretary of state, secretary of defense. The plan to rebuild Europe after the War is associated with his name.

3. General of the Army, Omar Nelson Bradley (1893–1981). Outstanding World War II general, known as the "soldier's general." Later chairman of the Joint Chiefs of Staff.

4. Dean Rusk (1909–94). Served in WWII in Southeast Asia as deputy Chief of Staff. Assistant secretary of state, 1949–52; secretary of state, 1961–69.

5. Victor Hugo (1802–85). French poet, novelist and dramatist. Most famous novel is *Les Miserables.*

6. Dr. Claude E. Forkner (1900–92), B.S., M.S. University of California Berkeley, Harvard Medical School. Research in universities in Germany and Great Britain. Cornell University Medical faculty.

7. Sheikh Jamal al-Din Abu Eshaq Inju (died 1357) is famed in Persian literature for being the patron of Hafez and Obeyd-e Zakani.

8. Dr. Jessie Marmorston (1897–1981). Emigrated from the Ukraine to the U.S.; M.D. University of Buffalo. Noted physician to key people in the film world.

9. Lawrence Weingarten (1898–1975). Executive producer at MGM film studio.

10. Yasha (Jascha) Heifetz (1901–87). Emigrated to the U.S. from Russia. One of the world's great violinists.

11. William Durant (1885–1957). American educator and author with his wife Ariel (1898–1981) of the highly popular *The Story of History.*

12. Harold Lamb (1892–1962). American author of popular history. Known for his partly fictionalized account of Omar Khayyam's life.

13. Louis B. Mayer (1885–1957). Born in Russia. Producer, vice president and general manager of MGM Studios, 1924–51.

14. Helen Adams Keller (1880–1968). American author. Lost her sight and hearing through an illness when nineteen months old. Under the guidance of Anne Sullivan Macy she became able to speak and graduated with honors from Radcliffe College in 1904.

15. Dr. Frank Glen (1901–82). Washington University School of Medicine, interned in surgery in Rochester; Boston and New York. Surgeon-in-chief at New York Hospital in 1947.

16. Mrs. Eleanor Roosevelt had been appointed the U.S. representative on the Human Rights Commission of the United Nations.

17. Mohammad Hasan Mirza b. (born Tabriz 1900, died 1942). The last Qajar crown prince of Iran. Third son of Mohammad Ali Shah.

18. Philip K. Hitti (born Lebanon 1886, died 1978). Professor of Semitic Literature and chairman of the Department of Oriental Languages at Princeton.

19. T. Cuyler Young. Professor of Persian Language and History at Princeton. Chairman of Near Eastern Studies at Princeton, 1954–69.

20. In 1950 a commission was established to rank all senior members of the government on the bases of their honesty and competence. There were very few in A, the highest category, and many in B and some in C.

21. Dr. Maryanne Payne (1913–). B.A., M.A., PhD., M.D. Professor Cornell University Medical College.

22. Abdolhoseyn Dehqan had served as Mosaddeq's private secretary during the latter's governorship of Fars Province (1921).

23. Earl Warren (1891–1974). Attorney general of California, 1939–43; governor 1949–53; chief justice of the U.S. Supreme Court, 1953–69.

24. General Patrick Jay Hurley (1883–1963). A self-made millionaire, lawyer and oil man. Served as secretary of war 1929–33 and ambassador to China under Franklin D. Roosevelt. FDR's special envoy to Iran in 1943. Was alarmed over the growing influence of Britain and Russia in Iran.

25. Dr. J. Robert Oppenheimer (1904–67). An American physicist who headed the Manhattan Project at Los Alamos Laboratory where the first atomic bomb was developed. In 1947 he became the director of the Institute for Advanced Studies at Princeton.

26. General David Sarnoff (1891–1971) Born in Minsk and came to the United States with his family. He studied electrical engineering and became general manager of Radio Corporation of America. He pioneered many aspects of the modern communications industry.

27. Dore Schary (1905–1980). Born Newark, NJ. Producer, screenwriter and playwright. Head of MGM 1951-59.

28. Gabriel Pascal (1894–1954). Born in Transylvania. Film producer. Had the sole rights to adapt George Bernard Shaw's plays to films.

29. George Bernard Shaw (1856–1950). Born in Dublin. Major twentieth-century playwright. His most popular plays are *Candida, Major Barbara* and *Pygmalion.*

30. Cornelius Jackson. Head of the William Morris Agency.

31. Gail Patrick (1911–80). Film actress born in Alabama.

32. Ronald Charles Colman (1891–1958). Actor born in England. Academy Award for best actor in 1949.

33. Jacqueline Cochran (1906–70). One of the most important female pilots of her time. The holder of several distance, speed, and altitude records.

34. Captain Charles Yeager (1923–). A famed test pilot, whose breaking of the sound barrier is dramatized in Tom Wolfe's book *The Right Stuff.* Yeager retired from the air force in 1975 with the rank of brigadier general.

35. Eugene O'Neill (1888–1953). American playwright born in New York. Best known works: *Strange Interlude, Mourning Becomes Electra* and *Long Day's Journey into Night.* Nobel Prize for literature, 1936.

36. Aeschylus (circa 525–456 B.C.E.). Greek dramatist. Best-known plays: *The Persians, Prometheus Bound* and the trilogy *(The Oresteia): Agamemnon, The Libation Bearers,* and *The Eumenides.*

37. Morgan Shuster, a lawyer from Washington, D.C., was employed by the Iranian government in 1911 to set its finances in order. The Russians amassed troops at its borders and issued an ultimatum demanding Shuster's dismissal. *The Strangling of Persia* is Shuster's account of his experience.

JONG
Random Notes on Various Topics

This part of Dr. Ghani's memoirs is known in Persian as a jong *(or random notes on various topics). These notes were written roughly in June and July 1944, when British and Russian troops occupied Iran, vying for influence that was tantamount to control. Dr. Ghani was a recognized authority on Persian poetry, and his comments on classical authors like Khayyam, Sa'di and Hafez are regarded as significant today, more than half a century after his death. The topics of the jong evince Dr. Ghani's wide-ranging knowledge on a variety of topics. Among them are:*

1. The poetry of Iranian writers, including a poem by Hafez previously selected by the eighteenth-century ruler of Fars and adjacent provinces Karim Khan Zand for Hafez's tombstone in Shiraz.

2. "Time" as defined by Aristotle (384–22 B.C.E.). More than twenty centuries later, the French mathematician Laplace (1749–1827) and still later Jules Henri Poincaré (1854-1912) defined "time" in ways that do not differ greatly from Aristotle's definitions.

3. Arabic poetry.

4. Naturalism in nineteenth-and twentieth-century literature and the novels of Emile Zola (1840–1902) and Alphonse Daudet (1840–97).

5. Roman architecture.

6. The nature and evolution of Iranian miniature painting.

7. The "First Principles" of Herbert Spencer (1820–1903) and the essays of Ralph Waldo Emerson (1803–82).

8. Gothic art.

9. Fanaticism and bigotry in religion, politics, taste, etc.

10. Molière's (1622-73) *Tartuffe.*

11. A comparative analysis of Hafez, Sa'di and Khayyam.

12. Absurd titles and honorifics of the Qajar era.

13. Raphael (1483–1520) and Dante (1265–1321).

14. Determinism in Persian poetry.

In addition to these topics, Dr. Ghani, drawing on his remarkable command of Persian and English, commented on the translation of Hafez's odes by Gertrude Bell. Dr. Ghani's suggestions are particularly insightful in pointing out where the translator went wrong. From the 197 pages in the original Persian, we have selected the following comments. As is the case in the rest of the memoirs, the entries in the jong are dated.

SATURDAY 17 JUNE 1944

<...>

Unquestioning faith in any form of belief, be it religious, political, scientific, or in matters of taste, is a mark of shallowness. The truly intelligent never succumb to absolute certainty about anything, just as they do not deny anything absolutely. Sadly in our time there are many manifestations of blind zeal in religion, in the choice of political party or faction, and in trivial matters.

About fifteen years ago, Hajj Fazel, one of the major theologians and jurists of Mashhad, passed away at the age of eighty or perhaps more. Hajj Fazel studied illuminatist philosophy with Hajj Mirza Hasan Shirazi and the legendary Hajj Molla Hadi Sabzevari. In addition to having a superior feel for literature and a knowledge of history, Hajj Fazel was uncommonly clever and playful. His eldest son, Sheikh Hasan, abandoned the traditional clerical education to study ophthalmology in Tehran. He returned to Mashhad as Dr. Hasan Khan. Hajj Fazel's younger son studied religious law with his father and attended traditional schools. He was to be sent to Najaf for advanced theological studies, but his older brother objected, saying that it would be better if the boy went to Tehran for a modern education. Hajj Fazel said to his older son, "You have changed the course of your life, your clothes, and become a Khan, but I want your brother to succeed me." Dr. Hasan Khan said, "Father, the market for clerics is slowly drying up. By the time brother finishes his education in Najaf, people will have no use for clerics." Hajj Fazel said, "My dear son, how can you be so naïve? Do you think that the simpletons in this country will stop breeding all of a sudden? As long as people continue to lay golden eggs, there will always be rogues and cheats."

Today the situation has only changed superficially. We do not have a large group of clerics but political and social leaders who use the same old hypocritical ploys to cheat people. The poor dupes are generally not sophisticated enough to recognize the venality and corruption of their leaders. They just go on being sheep ready to be sheered. <…>

<…>

MONDAY 19 JUNE 1944

<…> *Tartuffe*, the comedy by Molière,[1] was first seen by the general public on 5 August 1667. <…> Originally consisting of three acts, the author added two others after a private performance for the king three years earlier.

The play is about a man called Tartuffe, inwardly a conniving priest, outwardly the picture of piety, who victimizes the gullible Monsieur Orgon and his mother, Madame Pernelle. After gaining Orgon's trust, Tartuffe becomes the virtual lord of Orgon's household. He contrives to marry Orgon's daughter, Mariane, and in that way become heir to all her father's property. Not satisfied with the daughter, Tartuffe even tries to seduce Orgon's wife, Elmire. After these and other misadventures, Orgon's eyes are opened to Tartuffe's true nature. He tries to regain control of his property, but on the strength of a document attesting to Tartuffe's legal possession of the house, the false priest demands that the authorities evict the Orgon family. The play ends when the king intervenes on the Orgons' behalf and sends Tartuffe to prison.

Tartuffe was first performed privately for Louis XIV on 12 May 1664. Though the king enjoyed it, others thought the play's anti-clerical content too artful for the common people, who might have trouble distinguishing true belief from hypocrisy. As a result Louis only allowed *Tartuffe* to be performed before the nobility. Finally after considerable effort including adding two acts and changing the comedy's name to *The Impostor,* Molière managed to mount the first public performance mentioned above. <...>

Molière's greatness like that of all superb writers is based on the timelessness of his writings. He had an uncanny understanding of humanity, and his comedies are subtle and exacting studies of human values, habits and foibles. <...>

<...>

Human nature is the same all over the world. We all share in varying degrees, the same base impulses: greed, pretension, hypocrisy, etc. How these manifest in people depends on the era in which they live, their social conditions and their levels of intelligence. This is also the case for positive human traits, humility, candor and honesty. As Rumi says,

The spring is one whether saline or sweet,
That feeds humans till their Maker they meet.

Individuals and nations come and go. But the one thing that is eternal is the kind of creatures we are, the mix of good and bad that forms us. The greater the intellectual and spiritual decline of a particular nation, the more fertile the ground for Tartuffes, the posers and cheats that feed on human naïveté.

Another point is that every Tartuffe conforms to the peculiarities of his time. In eleventh-century Iran, for example, when clerics and religion were held in high regard, Moslem Tartuffes appeared in clerical robes. They styled themselves defenders of all that was sacred and earned their livelihoods hypocritically prohibiting vice and promoting virtue. They so enraged Khayyam that he called the clergy of his day who traded in Islam "worse than infidels." Later when *erfan* (mysticism) became respectable, the Tartuffes of the world began to knock on the doors of the Sufi retreats, becoming the imperfect truth-seekers that made Hafez wail. <...>

Today public attention is trained on other things, issues like human rights, the rights of the oppressed. In some countries cries for economic and social justice have stirred people to action. They demand to know why there is inequality in the world. Why do large numbers suffer while others live in comfort? Why aren't the actions of the ruling classes bound by logic and fairness? These and scores of similar questions are all warranted, of course, but from the cacophony has emerged a new breed of Tartuffe, one who speaks of "protecting human rights," one who "considers the oppressed." Admittedly today there are some well-meaning people, but despite a surfeit of good intentions, their ability to reason is feeble. They embrace premises that everyone accepts, but become bogged down when they try to find solutions. <...>

<...>

MONDAY 26 JUNE 1944

<...> In general authors, whether ancient or modern, can fall into three categories: pessimists, idealists and realists. The pessimists take the measure of the world and find it an unmitigated disaster. Omar Khayyam, the mathematician, falls into this category. His writing, which is self-assured, stresses reason and logic. He spent a lifetime grappling with scientific truths but came to no conclusion about how life began or how it would end. The reason for human existence and strife remained a mystery to him, and the logic in the way the world worked always eluded him. His interest piqued, Khayyam pursued a

thousand and one questions, none of which he could answer. After all these efforts, he admits,

> *The circle that contains our coming and going*
> *Has neither beginning nor end in sight.*
> *Why this coming and why this going?*
> *No one has ever told us what is right.*

Khayyam's pessimism mocks the vain accumulation of knowledge:

> *Those who have become fonts of every learning,*
> *And among the select are like candles burning,*
> *Failing to find their way out of this deep,*
> *Call it a fairy tale and go to sleep.*

<...>

The pessimists are men of learning and scientists who spend a great deal of energy on fatiguing research that ends in their own bewilderment. In the beginning with a command of the basics, they are beguiled and avidly probe the depths of their specialties. The superficial among them, intoxicated by their command of the basics, proudly imagine that they have achieved some kind of breakthrough. But true people of learning pursue the course to its conclusion and ultimately admit that they experience a dead end and ignorance. Khayyam saw manifestations of meaninglessness and nothingness in everything. On the glories of spring, which delight every other human soul, he was moved to say:

> *This greenery that today is on view for us,*
> *Will be for whom to behold when it tops our graves?*

The questions of why nature undergoes growth and decay, why compounds form at one point only to decompose later on, and innumerable other "whys" consumed Khayyam's life. Unable to find answers satisfying to his merciless intellect, he despaired, and occasionally mocking creation's very workshop:

<...>

[The great Arab poet] Abu Ala al-Ma'arri[2] saw nothing in the world but evil and corruption, and for this reason shunned people, abhorred everything. He chose to pass his life as an ascetic. Ma'arri showed no passion for anything, never married, and considered continuing the species a crime. <...> Schopenhauer[3] thought that the most delicate feelings were based on the most trivial animal instincts. That which we term "fine emotion" he called "sexual desire"; that which sounds to our ears as the divine call of love to him appeared like the demonic howl of lust. <...>

The second group, the idealists, are by nature poets full of passion. Compared to the first group, these poets have a superficial understanding of science and are thus not burdened by its rigor. Instead they follow their feelings and intuitions. Typically they are believers, who do not allow reason or logic to intrude upon their religious views. They place philosophy and the intellect at the service of religious truth, and forgo anything that is resistant to the coloration of faith. Sa'di says that his pursuit of purity would be impossible were it not a quest for the Prophet Mohammad.

Indifferent to the constraints of reason, the idealists are, generally speaking, a contented and happy lot. Sometimes they complain of misfortune, a friend's passing or a longing for him, but they are not prey to the chronic gloom of the pessimists. Sa'di finds delight in the beauties of the fields in springtime and transmits his feelings to his readers. The origin or ultimate end of this blade of grass or that stream, or the purpose of all the variations in nature with the change of seasons does not concern him at all. A sensualist, he revels in beauty and dances in intoxication. Every line in this ode shows his euphoria:

> At dawn when night and day do not differ,
> How sweet the desert's verge and the sight of spring.
> Tell the cloistered Sufi to pitch his tent in the meadow;
> This is no time to sit at home and remain idle.
> The nightingales that cry with delight when the rose is in bloom…
> How long like the violet will your head nod in disregard?
> The shame is that while you sleep, the narcissus is wide awake…

In the end these are the words of a true believer, one supremely confident that man is the culmination of God's creation, one who thinks the entire universe is an accessory to his own exalted self. Sa'di's odes praise the Lord for the singular mercy He bestows on mankind:

> *Your bounty, Almighty God, is beyond counting;*
> *The grateful shall never thank You enough for Your gifts.*
> *You cover our misdeeds in so many layers that*
> *Were You to fault us, there would be no world.*

None of Sa'di's odes penetrates the beautiful surfaces of nature. Unlike Khayyam he does not see the horrifying sights that lurk below them. A woman's shapely body makes Khayyam think of death, the desert of annihilation; while to Sa'di her outward beauty is like "the balm of a flower garden," so intoxicating as to "make one lose his senses." The poetic sensibility of the idealists appeals to the general public because it is closer to the way they experience the world than is Khayyam's morbid introspection. People innately appreciate surface beauty but often lack the words to express their appreciation. When they read Sa'di they are charmed because he expresses their feelings with the rarest fluency and eloquence.

The third group of poets bridges the gap between the other two, meaning they are an amalgam of Khayyam and Sa'di. Their language rests on science and logic but at the same time is saturated with feeling and emotion. On one hand they are precise and insightful, while, on the other hand, they are, in every sense of the word, poets—full of passion, love and joy. Their ecstasy keeps them from lapsing into dry pedantry. As soon as they near the brink of Khayyam's pessimism, passion pulls them back. For example, Hafez perceives the same suffering and injustice in the world—and with the same acumen—that Khayyam does:

> *On the tulip bed one dawn, I asked the east wind,*
> *There are so many bloody shrouds—who are all the martyrs?*

Unlike Khayyam, however, Hafez does not descend into a depression nor does he depress his readers. The east wind immediately answers and holds him back from the nihilism of Khayyam.

Hafez, you and I are not privy to these secrets;
Tell us tales of red wine and sweet-lipped ones.

Khayyam's poetry also teaches to "be joyful," but goes no further. He himself is unhappy and often envies the uncurious, for they remain blissfully ignorant. Though Hafez does not shun introspection, his innate optimism and enthusiasm keep it from depressing him. Hafez is what Persians call a *rend*, a maverick who understands reality but does not let it weigh on his mind. Despite the many ways his poetry seems to resemble Khayyam's, careful comparison of the two makes Hafez's inherent optimism apparent. Some examples:

Speak of minstrels and wine, and search less for destiny's secret;
For no one has solved, nor will solve this puzzle with wisdom.
<...>
The sum of what is and what was is more than all of this;
Bring the wine for what makes the world is more than all of this.
For the few days we are allotted this time around,
Live well for a while, for this is not all there is to time.
We await you, O cupbearer, by the shores of this vast deep;
Take the chance, for this is not all there is between the cup and
    the mouth.
<...>

As was said, the difference between the optimism of Hafez and that of Sa'di is that Sa'di does not abandon the superficial beauties of the world, the characteristics of nature. For this reason he is joyous, and, like the nightingale, he sings deliriously and drunkenly to the rose. On the other hand, Hafez peers deeper, <...>, and perceives the worthlessness and triviality of the world. He conjures up the saddening scenes and the terrors arising from nothingness; however, his lyricism and poetic creativity prevent him from succumbing to depression. <...>

<...>

There is another class of Persian poets who have been very influential in Iranian literature and thought. These are the Sufis and the Gnostics. As a group they are all optimism and passion, forming what might be termed their own special breed of St. Francis of Assisis. They have achieved that peculiar Sufi state in which the individual makes divine bliss the governing principle of life. Figures such as Abu Sa'id Abu al-Kheyr, Farid al-Din 'Attar and Jalal al-Din Rumi consider reality "pure goodness" or "goodness pure"; that is to say, but for God they see nothing, believing that whatever exists is Him and but for Him there would be nothing. For this reason, they believe that there is no such thing as evil and that everything in existence is but a phantom, while the truth lies elsewhere. They so cultivate the self that they come to view themselves as one with God. All of Rumi's poetry is imbued with the awe and euphoria of the Sufis. <...>

FRIDAY 30 JUNE 1944

An Arab poet has said,

> *I indulge the spirit with vain hopes that elate it;*
> *Were it not for these, the compass of life would be very narrow.*

This, of course, is quite true. Hope broadens life and enriches it. But it is also a balancing of fear and expectation that can be spiritually tormenting. When the scale tips toward fear and despair, a kind of anguish results that makes life unbearable. And even if the scale tips toward hope, we still entertain nagging doubts about why we have not reached our goals in life. This awful sense of inadequacy is particularly harmful because it makes us question our own worth. It is as if unworthiness makes us begrudge ourselves the next drink of water, mouthful of food. The feeling leads us to demand with absolute certainty whether we will flourish or fail in the future—anything to escape doubt. <...>

The great comfort to mankind is in not having. I do not mean being in want, but not craving things and being tormented by how to

obtain them, or envying what others have. That type of not having is
hell. I mean not having in the sense of making the heart free of want.
This form of immateriality is the contentment of the dervish.

Hafez encapsulates the entire matter in one masterful couplet:

If there be profit in this market 'tis the dervish's;
O Lord, enrich me with his contentment and unworldliness!

Hafez had tasted everything life had to offer and, after all was said
and done, came to the dervish's bitter conclusion. <...>

But if Hafez had truly obtained everything he wanted, would he
still have craved what the dervish had? No, but is there actually a limit to human desire? Is it ever possible for us to reach the end of wanting? So the truth is as Hafez would have it. Sa'di also says, "They once
asked a dervish what his most fervent desire was. He said, 'When the
heart desires nothing.'" <...>

<...>

SATURDAY 1 JULY 1944

Scholars and critics have always recognized the centrality of meaning
in a writer's choice of words. Meaning is the soul of a literary work; it
is what profoundly moves readers and pierces their emotions. Words
that fail to convey the desired meaning are merely a series of modu-
lated sounds, nothing more.

Despite this, the sounds of words can be quite significant. The
rhythm of words has a special effect in its own right. The skilled
choice of words that sound right and go well together creates the kind
of pleasure one experiences in good music. At times, when expressed
with euphony, the most ordinary ideas leave deep and lasting impressions on readers.

Of course, writers must observe the balance between form and
meaning. Maintaining this balance, more than any taught rule or
principle of writing, depends on the writer's gifts and taste. So far as
the equilibrium between sound and meaning is concerned, one can
group the great Persian poets in three ways:

1. Among the first group, form takes precedence over meaning; that is, literary devices, the outward beauty of words, their rhythms, are superior to the meanings they convey. Their diction is exactly analogous to a woman of simple features, who adorns herself with the finest clothes, most elaborate make-up and costliest jewels. The well-known classical poets of the Turkic courts of Khorasan like Onsori (died circa 1040) and Farrokhi (died circa 1038) fall into this category, as does Sa'di in his odes.

2. The second group place content above form. Here the sublime messages of the poet exhausts the capacity of the words he chooses to convey them. As is said about Rumi, who is among the poets in this group, he tries to pour an ocean into a clay water jug. In the quatrains of Khayyam and the odes of Hafez, as well as others, especially the Gnostics, we also see how content overwhelms form.

3. The third group are the poets who maintain a balance between words and meaning. To make their points these poets avoid unnecessary complexity and multiplicity of forms. Ferdowsi's *Shahnameh* and those poems of Sa'di that people term "deceptively simple"—easy to understand but difficult to contrive. More often than not this description stems from Sa'di's keeping the balance between form and content.

Of course, these categories, being generalizations, can overlap. Most of Hafez's poetry places him in the second category; however, he occasionally writes verse that belongs in the third. But the master poets have one thing in common: however sublime or pedestrian, the language they all use is both beautiful and expressive. They are always fastidious about semantics and grammar and also attentive to the balance between word forms and meanings.

For the most part, contemporary Persian poets and prose writers are trite and commercial (except, of course, those few blessed with talent and a command of Arabic and Persian). Their writing fails to maintain the balance between form and content. <...> Without the slightest knowledge of the subject, they commit insipid things to paper that are not only offensive, but are also crimes of literature, toxic to young sensibilities. Such "authors" deride and are often hostile to the great figures of the past. With scant intellectual capital they try to establish their own "credibility" and ring in a new era of literature. But the circle of incompetents only manages to stitch a few things together. They also take turns praising and encouraging one another, and thus create a narcissistic world for themselves full of phantoms and tangled dreams.

<...>

TUESDAY 11 JULY 1944

<...>

Yesterday I was informed that there would be a seat on the plane to Beirut for Cyrus. After making the necessary preparations, I thought to ensure a blessing for the trip and to fulfill certain obligations, which are meaningful to me personally. Cyrus and I made three calls.

First, around eight, we visited Mrs. Batul Farmanfarmaian, whose son, also named Cyrus, is studying in Beirut. This extraordinarily refined and even-tempered lady showered my Cyrus with affection and gave him a gold pound coin for luck. After kissing him and having him pass under the Qur'an, Mrs. Farmanfarmaian said her goodbyes. When we were in the car, Cyrus remarked what a good woman she was, and I told him that he should become friends with his namesake in Beirut. <...>

Second, around nine, we went to Tajrish to visit Maryam Firuz (Farmanfarmaian). Whatever I say about this woman will do neither her beauty and grace nor her singular character justice. <...> She is the daughter of the late Abdolhoseyn Mirza Farmanfarma. This lady was also very affectionate toward Cyrus, and, after having him walk under the family Qur'an, she bid us farewell.

<...>

Cyrus Ghani with his father, Dr. Ghasem Ghani

Around 9:30 P.M. we visited the third person, the great and eminent historian and scholar Mohammad Qazvini. Cyrus is aware of our long scholarly collaboration. For exactly twenty years now my admiration for Qazvini's prodigious learning, meticulousness and instincts as a master textual critic has grown and grown. His firm grasp of Persian and Arabic, history, bibliography, the Qur'an and its commentaries is rare. He is also familiar with European linguistics; while his French is very good, he knows German and English as well. He has spent thirty-six of his seventy years living in London, Paris, Berlin and in Switzerland. One thing that is truly remarkable about Qazvini is that he never lets personal taste or bias cloud his scholarship. He always applies a healthy universality and skepticism to his work. When it comes to his scholarly judgment, he is inflexibly scrupulous and strict. Like Aristotle, who is said to have contradicted Plato, his teacher of twenty years, truth is his only yardstick. Qazvini is also indefatigable and adopts an extremely orderly approach to the tasks involved in historiography and textual criticism. When facing even what might be considered trivial questions, he will spend months marshalling the written sources. He is prodigious in his encouragement of other experts and scholars; but he cannot suffer fools or people without taste. At the same time, he is modest and humble.

Qazvini spoke for a few minutes to Cyrus, encouraging him in his studies and to become useful like his father. I told Cyrus to kiss his hand. Qazvini then kissed the boy's head and said goodbye. I took it as a good omen that the boy was so taken with him that it is difficult to put into words. <...>

SATURDAY 15 JULY 1944

<...>

Someone once asked Hajj Molla Hadi Sabzevari who was the greater, Jalal al-Din Rumi or Hafez? Molla Hadi begged the question, saying that he was not in a position to judge between the two masters. The questioner persisted, finally asking which of the two was further along on the path toward spiritual enlightenment? Molla Hadi replied, "As I said, it is beyond me to judge. One must refer to the poets' own words for an answer. Rumi says, 'From the very first, love was bloody and headstrong, / To escape all who approached from the outside.' While Hafez says, 'O cupbearer, fill the cup and pass the wine around, / For love seemed easy at first, but then came a thousand cares.' Rumi knew what was ahead the moment he began to probe, while Hafez thought it would be simple and only later learned of the difficulties." <...>

NOTES
JONG

1. Jean Baptiste Poquelin Molière (1622–1673). French playwright and social satirist. Best-known works: *The Misanthrope, Tartuffe, The Doctor in Spite of Himself.*
2. Abu Ala al-Ma'arri (973–1057). Arab poet born in Syria. Went blind in his youth. Author of *Ghislat al-Ghufran*, which has been compared to Dante's *Divine Comedy.*
3. Arthur Schopenhauer (1788–1860). German philosopher. Most famous work: *The World as Will and Idea.*

BIOGRAPHICAL DICTIONARY
CYRUS GHANI

The entries in this dictionary are limited to some of the Iranians mentioned in Dr. Ghassem Ghani's memoirs and diaries.

ADL, Mostafa (Mansur al-Saltaneh): b. 1882, d. 1950. From a prominent Tabriz family. Early education in Tabriz; later in Cairo and Paris where he studied law. On his return to Iran he joined the Ministry of Foreign Affairs and became consul in Tbilisi. From 1919 he served alternately at the Ministries of Foreign Affairs and Justice. In 1921 he was appointed deputy minister of justice in Seyyed Zia's Cabinet in the aftermath of the coup d'état. In 1927 at the urging of the minister, Davar, he headed a section at Justice to advise on the drafting of the Civil Code. In 1935 he moved back to the Ministry of Foreign Affairs, and between 1938 and 1941 served as minister to Berne and Rome. He briefly held the post of dean of Tehran University School of Law. From 1941 to 1945 he served in ministerial capacities in the Cabinets of Foroughi, Soheyli, Sa'ed, Bayat and Hakimi. As the most senior minister, he headed the Iranian delegation to the founding session of the United Nations in San Francisco in April 1945. Adl is best remembered for his drafting of sections of the Civil Code and his valuable textbook and commentary on the Code. An affable, quiet man who seldom strayed beyond his own area of expertise.

ADL, Professor Yahya: b. Tabriz 1908, d. 2002. Early education in Tabriz and Tehran. Medical studies in Paris, and became interne des hôpitaux. A fine surgeon whose talents were recognized in Tehran soon after he returned in 1939. He became an intimate friend and companion of Mohammad Reza Shah. He accompanied the Shah on his trips abroad and holidays in Iran. His association with the shah was cemented when he stood with him during the turbulent 1950s and in August 1953 accompanied the shah to the north for an ostensible holiday, during which the shah and Queen Soraya left Iran for Baghdad and Rome. In the late 1950s Adl was appointed head of the People's (Mardom) Party, the nominal opposition to Dr. Eqbal's National (Melliyun) Party. Appointed to the Senate for four consecutive terms. One of the few people who could speak fairly openly to the shah during the last fifteen years of his rule. Adl had a tragic personal life.

AFSHAR, Dr. Mahmud: b. 1892, d. 1983. Came from a prominent family in Yazd. As was the custom for well-to-do families from central and southern Iran, he was sent to Bombay at an early age to an English school. (From the late nineteenth century financially comfortable families from northern Iran were more likely to send their children to Russia.) Afshar returned to Iran after some three years and enrolled at the High Institute of Political Science in Tehran and later at the Dar al-Fonun (polytechnic). During the period from 1913 to 1919, studied at various Swiss colleges and in 1919 received his doctorate of law from the University of Lausanne. He had also become a fierce nationalist and political activist, who bitterly expressed his opposition to the 1919 Agreement proposed by the British in both pamphlets and public lectures. He returned to Iran in 1919 and with several like-minded friends, including Esma'il Mer'at and Ali Akbar Siasi, formed Iran Javan (Young Iran), a political activist group. He also taught at the High Institute of Political Science, the Dar al-Fonun and the Military Academy. In 1925 he founded the literary and historical journal *Ayandeh* (Future), which he edited and later turned over to his erudite son, Iraj Afshar. At the urging of Ali Akbar Davar, the then minister of justice, he accepted an appellate court judgeship. When Davar moved to the Ministry of Finance, Afshar served briefly as the head of the legal department. Second only to literature, he loved travel. An inveterate traveler, he made eight trips around the world, and it can safely be said that he visited nearly every country that existed then. Dr. Afshar is also known for his philanthropic bequests and a circle of friends that included most of the literary luminaries of his time.

AHI, Majid: b. Tehran 1886, d. 1946. Traditional schooling in Tehran. In 1907 he went to St. Petersburg where he studied law. He continued his education at Moscow University. On his return to Tehran he briefly worked as a translator at the Russian Legation. Soon afterward he entered the Ministry of Foreign Affairs. In 1915, he was appointed Commissioner for the Lianasoff Fisheries (Caviar) Concession, a post he held until 1918. At Davar's urging he transferred to the Ministry of Justice and was appointed an appellate judge (1928–33). He furthered his reputation as governor of Fars (1933–36) and minister of roads (early 1936). On completion of the Trans-Iranian Railway in 1938, he received one of the highest citations. He fell out of the shah's favor over the delay in the completion of the Tehran-Tabriz rail linkage and spent some nine months in the wilderness. Restored to favor and appointed minister of justice in the Mansur Cabinet (1940). After the invasion of Iran by Soviet and British forces in 1941, Mansur's Cabinet was dismissed. Reza Shah offered Ahi the prime ministership, which he declined. The unanimous choice of the Cabinet was Mohammad Ali Foroughi, to whose appointment Reza Shah acceded. Ahi remained as minister of justice in Foroughi's Cabinet and later Soheyli's Cabinet of 1941–42. His last appointment was that of ambassador to the USSR in August 1942. A highly capable civil servant, Ahi was esteemed by his contemporaries. He spoke excellent Russian and French. One of his daughters, Dr. Mehri Ahi, was one of the foremost Iranian scholars of Russian literature.

AHMAD SHAH: b. Tabriz 1896, d. Paris 1929. The seventh and last of the Qajar kings. He was the second son of Mohammad Ali Shah. He succeeded his father who was forced to abdicate in 1909. Because Ahmad Shah was under the legal age on his accession, the country was ruled by regents: first, by Ali Reza Khan Azod al-Molk and, later, by Abolqasem Khan Naser al-Molk. In 1914 he reached legal age. A weak individual, he was known for his greed, self-indulgence and indifference to the fate of his country. He made three trips to Europe where he felt more at home. He was no match for Reza Khan (later Reza Shah), a man of exceptional ability and strength. Ahmad Shah's reign was proof that of all forms of government, hereditary monarchies are the most uncertain, dependent upon the vagaries of biology. History records that monarchical dynasties often fail to produce heirs and successors who are capable of governing.

ALA, HOSEYN, FORMERLY ALA'I (Mo'in al-Vezareh): b. 1884, d. 1965. Son of Mohammad Ali Ala al-Saltaneh, former ambassador to London, minister of foreign affairs, and prime minister. Educated at home, then attended the prestigious Westminster public school in London. He was fluent in English and French. He joined the Ministry of Foreign Affairs in 1906 when his father was minister. He served briefly in the Cabinets of Hasan Mostowfi and Samsam al-Saltaneh (1918–19); minister to Madrid in 1918 and to Washington in 1921. Member of the fifth session of Parliament in 1925 and voted against the abolition of the Qajar dynasty, although he praised Reza Khan; minister of public works in 1927; minister to Paris in 1929; minister to London in 1934; minister of commerce in 1937; head of the National Bank; ambassador to Washington, 1945–50. He presented Iranian claims to the Security Council (1945-46) well, highlighting the case against Soviet aggression in Azerbaijan. After serving in Washington, he became minister of foreign affairs; prime minister and minister of court. Despite his loyal and steadfast service to Mohammad Reza Shah Pahlavi, he was forced to resign when he incurred the displeasure of the shah for his views on the riots of 1963. Later appointed to the Senate. A decent, well-meaning public servant, but susceptible to influence and wanting in substance.

ALAM, AMIR ASADOLLAH: b. Birjand 1919, d. 1977. Son of Mohammad Ebrahim Showkat al-Molk, hereditary amir of Birjand

and Qaenat. Elementary and secondary education in Birjand with tutors at home; later at the Agricultural College in Karaj. Married the daughter of a tribal grandee from Fars (Qavam al-Molk Shirazi) in 1939. Became an acquaintance of the crown prince, later Mohammad Reza Shah, when the latter returned from his schooling in Switzerland. First government post was governor of Sistan and Baluchestan in 1947 when he was still in his twenties. Barely thirty when he was appointed minister of interior in Sa'ed's Cabinet of 1949; later, in Rajab'ali Mansur's government he was appointed minister of agriculture. In Razmara's Cabinet he was appointed minister of labor. He became closer to the shah during the Mosaddeq era. Later he negotiated General Zahedi's resignation as prime minister. In Ala's Cabinet he served as minister without portfolio. When the shah introduced the two-party system during Dr. Eqbal's premiership, Alam formed the People's (Mardom) Party in opposition to Eqbal's National (Melliyun) Party. During these years, Alam preserved his position at the court, continuing as chamberlain at the Ministry of Court. In 1962 he resigned as head of the Pahlavi Foundation and was appointed prime minister. During his tenure as prime minister, he introduced the Six-Point Shah/People Revolution, which he put to a referendum. In 1963 he took personal charge of quelling the uprising mounted by the rebellious clergy. His usefulness as premier at an end, he was succeeded by Hasan'ali Mansur. He then became chancellor of the University of Shiraz. In 1966 he was appointed minister of court where, in effect, he exercised authority as a second prime minister. He kept this post until 1977 when illness forced him to resign. A man of utmost charm and guile, he was loyal to the shah and to his own intimate friends. Alam was decisive and courageous. He can be faulted, however, for his involvement in business transactions. His death deprived the shah of a trusted intimate at a time of crisis. Alam kept diaries illuminating his years as minister of court, the full text of which has been published in six volumes. The diaries were edited and superbly annotated by Dr. Ali Alikhani. A condensed one volume English translation came out in 1991.

ALAM, MOHAMMAD EBRAHIM (Amir Showkat al-Molk): b. Birjand c.1880, d. 1942. Son of Amir Alam Heshmat al-Molk. The family had virtually ruled the region for nearly two centuries as governors of Qaenat (with its seat in Birjand) and Sistan. He was educated at home and was well versed in Iranian literature, history and traditions. The family was very close to British officials in Afghanistan and northwestern India (now Pakistan) and remained faithful to their interests in the border regions. With the advent of Pahlavi rule and as the power of the central government grew, Alam became more mindful and cautious, demonstrating his loyalty to Reza Shah. He was awarded a high citation for his work with the Afghans on the question of an equitable division of the water rights to the Helmand River. He was appointed governor of the volatile Fars Province in 1937. In 1939 he was appointed minister of post and telegraph, a post he held for over two years. Alam was a pioneer of civic philanthropy. He established the first modern primary school in Birjand and later a secondary school, a separate girls school and a local army learning center for recruits. The family had been instrumental in heading off separatist movements in the region. Alam is remembered as the best example of the old school and the best of Iranian aristocracy. He was hospitable, generous, and an excellent raconteur, whose company was sought in every quarter. Although a believing Moslem, like most people from his stratum of Iranian society, appreciated fine wine. His love of fine carpets motivated him to establish a carpet-weaving workshop in Birjand, utilizing the Josheghan pattern and design.

AMIN al-DOWLEH, MIRZA ALI KHAN (Monshi Hozur, Amin al-Molk, Amin al-Dowleh): b. 1844, d. 1904. Son of Mohammad Khan Sinaki, a high-ranking member of the Ministry of Foreign Affairs. At age fifteen accompanied his father to Baghdad where he had been posted as envoy. Ali Khan later joined the Ministry of Foreign Affairs. He soon became a member of Naser al-Din Shah's court and accompanied the shah on his first trip to Europe in 1873. When Mozaffar al-Din assumed the throne in 1896, Amin al-Dowleh was appointed first minister. A noted reformist with liberal and constitutionalist sentiments. His grandson, Ali Amini, became prime minister in 1961.

AMINI, Dr. Ali: b. 1903, d. 1992. Fourth son of Mohsen Amini and grandson of Ali Khan Amin al-Dowleh (see previous entry). His mother, Ashraf al-Moluk (Fakhr al-Dowleh) [see following entry], was the daughter of Mozaffar al-Din Shah. Ashraf al-Moluk played a decisive role in young Ali Amini's life and nurtured his ambitions. Ali was sent briefly to Najaf for a traditional Islamic education. He then went to schools in Tehran and was tutored at home. He was sent to France where he received a doctorate of law. On his return he joined the Ministry of Justice but soon transferred to the Ministry of Finance where he was routinely promoted, reaching the rank of assistant minister and head of the customs administration. Having married Ahmad Qavam's niece (one of the daughters of Vosouq al-Dowleh), he served briefly as assistant prime minister in Qavam's Cabinet of 1942. He was subsequently elected to Parliament. He became minister of national economy in Dr. Mosaddeq's Cabinet of 1951. Amini soon resigned and, after the 1953 coup that toppled Mosaddeq, he became minister of finance in General Zahedi's Cabinet; member of the team that negotiated the new oil agreement; served briefly as minister of justice. In 1956 he was appointed ambassador to Washington, where he was regarded highly and made useful contacts with figures in the U.S. administration and Senate. He incurred the wrath of Mohammad Reza Shah and was removed when his name was linked with an unsuccessful attempt by Major General Vali Qarani to topple prime minister Manuchehr Eqbal. Amini spent some two years in political and self-imposed exile. In 1961 with the new administration of John Kennedy, Amini's name began to surface. The shah reluctantly appointed him prime minister in early 1961. Iran was in dire financial straits due to the mismanagement of previous governments. Amini's government was doomed when Washington refused to advance any economic assistance, and he could not reach an understanding with the opposition and the revived National Front. His government was a great disappointment. His Cabinet included mediocrities, some of whom he barely knew. He mounted an ill-timed anticorruption campaign, but unfortunately prosecuted the wrong people. Amini was an intelligent and shrewd politician with the right instincts and temperament. He had close contacts with various strata of society.

AMINI, Ashraf al-Moluk (Fakhr al-Dowleh), b. 1882, d. 1995. Ninth daughter of Mozaffar al-Din Shah. She married Mohsen Amin al-Molk (later Amin al-Dowleh), the son of Ali Khan Amin al-Dowleh, the famed reformist first minister of Mozaffar al-Din Shah. She bore him a daughter and several sons who achieved prominence, including the future prime minister Ali Amini. Her husband proved to be lethargic and she assumed responsibility for his large estate. She went through a complicated arbitration proceeding to retrieve ancestral lands in the Caspian region. She established the first taxi company in Tehran and two well-run primary schools. She was a remarkable lady. Reza Shah is alleged to have said the entire Qajar dynasty produced only two men: the founder of the dynasty, Aqa Mohammad Khan Qajar, who was a eunuch, and Fakhr al-Dowleh.

AMIR FARROKH, Seyyed Hadi (Salar Heshmat, later Amir Arfa'): b. 1861, d. 1950. Educated in traditional schools in Iran. He began his career as an assistant to Ebrahim Mo'tamed al-Saltaneh (father of Hasan Vosouq al-Dowleh, Ahmad Qavam al-Saltaneh and Abdollah Mo'tamed al-Saltaneh). Ebrahim Mo'tamed al-Saltaneh had served in almost all parts of Iran either as deputy governor or governor, thus Amir Farrokh became a seasoned administrator. When Qavam al-Saltaneh became governor of Khorasan, Farrokh became the equivalent of a deputy governor over a large part of the province, the seat of which was Sabzevar. He had learned how to tame the local grandees and the clergy. For a view of the way he governed and his innate intelligence, refer to the index. Amir Arfa' became a father figure for the young Dr. Ghasem Ghani.

AMIR KABIR, Mirza Taqi Khan Farahani (Amir Nezam): b. Farahan region ca. 1800, d. Kashan 1852. Gained government experience under the tutelage of Qa'em Maqam II and was sent on several diplomatic missions to Russia and Ottoman Turkey, where he visited a variety of educational, industrial and military institutions. He served as the principal advisor to Crown Prince Naser al-Din when he accompanied him from Tabriz to Tehran for the prince's coronation. The new shah appointed him first minister. Once in office he encouraged the development of the mining industry and established several small plants in Esfahan, Tehran and Sari. He reorganized the military and introduced budgetary and civil service reforms. He also initiated pioneering work in an effort to improve public health standards. One of his lasting achievements was the establishment of the first polytechnic educational institution (Dar al-Fonun) based on European models. This served as the only Iranian institution of higher learning for over half a century. His detractors and enemies, some of whom had been dismissed from court circles or had been shunned, convinced the all-powerful Queen Mother, Mahd'olia, that Mirza Taqi Khan had his eyes on the throne. He was exiled to Kashan and soon afterwards murdered at the shah's orders. A systematic planner and farsighted man of exceptional ability, he is considered the greatest statesman of nineteenth century Iran. Most historians maintain that Iran never fully recovered from the murder of Amir Kabir, which allowed foreign powers a freer hand to interfere in the country's affairs.

AMIR KHOSRAVI, MAJOR GENERAL REZAQOLI: b. probably in the Caucasus 1893, d. 1958. Joined the Cossack Brigade c. 1915. Reza Khan had taken an interest in the young officer for his pleasing personality, and his knowledge of Russian, French, and accounting. Soon he became Reza Shah's Russian interpreter and shortly thereafter the army's payroll master. In the late 1920s he was sent to Paris to study banking. He returned after a two-year course. He rose rapidly in the army and, by 1931, he was appointed managing director of the newly established Army Bank (first named the Pahlavi Bank). Subsequently, he was appointed managing director of the newly formed National Bank (Bank Melli Iran). He was promoted to Major General in 1939, and in the same year he became minister of finance. He held the post, which was probably beyond his capabilities, for nearly two years. Reza Shah gradually became disillusioned by Amir Khosravi's lack of understanding of the world economic situation. He fell into disfavor, when at a Cabinet meeting, it became clear that he was unaware that a vessel carrying part of the equipment of a steel plant purchased from Germany had been seized by the British Navy in the Arabian Sea. He was promptly dismissed. After World War II, he immigrated to the U.S. and settled in Long Island, New York.

AMUZEGAR, Dr. Jahangir: b. Tehran 1920. The eldest son of Habibollah Amuzegar from Estahban, Fars, who held ministerial rank, became senator from Fars and was one of the longest-serving judges on the Iranian Supreme Court. Jahangir attended primary and secondary school in Tehran. He received a B.A. in law from Tehran University and one in French literature from Iran's Teachers' College. In 1948 he received an M.A. in economics from the University of Washington in Seattle, and later a Ph.D. in economics from the University of California at Los Angeles in 1955. In 1956, he returned to Iran, and after a brief stint as economic advisor in the Plan Organization, he went back to the U.S. to resume his teaching. In 1960 he traveled to Tehran as a Brookings Research Professor, and later joined Dr. Ali Amini's cabinet first as minister of commerce and customs and then minister of finance. Returned to the U.S. in 1963 as ambassador-at-large and chief of the Iranian Economic Mission in Washington. Between 1973 and 1980 he simultaneously served as an Executive Director in the International Monetary Fund. In 1980-1984 he served as advisor to the IMF's Managing Director. He has taught at a number of U.S. universities including UCLA, the University of Michigan, Michigan State, American University, the University of Maryland, and Johns Hopkins. He is the author of seven books, of which the most recent are *The Dynamics of the Iranian Revolution* (1991), the most important work on the background and causes of the Islamic Revolution of 1979, *Iran's Economy under the Islamic Republic*(1993, 1997), and *Managing the Oil Wealth: OPEC's Windfalls and Shortfalls* (1999, 2001). Dr. Amuzegar is the author of some 75 articles in such scholarly magazines as *Foreign Affairs*, *Foreign Policy*, *Middle East Journal*, *Middle East Policy*, *SAIS Review*, *Social Research*, and *Washington Quarterly* on oil, OPEC, the Middle East, and Iranian affairs.

AMUZEGAR, Dr. Jamshid: b. Tehran 1923. Third son of Habibollah Amuzegar. Primary and secondary schooling in Tehran. His first three years of higher education were at Tehran University's College of Engineering. In 1944, during World War II, he set out on an arduous journey of nearly five months through South Asia and Australia, eventually reaching the East Coast of the U.S. He enrolled in Cornell University from which he graduated in 1946 with a degree in civil engineering. In 1948 he received his MS from the University of Washington in Seattle. Returned to Cornell, and in 1950 was awarded a Ph.D. in civil engineering. He returned to Iran in 1951 and worked for the U.S. Point Four Program; deputy minister of public health; 1955 minister of labor and social affairs; 1959–60 minister of agriculture; 1963 minister of public health; and 1965–74 minister of finance. One of his lasting contributions is the Direct Taxation Act of 1967. Though amended several times until 1974, the basic structure and concepts of the Act have not been altered by subsequent governments. The Act introduced two necessary and long-overdue concepts: taxation of aggregate income and a graduated income tax. The Act also differentiated methods and rates of taxation on income from various sources. After a brief stint at the Ministry of the Interior, Amuzegar was appointed prime minister in August 1977, during one of the most difficult periods in contemporary Iranian history. He resigned in September 1978 and has lived in the U.S. ever since. He is well versed in classical Persian literature.

ARAM, Gholam Abbas: b. Yazd 1899, d. 1984. Studied in local schools and later in Shiraz. Having learned some English he was employed by the British Military Police in southern Iran (an offshoot of the South Persia Rifles in World War I), which protected the transport of goods owned by British firms to and from India. Later he settled in India and worked for British concerns. In 1935 he moved to Tehran and joined the Ministry of Foreign Affairs. He was posted to London as third secretary and married an English woman. His next assignments were to Berne and in 1949 Washington, D.C., as first secretary. Returned to Tehran in 1954; 1956 counselor at

Iranian Embassy, Baghdad; 1956 ambassador to Japan; minister of foreign affairs in several governments beginning with Dr. Eqbal's Cabinet of 1959 and the cabinets of Amini, Alam, Mansur and Hoveyda; 1966–70 ambassador to Great Britain; 1974 ambassador to China. Aram owed his early rise to Hoseyn Ala's sponsorship and later to a knack of anticipating Mohammad Reza Shah's wishes. A cautious and capable functionary, he was unfailingly obedient to the dictates of the monarch.

ARDALAN, DR. ALIQOLI: b. ca.1901, d. 1986. Born to a well established and prominent family of Kurdestan. Studied in Tehran and later in Germany where he received a doctorate of law. In 1924 he joined the Ministry of Foreign Affairs. In 1929 he transferred to the Ministry of Justice for a brief period. Served as third and second secretary in Washington, later as counselor in Paris and Ankara. In 1949 was assistant minister of foreign affairs; 1955 Ambassador to the UN; later that year minister without portfolio in Ala's Cabinet; still later minister of industry and mines; then minister of foreign affairs. He was made ambassador to the U.S. in 1958. He was appointed successively ambassador to the USSR and West Germany; then retired. In 1977, after Hoveyda's resignation as minister of court, he was persuaded to succeed him in that very difficult position. He performed his tasks with great dignity. After the revolution of 1979, he was imprisoned by the Islamic regime for several years. An affable and capable diplomat, he performed very well under pressure.

ARYA, ABBAS: b. Kashan 1891, d. 1946. He studied in local schools and entered government service ca. 1929. He soon became known for his judgement and good sense and was consulted by high-ranking government officials, including military commanders in the field (e.g., Major General Habibollah Shaybani). Having attained considerable experience in private construction projects, he came to the attention of Reza Shah who appointed him director general of the Ministry of Public Works and later deputy minister of roads. He played an important part in the completion of the Trans-Iranian Railway. Falsely accused of accepting bribes, he was soon exonerated. Nevertheless, he resigned from government service and returned to his former construction business. He became a noted philanthropist and helped several great scholars, most notably the impoverished Mohammad Qazvini and Abbas Eqbal. He was held in the highest esteem by all who knew him, among whom were the Saleh family of Kashan, Seyyed Hasan Taqizadeh, Mohammad Ali Farzin and Dr. Ghasem Ghani. The late Alahyar Saleh often invoked Arya's name as the personification of integrity and honesty.

ASADI, Mohammad Vali (Mesbah al-Saltaneh): b. 1878, d. 1935. Worked as administrator and steward of Mohammad Ebrahim Alam (Amir Showkat al-Molk), whose ancestors had been in effect undisputed rulers of Qaenat and Sistan. In time, Asadi himself became a substantial landowner. Showkat al-Molk had Asadi elected to the fourth session of Parliament from Birjand. Asadi actively supported Reza Khan and the overthrow of the Qajar dynasty. He was also elected to the fifth and sixth sessions of Parliament. With the support of Teimurtash, he was appointed to one of the most prestigious and powerful positions, custodian of the Imam Reza Shrine and its vast endowments. Two of Asadi's sons married prime minister Foroughi's daughters. In 1935, a fateful year for Asadi, the shah issued a directive that men were to wear the Pahlavi hat in public. This directive prefigured another that banned the veil for women in public. Asadi believed that the ban was premature and would provoke reactions by the clergy and the masses. A senior ayatollah (Hoseyn Qommi) was sent to Tehran to mediate; however rumors of Ayatollah Qommi's arrest sparked riots. Efforts to pacify the people were ineffective. The army was called in and several hundred people were killed or wounded. Asadi was charged with conspiracy and dereliction of duty and, after a summary trial, was executed. He had falsely believed that his proximity to Reza Shah would spare him. Asadi was a highly intelligent, self-made man. His execution ended a promising public career.

ATABAK MIRZA ALI ASGHAR KHAN (Saheb Jam', Amin al-Molk, Amin al-Soltan, Atabak A'zam): b. ca. 1858, d. 1907. Son of Ebrahim Amin al-Soltan, Naser al-Din Shah's favorite butler, who had risen to become the shah's minister of court. On Ali Asghar's father's death in 1882, he was given his father's title Amin al-Soltan and became minister of court. He was later dubbed the seldom-granted honorific title of Atabak by Naser al-Din Shah. He also served as First minister under Mozaffar al-Din Shah, and briefly, under Mohammad Ali Shah. He was an efficient administrator and made certain that government coffers were always full. Naser al-Din Shah's third and last trip to Europe in 1888 created the need for funds. With the full approval of the shah he sold various concessions to British companies and nationals. These included the rights to shipping on the Karun River, mining concessions and the tobacco monopoly. In reaction to the wholesale auctioning of Iran's assets, the clergy encouraged a prohibition of tobacco use. To balance the scales, Atabak granted Russian companies a concession for navigation on rivers that empty into the Caspian Sea. Atabak was a highly intelligent and resourceful politician, but in pleasing the shah he had essentially mortgaged the country to foreign interests. As is usual with men of Atabak's influence, he made many enemies. He was assassinated by an anarchist in 1907.

AYN al-DOWLEH, SOLTAN ABDOL MAJID MIRZA: b. 1846, d. 1927. A grandson of Fath Ali Shah, he became close to Mozaffar al-Din Shah (r. 1896–1907) when the latter was heir to the throne. He was appointed first minister and held the office from 1903 to the end of 1905. His autocratic ways and dismissal of the demands of Constitutionalists led to civil unrest, which forced the shah to remove him. He became prime minister again for brief periods during the occupation of neutral Iran in World War I (1915 and 1917). An authoritarian figure to whom constitutional government was anathema.

AZODI, YADOLLAH (AMIR A'ZAM): b. Tehran c. 1890, d. ca. 1963. Son of Nosratollah Amir A'zam, grandson of Vajihollah Mirza, Sepahsalar, and great-grandson of Fath Ali Shah. Scion of grandees from Shahrud and Damghan who held vast estates for more than a century. He was educated in Tehran and, for a brief period, in Istanbul. He also spent a few years in Europe. After his father was murdered in a local dispute, his uncle, Ayn al-Dowleh, used his influence as first minister to have Azodi appointed governor of Shahrud, Semnan, and Damghan. He was given the title Amir A'zam. For a brief period his governorship included Gorgan Province. He married the daughter of Hasan Pirnia (Moshir al-Dowleh), who died within a few years. He later married the third daughter of Vosouq al-Dowleh, Turan, a highly intelligent and forceful woman who became his principal guide and advisor. His vast estate, which had been run down, was restored, and his finances were put in order. He entered the Ministry of Foreign Affairs in the early 1920s. In 1932 he was counselor at the Iranian Embassy in Washington and, in the ambassador's absence, served as chargé d'affaires; 1933 minister in Warsaw; then minister in Berlin. On his return to Iran he joined the Ministry of Finance under Allahyar Saleh as deputy head of the Opium Monopoly; 1941 deputy minister of roads in Qavam's Cabinet; 1944 minister to Brazil and accredited to several South American countries; minister to Spain; 1960 ambassador to Iraq; late 1960 minister of foreign affairs in Sharif Emami's Cabinet. Spoke French, German, and some English. A person of great charm.

BAHAR, MOHAMMAD TAQI (Malek al-Sho'ara): b. 1886, d. 1951. Probably the greatest Iranian poet of the twentieth century. He was also an important historian of Persian literature; his study of the evolution of *Sabkshenasi* (Persian prose style) is still one of the basic texts on the subject. His poetry is an amalgam of classical Persian poetry and modernist verse. Bahar was also a political activist and agitator, a journalist and pamphleteer. Some of his poetry has contemporary themes and is infused with strong political overtones. He was a polemicist who wrote sharp political barbs, and was jailed and put under house arrest several times. Bahar's journalism and pamphlets were strongly supportive of the constitutionalist cause. He became a professor of Tehran University from 1934 onward. He formed a political party (Democrat) in Mashhad. Served in the third and sixth sessions of Parliament; years later elected from Mashhad to the turbulent fifteenth session (1945–46); minister of education for a brief period in Qavam's Cabinet of 1945-6. Some of his poems are humorous pieces, and he also wrote some charming verse in the Mashhadi dialect.

BAYAT, Mortezaqoli (Saham al-Soltan): b. 1887, d. 1955. Came from a wealthy land-owning family of Araq with close connections to several prominent families, including the Mosaddeq and Vosouq families. He was a member of Parliament from the fifth to the tenth sessions and, on occasion, served as deputy speaker. He also held several ministerial positions. Became prime minister for a brief period, November 1944 to April 1945, as a compromise candidate. During the Soviet political interference, he served as governor of Azerbaijan; 1949 member of the first Senate; 1953–55 managing director and chairman of the board of directors of the National Iranian Oil Company. An affable man of leisure who left no distinct mark.

DAFTARI, Dr. Ali Akbar: b. 1900, d. 1947. Younger brother of Dr. Ahmad Matin Daftari; grandson of Mirza Hoseyn Vazir Daftar. Close relative of the Mostowfi and Mosaddeq families. Secondary education, Iran-German school. Doctorate of law from Berlin. Began career at Ministry of Public Works; then joined the Ministry of Foreign Affairs with a short stint at the Ministry of Justice under Davar; then back to Foreign Affairs; 1931 served in Washington; Berlin; Kabul; and in 1945 again in Washington as counselor. Spoke German, French and English. Read widely and was knowledgeable in international affairs. Died unexpectedly of a heart attack.

DARVISH, Abdolmajid (Taleqani): b. 1737, d. 1771. As Mir Emad Qazvini is generally accepted as the master of *nasta'liq* calligraphy, Darvish is the unsurpassed master of Shekasteh. Darvish trained a number of calligraphers, the most notable being Mirza Kuchek Esfahani. Darvish also dabbled in poetry under the pen name of Majid and Khamush. More than 1,500 verses by him have been identified.

DARVISH, Gholamhoseyn: b. Tehran 1872, d. 1926. His adopted surname derives from his father's habit of calling close friends "*darvish*" (mendicant). Studied the tar and setar (stringed instruments) with Aqa Hoseynqoli, the foremost tar master of the era. Darvish became a court musician and trained several others who went on to become masters, most notably Abolhasan Saba. Darvish, who sided with the constitutionalists, joined the government in exile in Kermanshah. In addition to being the greatest instrumentalist of his time, Darvish composed a large number of pieces for the tar. He experimented with the five-string instrument by adding a sixth string, giving it more resonance and variety. He traveled to London and Tbilisi and recorded some of his compositions; however, very few of these recordings remain. Most of his early compositions were tracked down and transcribed by the musicologist Colonel Alinaqi Vaziri.

DASHTI, Ali: b. Karbala 1896, d. 1981. Came from a clerical family. Educated in theological seminaries in Iraq. Made a name for himself by his vehement support of the 1919 Agreement but soon changed his mind. In 1922 he began publishing the newspaper *Shafaq-e Sorkh* (Red Twilight). A pen for hire, he began a series of articles castigating Ahmad Shah and became a spokesman for the republican cause. He also became a supporter of Reza Khan and was elected to the fifth session of Parliament. His credentials were vetoed by his colleagues for his past attempts at extortion and blackmail. He was, however, elected to the sixth through the eighth sessions of Parliament. After having fallen out of favor for a few years, he was appointed head of the censorship department in the Ministry of the Interior and the Police Department in 1937. After the abdication of Reza Shah in 1941, he was the first deputy to suggest, in a vituperative address, that the former shah not be allowed to leave Iran until he had given a detailed account of his wealth. He was appointed ambassador to Egypt; then appointed senator for several terms. He was minister without portfolio in Ala's government of 1951 and ambassador to Lebanon in 1962. Dashti was a popular writer. He was very witty but could also be quite vulgar in social encounters. Though not considered a literary scholar, he wrote several highly readable books on Iranian poets and an autobiography. One of his last works, *Twenty-Three Years*, a biography of the Prophet Mohammad, led to his arrest and torture at the hands of the Islamic regime.

DAVAR, Ali Akbar: b. 1885, d. 1937. The son of a minor court official. Karbala Ali Khan Khazen al-Khalvat who served as custodian of the family quarters of Mozaffar al-Din Shah. Due to his position, he was able to get his son Ali Akbar admitted to the Dar al-Fonun in 1900. Davar studied law and graduated in 1908. He joined the Ministry of Justice as a judge on the provincial court. By 1910 he had become the public prosecutor of Tehran. He worked briefly for a newly established newspaper *Sharq* (The East), which was edited by an ambitious neophyte, Seyyed Zia (al-Din). Davar criticized the government in his articles and supported the program of the Democrat Party members in Parliament. In 1910 Davar volunteered to supervise two young sons of a wealthy Tabriz merchant, Hajj Ebrahim (Panahi), who were on their way to study in Switzerland. After perfecting his French, Davar entered the University of Geneva where in 1914 he received a post-graduate degree. Davar chose to remain in Switzerland during World War I. After the war, he campaigned for Iran's representation at the Paris Peace Conference and advocated the right of Iran's representative to be heard regarding the material damages the country suffered at the hands of British, Russian and Ottoman forces. He also formed an activist committee against the 1919 Agreement proposed by the British.

Davar returned to Iran in 1921 without having received his doctorate but having immersed himself in Western literature of social change. In January 1923 he started the newspaper *Mard-e Azad* (The Free Man) and soon thereafter founded the Radical Party, which attracted hundreds of young Iranians. The party members were mostly reformists and modernizers. Young Iranians read the newspaper, especially its editorials, which were filled with taunts against the entrenched establishment. These editorials also maintained that rapid progress in Iran was a possibility in a relatively short period of time. Davar married Nur al-Dowleh, the widowed daughter of Sheikh Mohsen Khan Moshir al-Dowleh. Through the influence of his wife's family, Davar was elected to Parliament from Varamin, a farming district not far from Tehran. Once in Parliament he grew close to Teimurtash and Firuz, leading modernists of their era. Davar was one of the key sponsors of a bill to transfer the powers of the commander in chief of the armed forces from Ahmad Shah to the office of the prime minister. He was also one of the early proponents of a law to change the royal dynasty. After Reza Shah's coronation, Davar resigned his seat in Parliament and was appointed minister of public works. He demonstrated his skills by drafting enabling legislation for the construction of the Trans-Iranian Railway and for the establishment of the School of Commerce. In February 1927, having shown organizational ability and boundless energy, he was appointed minister of justice. He revamped the judiciary and established several committees of the learned jurists of the day to draft Civil Code. Five years (1927–32) of work resulted in a marvel of draftsmanship, which survives today except for amendments passed by the present rulers of Iran on the legal age of marriage. In March 1933 Davar headed a four-member Iranian delegation to the League of Nations at Geneva where he defended Iran's right to cancel the inequitable 1901 Oil Agreement. Davar was appointed minister of finance in September 1933. His contribution at Finance was the establishment of several government monopolies for international trade and barter. These would last until such time as Iran had a middle class with sufficient wealth to handle international trade and commerce.

After Reza Shah had assumed the throne, most expected that it would only be a matter of time before Davar became prime minister. At the outset Reza Shah turned to Foroughi, then Hedayat and then to Foroughi once more—both predictable statesmen. Davar was further disappointed when Foroughi was dismissed and Jam succeeded him. He then knew that the shah would never select him as prime minister. Reza Shah expected miracles from Davar while he continued at Finance. The sheer strain of twelve years of overwork and Reza Shah's ever-increasing demands and taunts caused Davar to commit suicide on 10 February 1937.

After his first wife's death in 1931, Davar married Mehranvar Shabahang. He had three children, a daughter from his first marriage and two sons from the second. Davar was one of the great figures of twentieth-century Iran.

DEHKHODA, ALI AKBAR: b. Tehran 1879, d. 1955. Studied at the Political Science School under the supervision of Mohammad Hoseyn Foroughi (Zoka al-Molk I), the father of Mohammad Ali Foroughi (Zoka al-Molk II); later studied with the renowned jurist and theologian Sheikh Hadi Najmabadi. Spent some two years in Europe, primarily Vienna, and learned German. He later accompanied Mo'aven al-Dowleh I (Ghaffari) to the Balkans, which sharpened his interest in etymology. In other trips abroad he acquired greater sympathy for governments that are responsive to their people's needs. On his return to Iran he threw in his lot with the constitutionalists and started the newspaper *Sur-e Esrafil* (Gabriel's Trumpet), which was backed by friends who thought as he did. Dehkhoda's contributions to the paper under the heading *Charand va Parand* (Prattle 'n Rattle) were the most interesting. These pieces mocked the ruling order of the day. The authorities soon stopped the publication, and Dehkhoda together with other rebellious thinkers, including Seyyed Hasan Taqizadeh, sought refuge at the British Legation. Dehkhoda was able to flee to Switzerland, where he learned some French. After Mohammad Ali Shah's ouster in 1909, he returned to Tehran. He was elected from Kerman to the second session of Parliament. Later he had some secondary jobs at the Ministry of Education and briefly at the Ministry of Justice. He taught for a short time at the Political Science School and, in the mid-1930s, became dean of the School of Law at Tehran University. He then embarked on his magnum opus: the *Loghatnameh*, an encyclopedic dictionary of Persian and Arab culture, language, literature, history, geography, cosmology and philosophy. Besides the *Loghatnameh*, he was the author of several other works on Iranian language and culture. He was one of the original members of the "wise and learned" men who held weekly, informal gatherings with Mohammad Reza Shah to acquaint the young shah with various aspects of Iranian history and culture. Dehkhoda maintained close relationships with people from a wide spectrum of Iranian society. Before his death, Dehkhoda appointed Dr. Mohammad Mo'in, a noted scholar, as chief editor of the *Loghatnameh*.

DEHQAN, ABDOLHOSEYN: b. 1898, d. 1990. Son of Mohammad Baqer Khan, a landowner who became the head steward and administrator for the vast properties of Qavam al-Molk Shirazi. Over the years the family prospered and became the owners of a large estate in Shiraz. Dehqan was first educated at the Tarbiat School and then, with his two brothers, was sent to Beirut. There he and Dr. Ghani formed a close friendship, which lasted their entire lives. Abdol Hoseyn Khan received his B.A. from the American University in Beirut and spent 1927–8 in Paris. Members of the Dehqan family were known for their integrity. Dehqan served briefly as special assistant to Dr. Mosaddeq when he was governor of Fars in 1921. Their friendship continued into the late 1950s.

EBTEHAJ, ABOLHASAN: b. Rasht 1900, d. 1998. Second son of Ebtehaj al-Molk. Studied in Rasht, Beirut and, briefly, Paris. Father was murdered by thugs. Ebtehaj began his career c. 1920 as an interpreter for British troops in Gilan, who were trying to oust Russian Bolshevik forces in the region. Joined the British-owned and operated Imperial Bank of Persia circa 1920; was transferred to Tehran in 1925 and promoted to chief inspector. Dissatisfied because Iranian employees at the bank were considered second rank, he resigned in 1936; headed the Mortgage Bank; 1938 became government inspector at Bank Melli (National Bank) and in 1942 its governor; 1944–45, Iran's representative to the Breton Woods Monetary Conference. Negotiated with the Imperial Bank and was able to reduce the period of the British bank concession by two years. He argued that the original concession was based on the lunar year and thus 600 days shorter than it would have been had it been based on the solar calendar. Removed from office in 1950; appointed ambassador to France in 1952. Worked for the International Monetary Fund in Washington. Late in 1954 appointed Head of the Plan Organization. Initiated several vital economic development projects, most of which came to fruition in the 1960s and 1970s. Lost the confidence of the shah as he opposed the burdensome military expenditures and was forced to resign in 1959. Imprisoned by the Amini government on ludicrous charges. Upon his release he went into private banking, founding the Iranians' Bank with City Bank of New York as a minority shareholder. One of the most forceful and principled public servants of the Pahlavi era, he was the father and engine of vital economic projects. Ebtehaj's brothers were also prominent. Golamhoseyn Ebtehaj was one of the first heads of the Tourist Organization, Tehran's mayor and a sponsor of a national airline. His younger brother, Ahmad Ali, was a successful contractor/consulting engineer and industrialist.

ENTEZAM, ABDOLLAH (formerly Entezam Vaziri): b. Tehran 1896, d. 1993. Son of Entezam al-Saltaneh and nephew of Hasan Ali Ghaffari Mo'aven al-Dowleh. Studied in Iran. Entered Ministry of Foreign Affairs. His first postings were to Washington, Berne, Warsaw and Prague. While in the US, he married an American and had two children, a daughter and a son, Hume Horan, who later became U.S. ambassador to Saudi Arabia. In late 1945, early 1946, he reopened the Iranian diplomatic mission in Germany; 1946 minister to Warsaw. In

1955 minister of foreign affairs in Ala's Cabinet while also being designated deputy prime minister. After the death of Bayat, Entezam became managing director and chairman of the board of the National Iranian Oil Company (NIOC) 1957–63. He incurred the shah's displeasure by urging a conciliatory policy toward the clergy in the uprising of June 1963. He lived in obscurity, but found happiness in his second marriage to a like-minded Iranian. In 1978 the shah pleaded with him to become prime minister. He refused but accepted the post of NIOC chairman. Entezam was a soft-spoken, literate, and principled man who, in his later years, became a devotee of Jalal al-Din Rumi.

ENTEZAM, NASROLLAH: b. 1900, d. 1981. Younger brother of Abdollah Entezam, the previous entry. Studied in Tehran. Joined the Ministry of Foreign Affairs. Served in London and Berne. In 1933 secretary of the Iranian delegation to the League of Nations headed by Davar that was charged with negotiating Iran's oil dispute with Britain. In 1941 Entezam became chief of protocol at the Ministry of Court. Was minister of health, roads and foreign affairs. Member of delegation for the founding of the UN in San Francisco 1945; representative on the UN commission for Palestine 1947; ambassador to the UN, Washington, London, Paris. After retirement he wrote a segment of his memoirs that contains an invaluable section on several key figures in contemporary Iranian history, notably Mostowfi, Davar, and Hoseyn Ala. A charming and dapper man, recognized as a seasoned and respected diplomat.

EQBAL, DR. MANUCHEHR: b. Mashhad 1909, d. 1977. Son of Abu Torab Eqbal. Educated in Mashhad and Tehran. Sent to Paris in 1927 to study medicine. He returned in 1933 and worked for the military medical corps. He later established a private practice while teaching at Tehran University Medical School. His eldest brother, Ali Eqbal, who was a member of Parliament from Mashhad for several terms, introduced him to political figures of the day and greatly assisted his career. Dr. Eqbal gained access to the court of young Mohammad

Reza Shah. By 1942 he was appointed undersecretary of the Ministry of Health in Ahmad Qavam's Cabinet. In 1945, again in a Qavam Cabinet, he became minister of health. Thereafter he rose rapidly in the cabinets of Sa'ed and Hazhir, becoming minister of education, roads, and governor of Azerbaijan. In 1953 he became senator; 1955 chancellor of Tehran University, while serving as minister of court; 1957 prime minister. Political unrest led to his resignation, and he left Iran. He was appointed ambassador to UNESCO and in 1963 chairman of the board and managing director of NIOC, a position he held until his death. Appointed head of a political party (the National or Melliyun Party). He was blindly loyal to the shah, who began to ignore him in later years. He presided over NIOC when the Iranian oil industry reached its highest level of production and income. However, though personally honest, the most egregious instances of corruption occurred during his tenure. Stiff, arrogant, and aloof during the latter part of his career, he had some personal charm and was loyal to his friends and mentors.

EQBAL ASHTIANI, Abbas: b. Ashtian 1896, d. 1955. Born to a destitute family, but through sheer determination and sacrifice received a primary and some secondary education. (For almost a century the Ashtian region had one of the highest literacy rates in Iran.) He then came to Tehran and studied at the Dar al-Fonun. In 1925, with some knowledge of French, he became secretary for a group of Iranian army officers traveling to Paris to study at  military schools. While there, he received a degree at the Sorbonne. During his time in Paris, he scoured the oriental sections of all major libraries taking copious notes on rare manuscripts. He met the great scholar Mohammad Qazvini who had been living in Paris for some time. Dr. Ghani and Eqbal met with Qazvini twice a week for free-ranging conversations during which they benefited from Qazvini's erudition. After returning to Iran, Eqbal taught at the Dar al-Fonun. In 1942 Eqbal, Qazvini and Dr. Ghani published the quarterly *Yadegar* (Memento), which covered a range of literary and historical topics that were mostly written by Eqbal. Eqbal's major work is *Tarikh-e Moghol* (History of the Mongols). He is also responsible, with some assistance from Dr. Ghani, for a nearly complete biography of Amir Kabir (it was edited by Iraj Afshar and published posthumously). There are some twenty other works, mostly textbooks and a considerable number of articles. His dire financial situation forced him to serve as cultural attaché in Ankara and Rome. Never fully appreciated during his lifetime, he was virtually ignored by the then Iranian ambassador in Rome. Eqbal was one of the foremost scholars of Persian and the foremost historian of Iran in the modern era.

ESFANDIARI, Hasan (Hajj Mohtashem al-Saltaneh): b. ca. 1865, d. 1944. Came from a prominent family with roots in both northern and southern Iran. His grandfather had served as private secretary to Abbas Mirza, the heir to the throne. His father had been a fixture at the Ministry of Foreign Affairs and from its inception served as permanent undersecretary for nearly two decades. After Esfandiari joined the ministry in 1885, he was sent as a member of the Iranian delegation to Berlin circa 1889, where he met Otto von Bismarck; 1895 consul in Bombay; 1897 undersecretary

of the Ministry of Foreign Affairs; 1905 accompanied Mozaffar al-Din Shah to Europe; 1901 minister of justice; 1911 minister of foreign affairs; 1912 to 1917 he alternated between being minister of foreign affairs and minister of finance; and then governor of Azerbaijan. He opposed the British and Russian occupation during World War I, and when he objected to the 1919 Agreement, he was exiled to Kashan for a year. When the Vosouq government fell, he became minister of education 1922–23; 1926–29 finance; from 1930 a member of Parliament; and 1935–42 speaker of Parliament. He played a key role in persuading Parliament to ratify the tripartite treaty between Iran, Great Britain and the Soviet Union. The agreement laid the foundation for the withdrawal of the occupying forces from Iran at the end of World War II. Well read, he was the author of several treatises on law and ethics. He was a decent and respected figure who was helpful to his constituents and trusted by his peers. He was a superb master of the art of calligraphy.

ESKANDARI, Soleyman Mirza: b. c.1873, d. 1943. His great grandfather was a son of Fath Ali Shah. He was probably educated by tutors at home. Worked briefly with the police and, later, in the customs administration. In 1906 he was elected to the second session of Parliament and reelected to the third through the fifth sessions. In the second Parliament he gained adherents and prominence when he voted to reject the tsarist ultimatum demanding the dismissal of the American financial advisor Morgan Shuster who had put the Iranian fiscal situation in some sort of order and saved the country from bankruptcy. Eskandari was exiled to Qom by the regent Naser al-Molk. After his exile, he was elected to the third session of Parliament but was forced to flee to Baghdad and later to Istanbul as he opposed the British and Russian occupation of Iran during World War I. He returned to Iran in 1917 and began to incite tribes in the south to hamper British forces. The British arrested and exiled him to India. He was allowed to return and immediately campaigned for a seat in Parliament. He was elected to the fourth session and the fifth. He became close to Reza Khan and fought for the abolition of the Qajar dynasty. While in Parliament, Eskandari headed the Socialist bloc. Despite his support of Reza Khan as prime minister and later as shah, the king never took Eskandari seriously. While other socialists occupied ministerial posts, he was ignored. During the period 1923–24, he worked at the Ministry of Education but was ill suited for it. In October 1927, the tenth anniversary of the Russian Revolution, Eskandari was sent to Moscow in a semiofficial capacity. He lingered in Europe for a time but, financially pressed, returned to Tehran in the late 1930s where he opened a grocery store. In 1941 after the Russian and British occupation of Iran and Reza Shah's abdication, he was elected chairman of the newly formed Tudeh (Communist) Party. He was aging by this time and was assisted by his nephew Iraj Eskandari (who later became the head of the Party). Soleyman Mirza had little formal education, but he was a compelling orator. He possessed an excellent temperament but a mediocre mind. In Iran he was an anomalous combination: socialist, prince and communist.

FARHAD MO'TAMED, Dr. Ahmad: b. 1902, d. ca.1971. Son of Abdol Hoseyn Moshir Akram and great-grandson of Farhad Mirza Mo'tamed al-Dowleh, a learned Qajar prince. Early education was in Tehran; later in Germany he received a degree in medicine, with a specialization in radiology. He was professor at Tehran University and the most renowned radiologist in Iran. He became chancellor of the university. He was one of the few university chancellors who objected to government surveillance of student activities.  He survived government pressure for nearly six years but eventually resigned. A well-traveled man with an interest in the arts.

FARMANFARMAIAN, Cyrus: b. Tehran 1929. Son of Abdolhoseyn Mirza Farmanfarma, former governor of several provinces, prime minister and one of the most prominent political figures of late nineteenth century and early twentieth century Iran. Primary school in Tehran; secondary schooling in Beirut and London. B.S. and M.S. in mathematics and physics, University of Colorado. Managing director of Pasteurized Milk Company of Abadan; later managing director of Pars Oil Company while serving on the boards of directors of several other industrial enterprises. Author of *Vector Analysis;* taught physics at National (Melli) University. Translated nine textbooks from English into Persian, some written by Nobel Prize winners in mathematics and physics, including *Higher Mathematics* by E. S. Sokolnikoff; *Atomic Physics* by Henry Swat; and *Dreams of a Final Theory* by Steven Weinberg. After the Islamic Revolution, he showed great strength and resolution in assisting some members of his family and many friends under trying circumstances.

FARMANFARMAIAN, Khodadad: b. Tehran 1928. Son of Abdolhoseyn Mirza Farmanfarma. Elementary education in Iran; secondary education in Beirut; B.A. and M.A. in economics, Stanford University, and Ph.D. University of Colorado. From 1952 to 1958 instructor in economics at the University of Colorado and Brown University; 1955–58 university fellow at Harvard; 1958 lecturer at Princeton; 1958–60 head of Economic Bureau and later deputy managing director of Plan Organization for Economics and Finance; 1958–66 lecturer at Tehran University; 1964–68 deputy governor of Central Bank of Iran; 1968–70 governor of Central Bank; 1970–73 managing director of Plan and Budget Organization of Iran; 1973–79 chairman of the board of a private bank. After the Islamic Revolution, 1981–84 adjunct professor at the Fletcher School of Law and Diplomacy; 1984 to present chairman of Amas Bank in London. He was instrumental in bringing back to Iran numerous Iranians who were pursuing careers in the U.S.

FARZIN, Mohammad Ali: b. ca. 1878, d. 1942. Son of Mirza Masih Esfahani. He was educated in Tehran. Because early in his career he worked at the European Club, he became known as Mohammad Ali "Kolub." Farzin worked in various regional finance departments.

Elected to the third Parliament in 1914. During World War I he, along with many nationalists of the day, left Tehran for Kermanshah in opposition to the Russian and British occupying forces in Iran. He was appointed minister of finance of the Government in Exile headed by Nezam al-Saltaneh Ma'afi. Later he traveled to Berlin and joined a group of like-minded Iranian exiles. He was instrumental in raising funds for a new expatriate Persian journal *Kaveh,* which became an effective vehicle for exposing British and Russian machinations in Iran. Returned to Iran circa 1922 and was appointed undersecretary of finance; 1924–28 minister of finance; 1929 ambassador to Kabul but did not go to Afghanistan because of an impending revolution; 1929 acting minister of foreign affairs and, later the same year, minister of finance; 1930 minister to Germany, but recalled as Reza Shah was upset with articles appearing in a Munich newspaper; 1933 member of the board of directors of the National Bank (Bank Melli) and governor of the National Bank in 1939. After Reza Shah's abdication, he was appointed minister of court in September 1941. His task was made more difficult as he remained in disfavor with the British Legation. His home was the center for a group of cultured figures that met regularly once or twice a week; among them were Mohammad Ali Foroughi, Colonel Alinaqi Vaziri, Dr. Ghani and, after he returned from Europe, Mohammad Qazvini. Farzin was a literate man who had studied most Iranian poets in some depth. A man of charm and good will, he was highly respected for his discretion, probity and sense of humor.

FAYYAZ, Dr. Ali Akbar: b. 1898, d. 1971. Father was a noted clergyman. Fayyaz had studied in a seminary intending to pursue a clerical path; but he changed course and entered government service as an assistant administrator of the Imam Reza Shrine in Mashhad. Studied at Tehran University. He collaborated with Dr. Ghani in a revised and annotated edition of one of the most important histories of medieval Iran *Tarikh-e Beyhaqi* (The History of Ghaznavid Kings). He served for one term as Member of Parliament. He was invited to teach for a brief period at al-Azhar University in Cairo; later taught at the University of

Mashhad; and published several works on medieval Iran. Dr. Fayyaz wrote a moving eulogy on the occasion of Dr. Ghani's death.

FOROUGHI, MOHAMMAD ALI (Zoka al-Molk II): b. 1873, d. 1942. The son of the learned Zoka al-Molk I, who had been in government service during the rule of Naser al-Din Shah. In 1907, after the death of his father, the title Zoka al-Molk was conferred on Mohammad Ali. He began his career as the editor of *Tarbiat* (Education), a journal his father founded. In 1906 he joined the semisecret group Jame'eh-ye Adamiat (The Humanist Society), which had been active in the constitutional movement. The society was disbanded with the shelling of Parliament in 1908. Soon afterward Foroughi with some Iranian notables and some French expatriates working in Iran formed the first official Freemason lodge in Iran. The lodge continued to support the constitutionalist cause and soon had many more members. Foroughi was elected to the second Parliament (1909–11). Through the influence of his Masonic brothers, he served briefly as president of Parliament. After the forced disbanding of Parliament over the Russian ultimatum to have the American financial advisor Morgan Shuster dismissed, Foroughi was appointed minister of justice in several Cabinets from 1911 to 1915. Between ministerial appointments Foroughi served on the highest court in Iran and continued teaching at the Political Science School. In 1919 he was a member of the delegation to the Paris Peace Conference. Between 1923 and 1924 he was minister of foreign affairs; 1924–25 minister of finance; 1925 acting prime minister; 1925–26 prime minister; 1927 minister of war; 1928 ambassador to Turkey where he negotiated a binding settlement of Iran-Turkish frontiers; 1930-31 ministerial posts; 1932 again prime minister; 1935 forced to resign. Foroughi also resigned as the chairman of Farhangestan (the Iranian Academy of Culture). Between 1936 and August 1941, he devoted his time to literary pursuits. During this period he collaborated with Dr.

Ghani to produce a collection of Omar Khayyam's poetry containing 178 quatrains that their research showed to be the authentic work of the poet. There is also an epilogue that analyzes some of the poems. In August 1941, with the invasion of Iran by Soviet and British forces, Reza Shah had to turn to Foroughi, who became prime minister on 28 August. Foroughi played a pivotal role in maintaining stability after Reza Shah's abdication and the passing of the crown to Mohammad Reza Shah. Equally important was his role in negotiating the tripartite agreement between Iran, Great Britain and the Soviet Union, which ensured the evacuation of foreign troops from Iran at the end of World War II. He lost his majority in the Iranian Parliament and resigned. He briefly served as Mohammad Reza Shah's second minister of court. He was ambassador designate to Washington in 1942 when he died of a heart attack.

Foroughi was that rare amalgam of scholar and diplomat. His book on the evolution of philosophical thought in Europe is a classic. He appeared distant and preoccupied but had a logical mind that weighed and analyzed every nuance of thought and action.

GANJI, Aqabala Khan (Salar Mo'tamed): b. Qazvin ca. 1870, d. 1936. His father was administrator of the vast estate of Soltan Hoseyn Mirza Nayer al-Dowleh in Qazvin. Nayer al-Dowleh also had a large estate in Nishapur. Salar Mo'tamed and his father moved to Nishapur and in time they became large landowners. Kamal al-Molk, who had been disillusioned by officials and some of his friends in Tehran, was seeking a retreat to live out his remaining days. Salar Mo'tamed welcomed Kamal al-Molk and placed one of his properties, Hoseynabad, a small village a few kilometers outside Nishapur, at his disposal. This singular act of hospitality made Ganji a legendary figure. He was also helpful in repairing some early-nineteenth-century buildings, which had been neglected. His sons were all educated abroad and the eldest, Jamal Ganji, became minister of roads in Dr. Amini's Cabinet of 1961.

GHAFFARI, Gholamhoseyn (Saheb Ekhtiar): b. 1859, d. 1947. Son of Mirza Hashem Khan Amin al-Dowleh and nephew of Farrokh Khan Amin al-Dowleh, figures of note in the Qajar era. A prominent

Kashan family that goes back nearly thirty generations; they had served the Qajars from the reign of Fath Ali Shah at the beginning of the nineteenth century. Gholamhoseyn was born on Ashura, the day commemorating the martyrdom of the third Shiite Imam, Hoseyn. Thus Naser al-Din Shah ordered that the boy be called Gholamhoseyn (servant of Hoseyn). He received a traditional education and became well versed in Persian and Arabic literature. Even as a youngster he was frequently at the court of Naser al-Din Shah and was in the official entourage during the shah's last trip to Europe. He was also in the royal entourage when the shah was assassinated in 1896. When Mozaffar al-Din succeeded his father, Gholamhoseyn was appointed minister of court. In 1899 he served briefly as minister of justice. He was dubbed Saheb Ekhtiar (Master of One's Own Will) by Mohammad Ali Shah, a title that was seldom granted in the Qajar era and that derives from the days of Nader Shah (r. 1736–47). Appointed Governor of Fars, later of Khorasan and Sistan. A close friend of Hasan Mostowfi (Mostowfi al-Mamalek), who was prime minister numerous times. He served as minister of war in one of Mostowfi's Cabinets. Saheb Ekhtiar was a decent and honorable man and respected by all. He was the proper choice for Reza Shah as representative of the nobility at official court functions and royal audiences.

GHAFFARI, Mohammad (Kamal al-Molk): b. Kashan c.1851, d. 1940. Son of Mirza Bozorg Kashani and scion of the old and influential Ghaffari family of Kashan, which has contributed diplomats, civil servants and three painters of note. He came to Tehran in early youth and studied at the Dar al-Fonun. His drawings and paintings came to the attention of Naser al-Din Shah on one of his visits to the school, and young Mohammad became one of several court painters. His uncle, Abolhasan Khan Naqqashbashi (Sani' al-Molk), was the premier painter of the era. After his uncle's death, Mohammad assumed his position, and in 1892 was awarded the title Kamal al-Molk (Perfection of the Realm). In 1896 when Mozaffar al-Din Shah came to the throne he ordered Kamal al-Molk to paint portraits of his father in compromising situations. Mozaffar al-Din Shah had ascended to the throne at an advanced age and harbored great hostility

Photo signed: "Memento to Cyrus Ghani, the former Kamal al-Molk"

toward his father, Naser al-Din Shah, for having ignored him and having ruled for forty-eight years. Kamal al-Molk feigned illness and paralysis of one arm and asked to be allowed to travel abroad. He went to Florence and Paris where he stayed for nearly three years, studying the masters. He trained the best Iranian painters of the 1920s and 1930s: Haydarian, Hoseyn'ali Vaziri, Mo'ayyed Pardazi and Sadr al-Din Shayesteh. Kamal al-Molk is remembered not only for his superb paintings, most of which are housed in the Iranian Parliament, but also for the strength of his character. He was able to say no to monarchs, ministers and other powerful people of his day, including his Masonic brethren.

GHASEMZADEH, Dr. Ghasem: b. Baku 1888 of Iranian parents, d. 1961. Doctorate of Law from St. Petersburg University. With the outbreak of the Russian Revolution, several former tsarist provinces declared independence and Ghasemzadeh became a candidate for the presidency of the Azerbaijan Caucasus. When the Bolsheviks consolidated their power, all insurrections were put down. Ghasemzadeh and his wife escaped to France, where he received another doctorate of law. In 1931 he became an Iranian citizen. In 1935 he began teaching French and Russian at the newly established Tehran University. He later taught constitutional law. In 1942 he became dean of the Faculty of Law and in 1949 he was elected to the Senate. His classic book on Iranian constitutional law is still unsurpassed for its incisive analysis. Dr. Ghasemzadeh is also remembered for his knowledge of the constitutional law of several countries, and as a great teacher.

GOLSHAYAN, Abbasqoli: b. 1902, d. 1990. Son of Rezaqoli who came from a Qajar military family in Damghan. He was educated by tutors at home at the Dar al-Fonun and later at the Political Science College (newly established in 1919) run by French teachers in Tehran. His first position was at the Ministry of Justice as translator for Monsieur Perny, a French legal scholar employed by the ministry as advisor for the enactment of necessary legislation. His hard work and long hours soon came to the attention of the new minister of justice,

Ali Akbar Davar. Golshayan became in effect Davar's private secretary. He worked feverishly, sometimes through the night, and accompanied Davar on his inspection tours to various parts of the country. Soon he became a confidant of Davar. As a reward for his devotion and labors, Davar appointed him to the prosecutor's office in Tehran. When Davar moved to the Ministry of Finance in 1933, Golshayan was among the favorites he took along with him. Within three years he became director general of the ministry. Two years after Davar's suicide, Golshayan had risen to become deputy minister of finance (1939). In 1941 he served as acting minister and, after a few months, was appointed minister of finance. Later he served as minister of commerce, minister of justice, governor of Fars, and governor of Azerbaijan. In 1948 he became governor of Khorasan; 1949–50 minister of finance, during which time he negotiated the Golshayan-Gass Oil Agreement. When Parliament did not ratify the agreement, his reputation suffered. In 1953 he was appointed to the Senate and in 1956 he became minister of justice again. When he refused the governorship of Azerbaijan, he incurred the displeasure of the shah and retired involuntarily. Golshayan was an experienced and efficient administrator with backbone.

HAKIMI, Ebrahim (Hakim al-Molk): b. Tabriz ca. 1869, d. 1959. Father, Abolhasan Hakimbashi, was physician to Mozaffar al-Din, the crown prince in Tabriz. His primary education was in Tabriz. During the period of 1888–92, he attended Dar al-Fonun where he learned some rudimentary medicine. In 1892 he traveled to Paris where he stayed some seven years and received a degree in medicine. He married a French woman and fathered a son who later became a dentist  in Paris. He returned to Iran in 1899 and became a physician (Tabib Hozur) to Mozaffar al-Din Shah whom he accompanied on his trip to

Europe. When his uncle who had been the senior physician to the shah died, he succeeded him and received the latter's title: Hakim al-Molk. In 1904 he served briefly as governor of Gilan. He was elected to the first Parliament and demonstrated pronounced constitutionalist sympathies. Upon the shelling of Parliament by Mohammad Ali Shah, he sought asylum at the French Embassy. After Mohammad Ali Shah's ouster, Hakim al-Molk was elected to the second Parliament. Together with Mohammad Ali Foroughi he became a tutor for the underage Ahmad Shah. He was also elected to the third Parliament and held two ministerial posts. After the 1921 coup, Seyyed Zia put him in prison, and during Reza Shah's rule, he received no government appointments. He became prime minister in 1945 and 1947 for brief periods. In 1949 he was appointed minister of court. He served three terms in the Senate and was president of the Senate for a term. Hakim al-Molk was decent, honorable and respected. He was a prominent figure on the political scene for nearly sixty years.

HAZHIR, Abdolhoseyn: b. ca. 1898, d. 1949. Son of a *Feda'i* (one willing to sacrifice himself for the constitutionalist cause), who had known Seyyed Hasan Taqizadeh. There are various versions of his ancestry. Some sources refer to his father, Mohammad Vosouq Khalvat, as an employee of the royal *andarun* (inner quarters), where the wives and concubines of the Qajar shahs (Mozaffar al-Din Shah) resided. Hazhir attended the Dar al-Fonun and later the Political Science School, and then joined the Ministry of Foreign Affairs. Either seconded by the ministry or with the ministry's consent, he became a translator at the Soviet Embassy, where he stayed for some six years. Taqizadeh, then minister of roads, offered him a position. When Taqizadeh became minister of finance, he had Hazhir transferred. Later Hazhir caught the attention of Davar at finance who appointed him as manager of the government-owned Textile Monopoly. Hazhir's progress continued: head of Industrial and Agricultural Bank; director of Exchange Control Commission; minister of roads, interior and finance in the governments of Foroughi, Soheyli, Sa'ed, Hakimi and Qavam. Eventually he became prime minister and finally minister of court, when he was assassinated by a religious fanatic. (His assassin, Seyyed Hoseyn Emami, had murdered the noted jurist and scholar Ahmad Kasravi but was set free because some members of the clergy deemed Kasravi an apostate.) Hazhir is a highly controversial figure in twentieth-century Iranian politics. He was close to the highest circles of the Iranian court and also the British Embassy.

HEDAYAT, General Abdollah: b. Tehran c.1902, d. 1968. Second son of Gholam Reza Khan (Mokhber al-Dowleh II). Military school in Tehran, then sent abroad by the government. Completed a term at St. Cyr and, later, at the École de Guerre. On his return to Iran in 1931 he received routine promotions. In 1940 he was a brigadier general and upon the invasion of Iran in 1941, he was made deputy head of the armed forces. He established a name for himself and was lauded for his patriotism by staying at his post. In 1946 he headed a team of officers going to Washington, D.C., for the purpose of modernizing Iran's obsolete military stockpiles. In 1947 he was promoted to major general; he became minister of war in Razmara's 1950 Cabinet and in 1954 was promoted to lieutenant general. In 1958 Hedayat became full general, the first Iranian officer to hold the rank. Soon there was a conflict with the shah over the number and authority of U.S. military advisors and the legal immunity of members of the American Armed Forces from prosecution under Iranian law. There were also lingering doubts in the shah's mind about Hedayat's close relations with the late General Razmara (Razmara's wife was related to the Hedayat family). He was removed from active duty and appointed to the Senate. He was later charged with corruption based on trumped up charges over a minor temporary army housing project in Azerbaijan. Hedayat was convicted and spent nearly two years in prison. Upon his release he was a broken man. One of the very best officers of the Pahlavi era and highly respected. He was well versed in Iranian history and spoke good French and some English.

HEDAYAT, Dr. Major General Karim: b. 1879, d. 1969. Son of Nayer al-Molk I. Preliminary schooling in Tehran. Traveled to France. Graduated from Lyon University with a degree in medicine. On his return to Iran, entered the army and soon became administrator of the army hospital in Tehran with the rank of colonel. Promoted to brigadier general and administrator of the health department of the armed forces. Later promoted to major general. He spent most of his late years in Shiraz. An excellent physician and administrator, and a widely read man of letters; he created one of the good private libraries of Iran.

HEDAYAT, Khosrow Bahman: b. Tehran ca.1904, d. 1973. Brother of General Abdollah Hedayat, son of Gholam Reza Hedayat (Mokhber al-Dowleh II) and scion of a family of public servants from the early Qajar era. Secondary school in Tehran. Degree in mechanical engineering from Belgium. On his return to Iran was employed by the Ministry of Roads and by the late 1930s he became administrator of railways in Azerbaijan. In 1946 he was appointed head of the Trans-Iranian Railway. He was a member of Qavam al-Saltaneh's Democrat Party and formed an association of railroad workers that was akin to a labor union. With their support, he was elected to the fifteenth Parliament. Deputy minister of roads in 1955 and in 1957 deputy managing director of the Plan Organization. With Ebtehaj's resignation, he headed the Plan Organization as the prime minister's deputy minister without portfolio in 1962; ambassador to Belgium; vice chairman of the board of NIOC; his last post was roving ambassador in Europe. A capable administrator, he became head of the Plan Organization at a very difficult time. The senior staff was disheartened by Ebtehaj's forced resignation, and only Hedayat's adroit moves and winning personality restored confidence.

HEJAZI, Lieutenant General Abdolhoseyn: b. 1907, d. ca.1969. Attended St. Cyr in 1924. Began his career in the gendarmerie, but transferred to the regular army. He was an instructor at the military academy, Tehran. After 1941 he received steady promotions. Made a

name for himself for his strong measures against Tudeh Party sup-
porters. His career took off after a crucial event in 1946 when
Ahmad Qavam, the prime minister, appointed Mozaffar Firuz, his
chief parliamentary deputy, as minister of labor and propaganda.
Firuz had begun to attack and belittle senior military officers.
Hejazi, then a colonel, was sent to warn Firuz to cease attacking the
military. Firuz, probably with Qavam's tacit approval, removed
Hejazi from active command and imprisoned him for insulting a
Cabinet minister. Qavam backed off after senior military officers
demanded Hejazi's release. Another consequence of the event was
Qavam's dismissal of General Hasan Arfa' from his post as chief of
staff of the armed forces. Hejazi was subsequently promoted to
brigadier general. He became close to the shah and accompanied
HIM on his trip to the U.S. in November 1949. Was head of the
Military Bureau of the shah and in 1962 was promoted to full
General. Hejazi had a tragic family life.

HEKMAT, Ali Asghar: b. Shiraz 1893, d. 1980. Eldest son of
Ahmad Ali Hekmat al-Mamalek. His early education was in tradi-
tional Iranian schools. Came to Tehran and briefly studied Islamic
law and philosophy with the noted cleric Mirza Taher Tonakaboni.
Studied at the American school where he received a diploma. Wrote
articles for various newspapers. In 1918 he entered the Ministry of
Education and for a short time taught English at secondary schools.
He came to the attention of Davar when he joined the latter's Radical
Party. In 1925 he was a delegate from Shiraz to the Constituent
Assembly that proclaimed Reza Khan the shah. Davar had him transferred to the Ministry of Justice. He was sent on a government
scholarship to Europe. After a brief stay in Paris he moved to London
where he studied English literature. In Foroughi's 1933 Cabinet,
Hekmat became acting minister and later minister of education. His
five years at the ministry was a golden era. In his tenure the Iranian
educational structure underwent dramatic changes. Several institutions were established: the Teacher's College, Tehran University,
Farhangestan (the Iranian Academy of Culture), the Museum of

Antiquities, the Museum of Anthropology and the National Library. In 1939 he became minister of interior, a post he held in the cabinets of Jam and Matin Daftari. He held ministerial positions in Foroughi's 1941 Cabinet, as well as in the Cabinets of Soheyli, Sa'ed, Zahedi, and Eqbal. His last ministerial post was minister of foreign affairs in 1958 (a post he had held in previous cabinets). By most accounts Hekmat was not easy to work with, but he is an important figure of the 1930s. His contribution to the founding of Tehran University was his greatest accomplishment. He was minister of education when regulations for the removal of the veil in schools came into effect. His last position was ambassador to India where he was a success. His major literary work is an abridged and annotated Persian translation of E. G. Browne's famed *A Literary History of Persia*.

JAHANBANI, Lieutenant General Amanollah: b. ca. 1890, d. 1974. Son of Amanollah Mirza (Zia al-Dowleh), a descendant of Fath Ali Shah who committed suicide in 1917 at the British Consulate in Tabriz. He had sought asylum at the consulate protesting the mass murder of civilians by Russian troops on the streets of Tabriz. Young Amanollah had trained in the artillery school in 1907 and military college in Russia in 1910. He returned to Iran in 1916 and enlisted in the Cossack Division. Had served as aide-de-camp to Colonel Starosselsky, the commander of the division. He sided with Reza Khan in the coup of 1921. Became brigadier general in 1922 when he distinguished himself in operations against the rebel highwayman Semitqu. In 1928 he became commander of the Eastern Division. Later that year was sent to France to the Staff College. Accompanied Reza Shah on his trip to Turkey in 1934. minister of interior in 1941; late 1941 minister of post and telegraph; 1942 minister of war. Commandant of the Military Academy, and senator from 1949 until his death. A fine officer with a distinguished career. Spoke perfect Russian and fluent French.

JAM, Mahmud (Modir al-Molk): b. Tabriz ca. 1884, d. 1969. From an old Persian family that had settled in Tabriz. He began his career as an apprentice to a French pharmacist in Tabriz. Having learned French he came to Tehran and worked as a translator at the French Legation for some eight years. He came to the attention of Vosouq al-Dowleh and in 1919 was appointed administrator of grain storage and distribution. In 1921 Hasan Pirnia (Moshir al-Dowleh) appointed him treasurer general as he had shown a talent for recording inventory and accounting. Later that year he became foreign minister in Seyyed Zia's Cabinet. Then served successively as minister of finance; governor of Kerman, and governor of Khorasan; minister of interior in 1933; and prime minister 1935–39. Jam became minister of court 1939–41; ambassador to Egypt; 1945 minister of court again; ambassador to Italy; and appointed as senator. A dedicated public servant with a most pleasing demeanor. His son, Lieutenant General Fereydun Jam, was one of the very best officers of his time and showed integrity and backbone.

KASHANI, Ayatollah Seyyed Abolqasem: b. ca. 1882, d. 1961. Son of a notable cleric, Seyyed Mostafa Kashani. Began his clerical studies in Tehran; made a pilgrimage to Mecca and on his return journey remained in Karbala. Studied under Akhund Molla Mohammad Khorasani, a renowned Islamic scholar. In World War I British forces attacked Iraq, then an Ottoman province. The Shiite clergy mobilized the masses and put up a fierce resistance. The British dropped poison gas from airplanes and ultimately quelled the rebellion. Kashani lost his father in the struggle. He settled in Najaf and Kazemeyn and continued anti-British activities. He was able to flee to Iran where he continued to preach against the British. He played a part in the rise of Dr. Mosaddeq and, later, a key part in his weakening and ouster. He was not a noted scholar, but the first thoroughly modern political cleric in Iran.

KASRAVI, AHMAD: b. Tabriz 1890, d. 1946. Came from a clerical family and was sent to a seminary. During the constitutional movement, while still in his teens, his (as opposed to the rest of his family's) sympathies were with the constitutionalists. By 1914 he discarded his clerical garb and attended the American School where he taught Arabic and learned English. In 1916 he traveled to the Caucasus and stayed in Tblisi, where he was influenced by Russian, Armenian and Georgian intellectuals and read widely. He returned to Tabriz where he became a teacher and joined Khiabani's separatist movement, but was soon disillusioned and left them. Came to Tehran where he was employed by the Ministry of Education and became an advocate of Esperanto (a proposed international language). Joined the Ministry of Justice and Davar appointed him to head the Justice Department in Khuzestan. In 1925 Kasravi wrote articles supporting Reza Khan's attempt to end Sheikh Khaz'al's autonomous rule in Khuzestan. In 1927 Davar appointed him attorney general of Tehran. After a few years Kasravi resigned and went into the private practice of law. He published the magazine *Peyman* (Pledge) in 1933 and briefly taught languages at Tehran University. After Reza Shah's abdication, Kasravi represented Colonel Mokhtari, former head of police, and his henchman, a pseudo-doctor named Ahmadi, in an important court case. He formed the political party *Azadegan* (Free People), which died after a brief time. He began to challenge the fundamental beliefs of Iranian Moslems. He also attacked mysticism and classical Persian poets, not sparing even the masters such as Hafez, Sa'di and Mowlana. The threats made by Shiite zealots on Kasravi's life succeeded in March 1946. Kasravi has left behind a series of important books: *History of the Constitutional Movement in Iran, Five Hundred Years of History in Khuzestan, Eighteen Years in the History of Azerbaijan,* and *The Unknown Kings.*

KAZEMI, BAQER (Mohazzeb al-Dowleh): b. 1887, d. 1973. Studied at the Political Science School. Joined Ministry of Foreign Affairs ca.1918. Counsel to the Iranian Legation, Washington, D.C., 1925. In 1930 appointed deputy minister of roads; then acting minister; 1931 minister; 1932 minister to Baghdad; 1933 minister of foreign affairs in Foroughi's government; 1937 governor of East Azerbaijan; 1938 minister to Afghanistan; 1939 ambassador to Turkey. Thereafter he headed several ministries: 1941 public health; 1942 finance; 1944 education. He was a delegate to the founding session of the United Nations at San Francisco in 1945; thereafter minister to the Scandinavian countries; 1951 minister of education. In Dr. Mosaddeq's first government he served as minister of foreign affairs, minister of finance, and ambassador to France. No post after the coup d'état of 1953, as he had sided with Mosaddeq. A man of considerable energy.

MAKKI, HOSEYN: b. Yazd 1911, d. 1981. Educated in Yazd and Tehran secondary schools. After Reza Shah's abdication, he published articles in leading Tehran newspapers and soon had a devoted following. He was the author of two books: the first on Ahmad Shah and the second on Amir Kabir. Both were devoid of primary sources, loosely researched with fanciful conclusions. They were, however, engaging and attracted a large readership. The book on Ahmad Shah depicted him as a hero who was deposed because he had principles and opposed the 1919 Agreement with the British. Worked briefly for the Iranian National Railway. One of the founders of the Iran Party. He subsequently joined Ahmad Qavam's Iran Democrat Party and was elected to the fifteenth session of Parliament. He disassociated himself from the Democrat Party and became a supporter of the National Front and an adherent of Dr. Mohammad Mosaddeq. He was briefly secretary general of the National Front. He soon broke with Dr. Mosaddeq and considered himself a potential prime minister. He was even courted by Mohammad Reza Shah. Too ambitious with limited substance, he soon faded away. Makki is also the author of a seven-volume history of Iran from the 1921 Coup, and the fall of the Qajars to the abdication of Reza Shah. The book is a chronological recitation of events.

MANSUR, Rajab'ali (Mansur al-Molk): b. ca. 1886, d. 1974. Attended the Political Science School and entered the Ministry of Foreign Affairs in the British section. By 1917 he had become the director of the English section and in 1919 under secretary of the ministry. With the foreign minister, Firuz (Nosrat al-Dowleh), in London accompanying Ahmad Shah, Mansur became acting minister. He then moved to the ministry of interior as under-secretary. In 1920 he was awarded the c.b.e. by the British government. His rise was swift: 1927–31 governor of Azerbaijan; 1931 minister of interior; 1933 minister of roads. He was arrested in 1936 and charged with misappropriation of funds. He was acquitted of the charge and was appointed minister of industry and mines in 1938. He became prime minister in 1940. After the Soviet and British invasion of Iran in September 1941, he was forced to resign. In February 1942, he became governor of Khorasan where he served nearly three years. There were charges of misappropriation and he was recalled. In 1945 he became governor of Azerbaijan; in 1950 prime minister for a brief period; then in succession ambassador to Italy, to Turkey and to Switzerland. One of the most controversial politicians of the era. His son, Hasan'ali Mansur, became prime minister in 1964 and was assassinated by a religious/political fanatic in 1965.

MASOUDI, Abbas: b. 1895, d. 1974. From a prosperous family of tradesmen of meat products. Studied at the Dar al-Fonun. Teimurtash, then minister of court, had always wanted a European-model newspaper that would devote itself to daily events in Iran and abroad. In 1926 a license to run such a newspaper was issued to young Abbas and his elder brother. The paper was called *Ettela'at* (Information). It soon became the leading newspaper across the country and a semiofficial organ of the government of the day. By the late 1950s it had expanded, adding dailies in English and French, and several weekly and monthly magazines based on Western prototypes. Prior to that, by the late 1940s, the family had also become a political force in Tehran and some other cities. Masoudi was elected to Parliament from the tenth to the fifteenth sessions. In 1949 he was elected to the Senate, a position he held until his death. He traveled extensively and wrote accounts of his travels. A self-made man, competent, energetic and farsighted.

MATIN DAFTARI, Ahmad (Etezad Lashkar, later Matin al-Dowleh): b. ca. 1896, d. 1971. From a distinguished Iranian family with roots in the late eighteenth century beginning with Mirza Mohsen Ashtiani. Related to the Vosouq, Mosaddeq, Mo'aven, Farhad, Mo'tamed, Dadvar, Shokuh and Maykadeh families. Matin Daftari was a nephew of Dr. Mosaddeq and married his daughter. Primary education in traditional schools, later the Iran German School. Joined the Ministry of Foreign Affairs and worked at the German Legation as a translator. At Davar's urging he moved to the Ministry of Justice. Davar sent him to France in 1929 to study trial procedures. He received a doctorate and returned to Iran in 1931. In 1932 director general of the Ministry of Justice; 1934 under secretary; and 1936 minister of justice. member of the Mission to Egypt for the wedding of the crown prince to princess Fawzia. Prime minister in 1939 for about eight months. In 1943 during the occupation of Iran by British and Soviet forces, he was arrested and imprisoned by British forces for suspected pro-German bias, and subsequently released. Accompanied Dr. Mosaddeq to New York and later to The Hague to defend the nationalization of the oil industry. After the 1953 Coup, Matin Daftari became a senator. He is the author of an important book on Iranian rules of civil procedure.

MAYKADEH, Soleyman Khan: b. c. 1870, d. c.1928. Scion of a prominent family from western Iran that was involved in affairs of state from the early nineteenth century. Educated in Iran and later in Germany. On his return he joined the Ministry of Finance. He had acquired a reputation for honesty and competence when he had been in charge of the finances of the military. He had been a firm supporter of the constitutional cause and imprisoned by Mohammad Ali Shah. After the ouster of Mohammad Ali Shah, Maykadeh was elected to the third session of Parliament. With the outbreak of World War I, all of western Iran became a battleground. The Ottomans invaded western towns and Britain and Russia, whose forces were already in Iran, landed more troops despite Iran's declaration of neutrality. Some prominent Iranian nationalists left the capital and established a government in exile. Fearing arrest, they moved to Iraq, greater Syria and Istanbul. Soleyman Khan was one of the most active of the group. At the end of World War I, the nationalists gradually returned to Iran. After the 1921 Coup, Soleyman Khan served as governor of Esfahan and later of Mazandaran.

MEER IRVANI, DR. YOUSEF: b. 1882, d. 1968. Born to a well-to-do Iranian family in Erivan in tsarist Russia. His primary and secondary education took place in Russian schools. In 1908 he was sent to Switzerland to complete his studies and in 1914 received a medical degree from the University of Lausanne. He then decided to continue his studies in surgery and worked at the Lausanne hospital with noted surgeons of the day for five additional years. Ali Akbar Davar who was studying and living in Geneva at that time would often travel to Lausanne to attend the lectures of a noted sociologist. A close friendship developed, and Davar urged Dr. Meer to go to Tehran where he was needed. Meanwhile the October revolution in Russia had deprived the Meer family of their possessions. Meer went to Iran in 1919 and soon began his medical practice. He married Dr. Mohammad Mosaddeq's niece, a granddaughter of Najm al-Saltaneh who had established a charitable hospital in Tehran. Soon his fame as a surgeon spread. Davar introduced him to Reza Khan (later Reza Shah) and Meer became the head of the Ahmadieh Hospital, the only military hospital in Tehran at the time. By 1939 he was a professor at the newly established Tehran University as well as head of surgery at Sina and Najmieh hospitals. Dr. Meer pioneered modern surgery in Iran, having worked at the outset under difficult and primitive conditions. Dr. Meer spoke French and Russian fluently, was conversant with European and Iranian literature, and was highly respected by an elite literary circle in Tehran. He had a lifelong friendship with Dr. Ghani. He is survived by twin sons, Ali Mohammad and Mohammad Ali, both noted surgeons in Iran, daughter Homa and several grandchildren, among whom is a third-generation surgeon.

MER'AT, Esma'il: b. 1891, d. 1949. Son of Mer'at al-Mamalek, a prominent figure in the late Qajar era. Primary and secondary education in Tehran. In 1911 he was sent to France and received a university degree in mathematics. On his return he taught mathematics and physics at the Dar al-Fonun. He also joined the Ministry of Education. In 1928 he served as supervisor of the first group of Iranian students sent to France during the early Reza Shah era. He returned in 1935 having acquired the reputation for being a dedicated and caring advisor and a competent supervisor. He was appointed head of the Bureau of Higher Education. In 1937 he served briefly as governor of Kerman. In 1939 became acting minister of education and was appointed minister the following year. He held the position in the governments of Matin Daftari and Mansur. As minister he introduced a curriculum for secondary schools based on the French model; established several new schools in Tehran and the provinces; introduced new textbooks and updated old texts for primary and secondary schools; and also initiated a sports curriculum and a Boy Scout program. After World War II, he was appointed cultural representative and supervisor of Iranian students in the U.S.

MESBAHZADEH, Dr. Mostafa: b. Shiraz 1909. Studied law in Tehran. Sent to Europe on a government grant and obtained a doctorate in 1941. Around the time of his return to Iran, the skilled writer Abdolrahman Faramarzi had obtained a license to publish *Kayhan*, a daily newspaper. Mesbahzadeh became its editor in chief. The paper was published two or three times a week at irregular intervals. In 1942, when Ahmad Qavam was prime minister, shortages of food (bread in particular) caused a riot. Part of the flour normally used to bake bread was allotted to the Russian and British occupying powers. Widespread looting and arson ensued, and even Qavam's residence was set on fire. Faramarzi, who had written several editorials sharply denouncing the government of the day, was removed as publisher of *Kayhan*, and a new publishing license was issued in the name of Mesbahzadeh. With the financial assistance of the shah *Kayhan* thrived and became a serious rival of *Ettela'at* (see Masoudi), soon surpassing it in circulation. Both Mesbahzadeh and Faramarzi became members of Parliament, and Mesbahzadeh later became a senator. *Kayhan* is still published in Tehran and London under completely different management.

MOGHADDAM, Gholamreza: b. Tehran 1926. Primary and secondary education in Iran. B.A. in economics from Upsala College in the U.S.; 1956 Ph.D. in economics, Stanford University; teaching assistantship at Stanford; served briefly at the International Monetary Fund. Returned to Iran and became the senior economist at the Plan Organization; 1960 deputy minister of commerce; later deputy governor of the Central Bank of Iran. Returned to the U.S. and served as senior economic advisor at the IMF for six years. He was urged to return to Iran and was appointed deputy director of the Plan Organization from 1969 to 1973. He was the founder, chairman and president of the Development and Investment Bank of Iran, which provided loans and equity capital for private manufacturing enterprises. Shortly after the 1979 revolution in Iran, Moghaddam returned to the IMF and served in various capacities, including advisor to the Bank of Jamaica. One of the foremost economists of Iran, he advocated a sound and deliberate approach to economic growth, allocation of resources and the oil income of the 1970s.

MOSADDEQ, Dr. Mohammad (Mosaddeq al-Saltaneh): b. 1882, d. 1967. Descended from one of the most notable families of public servants. Son of Hedayatollah Vazir Daftar, a prominent figure of the Naser al-Din Shah period. His mother, Malektaj Najm al-Saltaneh, was the daughter of Firuz Mirza Farmanfarma, the sixteenth son of Crown Prince Abbas Mirza. Dr. Mosaddeq was the great-grandson of Mirza Kazem Ashtiani and hence was related to most prominent families of the era. Studied in Switzerland and received a doctorate in law. He had begun his career as the administrator of finances in Khorasan at a relatively young age. (His father and grandfather had also been involved in the administration of finances.) On his return from Europe he was appointed governor of Fars and later of Azerbaijan; held most key ministerial posts. As a member of Parliament he led a movement to nationalize the oil industry, provoking the animosity of the British government. Prime minister 1951–53. Toppled by Britain and the U.S. One of three or four dominant and influential political figures in twentieth-century Iranian history. His influence was felt in every major capital of the world. His legacy remains undiminished.

NAFISI, Dr. Ali Asghar (Mo'addeb al-Dowleh): b. ca. 1872, d. ca. 1949. Eldest son of Nazem al-Ateba, court physician to Naser al-Din Shah and Mozaffar al-Din Shah. Secondary education at the Dar al-Fonun. Studied medicine at the Lyon and Paris universities. On his return he established a successful practice in Tehran. In Seyyed Zia's short-lived 1921 Cabinet he was appointed head of the nascent Ministry of Health and Welfare, the first to hold the post. He gained the confidence of Reza Shah, becoming the semiofficial physician at court and treating some members of the royal family. He acted as the guardian and minder of Crown Prince Mohammad Reza, accompanying him to Le Rosey in Switzerland in 1931 and returning to Tehran with the crown prince in 1936. He was in the entourage that went to Cairo for the marriage of the crown prince and Princess Fawzia of Egypt.

NAJM, Abolqasem (Najm al-Molk): b. 1892, d. 1960. Born to a family of amateur astronomers (the family name Najm means "star"). Studied mathematics and astronomy, and later graduated from the Political Science School. In 1911 entered the Ministry of Foreign Affairs where he became chief accountant. In 1930 transferred to the Ministry of Finance and was promoted to assistant minister; later in 1933 became deputy minister. Minister to Berlin in 1936. Most researchers hold him responsible for faulty reporting from Berlin. He purportedly had heard that Afghanistan intended to change its name to Ariana or Iranistan, which greatly agitated the Ministry of Foreign Affairs and Reza Shah. A directive was issued to all foreign governments to cease referring to Iran as "Persia." The background to the issue has not been thoroughly researched. Najm returned the same year and became director general of the Ministry of Industry and Crafts. Minister to Tokyo in 1940; 1943–45 ambassador to Kabul;

minister of foreign affairs in Hakimi's government of 1945; 1948 minister of finance; ambassador to Paris; governor of Khuzestan. Despite his extensive government service in Iran and abroad, Najm's reputation rests with his service at the Ministry of Finance. He became known for being frugal in dispensing public funds.

NEMAZI, Mohammad: b. Bombay 1895, d. 1972. Son of Mohammad Hasan Nemazi of Shiraz. Attended traditional schools, but mostly self-educated. Later he worked in Hong Kong and Shanghai before settling in the U.S. in 1939 when he was appointed economic counselor at the Iranian Legation in Washington, D.C. on a pro bono basis. He had built a highly successful trading and shipping concern. Returned to Iran in 1953 and was appointed minister without portfolio in Zahedi's Cabinet and later in Ala's Cabinet of 1955. He was noted for his philanthropic works. With his own funds he built a piped water system for his hometown of Shiraz (the first such system in Iran). Also in Shiraz established a large modern hospital with a fine medical college. Later in his life he established a textile factory in the Qazvin area. Highly intelligent and well informed in international trade and finance.

QAVAM, Ahmad (Qavam al-Saltaneh): b. ca. 1875, d. 1955. The second of three brothers; the oldest was Vosouq al-Dowleh, the youngest Abdollah Vosouq (Mo'tamed al-Soltaneh). Ahmad Qavam's rise was as swift as his elder brother's. Minister of interior in 1911, when he made a valuable contribution by establishing the Iranian Gendarmerie under Swedish officers. He became known as a capable administrator. During the period 1914–18, he held two ministerial positions: Interior and finance. He was appointed governor of Khorasan (1918–21), when there were general unrest and sporadic separatist movements in the province. After the fall of Seyyed Zia, he was appointed prime minister. He was again prime minister in 1922 and 1923. He was accused of plotting the ouster of minister of war Reza Khan and sent into exile abroad. After being allowed to return, he settled on his properties in the northern part of the country in March 1930. He became prime minister in 1942 but was forced to resign when there were bread riots. Prime minister again in 1946 coming to terms with the Soviets, weakening the Soviet installed government of Azerbaijan. However, having lost a dispute with the shah over civilian control of the armed forces, he was forced to resign. He was again appointed prime minister in 1952 but was forced to step down in the face of a mass uprising. One of the most dominating public figures of twentieth-century Iran. He was an able administrator; daring and highly ambitious. One of the finest calligraphers in Iran, the proclamation issued by Mozaffar al-Din Shah granting the constitution is in his hand.

Detail showing the signature from a fine example of Qavam al Saltaneh's calligraphy

QAVAM, EBRAHIM (Qavam al-Molk II): b. Shiraz ca. 1888, d. 1972. Son of Habibollah Khan (Qavam al-Molk). The family dates back to mid-eighteenth century; influential in Fars as head of the five Arab tribes (Arabic "Khamseh"). Traditionally they constituted the opposition to the Qashqa'i tribe headed by Esma'il Khan Sowlat al-Dowleh. The Qavam family always had British backing. Qavam inherited vast estates and the position of titular head of the five Arab tribes of Fars. The family exercised such inordinate power in the region that Reza Shah thought it advisable to have Qavam in Tehran, not in Fars close to his ancestral lands, and had him elected to Parliament. In 1937 Ebrahim's eldest son Ali Mohammad married Reza Shah's daughter

(Princess Ashraf), twin sister of Mohammad Reza Shah. The marriage did not work out, and, after Reza Shah's abdication, they were divorced. Qavam's daughter, Malektaj, married Asadollah Alam, who had been a confidant of Mohammad Reza Shah from his youth, and later became prime minister and minister of court.

QAZVINI, MOHAMMAD: b. Tehran 1877, d. 1949. The eldest son of Abdolvahab Qazvini, a noted scholar of the day. Abdolvahab had worked for the Government Publication Bureau, which was engaged at the time in the preparation of an encyclopedia of notable Iranian and Islamic personages. Abdolvahab died while Mohammad was still young and the family was sustained by a small pension from the government. Mohammad Qazvini was a serious student destined to become a clergyman. Soon his horizons widened and surreptitiously he enrolled at the French-run Alliance School in Tehran to learn French. His younger brother, Ahmad, had learned enough English to manage the London offices of an Iranian merchant. Mohammad decided to travel to London, having been tempted by Ahmad's talk of great libraries in England housing thousands of unpublished Persian and Arabic medieval texts. His brother sent a small sum to cover Mohammad's travel expenses. He left Iran in 1904 for a stay abroad that was to last thirty-five years. Soon after Mohammad's arrival in England he came to the attention of E. G. Browne, the leading Orientalist of the time at Cambridge University. Mohammad's erudition was acknowledged by other Western scholars, and he was given the task of annotating several manuscripts, most notably the three-volume history *Tarikh-e Jahan Goshai Jovaini*, which was published in 1911, 1915 and 1936. Mohammad spent the duration of World War I in Switzerland and Germany. From 1920 to 1939 he lived in Paris, and then he returned to Iran in 1939. In collaboration with Dr. Ghasem Ghani, he published a scholarly edition of the poems of Hafez in 1941, which remains the most reliable text of Hafez's poetry. Mohammad Qazvini's knowledge of Persian literature was unsurpassed. He is generally regarded as the foremost literary scholar of twentieth-century Iran.

RAZMARA, LIEUTENANT GENERAL HAJALI: b. 1900, d. 1951. Son of a former cavalry officer, one of fourteen children, two of whom also served in the military. Related to the Hedayat family (Razmara married the sister of Sadeq Hedayat, the novelist who greatly influenced Persian writers of the twentieth century). He studied at St. Cyr, the French military academy, and on his return to Iran became military governor of the Khamseh Tribe in Fars. He later led a military operation to suppress a Kurdish insurrection. A favorite officer of Reza Shah. In 1941 commanded the First Division stationed in Tehran. When Russia and Britain invaded Iran in 1941 and Soviet forces reached Qazvin, pausing on their way to Tehran, Razmara and Brigadier General Abdollah Hedayat remained at their posts, while some commanders were abandoning theirs. He became chief of the general staff in 1943. For reasons not entirely clear, Mohammad Reza Shah never completely trusted Razmara. This mistrust grew after the incident involving the arrest of Colonel Hejazi (see Hejazi). By 1947 the shah and Razmara reached a modus vivendi and the general became the supreme authority in the military. Prime minister in 1950. Assassinated by a religious fanatic in 1951. Razmara was one of the best officers of the era. He read widely and knew Iran well. Highly ambitious, he made some important improvements in the military. There have been persistent but unsubstantiated rumors that he was implicated in the 1949 assassination attempt on the shah. Wrote several books on the geography and topography of Iran.

SADIQ, DR. ISA (Sadiq A'lam): b. ca. 1892, d. 1975. Studied at the Dar al-Fonun. Studied in France on government scholarship, ca. 1921. Went to England (ca.1922) and worked for some four to six months as secretary to the Orientalist E. G. Browne at Cambridge University. Returned to Iran and joined the Ministry of Education. In 1930 he attended Columbia University in New York and received a doctorate in education. On his return (ca.1931–2), he was appointed head of Tehran's École Normale (Teacher's College). Minister of education in Foroughi's Cabinet of September 1941. Briefly served as acting head of Tehran University; 1943, 1944, 1947 minister of education; beginning in 1949, senator for five consecutive terms. A decent man and an honest public servant who contributed greatly to the expansion of educational facilities and more important to the training of competent teachers.

SA'ED MARAGHE'I, Mohammad (Sa'ed al-Vozara): b. Maragheh 1885, d. ca.1973. Educated in the Caucasus. Joined the Ministry of Foreign Affairs and thereafter served in consular capacities in the region: Tblisi and Batum; and in 1927 acting general counsel in Baku. Head of the Soviet section of the Ministry of Foreign Affairs in 1933; 1934 charge d'affaires in Moscow; 1936 minister to Rome; 1938 ambassador to Moscow. Minister of foreign affairs in the Qavam Cabinet of 1942 and in the Soheyli Cabinet of 1943. Prime minister in March 1944, but lost parliamentary majority and resigned the same year (the reason for the loss was the Soviets' demands for an oil concession in northern Iran). Prime minister again in 1948; 1950 ambassador to Ankara; thereafter appointed to the Senate. His extremely amiable exterior masked an experienced and shrewd diplomat and politician.

SALEH, Alahyar: b. Kashan ca.1900, d. 1980. Studied at the American College in Tehran. Advisor at U.S. Legation in Tehran; joined the Ministry of Justice, then transferred to Finance. Director of the Opium Monopoly, later Tobacco Monopoly. He was one of Davar's protégés. Sent to Washington, D.C., in 1941 on an economic mission; returned late the same year. He could not work with Dr. Millspaugh, the American employed as director general of Iranian finances, and Saleh resigned from his post as minister of Finance in Soheyli's 1943 Cabinet. Member of the Iranian delegation to the founding of the United Nations in 1945; minister of finance late the same year; and 1946 minister of justice. Because he was seen as pro-American, the British never regarded him highly. Ambassador to the U.S. in 1952, he resigned after the coup that toppled Mosaddeq in 1953. Asked by General Zahedi to stay on, he declined. In a relatively free parliamentary election he won a seat from Kashan in 1960. In

1979 amidst growing civil unrest, he was offered the prime minister-ship, which he declined. A man of principle and extraordinary decency. He was highly respected and the de facto elder statesman of the revived National Front. Spoke English well and some French.

SAMI'I, HOSEYN (Adib al-Soltaneh II): b. Rasht ca. 1875, d. 1954. From a large land-owning family that had moved from Azerbaijan to Gilan in the late eighteenth century. His father, Hasan, a prominent landowner, had the title of Adib al-Saltaneh I. Hoseyn received a tra-ditional Iranian education in Rasht and then attended the Dar al-Fonun. He entered government service in 1898 at the Ministry of Foreign Affairs but soon transferred to the Ministry of the Interior and served briefly as governor of Rasht. In 1915 he joined the govern-ment in exile as minister of interior and after a short stay in Kermanshah went into self-exile in Syria. He returned to Iran in 1918. When Reza Khan became prime minister in 1923, Sami'i served as assistant prime minister until 1924; 1924 minister of justice; 1927 minister of interior; 1931 governor of Azerbaijan. After Teimurtash's dismissal, he served in effect as head of Reza Shah's court (1935–38). Incurred Reza Shah's displeasure over the management of the ban-quets celebrating the crown prince's wedding to Princess Fawzia, but soon returned to favor. He became governor of Western Azerbaijan in 1939; later ambassador to Kabul; several ministerial posts between 1942–1943; and 1943–44 grand master of ceremonies at court. Sami'i was a learned man who wrote several books on Persian grammar and prose, a short memoir on his years in self-exile, and dabbled in poet-ry. A highly respected public servant whose services and counsel were prized for more than forty years.

SEPAHBODI, ANUSHIRVAN: b. ca. 1900, d. 1980. The grandson of Ayn al-Molk, a Qajar nobleman from his marriage to Ezzat al-Dowleh, the sister of Naser al-Din Shah (formerly the wife of Amir Kabir). Educated in Tehran. Entered the Ministry of Foreign Affairs in 1927. Served in several Russian cities as vice consul and consul for some five years; 1929–33 minister in Berne; 1933–34 undersecretary at Ministry of Foreign Affairs; later in 1934 minister to Rome; 1936–1938 ambassador to Moscow; July 1938 minister in Paris (also accredited to Spain); ambassador to Turkey; 1945 minister of foreign affairs; 1946 minister of justice; 1946–47 ambassador to Paris. One of the most astute and experienced diplomats at the Ministry of Foreign Affairs. He was dignified and spoke very good Russian and French.

SHAHROKH, Arbab Kaykhosrow: b. Kerman ca. 1875, d. ca. 1940. An Iranian Zoroastrian. Educated at the American School in Tehran. Worked in Bombay for several years. Returned to Tehran and was employed as one of the managers of the Arbab Jamshid Bank (owned by one of the wealthiest and senior Zoroastrians of Iran). He was elected to the second Parliament and soon became prominent for his nationalist views and his integrity. Was elected to every term of Parliament as the representative of the Zoroastrian community until his death. Traveled often to Europe and the U.S. As the administrator of Parliament buildings and gardens, he negotiated the transfer of Kamal al-Molk's paintings to the Parliament. A wealthy man, he was known for his energy and honesty. He died in unusual circumstances in about 1940. None of his six sons ever achieved his stature. The youngest, Bahram, a mysterious adventurer, lived in Germany during World War II and was the Persian announcer on German shortwave radio transmissions to Iran.

SHAYBANI, Major General Habibollah: b. Kashan 1885, d. 1945. Son of Nazem al-Dowleh. Received a solid Iranian education in Kashan. In 1906 he was sent to St. Cyr Military Academy and graduated in 1910. Remained in France and joined a French regiment for further training. Returned to Iran in 1913 and joined the Swedish-commanded gendarmerie. Highly regarded by Swedish officers, he was promoted to captain and in 1914 became a major. He was strongly anti-Russian and opposed the Allied occupation of Iran during World War I. He joined the Mohajerin (Exiles) and lived in self-imposed exile in Turkey until the war ended in 1918. He rejoined the gendarmerie and established contact with Reza Khan. As head of the

Bagh-e Shah Garrison, he played a key role in the success of the 1921 Coup. After the coup he was promoted to the rank of colonel. He fought against Kuchek Khan's separatist forces in Gilan and later against the warlord Simitqu. Promoted to brigadier general in 1922. In 1923 he was sent to France to lead a group of Iranian military students. He entered the French Staff Officer's College and graduated with distinction in 1925. In 1926 he became chief of the Iranian General Staff. He refused to sign the execution order of the military tribunal condemning Colonel Puladin of plotting to assassinate Reza Shah. Shaybani resigned from his office. He was asked to return, promoted to major general, and played a crucial role in Reza Shah's efforts to create a modern army. He commanded the army in Fars when it successfully quelled the Qashqa'i rebellion. In 1930 he commanded operations in the Mamasani district against the Kohkiluyeh tribes. Although the revolt was put down, the army suffered 500 casualties. He was court-martialed for the conduct of the operations and sentenced to a prison term of two years but was pardoned and allowed to leave Iran. He went to Berlin and was likely killed during the heavy bombardment of Berlin in 1945. His death was confirmed by the late Abdollah Entezam who reestablished the Iranian legation in Stuttgart in 1947. Shaybani was probably the finest Iranian military officer of his era. He also had a literary side. Mohammad Qazvini, Abbas Eqbal, and Dr. Ghani, who met regularly in Paris, have all praised his knowledge of Persian history and literature. He spoke French fluently and had a good knowledge of French literature.

SHOKUH, HOSEYN (Shokuh al-Molk): b. ca. 1880, d. ca. 1955. A cousin of Vosouq al-Dowleh. Educated in Tehran. Held positions in various ministries. Chief secretary to prime ministers 1919–23. Head of Reza Shah's Special Office 1928–41. Accompanied Reza Shah on his state visit to Turkey in 1934. He remained head of Mohammad Reza Shah's Special Office until his death. Capable and ideal for his position; known as the "soul of discretion."

SOHEYLI, Ali: b. ca. 1895, d. 1959. Little is known about his youth other than that he was educated in Russia. In 1931 he was appointed deputy minister of roads under Baqer Kazemi. Late in 1933 he transferred to the Ministry of Foreign Affairs as deputy minister when Kazemi was appointed foreign minister. He served several times as acting minister in Kazemi's absences. Was minister to London in 1937; early 1939 governor of Kerman; six months later ambassador to Kabul; minister of foreign affairs in Foroughi's Cabinet of 1941; prime minister for short periods in 1942 and again in 1943. Later accused of corruption and exceeding his authority. An inquiry proved inconclusive and he was absolved. In 1946 became Ambassador to Paris; 1948 minister without portfolio; 1953 ambassador to London. In the second volume of his memoirs, *Full Circle,* Anthony Eden praises Soheyli for his support of Britain in the Iranian oil nationalization dispute. Soheyli was a knowledgeable and efficient functionary. He played an important part in the conclusion of the agreement among Iran, Great Britain and the Soviets that Russian forces would evacuate Iran within six months after the end of World War II. His name is tarnished, however, by the activities of his Russian-born wife who acted as an agent for foreign firms, including the John Mowlem Construction Company. British Foreign Office documents implicate her in other ventures without mentioning her husband's complicity.

TADAYYON, Seyyed Mohammad: b. Birjand ca.1884, d. 1951. Educated in Birjand and Tehran intending to become a clergyman. But his interests changed and he established a secular school that he named Tadayyon (Being Faithful; later adopted as his family name). He wrote articles in the newspapers of the day and supported the constitutional movement. He was elected to the fourth Parliament from Tehran and became one of the leaders of the "Democrat" faction. He was elected to the fifth and sixth sessions of Parliament from Birjand. He played a key part in the abolition of the Qajar dynasty and in the establishment of the Pahlavi monarchy. Tadayyon was appointed minister of education both in the Mostowfi and the Hedayat cabinets and served for more than a year. He instituted some important reforms in school curricula, most notably a mandatory hour of physical exercise. Foreign-run schools were required to teach Persian language and Iranian history. Tadayyon's relationship with Teimurtash, the powerful minister of court, became strained and he resigned. He served for a year as governor of Kerman and then disappeared from the scene until after Reza Shah's abdication. He served as minister of education in Foroughi's Cabinet of September 1941 and held various ministerial posts until 1943. He was accused of malfeasance when minister of food supply, but was tried and acquitted. He served in Sa'ed's Cabinet of 1948 as minister without portfolio and later as a member of the first Senate.

TAHERI, Dr. Hadi: b. Yazd ca. 1888, d. 1957. He came from a clerical family. Taheri became a wealthy man—a landowner and proprietor of various businesses in Yazd. Served in Parliament for several terms. In the thirteenth session he was elected as one of the vice presidents. In the fourteenth he was one of the most influential members and instrumental in the election of Seyyed Zia al-Din to that session in 1943. Taheri was strongly anti-Russian and considered one of the most pro-British deputies. He briefly served as minister without portfolio in Sa'ed's Cabinet of 1948. He and Seyyed Kazem Jalili, the senior deputy from Yazd, controlled the key decisions taken by Parliament at the time.

TAQAVI, Seyyed Nasrollah (also known as Akhavi Tehrani): b. Tehran 1863, d. 1947. Studied with some of the leading Shiite theologians of the day. An early supporter of the constitutional movement, he was elected to the first (founding) term of the Iranian Parliament. He was reelected to the second and third Parliaments. Appointed head of Iran's Supreme Court. He gained a reputation as a farsighted jurist and was praised for his lack of bias and his measured opinions and judgments. One of the founders of the National Library. He was a prominent member of the group of scholars who met regularly with the young Mohammad Reza Shah to acquaint him with Iranian history and literature. He was the author of several learned treatises on law. Highly respected by the elite and the erudite of the day.

TAQIZADEH, Seyyed Hasan: b. Tabriz ca.1880, d. 1967. The son of a preacher, he began his education as a student of theology and wore the clothing of a clergyman. In 1905 he traveled to the Caucasus, later to Istanbul, Cairo and Damascus. By the time he returned to Iran, he had become a confirmed constitutionalist and began advancing his views in Tabriz. He was one of the founders of the Tarbiat School in Tabriz, which promulgated the cause of constitutional government. He was elected to the first Parliament and became one of its most prominent members despite his youth. In the aftermath of the shelling and closing of Parliament by the new king Mohammad Ali Shah, Taqizadeh sought asylum at the British Legation. He was allowed to leave Iran under an amnesty. After Mohammad Ali Shah was deposed, Taqizadeh was elected to the second Parliament in 1909. He went to Europe in 1910 and did not return to take his seat in the third and fourth Parliaments to which he had been duly elected. He lived mostly in Berlin where he edited the influential journal *Kaveh,* which advocated modernism and adoption of Western values. For this, middle-ranking clergy regarded him as an apostate. After his return to Iran in 1924, he was elected to the fifth and sixth Parliaments. He traveled to the United States as the Iranian representative to the Philadelphia Trade Exhibition. On his return to Iran he was appointed governor of Khorasan in January 1929. He was recalled the same year and appointed minister to London where he served for some eleven months to April 1930. Appointed minister of roads and soon thereafter minister of finance. He fell into disfavor in September 1933 and was removed from office. But soon afterwards he was appointed minister to Paris. After being recalled from Paris in August 1934, he obtained a leave of absence. He had no post until appointed minister to London by Foroughi in September 1941. He returned to Iran in 1946 and was elected from Tabriz to the fifteenth session of Parliament. In a speech to Parliament, he maintained that he had signed the agreement in 1933 that extended the duration of the Oil Concession under duress, against his better judgment. He was elected to the Senate in 1949 and was appointed its president. Taqizadeh was not an exceptional administrator and was not at his best when under pressure. He was, however, one of the most learned men of his day. Though he wrote and published little, some of his works have attained the status of classics. He also had an interest in science. In 1959 he gave a lecture at a private club in Tehran (Mehregan) on the evolution of the constitutional movement in Iran. Lucid and comprehensive, it is among his finest works.

TEIMURTASH, 'ABDOLHOSEYN (Moazez al Molk II, later Sardar Moazam): b. Khorasan, 1879, d. 1933. The son of a minor tribal chieftain, Karimdad Khan Nardini (Moazes al Molk). Teimurtash was sent as a child to a preparatory school in tzarist Russia (Eshqabad) and later to the military college in St. Petersburg. He became fluent in Russian and French. On his return to Iran he immersed himself in Persian literature and history, which more than compensated for his lack of a formal Persian education. He served briefly at the Ministry of Foreign Affairs as a Russian translator. A fortuitous marriage to the niece of the Regent, Azod al Molk, a close relative and ward of the then governor of Khorasan, Nayer al Dowleh, served him well. He was elected to the second through sixth sessions of Parliament from Nishapur in Khorasan. He had declined to serve in the sixth session as he had been appointed minister of court of Reza Shah in 1926. By the time he entered Parliament he had become an effective public speaker. He was forceful and quick-witted. It was inevitable that Teimurtash would be propelled into prominence. He was appointed governor of Gilan Province by Vosuq al-Dowleh in 1919. Later, after brief service as minister of Justice, he was appointed governor of Kerman in 1923. After Reza Khan became prime minister, Teimurtash served as minister of public works. Upon Reza Khan's accession to the throne, Teimurtash was appointed minister of court where he became virtually the shah's alter ego. Teimurtash came closer than anyone else to sharing power with Reza Shah, who is alleged to have said, "Teimurtash's word is my word." Never before or afterward did Reza

Shah delegate so much authority to any single person. He fell from grace and was removed as minister of court in December 1932. He was accused and convicted of bribery and misuse of foreign currency regulations. It is certain that Teimurtash was murdered while in prison in September 1933. A man of great charm and intellect Teimurtash also had certain flaws of character. As a twentieth-century modernist, he together with Ali Akbar Davar were Reza Shah's principal advisors in the creation of a modern Iranian state. Teimurtash had a daughter and three sons from his first wife and two daughters from his second wife. Iran, his eldest daughter, was well versed in Iranian and European literature.

VAKILI, Ali: b. Tabriz 1897, d. 1968. As an enterprising young man he began exporting carpets; later, by becoming an agent for U.S. products, he became wealthy. His name is remembered, however, in connection with government-owned companies begun by minister of Finance Davar. Davar realized that there was not enough capital in the private sector to form companies to give a boost to the national economy. To stimulate commercial activity he formed government companies. Several companies including carpet weaving and textile manufacture were established. Vakili served on their boards and guided their activities. He was later appointed head of the Tehran Chamber of Commerce and member of Parliament from the ninth to the twelfth sessions and the fifteenth session. He was appointed to four Senate terms. After World War II, he lived in the United States for a period and expanded his import business.

VAZIRI, Colonel Alinaqi: b. 1887, d. 1969. Son of Mir Panj (Brigadier General) Musa Khan. In his youth he studied music with a French pianist at the St. Louis School in Tehran. He later joined the gendarmerie and rose to the rank of lieutenant colonel. During the constitutional struggle, he resigned his commission and joined the forces that ousted the absolutist Mohammad Ali Shah. At the end of World War I, he traveled to Europe and spent three years in France and two years in Germany studying music. On his return in 1923 he established a music school, which attracted a generation of talented musicians including Javad Ma'rufi, Abdolali Vaziri, Ruhollah Khaleqi and Abolhasan Saba. Vaziri's favorite instrument was the tar, though he played the setar, violin, and piano with equal facility. His greatest contribution was to use standard notation to transcribe music that had been part of the oral tradition in Iran. Vaziri was a highly literate man who had studied Hafez and Rumi in depth. He set several of Hafez's odes to music and often sang his compositions to friends with his melodious voice.

VOSOUQ, HASAN (Vosouq al-Dowleh): b. 1868, d. 1951. Son of Ebrahim Khan Mo'tamed al-Saltaneh, grandson of Mohammad Qavam al-Dowleh Ashtiani, one of the most prominent Iranian families of the last two centuries. His father's family produced three prime ministers: Hasan Mostowfi, Ahmad Matin Daftari and Mohammad Mosaddeq. On his mother's side two prime ministers: Ali Khan Amin al-Dowleh and Ali Amini. His brother, Ahmad Qavam, was prime minister on five occasions. Vosouq lost his mother at an early age and was raised by Amin al-Dowleh. Received a traditional Iranian education. He followed his father's footsteps and soon became the financial administrator of Azerbaijan Province. Elected to the first and second terms of Parliament; 1909 he was chosen to be a member of the committee that governed the country after the abdication of Mohammad Ali Shah; minister of justice in 1909 and later minister of finance; 1911 he became minister of foreign affairs; during the period 1911–15 he held several ministerial portfolios. Prime minister from August 1916 to May 1917 and again from August 1918 to June 1920, when he negotiated the infamous and widely unpopular 1919 Agreement between Great Britain and Iran. Lived in Europe from June 1920 to early 1926; was appointed minister of finance in the summer of 1926; and elected to the seventh session of Parliament 1928–30. In 1936 he succeeded Foroughi as president of Farhangestan (The Iranian Academy of Culture). A man of exceptional ability, he pacified Iran after World War I when bandits controlled most roads to and from major towns. His reputation, however, will always suffer because of his advocating the 1919 Agreement and the fact that he and two of his ministers received compensation. Vosouq was also a minor poet. Some of his verses gained great popularity.

YAZDANPANAH, Lieutenant General Morteza: b. Tehran ca. 1884, d. 1973. His father was a colonel in the army. Attended Cossack Cadet School and learned some Russian. His knowledge of the language led to steady promotions. By 1921 he was a brigadier general. He was with Reza Khan in the days preceding the 1921 Coup and rode with him to Tehran. Very close and loyal to Reza Shah who treated him as a protégé, though on at least one occasion he fell into disfavor. In 1928 promoted to major general and chief inspector of the army. Later commander of the gendarmerie and head of the military academy. He maintained that Reza Shah, prior to leaving Iran, had given the names of trustworthy people to Mohammad Reza Shah. He was loyal to the young shah as he was to his father. In 1942 appointed commander of the Tehran Garrison and promoted to lieutenant general. Held numerous ministerial posts. Entrusted with conducting the coronation ceremonies of Mohammad Reza Shah, which were handled with tact and good taste. Yazdanpanah was highly regarded by fellow officers and known for his honesty. A nationalist of the old school, he suspected the motives of all foreign countries.

ZAHEDI, Lieutenant General Fazlollah: b. Hamadan ca. 1890, d. 1964. Father was the administrator of the large estate of Abolqasem Qaraguzlu (Naser al-Molk II; regent until 1915 under Ahmad Shah). In his early youth he supported the constitutional movement and was injured in skirmishes with pro-Mohammad Ali Shah forces. He joined the Cossack Brigade and as a lieutenant came to the attention of Reza Khan who was the commander of forces in Hamadan. Zahedi's rise was swift and by 1922 he commanded troops in Shiraz. By late 1924 he was a brigadier general cited for bravery in battle. He commanded troops sent to Khuzestan to disarm followers of Sheikh Khaz'al, the rebellious, British-backed ruler of the province. In 1925 the province was pacified and Khaz'al was sent to

Tehran under armed escort. Zahedi gained fame for his exploits and in 1926 commanded troops in Rasht where he eliminated the remnants of Kuchek Khan's Jangalis (rebels). He fell afoul of Reza Shah in 1929 and was arrested; soon was pardoned and restored to full rank. Appointed chief of police in 1931. When several prisoners escaped, Zahedi was dismissed. He left the military for business and imported Ford cars into Iran. In 1935 he was a member of a commercial delegation to the USSR. After Reza Shah's abdication, he rejoined the army, was appointed head of the gendarmerie, and shortly thereafter commanded troops in Esfahan. British Intelligence arrested Zahedi in 1942, accused him of working with German fifth columnists, and exiled him first to Iraq and then to Palestine for the duration of World War II. He was released in 1945 and reentered the army as Inspector of armed forces. Chief of Staff Lieutenant General Razmara put him on the retired list in 1949. He was activated a year later. He supported National Front candidates including Dr. Mosaddeq in the 1951 parliamentary elections. Appointed minister of interior in Mosaddeq's Cabinet of 1951. Beginning in 1952 he had a falling out with Dr. Mosaddeq and sought to become prime minister. Relations between them worsened and a warrant for Zahedi's arrest was issued. He sought asylum in Parliament and was protected by Ayatollah Kashani. He later went into hiding in Tehran. General Zahedi was the key individual in the 1953 Coup engineered by British and U.S. intelligence agencies that overthrew Dr. Mosaddeq's government and enabled the shah to return to Iran. Zahedi was then appointed prime minister. The shah had never been comfortable with him and, after two years in office, Zahedi was forced to resign in 1955. He was in effect exiled to Switzerland with the title of ambassador to the UN headquarters in Geneva. General Zahedi's first wife was the daughter of Hoseyn Pirnia (Mo'tamen al-Molk); they had two children: Ardeshir and Homa. Ardeshir served as ambassador to the U.S., later London; minister of foreign affairs and a second term as ambassador to Washington.

PUBLISHED WORKS BY DR. GHASEM GHANI

BOOKS

Ebn Sina (Avicenna). Tehran, 1936.

Discourse on Psychology. Tehran, 1936.

Rubaiyat-e Omar Khayyam; research and annotation by Mohammad Ali Foroughi and Dr. Ghasem Ghani. Tehran, 1941.

Divan-e Hafez; research and annotation by Mohammad Qazvini and Dr. Ghasem Ghani. Tehran, 1942.

Bahs dar Asar va Afkar va Ahval-e Hafez (A Study of the Works, Thoughts and Life of Hafez). Tehran, 1942.

Tarikh-e Tasavvof dar Islam az Sadr Eslam ta Asr-e Hafez (The History of Mysticism from the Beginning of Islam to the Age of Hafez). Tehran, 1943.

Tarikh-e Bayhaqi (The History of Bayhaq); research and annotation by Dr. Ghasem Ghani and Dr. Ali Akbar Fayyaz. Tehran, 1945.

Bahsi dar Tasavvof (A Discourse on Mysticism); published posthumously. Tehran, 1954.

Divan-e Hafez; annotated by Dr. Ghasem Ghani; published posthumously. Tehran, 1977.

Yaddashtha-ye Dr. Ghasem Ghani (The Memoirs of Dr. Ghasem Ghani); 12 vols. London 1981-85.

Namehha-ye Dr. Ghasem Ghani (The Letters of Dr. Ghasem Ghani); London, 1989.

ARTICLES

"Reynold A. Nicholson," in *Studies in Islamic Mysiticism* published by the Farhangestan, Tehran, 1939.

"Comprehensive Education," in *Publication of the Ministry of Education.* Tehran, 1944.

"The Turkmenchai Treaty," in *Yadegar,* Tehran,1944.

Biorgraphy of Hajji Molla Hadi Sabzevari," in *Yadegar,* Tehran, 1944

"Biography of Fathali Khan Sheybani," in *Yadegar,* Tehran, 1944.

"George Louis Buffon: Discours sur le Style," in *Yadegar,* Tehran, 1944.

"Biography of Mohtashem al-Saltaneh Esfandiari," in *Yadegar,* Tehran, 1944.

"History of Islamic Medicine," in *Yadegar,* Tehran, 1945-48.

"Letters of Mohsen Khan Moshir al-Dowleh to Naser al-Din Shah," in *Yadegar,* Tehran, 1945.

"Eugenics," in *Yadegar,* Tehran, 1945.

"Mohammad Qazvini," in *Yaghma,* Tehran, 1950.

"Kamal al-Molk," in *Yaghma,* Tehran, 1950.

"Cycles of Iranian Painting," in *Yaghma,* Tehran, 1951.

TRANSLATIONS

Thaïs by Anatole France. Tehran, 1929.

La Révolte des anges, by Anatole France. Tehran, 1939.

La Rôtisserie de la Reine Pédauque, by Anatole France. Tehran, 1943.

INDEX OF NAMES

487

ABOUT THE EDITOR AND TRANSLATOR

CYRUS GHANI is a lawyer and scholar specializing in Iranian studies. He is the author of *Iran and the Rise of Reza Shah* (1998), and *Iran and the West: A Critical Bibliography* (1987). He edited twelve volumes of *The Memoirs of Dr. Ghasem Ghani* in Persian (1989–97). A film afficianado, he most recently has written *My Favorite Films* (2004). He was born in Iran and has lived in Tehran, Los Angeles, London and New York City, where he now resides.

PAUL SPRACHMAN is Vice Director of the Center for Middle Eastern Studies at Rutgers University. He has taught and lectured in Iran, is the translator of several works including Jalal Al-e Ahmad's *Plagued by the West* (1982), and is the author and translator of *Suppressed Persian: An Anthology of Forbidden Literature* (1995).